STATE
LEGISLATURES
TODAY

POLITICS UNDER
THE DOMES

STATE LEGISLATURES TODAY

POLITICS UNDER THE DOMES

Peverill Squire
University of Missouri

Gary Moncrief
Boise State University

Longman
Boston   Columbus   Indianapolis   New York   San Francisco
Upper Saddle River   Amsterdam   Cape Town   Dubai   London   Madrid
Milan   Munich   Paris   Montreal   Toronto   Delhi   Mexico City
Sao Paulo   Sydney   Hong Kong   Seoul   Singapore   Taipei   Tokyo

Editor-in-Chief: Eric Stano
Marketing Manager: Lindsey Prudhomme
Production Manager: Holly Shufeldt
Project Coordination, Text Design, and Electronic Page Makeup:
   GGS Higher Education Resources, a Division of PreMedia Global, Inc.
Full-Service Project Management: Aparna Yellai,
   GGS Higher Education Resources, a Division of PreMedia Global, Inc.
Cover Art Manager: Jayne Conte
Cover Designer: Bruce Kenselaar
Cover Photo: Shutterstock
Text and Cover Printer: R.R. Donnelley & Sons/Harrisonburg

Library of Congress Cataloging-in-Publication Data
Squire, Peverill.
   State legislatures today : politics under the domes / Peverill
Squire, Gary Moncrief. — 1st ed.
       p. cm.
   Includes bibliographical references and index.
   ISBN-13: 978-0-13-603355-4 (alk. paper)
   ISBN-10: 0-13-603355-5 (alk. paper)
   1.   Legislative bodies — United States — States.   2.   U.S. states —
Politics and government.   I. Moncrief, Gary F.   II. Title.
   JK2488.S695 2010
   328.73—dc22

                                                                    2009028585

Longman
is an imprint of

www.pearsonhighered.com

ISBN-13: 978-0-13-603355-4
ISBN-10: 0-13-603355-5

CONTENTS

CHAPTER 3

THE CHANGING JOB OF STATE LEGISLATOR 74

CHAPTER 4

LEGISLATIVE ORGANIZATION ACROSS THE STATES 122

CHAPTER 6

THE LEGISLATIVE CONTEXT 197

CHAPTER 7

ARE STATE LEGISLATURES REPRESENTATIVE INSTITUTIONS?   235

PREFACE

Amid the steepest economic downturn in generations, state governments faced massive shortfalls in their budgets by the beginning of 2009. There was little hope that the problems would subside by 2010 or even 2011. In state after state, painful decisions had to be made about what programs to cut and by how much, and what taxes (if any) to increase and by how much. These decisions affect citizens in direct and meaningful ways. Ultimately, it is the state legislature's job to make them.

At the same time that the legislatures were struggling with these fiscal concerns, they were addressing a myriad of other issues, including repealing the death penalty (New Mexico), legalizing same-sex marriage (Maine, New Hampshire, and Vermont), and requiring public utilities to make greater use of renewable energy sources (Colorado). At least nine state legislatures passed bills that banned text messaging while driving. Maryland became the first state to expand its hate crime law to include attacks on the homeless. Indiana passed a law to restrict and regulate puppy mills. Decisions made by state legislators impact almost every aspect of people's daily lives: the taxes they pay, the education they receive, the roads they drive, and the health and safety of their communities.

Despite the importance of state legislatures, Americans know very little about the institutions and the people who serve in them. Our goal in this book is to help fill that gap. We have sought to write a book that conveys the importance of state legislatures while also highlighting their fascinating variety.

Because so much has been written about the U.S. Congress and, until recently, so little about state legislatures, most people assume that all American legislatures are alike (and a lot like Congress). Although the state legislatures share some commonalities among themselves, they are decidedly not all the same. We set out to demonstrate this fact, armed with a recent surge in academic research on state legislatures and an ample collection of examples and anecdotes about individual legislatures and legislators. At the same time, we chose to organize the chapters in this volume in such a way that it parallels the way most textbooks on Congress are structured. This facilitates the use of this book on state legislatures as a comparative counterpoint to congressional texts in Congress courses. In each chapter, we strive to point out the ways state legislatures are similar and, more importantly, the ways they are different from the national legislative institution.

But this book is not just about how state legislatures compare and contrast with Congress. It is, ultimately, a book about the fascinating variation one finds in legislative structure and operations. Simply put, no government institution varies as much from one state to another as does the state legislature. One of our main objectives in writing this book is to convey these contrasts and to identify their consequences, and we have sought to do this in a way that is both informative and engaging.

One of the distinguishing features of the book is the use of boxes to highlight and engage students in the key points of each chapter. These "Politics Under the Domes" boxes are case studies, personal stories, or vignettes that provide texture and human dimension to our subject. We hope the readers enjoy these features as much as we enjoyed writing them.

In bringing a book such as this one to print, many debts—intellectual and otherwise—are incurred. Gary Moncrief wishes especially to acknowledge the mentoring role of Malcolm E. Jewell, his major professor at the University of Kentucky and one of the pioneers in state legislative research, and Donald R. Matthews. Don Matthews became a friend and mentor during a period as visiting professor at the University of Washington. One of the most influential political scientists of his time, he was also a wonderful person with a remarkable mind and very kind heart. More recently, Moncrief spent a semester at the Center for American Women and Politics and the Eagleton Institute of Politics at Rutgers University, and that time was instrumental in helping develop parts of this project. Deborah Walsh (CAWP) and Ruth Mandel (Eagleton) were extremely helpful, and the opportunity to talk with Alan Rosenthal on a near-daily basis was an education in itself.

Peverill Squire wishes to acknowledge his great fortune in having had the opportunity to learn from Ray Wolfinger and Nelson W. Polsby while he was a student at the University of California, Berkeley. Unparalleled as scholars, they gave him the opportunity, guidance, and encouragement to develop his own set of scholarly interests in his own way. He is indebted to each of them. While on the faculty at the University of Iowa he benefitted greatly from the collegiality of Pat Patterson, and, especially, Jerry Loewenberg. Squire's contribution to this book was aided by a semester leave provided by the Department of Political Science at the University of Missouri and, during that leave, by the continued use of his old office by the Department of Political Science at the University of Iowa.

Eric Stano and the staff at Pearson Longman also deserve our thanks for their professionalism throughout the process of turning concept into book. In particular, we would like to thank Holly Shufeldt, Danielle Shaw, and Aparna Yellai. The greatest debt of all, however, is to our wives, Janet and Heidi, for their constant support and encouragement.

Peverill Squire
Gary Moncrief

99 CHAMBERS AND
WHY THEY MATTER

On February 26, 2007, Arkansas Representative Steve Harrelson (D-Texarkana) introduced House Concurrent Resolution 1016, a measure titled, "Declaring 'Arkansas's' as the Correct Form of the Possessive Form of the Name of Our State." Rep. Harrelson's seemingly inconsequential proposal generated an enormous amount of media attention, much of it lightly jabbing the legislature for spending valuable time on such a trivial matter.[1] The measure even spawned a grammatical controversy, with the Clinton School of Public Service at the University of Arkansas sponsoring a debate on the issue.[2]

Why had Rep. Harrelson chosen to risk public ridicule by pushing "Arkansas's" over "Arkansas'"? The representative admitted that an elderly friend had "asked me to introduce a resolution to amend the 1881 Arkansas General Assembly resolution recognizing the state's pronunciation (Ark-an-saw rather than ar-KAN-sas) to include appropriate usage of the word in the possessive case."[3] Harrelson was not, however, oblivious to the reception his measure was apt to receive. When the proposal came before the House, he confessed to his colleagues that "I know a lot of the attention that has been given to this resolution has reflected poorly on us as a Legislature, and for that I apologize. . . . Yes, there are more pressing matters we can deal with."[4] Nonetheless, the measure passed without opposition on a voice vote.

For many people in Arkansas, the debate over whether the possessive of the state's name ought to have a second "s" may be all they know or recall about the 2007 legislative session. Yet any assumption that the legislature had frittered away its time on silly issues would be seriously misguided. By the time the Arkansas state legislature had ended it 86-day session, it had actually accomplished a great deal. Bills had been passed to provide close to $400 million in general tax relief, allocate $456 million for school building maintenance and new equipment, and give an additional $100 million in funding for public education. A merit pay program for teachers was initiated. The state sales tax on groceries was cut in half, and thousands of poorer state residents were removed from the tax rolls. Manufacturers in the state saw the sales tax they pay on utilities reduced by 2 percent. The homestead exemption enjoyed by most homeowners was increased by almost 17 percent. Overall, legislators from both parties expressed satisfaction with the legislature's performance.

Arkansas is not a special case. Every state legislature suffers from an image problem. Constituents often take note of their activities only when something frivolous such as the "apostrophe war" gains media attention. Yet the decisions made by state legislatures impact every aspect of Americans' daily lives in fundamental ways, including the taxes they pay, the education they receive, the roads they drive, and the health and safety of their communities. Despite the importance of the decisions made by them, Americans know almost nothing about their state legislatures or their legislators.

This book is an effort to remedy this deficiency by examining state legislatures and state lawmakers in some depth. We begin in this chapter by placing state legislatures in their proper historical context, demonstrating that although the original state legislatures and the U.S. Congress had much in common when they were first established, they have evolved over the past two centuries to become different kinds of legislative organizations. We then provide a primer on the 50 state legislatures today, highlighting their variety of institutional sizes and structures, again to emphasize the point that state legislatures are not simply copies of Congress. The final section provides an outline for the rest of the book.

STATE LEGISLATURES IN HISTORICAL CONTEXT

State legislatures as a group have a much longer history than does the U.S. Congress. Indeed, by the time Congress first met in 1789, the original state legislatures had already been in existence for 13 years. But the age discrepancy is actually greater than that because the original state legislatures evolved directly from their colonial predecessors.[5] In the case of Virginia, its colonial assembly first met in 1619, meaning the legislature enjoyed a 157-year history even before American independence was declared.

This history is important to appreciate because it means that state legislatures are not simple imitations of Congress. Indeed, in some notable regards, the evolutionary relationship actually runs the other way. The design of the Congress created in the Constitution owes much more to the original state legislatures than it does to its predecessor Congress under the Articles of Confederation.[6] That the founders drew on the state legislative experience in writing the Constitution should not be surprising because of the 39 men who signed that document, 18 had served in colonial legislatures and 32 had served in state legislatures.[7] Yet the similarity between the Congress and the original state legislatures is ironic because many of the men who wrote the

Constitution, most notably James Madison and George Mason, distrusted the state bodies because they thought they wielded too much power in state government.[8]

As can be seen in Table 1-1, the most obvious similarity between the first state legislatures and Congress was the number of houses. Similar to 11 of the original 13 state legislatures, the Constitutional Congress was created as a bicameral body. In contrast, the Congress under the Articles had been unicameral. The two houses of Congress were also given the names most commonly used in the states.

There were other similarities. The U.S. Senate was given longer terms than the U.S. House; upper houses in four states had longer terms than their lower houses.[9] U.S. Senators were given six-year terms, longer than any upper house terms in the states. The Senate's terms, however, were three times longer than those for the lower house, as were those for Delaware's upper house members. And although all but one state legislature had either six-month or one-year terms for the members of their lower houses—the Congress under the Articles also had one-year terms—South Carolina gave its state representatives the same two-year term that members of the U.S. House were granted.

Other significant provisions of the U.S. Constitution regarding Congress appear in earlier manifestations in the original state constitutions. While separation of powers among the legislature, executive, and judiciary appeared in each state constitution, these institutions were fused under the Articles. In the U.S. Constitution, individual members of Congress were each given an equally weighted vote, just like their state legislative counterparts. In the Congress under the Articles, each state, not each lawmaker, got a vote. Another noteworthy similarity is the provisions allowing each house to adopt its own rules and to select its own leaders, powers that enhance legislative independence from other governmental entities. State legislatures were given explicit authority to select their own leaders in 10 state constitutions and to devise their own rules in five constitutions. Thus, the leadership selection and rulemaking provisions put in the U.S. Constitution are similar to those that appeared in many of the first state constitutions.

Another important provision in the U.S. Constitution involves the power to originate tax legislation. The idea that "money bills," as they were called, should originate in the lower house was well rooted in American history; colonial assemblies successfully claimed exclusive origination privileges early in many of their histories. The majority of the original state constitutions continued the tradition by granting the lower house exclusive rights to initiate tax legislation. Most state constitutions forbade the upper house from amending tax bills. The Constitutional Convention, however, opted for the process established in Delaware and Massachusetts, in which tax bills originated in the lower house, but the upper house could amend them. Indeed, the language in the U.S. Constitution on this score is virtually identical to that in the Massachusetts Constitution.

TABLE 1-1   THE ORIGINAL 13 STATE LEGISLATURES (IN ALPHABETICAL ORDER)

STATE	CAMERAL STATUS	LOWER HOUSE NAME	LOWER HOUSE MEMBERSHIP SIZE[a]	LOWER HOUSE TERM OF OFFICE	UPPER HOUSE NAME	UPPER HOUSE MEMBERSHIP SIZE[a]	UPPER HOUSE TERM OF OFFICE
Connecticut	Bicameral	House of Deputies or Representatives	200	6 months	Council	12	1 year
Delaware	Bicameral	House of Assembly	21	1 year	The (Legislative) Council	9	3 years
Georgia	Unicameral	House of Assembly	90	1 year	N/A	N/A	N/A
Maryland	Bicameral	House of Delegates	80	1 year	Senate	15	5 years
Massachusetts	Bicameral	House of Representatives	Variable	1 year	Senate	40	1 year
New Hampshire	Bicameral	House of Representatives or Assembly	Variable	1 year	Council	12	1 year
New Jersey	Bicameral	General Assembly	39	1 year	Legislative Council	13	1 year
New York	Bicameral	Assembly	70	1 year	Senate	24	4 years
North Carolina	Bicameral	House of Commons	70	1 year	Senate	32	1 year
Pennsylvania	Unicameral	House of Representatives	78	1 year	N/A	N/A	N/A
Rhode Island	Bicameral	House of Deputies	55	6 months	Council or Assistants	12	1 year
South Carolina	Bicameral	General Assembly	199	2 years	Legislative Council	13	2 years
Virginia	Bicameral	House of Delegates	126	1 year	Senate	24	4 years

Source: See the initial state constitution for each state (1776 version for South Carolina) except for Connecticut and Rhode Island. For Connecticut, see Purcell (1918, pp 188–89), for Rhode Island, see Bartlett (1863) and Polishook (1969, pp 22–23).

[a] A few constitutions provided explicit membership sizes. Most have to be calculated using the number of counties in each state (or towns, in the case of most New England states) at the time the particular constitution was adopted.

Finally, although most state constitutions did not grant their governors a veto power, three states did: South Carolina, New York, and Massachusetts. The veto power given to the president in the Constitution is the same as that granted to the governor of Massachusetts. Indeed, the language used in the Constitution is lifted almost verbatim from the Massachusetts Constitution.

Congress, then, initially starts out looking like the state legislatures rather than the other way around. Moreover, at the beginning, Congress was not seen as being more important or powerful than the state legislatures. For instance, although Jonathan Dayton was elected to serve as a member of the U.S. House of Representatives from New Jersey in 1788, he declined the office to serve instead as speaker of the New Jersey Assembly. Even into the early nineteenth century, it was not unusual for a member of Congress to give up his seat to take a state level post.[10] Once the Congress under the Constitution was established, however, it began to exert occasional influence on state legislative organization. When Georgia adopted its second constitution in 1789, for example, the state legislature was made bicameral, largely to emulate the new federal structure.[11] Over the next century, however, Congress and the state legislatures generally began following separate evolutionary paths.

STATE LEGISLATIVE EVOLUTION
IN THE NINETEENTH CENTURY

During the nineteenth century, state legislatures experienced two significant evolutionary trends. One was that existing legislatures underwent extensive organizational transformations. Many of these changes were forced on state legislatures by disaffected political elites and electorates who were disgusted by the legislatures' perceived (and in many cases, real) abuses of power. Thus, as state constitutions were revised or replaced, provisions were adopted that required specific legislative procedures be followed, almost all of which greatly constrained legislative power in the policymaking process.[12]

The second trend was that the number of American state legislatures increased substantially, with 29 of them being created between 1803 and 1896 as new states were admitted to the union. All of the new state legislatures were established as bicameral bodies because it was widely thought at the time that a second house prevented, or at least slowed down, the passage of bad legislation.[13] (Similar to Georgia, the Pennsylvania legislature became bicameral when the state adopted its second constitution in 1790. Vermont, the fourteenth state, kept its unicameral legislature until 1836.) Most importantly, the new state legislatures were created to look like existing state legislatures.

Most of the state legislatures established in the nineteenth century originated as territorial bodies, typically set up in primitive settings. As a young reporter in Nevada, for example, Mark Twain observed that in the building used for the first territorial assembly meeting, a local merchant "furnished pine benches and chairs for the legislature, and covered the floors with clean saw-dust by way of carpet and spittoon combined. . . . A canvas partition to separate the Senate from the House of Representatives was put up by the Secretary."[14] Even when they became state legislatures, these fledgling institutions were often rowdy and unmanageable. For instance, during the inaugural session of the Arkansas House of Representatives in 1837, Speaker of the House John Wilson and Representative Joseph Anthony became so angry with each other during a legislative debate that Wilson left the speaker's chair and lunged for Anthony on the house floor. In the ensuing fight, both men drew hunting knives, and Wilson stabbed Anthony to death.[15] Such outrageous behavior was not unusual. The first session of the California legislature in 1849 was labeled the "Legislature of a Thousand Drinks" because at the end of each session, one committee chair would encourage his colleagues to adjourn to the whisky kegs he kept stashed just outside the meeting hall and to "take a thousand drinks."[16] Reputedly, California's first lawmakers "appeared in the legislative halls with revolvers and bowie knives fastened to their belts and were drinking, rioting, and swearing nearly all the time."[17]

But even with primitive facilities and boorish members, organizationally, the new legislatures were anything but rudimentary. The new state legislatures in the nineteenth century were closely modeled after their existing peer institutions. The generational impact of older state legislatures on newer ones is clearly seen in two areas: committee systems and rules of procedure.

The first state legislatures made limited use of standing committees—committees that continue to exist from session to session—to process their work. In Massachusetts, for example, standing committees appeared in 1777, and a "fairly elaborate system had developed by 1790."[18] Thus, in the original state legislature, standing committee systems evolved over time. In contrast, state legislatures created just after the revolutionary era adopted standing committee systems either at their inception or shortly thereafter. Legislative journals provide no evidence of standing committees in the Ohio House of Representatives in 1815, but by 1832, they reveal 14 standing committees.[19] But by the middle of the nineteenth century, newly established state legislatures instituted standing committee systems from their start. During the Iowa legislature's first session in 1846, for example, there were 15 standing committees in the House and 16 standing committees in the Senate.[20] Clearly, standing committee systems had become standard in American legislatures by the 1840s, and they were created immediately in all new lawmaking bodies.

The pedigree of legislative rules and procedures is somewhat more complicated to trace. An examination of the rules in the early Indiana state legislature, for example, reveals: "The first general assemblies drew their rules from those adopted by the House of Representatives during the first territorial assembly in Indiana in 1805. These were in turn based upon rules adopted by the first session of the House of Representatives of the Northwest Territory in 1799."[21] The rules of the Northwest Territory House were direct descendents of the rules developed during the first session of the U.S. House. Similar inheritance patterns were evidenced in other state legislatures.[22] A generation later, legislative procedures in the newly established Iowa territorial legislature were again rooted in the rules developed by existing legislatures. In the Council—the upper house of the territorial legislature—members used *Jefferson's Manual*, written when Thomas Jefferson was president of the U.S. Senate and based on British parliamentary precedents, as the source for legislative rules and procedures in their first session, and they formally recognized those rules as governing their procedures in their second session. During the transition in Iowa from territory to state, legislative procedures essentially carried over virtually unchanged. In the new state Senate, the territorial rules of procedure were adopted with only a few minor modifications.[23]

By the end of the nineteenth century, state legislatures were well-developed institutions, complete with standing committee systems and sophisticated rules and procedures. In that sense, they looked much like Congress. But, although state constitutions were rewritten to rein in state legislative powers, the U.S. Constitution was left untouched in regards to congressional organization, and the Thirteenth, Fourteenth, and Fifteenth Amendments, which were added to it in the aftermath of the Civil War, expanded congressional powers (although it was decades before these new powers were exploited). Toward the end of the century, Congress also began to professionalize, greatly increasing its informational resources and, in turn, its impact on the policymaking process. Thus, during the course of the nineteenth century, the power of state legislatures waned while Congress was becoming a more powerful institution.

STATE LEGISLATIVE EVOLUTION IN THE TWENTIETH CENTURY

It was only in the twentieth century that state legislatures began to view Congress as a model to be emulated. This was not necessarily because Congress was deemed more visible or important but because Congress became a more professional organization that was well equipped to meet the policy challenges it faced. The story of state legislative evolution over this time was one of a lagging effort to effect similar organizational improvements.

As we will discuss in greater depth in Chapter 3, legislatures that are deemed professional meet in unlimited sessions, provide superior staff resources, and pay members well enough to allow them to pursue service as their vocation. It is important to note that a professionalized body does not have to be a career body, one in which members want and expect to serve for many years. Even when professionalization standards are met, members may, of their own volition, opt to serve for only short periods, as was the case in the California legislature even before the imposition of term limits.[24]

The evolution of state legislatures in the twentieth century is, however, linked to professionalization. At the beginning of the twentieth century, the vast majority of state legislatures were very similar to each other, with low levels of professionalization. They paid their members little, met for relatively few days, and had no staff. Over the next century, substantial differences emerged across the states.[25] The state legislatures in a few states, all with large populations, became well-paid, full-time bodies, with large staffs, much like the U.S. Congress. Many legislatures improved their lot, at least a little. Some legislatures, however, failed to change much at all.[26] Thus, by the beginning of the twenty-first century, state legislatures as institutions varied from one another, as well as from Congress.

STATE LEGISLATURES TODAY

What are the basic characteristics of state legislatures today? None is referred to as "Congress." As documented in Table 1-2, just over half of the states call their lawmaking body the "Legislature." The majority of the rest are referred to as the "General Assembly." North Dakota and Oregon blend the two names with the "Legislative Assembly." Finally, Massachusetts and New Hampshire use the seemingly archaic title, the "General Court." This label was used in the colonial era and was grounded in the fact that lawmaking bodies at that time performed both legislative and judicial functions. Indeed, the separation between the two branches actually sharpened only in the twentieth century. Divorces, for example, could be granted by many state legislatures until the mid-nineteenth century and in a few states even into the early decades of the twentieth century.[27]

NUMBER OF HOUSES

Perhaps the most fundamental question about the structure of a legislature is how many houses it has. As Table 1-2 shows, bicameral legislatures are a fixture at the state level. Every state legislature, except for Nebraska, has two houses. Importantly, similar to the two houses in Congress, both houses in the 49 bicameral state legislatures are powerful, and both must pass bills for them to become law. (Bicameral legislatures in other countries often have only one house that is powerful, as in, for example, Canada, Great Britain, and Japan.) As noted previously, one reason for the prevalence of bicameral

TABLE 1-2 THE 50 STATE LEGISLATURES (IN ALPHABETICAL ORDER)

STATE	LEGISLATURE NAME	UPPER HOUSE NAME	UPPER HOUSE SIZE	UPPER HOUSE TERM	LOWER HOUSE NAME	LOWER HOUSE SIZE	LOWER HOUSE TERM	LOWER HOUSE MEMBERS PER SENATOR
Alabama	Legislature	Senate	35	4	House of Representatives	105	4	3.00
Alaska	Legislature	Senate	20	4	House of Representatives	40	2	2.00
Arizona	Legislature	Senate	30	2	House of Representatives	60	2	2.00
Arkansas	General Assembly	Senate	35	4	House of Representatives	100	2	2.86
California	Legislature	Senate	40	4	Assembly	80	2	2.00
Colorado	General Assembly	Senate	35	4	House of Representatives	65	2	1.86
Connecticut	General Assembly	Senate	36	2	House of Representatives	151	2	4.19
Delaware	General Assembly	Senate	21	4	House of Representatives	41	2	1.95
Florida	Legislature	Senate	40	4	House of Representatives	120	2	3.00
Georgia	General Assembly	Senate	56	2	House of Representatives	180	2	3.21
Hawaii	Legislature	Senate	25	4	House of Representatives	51	2	2.04
Idaho	Legislature	Senate	35	2	House of Representatives	70	2	2.00
Illinois	General Assembly	Senate	59	4[a]	House of Representatives	118	2	2.00

(Continued)

9

TABLE 1-2 (CONTINUED)

State	Legislature Name	Upper House Name	Upper House Size	Upper House Term	Lower House Name	Lower House Size	Lower House Term	Lower House Members Per Senator
Indiana	General Assembly	Senate	50	4	House of Representatives	100	2	2.00
Iowa	General Assembly	Senate	50	4	House of Representatives	100	2	2.00
Kansas	Legislature	Senate	40	4	House of Representatives	125	2	3.13
Kentucky	General Assembly	Senate	38	4	House of Representatives	100	2	2.63
Louisiana	Legislature	Senate	39	4	House of Representatives	105	4	2.69
Maine	Legislature	Senate	35	2	House of Representatives	151	2	4.31
Maryland	General Assembly	Senate	47	4	House of Delegates	141	4	3.00
Massachusetts	General Court	Senate	40	2	House of Representatives	160	2	4.00
Michigan	Legislature	Senate	38	4	House of Representatives	110	2	2.89
Minnesota	Legislature	Senate	67	4	House of Representatives	134	2	2.00
Mississippi	Legislature	Senate	52	4	House of Representatives	122	4	2.35
Missouri	General Assembly	Senate	34	4	House of Representatives	163	2	4.79
Montana	Legislature	Senate	50	4	House of Representatives	100	2	2.00

TABLE 1-2 (CONTINUED)

STATE	LEGISLATURE NAME	UPPER HOUSE NAME	UPPER HOUSE SIZE	UPPER HOUSE TERM	LOWER HOUSE NAME	LOWER HOUSE SIZE	LOWER HOUSE TERM	LOWER HOUSE MEMBERS PER SENATOR
Nebraska	Legislature (Unicameral)	N/A	49	4	N/A	N/A	N/A	N/A
Nevada	Legislature	Senate	21	4	Assembly	42	2	2.00
New Hampshire	General Court	Senate	24	2	House of Representatives	400	2	16.67
New Jersey	Legislature	Senate	40	4[b]	General Assembly	80	2	2.00
New Mexico	Legislature	Senate	42	4	House of Representatives	70	2	1.67
New York	Legislature	Senate	62	2	Assembly	150	2	2.42
North Carolina	General Assembly	Senate	50	2	House of Representatives	120	2	2.40
North Dakota	Legislative Assembly	Senate	47	4	House of Representatives	94	4	2.00
Ohio	General Assembly	Senate	33	4	House of Representatives	99	2	3.00
Oklahoma	Legislature	Senate	48	4	House of Representatives	101	2	2.10
Oregon	Legislative Assembly	Senate	30	4	House of Representatives	60	2	2.00
Pennsylvania	General Assembly	Senate	50	4	House of Representatives	203	2	4.06
Rhode Island	General Assembly	Senate	38	2	House of Representatives	75	2	1.97
South Carolina	General Assembly	Senate	46	4	House of Representatives	124	2	2.70

(Continued)

TABLE 1-2 (CONTINUED)

STATE	LEGISLATURE NAME	UPPER HOUSE NAME	UPPER HOUSE SIZE	UPPER HOUSE TERM	LOWER HOUSE NAME	LOWER HOUSE SIZE	LOWER HOUSE TERM	LOWER HOUSE MEMBERS PER SENATOR
South Dakota	Legislature	Senate	35	2	House of Representatives	70	2	2.00
Tennessee	General Assembly	Senate	33	4	House of Representatives	99	2	3.00
Texas	Legislature	Senate	31	4	House of Representatives	150	2	4.84
Utah	Legislature	Senate	29	4	House of Representatives	75	2	2.58
Vermont	General Assembly	Senate	30	2	House of Representatives	150	2	5.00
Virginia	General Assembly	Senate	40	4	House of Delegates	100	2	2.50
Washington	Legislature	Senate	49	4	House of Representatives	98	2	2.00
West Virginia	Legislature	Senate	34	4	House of Delegates	100	2	2.94
Wisconsin	Legislature	Senate	33	4	Assembly	99	2	3.00
Wyoming	Legislature	Senate	30	4	House of Representatives	60	2	2.00

[a]Illinois senate seats are divided into three electoral classes. In each 10-year period, a senate seat has two four-year terms and one two-year term.
[b]New Jersey senate terms are two years in the first election after redistricting each decade and are then followed by two four-year terms.

bodies in the states was the calculation that two houses allow for greater re-flection in the policymaking process. Legislation that passes one house must still pass the other house, inevitably slowing down the lawmaking process by requiring a separate house of legislators, elected independently from the members in the first house, to render judgment on a measure's merits. Thus, having two houses makes it more difficult for bills to become law because it increases the number of obstacles any proposal must pass. This can be a source of considerable frustration for supporters of a bill that passes one house but fails to make it out of the other house. Opponents of a measure, however, realize that a second house may prove to be their saving grace. A Missouri state senator, for example, recently expressed his disdain for a bill that passed his chamber by exclaiming, "I think it is time to send this piece of crap to the House and pray to God that for once they have more sense than this body."[28]

The existence of two houses that must each consider legislation forces the creation of rules to manage that dual consideration. Rules can dictate the sequencing of bill consideration and voting, such as the constitutional provi-sions currently found in 20 states that require the lower house to originate all revenue or tax bills.[29] There also are rules governing how conflicts between two houses are to be resolved, with, for example, several states making little or no use of conference committees with member for both houses but other states relying heavily on them.[30]

THE NEBRASKA EXCEPTION

Nebraska's unicameral legislature is the great exception among current state legislatures. When the state entered the union in 1867, its legislature was a bicameral body, like every other state legislature at the time. Indeed, the cur-rent state capitol, designed in 1920 and completed in 1932, has a second chamber. But in 1934, Nebraska voters overwhelmingly passed an initiative to change their bicameral legislature to a unicameral body. The idea had been pushed for some years by U.S. Senator George W. Norris (R-NE), who railed against what he saw as the corruption promoted by the actions of con-ference committees in bicameral legislatures. Other unicameral supporters, however, backed the idea because they thought one house would be more economical, a powerful appeal at a time when the country was in the depths of the Great Depression.[31] The unicameral legislature first met in 1937 with 43 members, a considerable reduction from the 133 members in its bicameral predecessor.

Voters hoped the switch would reduce the cost of running the legislature and make the legislative process more efficient. It is not clear, however, that the Unicameral functions more economically, efficiently, or effectively than other state legislatures.[32] For example, the Unicameral costs more to run per citizen than the larger two-house state legislature next door in Iowa. Still, in recent years, proponents of unicameral legislatures have promoted the idea in California, Iowa, Michigan, Minnesota, Pennsylvania, and South Dakota, albeit unsuccessfully.[33] In 2005, voters in Puerto Rico endorsed a proposed constitutional amendment to create a unicameral legislature, but the courts later scuttled the effort.[34]

But the Nebraska legislature is not only exceptional because of its single house. When unicameralism was adopted, the legislature was also changed to become a nonpartisan body, meaning that party labels do not appear on the ballot attached to candidate names. (Nonpartisan elections are usually associated with contests for local offices or judgeships. The Minnesota legislature, however, was also nonpartisan from 1914 to 1973.) Although most Nebraska voters know which candidate for the Unicameral is a Republican and which is a Democrat, after they are elected to office, members tend to downplay their partisanship. There are, for example, no party caucuses in the legislature; instead, groups are organized regionally, with members assigned to the Omaha, Lincoln, or West caucus based on the district they represent. Moreover, in recent years, Democrats have been elected as committee chairs and speaker even though they were in the minority. Finally, party does not explain how Nebraska legislators vote on bills.[35] Arguably, being nonpartisan may have a greater impact on the behavior of Nebraska legislators than the fact that they operate in a single house.

HOUSE NAME

Almost every state now calls its lower house the "House of Representatives." As Table 1-1 documents, the name was used in many of the original states, but several of them first used other names before switching to it.[36] A few states continue to use other names. California, Nevada, New York, and Wisconsin call their lower houses the "Assembly," while the lower house in New Jersey is called the "General Assembly." Both New Jersey and New York kept the "Assembly" name from their colonial legislature; the name spread to the other states because of the use of an older state's constitution as a model in the development of a new state's constitution—New York's in Wisconsin and California and California's in Nevada.[37] Finally, Maryland, Virginia, and West Virginia refer to their lower houses as the "House of Delegates." Virginia switched the name of its representative assembly to "House of Delegates" from the "House of Burgesses" when it declared independence in 1776. Neighboring Maryland adopted the same name, and West Virginia took it when it split from Virginia during the Civil War.

Every upper house today is called the "Senate." Thomas Jefferson first suggested the name in his proposed draft of Virginia's first constitution.[38] Although a few states initially referred to their upper house as a "Council" (or occasionally another name), they eventually switched to calling it the "Senate" as well.[39]

MEMBERSHIP SIZE

Currently, state legislative chambers range in size from very small (20 members in the Alaska state Senate) to very large (400 members in the New Hampshire House of Representatives, down from 443 as recently as 1942). As has always been the case, in each state, the lower chamber has more members than the upper chamber. But none of the lower houses is as large as the 435-member U.S. House of Representatives. And none of the 50 state senates is as large as the 100 member U.S. Senate; the largest is Minnesota's, with 67 members. Indeed, only 22 of the lower houses in the states are larger than the U.S. Senate. Perhaps surprisingly, there is no statistically significant relationship between state population size and the number of legislators in a state.[40] California, for example, has 120 state legislators, and New Hampshire has 424.

Typically, membership size is established in the state constitution. Some constitutions, such as Alaska's (Article 2, Section 1), are very specific: "The legislative power of the State is vested in a legislature consisting of a senate with a membership of twenty and a house of representatives with a membership of forty." Other state constitutions allow somewhat more flexibility. The New Hampshire Constitution (Part Second, Article 9), for example, states, "The whole number of representatives to be chosen from the towns, wards, places, and representative districts thereof established hereunder, shall be not less than three hundred seventy-five or more than four hundred." The state senate, however, is given a definite size (Part Second, Article 25): "The senate shall consist of twenty-four members." Perhaps the greatest flexibility is in Nevada, where the constitution imposes no limit on the number of legislators, leaving that decision to the legislature itself (Constitution of the State of Nevada, Article 4, Section 5): "It shall be the mandatory duty of the legislature at its first session after the taking of the decennial census of the United States . . . to fix by law the number of senators and assemblymen. . . ." The only constitutional restriction is "the number of senators shall not be less than one-third nor more than one-half of that of the members of the assembly."

Given that many state constitutions make it relatively easy to change the number of state legislators, it is not surprising that a majority of legislatures either increased or decreased their number of legislative seats in the past half century.[41] In contrast, both houses of the U.S. Congress remained the same size during this period. Many state legislatures changed membership sizes in the aftermath of the Supreme Court's 1964 decision *Reynolds v. Sims*, which, as discussed in Chapter 2, forced a number of states to alter the way they apportioned one or both houses.[42] Later, alterations in a few states were made to make legislatures smaller and, it was hoped, less costly and more efficient. In 1979, for example, the number of seats in the Massachusetts House of Representatives was reduced to 160 from 240, and in 1983, the Illinois House of Representatives experienced a one-third cut in the number of seats, to 118 from 177. More recently, in 2003, the Rhode Island legislature downsized both chambers of its legislature by 25 percent as mandated by the voters several years earlier.[43] Finally, a handful of states (notably Nevada, North Dakota, and Wyoming) tinker with the number of members in their legislature after each decennial Census.[44]

Adding or reducing the number of seats in a legislature involves an implicit tradeoff between legislative efficiency and representation, as Politics Under the Domes 1-1 discusses. But there is another consideration in setting the number of seats in each house that is usually ignored. Of the 99 state legislative houses, 61 are currently configured with an even number of seats. Indeed, in 23 states, both houses have an even number of seats. Given a two-party system, an even number of legislative seats enhances the possibility of a potential complication—a tied house. This happens more frequently than one might predict. Between 1966 and 2008, 38 chambers were tied at some point, creating considerable organizational difficulties.[45] Problems with managing the Washington state House, which has been tied three different times in the past three decades, have prompted so far unsuccessful calls for adding another seat to make an odd number.[46] And although we might assume that a tie would be avoided in the 38 houses that have an odd number of seats, the problem can still arise. In 2001, the 35-member Maine Senate found itself tied with 17 Democrats, 17 Republicans, and an independent who forced a power-sharing agreement with the two parties.[47]

What difference does varying membership size make? It is possible that the number of members influences organizational structures and rules. In a study of decision making in the 99 state legislative chambers, for example, it was found that party caucuses are more important in smaller chambers, and party leaders are more important in larger chambers.[48] More generally, another student of state legislatures observed:

> Size has its effects on the following: the atmosphere, with more confusion and impersonality in larger bodies and friendlier relationships in smaller ones; hierarchy, with more elaborate and orderly rules and procedures and greater leadership authority in larger bodies and informality and collegial authority in smaller ones; the conduct of business, with a more efficient flow and less debate in larger bodies and more leisurely deliberation and greater fluidity in smaller ones; the internal distribution of power, with more concentrated pockets possible in larger bodies and greater dispersion of power in smaller ones.[49]

Congressional scholars frequently cite differences in membership size to explain why the larger House developed much more rigid rules and procedures than did the smaller Senate.[50] An examination of 55 national legislatures reached a similar conclusion.[51] But this relationship does not appear to apply to state legislatures. If size alone matters in explaining the evolution of legislature rules and procedures, then most state legislative houses should

POLITICS UNDER THE DOMES 1-1

The Legislative Representation and Efficiency Tradeoff

In 2003, the Rhode Island House of Representatives was reduced to 75 seats from 100 seats, and the Senate to 38 seats from 50 seats. The chair of the Rhode Island commission that first recommended creating a smaller legislature observed, "The goal of the downsizing was to increase responsibility and give individual legislators an opportunity to influence decisions and be more effective in representing their constituents." Embedded in this rationale is an inherent but often unrecognized tradeoff. Having fewer members in a house gives each member a greater opportunity to influence legislative decisions. That is, being one of 75 lawmakers is better than being one of 100 lawmakers. At the same time, however, reducing the number of seats in each house means that each legislator will represent more constituents. In the case of the Rhode Island House, the reduction increased the average district size to roughly 14,000 people from 10,500 people. Consequently, in the smaller house, each legislator would be able to exercise greater power but would do so on behalf of more constituents.

One side or the other of this tradeoff is often acknowledged in debates over changes in membership size. A proponent of increasing the number of legislative seats in California, for example, recently touted the perceived benefits of smaller districts: "Smaller districts would mean candidates could conceivably . . . meet more voters face to face. It would also mean voters could stay in touch with their constituencies better." A few years earlier, a Rhode Island representative offered the flip side of this argument in opposing a reduction in seats: "If the legislature is downsized, future legislators will not be able to have the type of one on one contact that I have been privileged to have with the people of Pawtucket for the last eighteen years." Others in these debates focus on the anticipated impact of a change in membership size on legislative dynamics. For instance, an official with the League of Women Voters in Pennsylvania claimed in supporting a measure to reduce the number of seats in that state's legislature, "The present size is too large for individual [legislators'] opinions to be considered and too large for meaningful floor debate." Rarely, however, is the tradeoff between seats and district size explicitly recognized.

Moreover, practical concerns rather than theoretical ones often drive support for or opposition to a proposed change in legislative

(Continued)

POLITICS UNDER THE DOMES 1-1 (CONTINUED)

membership size. Many times, proposals for increasing the number of seats in a legislature are opposed because of the additional costs in salaries, staff, and equipment. Concomitantly, those pushing for a smaller legislature claim it will cost the state less money to run. But in many cases, there is more than just a concern with costs with these proposals. It is not unusual for there to be a desire to reduce the number of legislators as a way of limiting the number of officials who can exploit their positions. As a cynical letter to the editor supporting the reduction in the size of the Rhode Island legislature put it, "Fewer legislators means fewer brothers-in-law that have to be found state jobs." The comments of a Nevada National Association for the Advancement of Colored People leader, who opposed enlarging that state's legislature, are along the same lines: "Increasing the number of foxes guarding the henhouse does not mean the chickens are any safer. I don't know how many foxes we need." Given such sentiments, it is not surprising that proposals to downsize a state legislature often enjoy broad political appeal. In a 2007 survey, for example, 51 percent of Pennsylvanians supported a proposal to eliminate 53 state legislative seats; only 32 percent opposed the idea. Indeed, the proposed cut was popular with Republicans and Democrats alike. Pennsylvania state legislators, however, were not enthused about the measure and prevented it from coming up for a formal debate.

It is not clear that reducing the number of legislators produces a lower cost legislature or a more efficient legislative process. A decade after the dramatic reduction in the size of the Illinois House of Representatives, administrative costs had actually increased rather than decreased, and the number of bills introduced stayed about the same. One analysis attributed this outcome to the fact that the legislature's workload was driven by the size and diversity of the state, not by the size of the legislature. It may be that in this case, size does not matter.

Sources: Tom Barnes, "Lawmaker Cuts Still in Committee; Attempt to Fast-Track Bill Fails, *Pittsburgh Post-Gazette,* October 16, 2007; Tom Barnes, "Time at Hand to Downsize State Legislature?" *Pittsburgh Post-Gazette,* January 18, 2006; Alan Ehrenhalt, "'Rightsizing the Legislature," *Governing* (July 2001):6; David H. Everson, "The Cutback at 10: Illinois House Without Cumulative Voting and 59 Members," *Illinois Issues* 17 (July 1991), 13–15; Edward Fitzpatrick, "The Incredible Shrinking Legislature," *State Legislatures* 28 (July/August 2002), 51–54; Jane Ann Morrison, "Democrats' Proposal Draws Fire on First Day," *Las Vegas Review Journal,* May 11, 2001; Quinnipiac University Poll, "Pennsylvania Voters Back Rendell Plan to Hike Sales Tax, Quinnipiac University Poll Finds; Support to Reduce Lawmakers and Set Term Limits," May 30, 2007; State of Rhode Island and Providence Plantations, *Journal of the House of Representatives,* May 31, 2000; Sean Whaley, "Legislature Size May Spur Rift," *Las Vegas Review Journal,* July 7, 2000; and Steve Wiegand, "His Master Plan: More Legislators," *Sacramento Bee,* November 30, 2006.

operate with less-rigid rules like the similarly sized U.S. Senate, and only a handful of the really large bodies should be regimented, along the lines of the U.S. House. In fact, as discussed in Chapters 5 and 6, more state legislative chambers organize and proceed like the U.S. House than like the U.S. Senate, regardless of size.

Bicameral Size Differences

Perhaps the most underappreciated contrast between the two houses in bicameral state legislatures is the difference in membership sizes. The contrast in size between the two houses may affect their relationship because of differences in their relative capacities to gather and digest information. A house with far more members than its companion house enjoys considerably lower information acquisition costs, thereby conferring policymaking advantages on it.[52] Also, evidence suggests that disparities in membership size affect legislative productivity, with upper houses that are small in comparison to their lower houses creating substantial legislative bottlenecks.[53] Finally, as the ratio of lower house seats to upper house seats increases, state expenditures decrease.[54]

As shown in Table 1-2, the most common ratio between upper and lower house memberships in the states is one senator for every two lower house members, which is found in 16 states. But the ratios range from a low of one senator for every 1.67 representatives in New Mexico to a high of one senator for every 16.7 representatives in New Hampshire. Indeed, four state legislatures have higher ratios than the one senator to 4.35 House members found in the U.S. Congress.

Terms of Office

Term length is thought to influence member behavior, with longer terms giving legislators greater freedom from electoral pressures and shorter terms providing less freedom. Terms for state legislators have changed over time. In general, terms were lengthened over the course of the nineteenth century.[55] In Pennsylvania, for example, members of the House of Representatives were elected to one-year terms until the 1874 constitution, when two-year terms were instituted. In that same constitution, state senators were bumped up to four-year terms from three-year terms.[56] In most states, lower house terms were extended from one to two years. Typically, upper house terms were extended as well, although the number of years adopted often bounced around. Georgia, for example, kept changing the term of office for its upper house:

> Her first senators, provided for in 1789, were to be elected every third year. Annual election was substituted in 1795; this was changed to biennial in 1840 with the adoption of the biennial system; in 1868 the four-year term was substituted; and in 1877 return was made to the two-year term.[57]

Terms continued to change over the past century, as the current terms of office given in Table 1-2 reveals. Terms in 30 states are for two years in the lower house and four years in the state senate. But in 12 states, members of both houses are given two-year terms, and in five states, both houses get four-year terms. Nebraska legislators are given four-year terms. And in Illinois and New Jersey, state senators have shifting terms, with one two-year term and two four-year terms to accommodate redistricting every 10 years. A variety of other mechanisms are used to cope with redistricting in the other 37 states that have staggered electoral terms.[58]

Proposals to lengthen legislative terms have surfaced in several states in recent years. The arguments advanced by legislators in favor of longer terms revolve around the electoral burden imposed by two-year terms. An Arizona legislator noted that with two-year terms, "You're in a constant cycle." He thought longer terms would be beneficial because "you'd have a little less time to be worried about the campaign. You can concentrate on business and not running."[59] Other legislators see advantages in two-year terms. A West Virginia legislator argued that shorter terms "make closer to the people we represent," adding, "I do think the more often we run, the more responsible we are."[60] Rigorous analyses of state legislative elections reveal that legislators with two-year terms enjoy higher reelection rates than their colleagues with four-year terms, probably because less-frequent election cycles draw better challengers to a race.[61] Although legislators occasionally contemplate pushing for changes in their term lengths—usually longer terms—no state has done so since 1996, when North Dakota increased its lower house term from two to four years.

TERM LIMITS

Limits on the number of terms a state legislator may legally serve are not a recent idea. They were first imposed on the Pennsylvania legislature in 1776, where members could only serve four one-year terms over a seven-year period.[62] These first limits were, however, dispensed with when the state adopted its second constitution in 1790. But the notion of limiting state legislative service still held in various places around the country. Often called *rotation*, legislators in some districts during the nineteenth century were expected to serve only one or two terms and then step aside so that someone else, usually from another county in the district, could hold the seat. This political norm constituted an informal term limitation. More recently, rotation agreements were used in a few state legislatures, almost all in the one-party South. The U.S. Supreme Court's reapportionment decisions in the early 1960s effectively ended such pacts.[63]

Term limits were not seriously debated again until the late 1980s, and then they were adopted in 21 states with amazing speed.[64] As Table 1-3 shows, in 1990, voters in Colorado, Oklahoma, and California were the first

TABLE 1-3   STATE LEGISLATIVE TERM LIMITS WITH YEAR OF ADOPTION
AND YEAR LIMITS TOOK EFFECT[a]

TERM LIMIT	CONSECUTIVE SERVICE	LIFETIME BAN
6 years lower house 8 years upper house		Arkansas (1992, 1998 H, 2000 S)[b] California (1990, 1996 H, 1998 S) Michigan (1992, 1998 H, 2002 S)
8 years total	Nebraska (2000, 2006)[c]	
8 years lower house 8 years upper house	Arizona (1992, 2000) Colorado (1990, 1998) Florida (1992, 2000) Maine (1993, 1996) Montana (1992, 2000) Ohio (1992, 2000) South Dakota (1992, 2000)	Missouri (1992, 2002)
12 years combined in either one house or both houses		Oklahoma (1990, 2004)
12 years lower house 12 years upper house	Louisiana (1995, 2007)	Nevada (1996, 2010)

Source: Data from National Conference of State Legislatures.

[a]State courts in Massachusetts, Oregon, Washington, and Wyoming tossed out term limit measures passed by their voters. State legislators repealed term limits in Idaho and Utah.

[b]The first number in parentheses is the year term limits were adopted. The second number is the year term limits went into effect. The year they went into effect for different houses is designated by H for the lower house and S for state senate.

[c]Voters in Nebraska passed term limit measures in 1992 and 1994, but both were ruled unconstitutional by the state supreme court.

to impose term limits on their state legislators. Two years later, term-limit measures passed in all 12 states in which they appeared on the ballot, and they were adopted in six more states by 1995. There were, however, some bumps along the way. Nebraska voters had to pass term limits three times—in 1992, 1994, and 2000—because the Nebraska Supreme Court tossed out the first two versions on legal technicalities. Term-limit laws passed by the voters were also overturned by the state supreme courts in Massachusetts in 1997, Washington in 1998, Oregon in 2002, and Wyoming in 2004. Moreover, the term limit movement was pushed by voters, not legislators. Only in Utah and Louisiana did lawmakers place limits on themselves, and in Utah, they were pressured by the threat that voters would use a ballot measure to impose more stringent limitations. In every other state that adopted term limit, voters, not legislators, made the decision.

The political tide appears to have turned against the term-limit movement in recent years. Other than Nebraska, no state has adopted term limits since 1995. Mississippi voters rejected term limits in both 1995 and 1999;

North Dakota voters did likewise in 1996. In 2002, the heavily Republican state legislature in Idaho repealed the term limits voters had imposed eight years earlier (the repeal option is afforded to legislatures in only a few states).[65] In the general elections that fall, Idaho voters upheld the legislators' decision to remove term limits, although by only the thinnest of margins. Utah's Republican-controlled legislature repealed term limits in 2003 without much public dissent. Term limits, however, still appear to have political appeal elsewhere. Ballot measures to soften or eliminate term limits were rejected by voters in California in 2002 and 2008, Arkansas and Montana in 2004, Maine in 2007, and South Dakota in 2008.

Currently, 15 states impose term limitations, but the limits vary regarding their specifics. The differences revolve around the number of terms a legislator may serve and whether those term limits are lifetime bans or simply limits on the number of consecutive terms. For example, Louisiana and Nevada have 12-year limits in each house, and Arkansas, California and Michigan have more stringent limits of six years in the lower house and eight years in the upper house. Both Ohio and Missouri have eight-year limits in each house, but Missouri's is a lifetime limit while Ohio's is simply a consecutive term limit. Therefore, in Ohio, a termed-out legislator is eligible to hold office again after sitting out for four years. In Missouri, after a legislator reaches the term limit, his or her career in that house is over.

Assessing the effects of term limits is a complicated enterprise, partly because the nature of the term limit laws are not the same everywhere and partly because of the relative professionalization of the various legislatures before term limits went into effect. In other words, not all legislatures were the same before term limits, and therefore the precise effect will not be the same. Nonetheless, a careful, comprehensive multi-year study of term limits reported that some consequences of term limits are now pretty clear.[66] The most obvious consequence is greater turnover in most term-limited legislatures.[67] And this, in turn, has led to instability in standing committee systems. As discussed in Chapter 5, committees are a crucial element in the lawmaking process. The upshot, then is that "the informational, deliberative and gatekeeping roles of the committees are undermined by term limits."[68] Furthermore, strong evidence suggests that term limits put legislatures at a disadvantage in their relations with the executive branch.[69]

CONSTITUENCY SIZE

Since *Reynolds v. Sims*, all state legislative houses must be apportioned on the basis of population, meaning that all districts in a chamber in a state must have roughly the same population per legislator elected. States, however, vary greatly in population and in the number of legislators in their legislatures. Thus, it is not surprising that the range of constituency sizes across the 50 state legislatures is extraordinary. Using 2006 population figures, Tables 1-4 and 1-5

**TABLE 1-4 CONSTITUENCY SIZE BY STATE LOWER HOUSE CHAMBER, 2006
(FROM SMALLEST TO LARGEST)**

STATE	LOWER HOUSE SEATS	DISTRICT POPULATION[a]
New Hampshire	400	3,287
Vermont	150	4,159
Wyoming	60	8,583
Maine	151	8,752
Montana	100	9,446
North Dakota	94	13,529
Rhode Island	75	14,235
Alaska	40	16,751
West Virginia	100	18,185
Delaware	41	20,816
Kansas	125	22,113
South Dakota	70	22,341
Connecticut	151	23,211
Mississippi	122	23,857
Hawaii	51	25,206
New Mexico	70	27,923
Arkansas	100	28,109
Iowa	100	29,821
Utah	75	34,001
South Carolina	124	33,849
Oklahoma	101	35,438
Missouri	163	35,845
Minnesota	134	38,560
Maryland	141	39,828
Massachusetts	160	40,232
Louisiana	105	40,836
Idaho	70	41,899
Kentucky	100	42,061
Alabama	105	43,800
Georgia	180	52,022
Wisconsin	99	56,126
Nevada	42	59,417
Tennessee	99	60,998
Pennsylvania	203	61,284
Oregon	60	61,679
Indiana	100	63,135
Colorado	65	73,129
North Carolina	120	73,804

(Continued)

TABLE 1-4   (CONTINUED)

STATE	LOWER HOUSE SEATS	DISTRICT POPULATION[a]
Virginia	100	76,429
Michigan	110	91,779
Illinois	118	108,746
Ohio	99	115,939
New York	150	128,708
Washington	98	130,526
Florida	120	150,749
Texas	150	156,719
Arizona	60	205,544
New Jersey	80	218,114
California	80	455,719
Mean		64,229
Median		40,232

Source: Calculated by the authors using U.S. Census Bureau data for 2006.

[a]Arizona, Idaho, New Jersey, North Dakota, and Washington elect two lower house members in each upper house district; thus, each lower house member represents as many constituents as the corresponding upper house member, and that is the number reported here. Maryland, New Hampshire, South Dakota, Vermont, and West Virginia have "mixed" electoral systems with some single-member districts (SMDs) and some multi-member districts. For this table, the district population figure is calculated for the SMDs in those states, except for South Dakota. For more details, about the electoral districts in these states, see Table 1-6. Nebraska's unicameral legislature is considered as an upper house and not included in this table.

provide average constituency sizes for the 99 state legislative houses. At one extreme, the 40 California state senators each represent 911,439 people, an impressive number when put into proper context. California state senators represent over 220,000 more constituents than the average member of the U.S. House and more constituents than U.S. senators from Alaska, Delaware, North Dakota, South Dakota, Vermont, or Wyoming. Members of the Texas state Senate, with 758,316 constituents each, also have districts larger than the average U.S. House district. At the other extreme, many New Hampshire representatives have districts with as few as 3,300 people in them. Overall, state legislative districts in five houses have fewer than 10,000 people, and 13 houses have districts with more than 200,000 constituents.

What difference does constituency size make? At the extremes, being a California state senator is markedly different from being a New Hampshire representative for many reasons. Obviously, running for office differs between the two. As a state representative in New Hampshire observed about his relationship with the people in his district, "You personally knew them. I knew 60 percent of the people in my district."[70] A California state senator would have to personally know 546,863 people in his or her district to know 60 percent of his or her constituents!

TABLE 1-5 CONSTITUENCY SIZE BY AMERICAN UPPER HOUSE CHAMBER, 2006
(FROM SMALLEST TO LARGEST)

STATE	UPPER HOUSE SEATS	DISTRICT POPULATION[a]
North Dakota	47	13,529
Wyoming	30	17,167
Montana	50	18,893
Vermont	30	20,797
South Dakota	35	22,341
Rhode Island	38	28,095
Alaska	20	33,503
Nebraska	49	36,088
Maine	35	37,759
Delaware	21	40,642
Idaho	35	41,899
New Mexico	42	46,538
Hawaii	25	51,420
New Hampshire	24	54,787
Mississippi	52	55,972
Iowa	50	59,642
Kansas	40	69,102
Oklahoma	48	74,567
Minnesota	67	77,121
Arkansas	35	80,311
Utah	29	87,933
South Carolina	46	93,940
Connecticut	36	97,356
West Virginia	34	106,969
Louisiana	39	109,943
Kentucky	38	110,686
Nevada	21	118,835
Maryland	47	119,484
Oregon	30	123,359
Indiana	50	126,270
Washington	49	130,526
Alabama	35	131,401
Colorado	35	135,811
Massachusetts	40	160,930
Georgia	56	167,213
Wisconsin	33	168,379
Missouri	34	171,845
North Carolina	50	177,130

(Continued)

TABLE 1-5   (CONTINUED)

STATE	UPPER HOUSE SEATS	DISTRICT POPULATION[a]
Tennessee	33	182,994
Virginia	40	191,072
Arizona	30	205,544
Illinois	59	217,491
New Jersey	40	218,114
Pennsylvania	50	248,812
Michigan	38	265,675
New York	62	311,390
Ohio	33	347,818
Florida	40	452,247
Texas	31	758,316
California	40	911,439
Mean		150,582
Median		110,314

Source: Calculated by the authors using U.S. Census Bureau data for 2006.

[a]West Virginia elects two members in 15 of the 17 senate districts, and the number reported here is calculated for the 15 two-member districts. Vermont has a "mixed" electoral system with a few single-member districts (SMDs) and the rest multi-member districts. For this table, the district population figure is calculated for the SMDs. For more details, about the electoral districts in these states, see Table 1-6. Nebraska's unicameral legislature is considered an upper house and included in this table.

Constituency size also matters because as the number of constituents (and, we would assume, number of organizations and differing interests) in a district increases, more demands are made on a legislator. An increasingly important and time-consuming part of the job of legislators is helping constituents who come to them with problems. This is known as casework or constituent service. Casework involves everything from fielding complaints about potholes in the street to intervening on behalf of a constituent in a dispute with a state agency. Obviously, the constituent service workload increases with the district population. The way a legislator interacts with his or her constituents also changes; for example, contacts with lawmakers per constituent decline as district size increases, suggesting that voters may feel less connected to their legislators as the size of the legislative district increases.[71]

GEOGRAPHIC SIZE

There is another important way of thinking about district size. State legislative districts come in every geographic size and shape imaginable. The variation can be astounding. Take, for example, the maximum size difference. At one extreme, Alaska state senate district C encompasses close to 250,000 square miles, a size greater than every other state except for Texas. To visit the district's voters, the state senator has to travel by car, airplane, and ferry. One incumbent senator from District C tried to visit all of its towns, but after being gone from home for three months, she managed to only get to about 75 percent of them.[72] At the other extreme, legislative districts in smaller, more densely populated states may cover very little territory. New York Assembly District 73, for example, is about 50 blocks long and six blocks wide—not much more than a square mile or two—taking up just a sliver of Manhattan.

The geographic setting of a district can have obvious implications for representation. A Utah state senator commenting on the potential redrawing of his district noted, "But it's the geographic size that's the real problem. . . . It would be larger—geographically—than most of the New England states. How can you adequately represent all of the people, the area, of that?"[73] In contrast, a member of the Rhode Island House, an institution with very small districts in terms of land mass, told her colleagues, "I learn by listening and I listen to my voters over the fence, at the swimming pool. . . . My office is a shopping cart on Sunday afternoon at Stop & Shop."[74] Her Western counterparts with geographically large districts undoubtedly could not fathom the notion of running into most of their constituents at a local grocery store.

MULTI-MEMBER DISTRICTS

Currently, most state legislators are elected from single-member districts (SMDs). This has not always been the case. Earlier in American history, multi-member districts (MMDs) were the norm. MMDs and at-large districts were used to elect members of the U.S. House, even as recently as the 1960s.[75] At the state level, the use of MMDs was even more pronounced, particularly in lower houses. In the 1950s, for example, 39 of the 48 states used MMDs to elect at least some members of their state legislatures.[76] Over the next several decades, however, the use of MMDs declined, partly because of concerns that they made it more difficult for minority candidates to win office. By 2008, MMDs were found in just two upper senates and 10 lower houses, as shown in Table 1-6. At least 90 percent of all legislators are elected from MMDs in nine of these 12 chambers; the figure is greater than 50 percent in another three chambers. All told, roughly 21 percent of lower house members and 3 percent of state senators in the country are currently elected from MMDs.

Member behavior differs between MMDs and SMDs. Members in MMDs are more likely than their SMD counterparts to think of themselves as being "trustees," or representatives elected to act in the broader interests of their constituents rather than simply reflecting their preferences.[77] Legislators from MMDs claim to spend more time providing constituent services.[78] MMD legislators also bring home more government dollars to their constituents.[79] There are institutional effects as well. Political parties in the Illinois House, for example, were ideologically more diverse when the chamber was elected using MMDs than when SMD elections were used.[80]

TABLE 1-6 STATES USING MULTI-MEMBER LEGISLATIVE DISTRICTS IN 2007

STATE	CHAMBER	PERCENT OF MEMBERS ELECTED FROM MULTI-MEMBER DISTRICTS	NUMBER OF MULTI-MEMBER DISTRICTS	NUMBER OF MEMBERS ELECTED PER MULTI-MEMBER DISTRICT (RANGE)	TYPE OF MULTI-MEMBER DISTRICT SYSTEM
Arizona	Lower house	100.0	30	2	Plurality[a]
Idaho	Lower house	100.0	35	2	Post or Place[b]
Maryland	Lower house	83.0	47[c]	2–3	Plurality
New Hampshire	Lower house	97.0	91	2–13	Plurality
New Jersey	Lower house	100.0	40	2	Plurality
North Dakota	Lower house	100.0	47	2	Plurality[d]
South Dakota	Lower house	94.3	33	2	Plurality
Vermont	Lower house	56.0	42	2	Plurality
Vermont	Upper house	90.0	10	2–6	Plurality
Washington	Lower house	100.0	49	2	Post or Place
West Virginia	Lower house	64.0	22	2–7	Plurality
West Virginia[e]	Upper house	100.0	17	2	Plurality

[a]For example, if voters may vote for five candidates, then the top five vote getters are declared the winners.

[b]Voters cast more than one vote but only one for each place, position, or post on the ballot.

[c]Maryland has 47 electoral districts, all of which send three members to the House of Delegates. Voters in 31 districts cast three votes for three delegates from their district. Voters in one district (District 36) cast three votes, but each of the three counties in the district is contested as a separate seat, and voters may cast no more than one vote per county contest. The remaining districts are divided geographically into subdistricts. In 24 of these subdistricts, a voter casts a single vote to elect a single delegate. In 12 of these subdistricts, voters cast two votes to elect two delegates.

[d]Members of the North Dakota House of Representatives are elected to four terms. Each district elects two members using a plurality rule. District elections are staggered; odd-numbered districts are contested in one election, and even-numbered districts are contested two years later.

[e]In the West Virginia Senate, two members are elected from each of the 17 districts. Terms are staggered, so only one member is elected from each district during each election. Two districts (the 8th and 17th) are geographically coterminous, meaning voters in that district elect two senators every two years in a post or place system.

POLITICS UNDER THE DOMES 1-2

Domes?

State legislatures are often thought to simply be smaller versions of Congress. But as argued in this chapter and throughout the rest of the book, in many important regards, this notion is untrue. Similarly, although many Americans think of state capitols as being smaller versions of the U.S. Capitol, the reality is that they, too, vary in significant ways.

Along with skyscrapers, capitol buildings are an American architectural innovation. The original capitols were built in the colonial era. Indeed, the word "Capitol," derived from Capitoline Hill in Rome, was first applied to a building housing the government by a colonial Virginia governor. Most of the pre-independence capitols have disappeared from the scene, replaced by series of newer buildings. Still, several of the current state capitols predate the U.S. Capitol. Most state capitols, however, have been constructed since the U.S. Capitol took form, and many of them were greatly influenced by its architectural style. Thus, similarities between the U.S. Capitol and capitols in Arkansas, California, Idaho, Kentucky, Michigan, Minnesota, Missouri, Oklahoma, Pennsylvania, Texas, Utah, Washington, West Virginia, Wisconsin, and Wyoming are easy to see because all of them are some variant of the same American Renaissance style.

In other states, stylistic contrasts with the U.S. Capitol are obvious. Virginia's capitol, for example, is neoclassical style, Delaware's is Georgian Revival, and Iowa's is Beaux-Arts. Both Connecticut's and New York's are Victorian Gothic. Louisiana and Nebraska have Art Deco capitols built in the 1930s. North Dakota's International Style "Skyscraper on the Prairie" capitol (with an Art Deco interior) is of the same vintage. More recent capitols are even more distinctive. The New Mexico capitol, built in the 1960s, is a circular design intended to form the Zia, or Pueblo Indian sun sign. Hawaii's capitol, also constructed in the 1960s, is done in the International Style; inspired by the islands, it has an open center, suggestive of a volcano crater. None of these capitols would be confused with the U.S. Capitol. But perhaps the most unusual capitol is Alaska's. It differs from its counterparts because it is a converted federal office building rather than a structure designed specifically for its current purpose.

Several state legislatures do not meet in the state capitol. The North Carolina and Nevada legislatures each has its own building. Constructed in the 1960s and 1970s, both buildings are done in modern styles. In the

(Continued)

POLITICS UNDER THE DOMES 1-2 (CONTINUED)

mid-1980s, at the beginning of a major restoration project, the Alabama legislature was exiled from the state capitol and relocated to a state highway department building that was converted to meet its needs. The legislature has yet to return to the capitol.

Although there are substantial external differences in the buildings where state legislatures meet, there are important interior commonalities. Many of their significant architectural features reflect bicameralism. The lower house and senate chambers are usually on the same floor, physically separated by at least 100 feet, and opposite each other (although in Colorado and Wisconsin, they are perpendicular). More importantly, however, the chambers are comparable, if not in size than in accommodations, as befits institutions of equal stature. Additionally, in almost every capitol, the legislature is the dominant institution and is given more space and greater prominence than the other branches of government. Indeed, in recent years, state legislatures in both Mississippi and South Dakota have commandeered capitol offices used by people working for the governor, forcing them to move elsewhere.

Finally, what about the domes? The vast majority of state legislatures—41 of them—meet under a dome, as does the U.S. Congress. Many of those domes are strongly reminiscent of the Capitol dome. But again, some are very different. The capitols in Ohio and Oregon have flat domes. The Nevada Legislative Building has only a small token dome. And, of course, legislators in Alaska, Delaware, Hawaii, Louisiana, New Mexico, New York, North Dakota, Tennessee, and Virginia, are altogether domeless.

Sources: Charles T. Goodsell, *The American Statehouse* (Lawrence, KS: University Press of Kansas, 2001) and Henry-Russell Hitchcock and William Seale, *Temples of Democracy* (New York: Harcourt, Brace Jovanovich, 1976). See also the website *Cupolas of Capitalism* (http://www.cupola.com/html/bldgstru/statecap/). On Mississippi, see Patrice Sawyer, "Lawmakers Taking over Governor's Space in Capitol," *Clarion-Ledger*, October 3, 2001. On South Dakota, see Joe Kafka, "Turf Battles, Drunken Riders among New Laws," Associated Press State & Local Wire, June 28, 2006.

DIFFERENCES WITH CONGRESS

Clearly, state legislatures come in all shapes and sizes, none of which exactly mirror the size and shape of Congress. Moreover, their histories differ. Indeed, as Politics Under the Domes 1-2 discusses, even the buildings in which state legislatures meet are, at best, only reminiscent of the U.S. Capitol. Thus, understanding Congress is not sufficient for understanding state legislatures. State legislatures merit separate consideration and study.

FURTHER EXPLORATIONS OF STATE LEGISLATURES

Having come to understand how state legislatures as organizations evolved and what they look like today, the rest of this book is devoted to exploring important aspects of state legislative life in greater depth. Chapter 2 investigates state legislative elections, examining what it takes to get to the legislature and what it takes to stay there. Among the topics covered are redistricting, candidate recruitment, the emergence of women and minority candidates, competition for state legislative office, campaign finance, the power of incumbency, and the nature of campaigning for the legislature in different states. The chapter also explores the recent increase in party competition for chamber control in much of the nation and assesses the evidence of party realignment at the state legislative level.

Chapter 3 details the changing job description of state legislators and examines the substantial variation across the states in the sorts of legislative careers legislators pursue. The chapter begins by explaining and examining the concept of legislative professionalization. In doing so, we look at the roles pay, time demands, and staff and facilities play in legislative career decisions and look at how terms limits change career patterns in the states where they are in effect. We document how the face of the state legislature has changed significantly over time and explain what difference these occupational and demographic changes make. Problems surrounding legislative ethics are investigated as well. Finally, the concept of legislative career opportunity structures is introduced and analyzed.

Chapter 4 focuses on legislatures as organizations. We analyze the roles of political parties, legislative leaders, committees, and staff in structuring legislative decision making. Links are drawn between member careers and the ways legislatures are organized. One point highlighted in this chapter is that the structures found in Congress do not exhaust the organizational configurations of American legislatures. The diverse organizational forms found across state legislatures have strengths and weaknesses that merit examination.

The convoluted and often messy process by which legislation gets produced is described in Chapter 5. We begin with a discussion of where ideas for bills originate, explore how ideas get turned into proposals and how different legislatures process legislation, and conclude with an explanation of how members decide how to vote on bills. Major emphases of this chapter are the differences in legislative rules and procedures across the states and analyses of the policy consequences of those differences.

The main goal of Chapter 6 is to understand how legislators are influenced by a multitude of forces as they consider legislation. Topics covered are legislative relations with the governor, executive agencies, interest groups, courts, and the voters through the initiative and referendum processes. We discuss legislative oversight of the executive branch and the rise of legislative independence in policymaking. We examine how initiatives and referenda influence the legislative process by either forcing legislatures to act or by allowing them to pass the buck to the voters. Particular attention is paid to the effects of voter-passed tax and expenditure limits.

Finally, Chapter 7 tackles the question of how state legislatures today are to be judged. We look at different ways of measuring how the public assess their legislators and the institutions in which they serve. That is followed by an exploration of the sorts of information voters have about the state legislature. We finish with some thoughts on how well state legislatures perform as representative institutions.

ENDNOTES

1. For a sampling of comments from within Arkansas, see Paul Greenberg, "An Apostrophe Starts a War, " *Arkansas Democrat-Gazette*, March 4, 2007; Jay Grelen, "In a League with Jesus and Texas," *Arkansas Democrat-Gazette*, March 6, 2007; and Meredith Oakley, "Apostrophe Wars," *Arkansas Democrat-Gazette*, March 21, 2007. For a sampling of comments from outside Arkansas, see *Houston Chronicle*, "Lawmaker Possessed by Apostrophe," March 4, 2007; and Nathan Bierma, "Possessive is Nine-tenths Law in Arkansas's Statutes," *Chicago Tribune*, April 6, 2007.
2. See the Chronicle of Higher Education News Blog, "Silent Sibilant Is Focus of Possessive Debate at U. of Arkansas-Little Rock," March 13, 2007 (http://chronicle.com/news/article/1789/silent-sibilant-is-focus-of-possessive-debate-at-u-of-arkansas-little-rock).
3. See Steve Harrelson, "Arkansas's Grammar Lesson," January 23, 2007 (http://www.steveharrelson.com/blog/2007/01/arkansass-grammar-lesson.html).
4. The quote is from a widely distributed AP story, Mark DeMillo, "Arkansas House Backs Apostrophe Act," Newsday.com, March 6, 2007.
5. Peverill Squire, "Historical Evolution of Legislatures in the United States," *Annual Review of Political Science* 9 (2006): 19–44; Peverill Squire, and Keith E. Hamm, *101 Chambers: Congress, State Legislatures, and the Future of Legislative Studies* (Columbus, OH: Ohio State University Press, 2005).
6. Donald S. Lutz, "The Colonial and Early State Legislative Process," in *Inventing Congress: Origins and Establishment of the First Federal Congress*, ed. Kenneth R. Bowling and Donald R. Kennon (Athens, OH: Ohio University Press, 1999); Squire and Hamm, *101 Chambers*, 28–34.
7. Squire and Hamm, *101 Chambers*, 19.
8. William H. Riker, "The Heresthetics of Constitution-Making: The Presidency in 1787, with Comments on Determinism and Rational Choice," *American Political Science Review* 78 (1984): 1–16.
9. Squire and Hamm, *101 Chambers*, 29.
10. Nelson W. Polsby, "The Institutionalization of the U.S. House of Representatives," *American Political Science Review* 62 (1968): 144–168; Riker, "The Heresthetics of Constitution-Making," 462.
11. Alvin W. Johnson, *The Unicameral Legislature* (Minneapolis, MN: University of Minnesota Press, 1938), 32–33.
12. Squire and Hamm, *101 Chambers*, 35–39.
13. Laura J. Scalia, *America's Jeffersonian Experiment: Remaking State Constitutions, 1820–1850* (DeKalb, IL: Northern Illinois University Press, 1999), 107.
14. Mark Twain, *Roughing It* (New York: Oxford University Press, 1996 [1872]), 187–188.
15. Jeannie M. Whayne, Thomas A. DeBlack, George Sabo III, and Morris S. Arnold, *Arkansas: A Narrative History* (Fayetteville, AR: University of Arkansas Press, 2002), 113.
16. William H. Ellison, *A Self-Governing Dominion: California, 1849–1860* (Berkeley: University of California Press, 1950), 75.

17. Ellison, *A Self-Governing Dominion*, 76.
18. Ralph Volney Harlow, *The History of Legislative Methods in the Period Before 1825* (New Haven: Yale University Press, 1917), 66.
19. Squire, "Historical Evolution of Legislatures in the United States," 33.
20. John E. Briggs, "History and Organization of the Legislature in Iowa," in *Statute Law-making in Iowa*, ed. Benjamin F. Shambaugh (Iowa City, IA: State Historical Society of Iowa, 1916), 88–89.
21. Justin E. Walsh, *The Centennial History of the Indiana General Assembly* (Indianapolis, IN: The Select Committee on the Centennial History of the Indiana General Assembly, 1987), 92.
22. Squire, "Historical Evolution of Legislatures in the United States."
23. Briggs, "History and Organization of the Legislature in Iowa."
24. Peverill Squire, "Career Opportunities and Membership Stability in Legislatures," *Legislative Studies Quarterly* 13 (1988): 65–82; Peverill Squire, "Member Career Opportunities and the Internal Organization of Legislatures," *Journal of Politics* 50 (1988): 726–744; Peverill Squire, "The Theory of Legislative Institutionalization and the California Assembly," *Journal of Politics* 54 (1992): 1026–1054.
25. Squire and Hamm, *101 Chambers*, 81–86.
26. James D. King, "Changes in Professionalism in U.S. State Legislatures," *Legislative Studies Quarterly* 25 (2000): 327–343; Christopher Z. Mooney, "Citizens, Structures, and Sister States: Influences on State Legislative Professionalism," *Legislative Studies Quarterly* 20 (1995): 47–67; Peverill Squire, "Legislative Professionalization and Membership Diversity in State Legislatures," *Legislative Studies Quarterly* 17 (1992): 69–79; Peverill Squire, "Uncontested Seats in State Legislative Elections," *Legislative Studies Quarterly* 25 (2000): 131–146; Peverill Squire, "Measuring Legislative Professionalism: The Squire Index Revisited," *State Politics and Policy Quarterly* 7 (2007): 211–227.
27. Simeon E. Baldwin, "Legislative Divorces and the Fourteenth Amendment," *Harvard Law Review* 27 (1914), 699–700; Doris Jonas Freed and Henry H. Foster, Jr., "Divorce American Style," *Annals of the American Academy of Political and Social Science* 383 (1969): 73–75; Glenda Riley, "Legislative Divorce in Virginia, 1803–1850," *Journal of the Early Republic* 11 (1991): 51–67.
28. Matthew Franck, "Plan to Sell Loan Assets Clears Missouri Senate after Long Fight," *St. Louis Post-Dispatch*, April 26, 2007.
29. J. Michael Medina, "The Origination Clause in the American Constitution: A Comparative Survey," *Tulsa Law Journal* 23 (1987): 165–234, 166.
30. Malcolm E. Jewell and Samuel C. Patterson, *The Legislative Process in the United States*, 4th ed. (New York: Random House, 1986), 170; James R. Rogers, "An Informational Rationale for Congruent Bicameralism," *Journal of Theoretical Politics* 13 (2001): 123–152; Squire and Hamm, *101 Chambers*, 114–115.
31. See the discussion in Charlyne Berens, *One House* (Lincoln, NE: University of Nebraska Press, 2005), 36–41.
32. Jack Rodgers, Robert Sittig, and Susan Welch, "The Legislature," in *Nebraska Government and Politics*, ed. Robert D. Miewald (Lincoln: University of Nebraska Press, 1984); Tom Todd, "Nebraska's Unicameral Legislature: A Description and Some Comparisons with Minnesota's Bicameral Legislature," *Journal of the American Society of Legislative Clerks and Secretaries* 4 (1988). See also the analysis of the costs and benefits of a unicameral system produced by House Research office of the Minnesota House of Representatives (http://www.house.leg.state.mn.us/hrd/issinfo/nebunic.htm and http://www.house.leg.state.mn.us/hrd/issinfo/uni_bicam.htm).
33. Barry Bedlan, "Ventura Sends Scouts to Nebraska's 'Unicameral'," *Minneapolis Star-Tribune*, 16 April 1999; Mario F. Cattabiani, "Toward a Smaller Harrisburg," *Philadelphia Inquirer*, May 9, 2007; Robb Douglas, "Going Nebraska's Way," in *State Government 1993–94*. Thad L. Beyle, ed (Washington, D.C.: CQ Press, 1993); Bob Mercer, "Reforms Mulled for Legislature," *Rapid City Journal*, August 14, 1996; Stacey Range, "New Grassroots Efforts Focus on Eliminating State Senate," *Lansing State Journal*, April 16, 2005.
34. *Omaha World-Herald*, "A Tropical Unicameral? If Puerto Ricans Are Still Mad at Lawmakers in Two Years, Nebraska Could have Company in 1-House Club," July 24, 2005; Manuel Ernesto Rivera, "Puerto Rico Vote Favors Legislature Switch," *Los Angeles Times*, July 10, 2005.
35. John H. Aldrich and James S. Coleman Battista, "Conditional Party Government in the States," *American Journal of Political Science* 46 (2002): 164–172; Brian F. Schaffner, "Political

Parties and the Representativeness of Legislative Committees," *Legislative Studies Quarterly* 32 (2007): 475–497; Gerald C. Wright and Brian F. Schaffner, "The Influence of Party: Evidence from the State Legislatures," *American Political Science Review* 96 (2002): 367–379.

36. Robert Luce, *Legislative Assemblies* (Boston: Houghton Mifflin, 1924), 23.
37. Don W. Driggs and Leonard E. Goodall, *Nevada Government and Politics* (Lincoln, NE: University of Nebraska Press, 1996), 66; James D. Driscoll, *California's Legislature* (Sacramento, CA: Center for California Studies, 1986), 8; Frederic L. Paxson, "A Constitution of Democracy—Wisconsin, 1847," *Mississippi Valley Historical Review* 2 (1915): 3–24, 9.
38. Luce, *Legislative Assemblies*, 21.
39. Luce, *Legislative Assemblies*, 21–22.
40. Squire and Hamm, *101 Chambers*, 48.
41. Squire and Hamm, *101 Chambers*, 46–48.
42. *Reynolds v. Sims*, 377 U.S. 533 (1964).
43. Rhode Island Constitution, Article 7, Section 1 and Article 8, Section 1.
44. North Dakota, for example, downsized both chambers of its legislature in 2003 as a result of its redistricting process, going to 47 senate districts and 94 house districts from 49 senate districts and 98 house districts the decade before. Cost savings to the state were given as the rationale behind the reduction in the number of seats. See Janet Cole, "N.D. Legislative Districts Set, But Not Without Problems," *The Forum* (Fargo), December 1, 2001; and Joel Heitkamp, "Fewer Districts is the Right Way," *Bismarck Tribune* December 19, 2001. Redistricting also prompted New York to add a seat to its upper house in 2003, bringing the total number to 62. This time, the explanation was party politics. Adding a seat allowed the GOP senate majority to avoid eliminating a district upstate that they held and to create several districts in New York City that improved their party's prospects to win there. See Richard Perez-Pena, "Questions from Justice Department Delay Plan to Add District to New York Senate," *New York Times*, June 4, 2002.
45. This count in taken from The National Conference of State Legislatures, "In Case of a Tie......" (http://www.ncsl.org/LegislaturesElections/OrganizationProcedureFacilities/In CaseofaTie/tabid/17278/Default.aspx). This page also provides the National Conference of State Legislature's advice for how to manage such situations ().
46. David Postman, "Senators Take Aim at the Tie That Binds the State House." *Seattle Times*, June 12, 2001.
47. Francis Quinn, "Mellow (Mostly) in Maine," *State Legislatures Magazine* (July/August 2001): 24–26.
48. Wayne L. Francis, "Leadership, Party Caucuses, and Committees in U.S. State Legislatures," *Legislative Studies Quarterly* 10 (1985): 243–257.
49. Alan Rosenthal, *Legislative Life* (New York: Harper & Row, 1981), 132–134.
50. Ross K. Baker, *House and Senate*, 3rd ed. (New York: Norton 2001), 72, Roger H. Davidson, Walter J. Oleszek, and Frances E. Lee, *Congress and Its Members*, 11th ed. (Washington, DC: CQ Press, 2008), 28; Lewis A. Froman, Jr., *The Congressional Process* (Boston: Little, Brown, 1967), 7–15.
51. Andrew J. Taylor, "Size, Power, and Electoral Systems: Exogenous Determinants of Legislative Procedural Choice," *Legislative Studies Quarterly* 31 (2006): 323–345.
52. James R. Rogers, "Bicameral Sequence: Theory and State Legislative Evidence," *American Journal of Political Science* 42 (1998): 1025–1060.
53. Arleen Leibowitz and Robert Tollison, "A Theory of Legislative Organization: Making the Most of Your Majority," *Quarterly Journal of Economics* 94 (1980): 261–277.
54. Jowei Chen and Neil Malhotra, "The Law of k/n: The Effect of Chamber Size on Government Spending in Bicameral Legislatures, *American Political Science Review* 101 (2007): 657–676.
55. Luce, *Legislative Assemblies*, 113; Michael J. Dubin, *Party Affiliations in the State Legislatures: A Year by Year Summary, 1796–2006* (Jefferson, NC: McFarland, 2007).
56. John J. Kennedy, *The Contemporary Pennsylvania Legislature* (Lanham, MD: University Press of America, 1999), 2–3.
57. Luce, *Legislative Assemblies*, 119.
58. Squire and Hamm, *101 Chambers*, 62–63.
59. Chris Fiscus, "Legislators Discuss 4-Year-Terms Idea," *Arizona Republic*, January 28, 2003.
60. Fanny Seiler, "House Panel Passes Term Extension for Lawmakers,' *Charleston Gazette*, February 26, 2003.

61. William D. Berry, Michael B. Berkman, and Stuart Schneiderman, "Legislative Professionalism and Incumbent Reelection: The Development of Institutional Boundaries," *American Political Science Review* 94 (2000): 859–874; John M. Carey, Richard G. Niemi, and Lynda W. Powell, "Incumbency and the Probability of Reelection in State Legislative Elections," *Journal of Politics* 62 (2000): 671–700.
62. The Congress under the Articles of Confederation operated under similar term limits with three annual terms out of six years.
63. See Edwin L. Cobb, "Representation and the Rotation Agreement: The Case of Tennessee," *Western Political Quarterly* 23 (1970): 516–529; Malcolm E. Jewell, "State Legislatures in Southern Politics," *Journal of Politics* 26 (1964): 177–196.
64. See Jennie Drage Bowser and Gary Moncrief, "Term Limits in State Legislatures," in *Institutional Change in American Politics: The Case of Term Limits*, ed. Karl T. Kurtz, Bruce Cain, and Richard G. Niemi (Ann Arbor, MI: University of Michigan Press, 2007).
65. See Daniel A. Smith, "Overturning Term Limits: The Legislature's Own Private Idaho?" *PS: Political Science & Politics* 36 (2003): 215–220.
66. See Karl T. Kurtz, Bruce Cain, and Richard G. Niemi, ed., *Institutional Change in American Politics: The Case of Term Limits* (Ann Arbor, MI: University of Michigan Press, 2007).
67. Gary Moncrief, Richard G. Niemi, and Lynda W. Powell. "Time, Term Limits, and Turnover: Membership Stability in U.S. State Legislatures," *Legislative Studies Quarterly* 29 (2004): 357–381.
68. Bruce Cain and Gerald Wright, "Committees," in *Institutional Change in American Politics: The Case of Term Limits*, ed. Karl T. Kurtz, Bruce Cain, and Richard G. Niemi (Ann Arbor, MI: University of Michigan Press, 2007), 89.
69. Richard Powell, "Executive-Legislative Relations," in *Institutional Change in American Politics: The Case of Term Limits*, ed. Karl T. Kurtz, Bruce Cain, and Richard G. Niemi (Ann Arbor, MI: University of Michigan Press, 2007).
70. Norma Love, "Traditional Campaigns a Memory," *Concord Monitor*, October 21, 2002.
71. Peverill Squire, "Professionalization and Public Opinion of State Legislatures," *Journal of Politics* 55 (1993): 479–491.
72. Bill McAllister, "Alaska Senate District Tests Candidates' Stamina," *Stateline.org*, October 17, 2002.
73. Bob Bernick, Jr., "Expand Senate by 2 Says Lawmaker," *Deseret News*, July 13, 1999.
74. State of Rhode Island and Providence Plantations, *Journal of the House of Representatives*, May 31, 2000.
75. Stephen Calabrese, "Multimember District Congressional Elections," *Legislative Studies Quarterly* 25 (2000): 611–643.
76. Maurice Klain, "A New Look at the Constituencies: The Need for a Recount and a Reappraisal," *American Political Science Review* 49 (1955): 1105–1119.
77. Christopher A. Cooper and Lilliard E. Richardson, Jr. "Institutions and Representational Roles in American State Legislatures," *State Politics and Policy Quarterly* 6 (2006): 174–194.
78. Patricia K. Freeman and Lilliard E. Richardson, Jr., "Explaining Variations in Casework among State Legislators," *Legislative Studies Quarterly* 21 (1996): 41–56.
79. James M. Snyder, Jr. and Michiko Ueda, "Do Multimember Districts Lead to Free-Riding?" *Legislative Studies Quarterly* 32 (2007): 649–679.
80. Greg D. Adams, "Legislative Effects of Single-Member vs. Multi-Member Districts," *American Journal of Political Science* 40 (1996): 129–144.

STATE LEGISLATIVE CAMPAIGNS AND ELECTIONS

In 2006, Nicole Parra, a Democrat from Hanford, spent just over $2 million on her campaign for the California Assembly. At the same time, 3,000 miles away, Everett McLeod, Sr. (a Republican from Lee Township) spent $4,263 in his bid for election to the Maine House of Representatives. Both won.

In some respects, these two cases represent the extremes in American state legislative elections. Although the Parra campaign was not the most expensive state legislative race in 2006, it was one of the most expensive; Parra and her opponent spent more than $3 million between them. And the Maine House District 11 race was not the least expensive, but it certainly was on the low end of the spectrum. These two races represent the tremendous variation in state legislative races in the United States. As detailed in this chapter, there are a number of reasons for these differences.

Most of the laws pertaining to elections in the United States are determined at the state—not national—level. And because states created their electoral systems at different times and under different circumstances, not all state election procedures are the same. Indeed, people are often surprised to find out just how much electoral structures and procedures vary from state to state. This variation is clearly evident in state legislative elections. They may differ on their district size, district magnitude, redistricting practices, campaign finance laws, rules to determine winners, when elections are held, who is eligible to vote, and who is eligible to run for office.

Consider, for a moment, the California Assembly. As shown in Table 1-4, each Assembly district contains about 450,000 people (and California state senate districts contain at least 900,000 people). Representing a district of more than 450,000 people is a daunting task to be sure, but here we are interested in the campaign and electoral implications. Consider, for example, the cost of running for an Assembly seat. A good example is the 30th Assembly District in the southern part of the San Joaquin Valley, the district represented by Nicole Parra for six years.[1] Parra, a Latina who was born and raised in the valley, has impressive political credentials. Her father was a county supervisor and school board member in Kern County, California. Parra graduated from the University of California, Berkeley and attended law school at Catholic University in Washington D.C. and then served as a staff member for U.S. Representative Cal Dooley before winning her first election to the Assembly in 2002.

Parra represented a sprawling agricultural district that includes the farming communities of Delano, Hanford, Wasco, and a small part of Bakersfield. The district is 60 percent Hispanic and, although the district leans toward the Democrats, it is considered a competitive electoral district. Parra outspent her opponent $2 million to $1 million and won by a narrow 51.5 to 48.5 percent in the vote. Campaigning in a large, competitive district requires a lot of money. Because the candidate seeks to reach so many potential voters, she must run a "wholesale" campaign based on mass media. Table 2-1 breaks down the major campaign expenditures for the Parra campaign. This campaign looks a lot like a campaign for U.S. Congress or statewide office; note the reliance on broadcast media (both television and radio), professional consultants, polling, and fundraising.

TABLE 2-1   A TALE OF TWO CAMPAIGNS

	NICOLE PARRA, CALIFORNIA 30TH ASSEMBLY DISTRICT[a]	EVERETT MCLEOD, SR., MAINE 11TH HOUSE DISTRICT
2006 campaign expenditures	$2,075,713	$4,263
Opponent spent	$987,622	$8,179
Votes received	28,244 (of 54,771 cast)	1,785 (of 3,019 total cast)
Expenditure per vote received	$73.49	$2.39
Major expenditures	TV and cable air time and production: $590,000	Campaign signs and printing: $2,108
	Radio air time and production: $345,000	Gasoline for travel by car: $650
	Campaign consultants: $106,000	Newspaper ads: $576
	Fundraising events: $106,000	Flyswatters (1,000 count): $439
	Campaign staff salaries: $73,000	T-shirts: $196
	Polling: $25,000	Meals for campaign staff: $107
	Campaign literature and mailing: $27,000	

Sources: Figures calculated by the authors from the Maine Campaign Finance Access Site (http://www.mainecampaignfinance.com/public/home.asp), the California Secretary of State's campaign finance site (http://cal-access.ss.ca.gov/Campaign/), and the National Institute on Money in State Politics' database (http://www.followthemoney.org).
[a]The figures for the Parra campaign are estimates of the minimum amount spent in each category.

In contrast, Everett McLeod, Sr. was able to run a "retail" campaign in the 11th House District race in Maine. The 11th District is an upstate district, sharing an international border with the Canadian province of New Brunswick. There are only about 8,700 residents in each house district in Maine, and the residents of the 11th District are spread out in small towns and rural homes amid forested hills, streams, and lakes. Reaching voters in such a district is mostly a matter of driving from one small community to another and talking to people wherever a few of them are likely to gather. The campaign expenditures for the McLeod campaign were very different from those for the Parra campaign. The largest expenditure was for signs. The only media purchase was newspaper ads. Whereas Parra's campaign in California spent more than $900,000 on advertising through the airwaves (television and radio), the only thing waving in the air in McLeod's campaign were flyswatters imprinted with his name.

Legislators are not born as legislators; they are elected to the position. For the most part, they are simply citizens who have managed to successfully negotiate through a set of rules and circumstances that lead them from private citizen to elected public official. These rules and circumstances are not the same in all states. In other words, the electoral context differs. We use the term *electoral context* in a broad sense—to refer to the recruitment, nomination, campaign, and electoral phases of the process by which private citizens become public officials. Used in this way, the electoral context depends on the particular electoral rules of a state; on whether candidates are incumbents, challengers, or open-seat contestants; and on the processes by which candidates are recruited to run. In this chapter, we discuss the differences (and similarities) in this electoral context for state legislative candidates.

The electoral context shapes the nature of the electoral campaign. A second goal of this chapter is to discuss how state legislative campaigns are run. Ultimately, the electoral outcomes have implications for how the state legislature operates. In the final section of this chapter, we note how competition and turnover vary among the states.

DIFFERENCES IN ELECTORAL RULES

As mentioned earlier, some of the sources of variation in campaigns are related to variation in the electoral rules from one state to another. Not all states have the same rules—in fact, very few states have exactly the same rules. They may differ in at least the ways discussed below.

DISTRICT MAGNITUDE

District magnitude refers to the number of people being elected in a given legislative district. The most common case in U.S. politics is to elect one representative per district—known as a single-member district (SMD). But as noted in

Table 1-6, 10 states currently use multi-member districts (MMDs) for one or both of the houses. In almost all cases, these MMDs are simply two-member districts—for example, in New Jersey and Washington—where two representatives are elected in each district. But a few states have some larger MMDs. Maryland, for example, has many three-member districts (more than 30 of them), as well as some SMDs and some two-member districts. But the most prolific user of large MMDs is New Hampshire, where house districts range from single member (e.g., Merrimack District #3) to 13-member (Rockingham District #4). There are also six districts that elect eight members, two nine-member districts, a 10-member, and an 11-member district in New Hampshire.

In Chapter 1, we note that there are some differences in the way legislators from MMDs operate within the legislative institution compared with legislators from SMDs. In other words, there are some behavioral consequences. But there are also some electoral consequences to the choice of single versus MMDs. For example, the advantage of incumbency appears to be somewhat less in MMDs.[2] There is a tendency for "team campaigns" in MMDs—that is, campaigns in which all the candidates from one party pool their resources and urge the electorate to "block vote" (e.g., "Vote for the Republican team in District 5!"). Historically, MMDs appeared to make it more difficult for minority candidates to get elected, and for this reason, MMDs are no longer used in many states.[3]

TYPE OF PRIMARY ELECTION

In almost all states, primary elections are used to determine the party nominee for each office in the general election. The rules for primary elections, however, differ from state to state. For candidates, the most important differences are the rules for establishing candidacy, how the winner (nominee) is determined, which voters are eligible to participate, and the timing of the primary. This last issue is discussed in a separate section below. For now, we focus on the first three questions.

The rules for establishing candidacy are not the same in all states.[4] Table 2-2 shows some of the rules for filing as a major party (Republican or Democratic) candidate for the senate in selected states. There are differences in terms of the minimum age before one can run (18 years old in Montana and Massachusetts but 30 years old in Kentucky), the length of residence in the state (one year in Montana, six years in Kentucky), the length of residence in district (30 days in Nevada, two years in Illinois), and the cost of filing to run ($1,250 in Texas; $0 in Illinois).[5] These qualifications limit the potential pool of candidates and can become an issue during a campaign, as Politics Under the Domes 2-1 demonstrates.[6] Even the "window of opportunity" is very different across the states; for the 2006 primary election, a potential candidate in Massachusetts had about a 3.5-month window (February 14 to May 30) to file for the primary, but in Illinois, filing had to occur within an eight-day period (December 12 to 19).

TABLE 2-2   RULES OF CANDIDACY FOR STATE SENATE IN SELECTED STATES

STATE	MINIMUM AGE	MUST LIVE IN STATE FOR AT LEAST	MUST LIVE IN SENATE DISTRICT FOR AT LEAST	FILING FEE	DATES FOR FILING NOMINATION PAPERS (2006 ELECTION)
Illinois	21	2 years	2 years	None	December 12–19, 2005
Kentucky	30	6 years	1 year	$200	November 9, 2005–January 31, 2006
Massachusetts	18	5 years	At time of election	$300	February 14–May 30, 2006
Montana	18	1 year	6 months	$15	January 23–March 25, 2006
Texas	26	5 years	1 year	$1,250	December 3, 2005–January 2, 2006

Source: From various secretary of state or election board websites.

POLITICS UNDER THE DOMES 2-1

When Residency Requirements Bite

When the votes in the 37th Kentucky senate district contest were tallied on election night, November 2, 2004, the Republican candidate, Dana Seum Stephenson, outpolled her Democratic opponent, Virginia L. Woodward, by 1,022 votes. Stephenson and her supporters assumed that this victory would allow her to join her father, Senator Dan Seum (R-Louisville) and the rest of the Republican majority in the state senate. The day before the election, however, Woodward had filed a motion in the Jefferson Circuit Court to have Stephenson disqualified, arguing that she failed to meet the state's residency requirement. Because of the residency controversy, it would take well over a year to determine who would represent the 37th district in the Kentucky Senate.

The Kentucky Constitution sets a stringent residency standard for the state senate (Part 1, Section 32): "No person shall be a Senator who, at the time of his election, is not a citizen of Kentucky, has not attained the age of thirty years, and has not resided in this State six years next preceding his election, and the last year thereof in the district for which he may be chosen." It was Woodward's contention that Stephenson had not resided in the state for the required six years before becoming a candidate. The circuit court held an evidentiary hearing on November 3, the day after the election. There was an initial attempt by Senator David Williams, acting as the president of the Kentucky Senate, to argue that the court lacked jurisdiction in the matter, an assertion the court immediately rejected. During the hearing, it was determined that Stephenson had lived in Indiana from 1997 to 2001 while she pursued a master's degree at Indiana University Southeast. Moreover, she had bought a home in Jeffersonville, Indiana, and had not only registered to vote in Indiana but actually cast ballots there twice, had gotten an Indiana driver's license, and had paid in-state tuition. Stephenson's lawyer countered that during this time, she had come back to Kentucky often, even teaching at a school and attending church, and had always intended to return permanently. The lawyer also asserted that, in any event, the six-year residency requirement was unconstitutional.

On November 22, the Jefferson Circuit Court rejected all of Stephenson's arguments and ruled that she did not meet the residency requirement and was therefore not a bona fide candidate. The court ordered the Jefferson County Board of Elections not to count the votes for Stephenson. The court order, of course, meant that Woodward would win the seat.

Stephenson did not appeal the circuit court's decision. Instead, on December 7, she took her case to the state senate, arguing that the Kentucky constitution gave each house of the legislature authority over its own membership (Part 1, Section 38), "Each House of the General Assembly shall judge of the qualifications, elections and returns of its members. . . ." Stephenson calculated that the Republican majority in the senate would opt to seat her rather than her Democratic opponent, the circuit court's decision notwithstanding.

A week later, Woodward answered that move by asking the Franklin Circuit Court to hand down an injunction against Stephenson, Senate President Williams, and the State Board of Election, preventing them from handing the Republican the seat. Woodward, operating on the same assumptions as Stephenson about the likely outcomes in the two different venues, wanted to keep the case in the courts and out of the state senate. On December 21, the circuit court ordered the State Board of Elections to certify Woodward as the victor. At the same time, however, the court refused Woodward's request to prevent the state senate from considering the matter. A week later, the State Board of Elections followed the court's direction, unanimously certifying Woodward as the winner in the 37th district.

Woodward was sworn in privately on January 1, 2005, and then took her oath again along with the other new members of the senate in a public ceremony on January 4. Immediately after the swearing in, Senator Dan Kelly, a Republican, moved that the senate reject Woodward's election because she had not gotten the most votes. The Senate then

(Continued)

POLITICS UNDER THE DOMES 2-1 (CONTINUED)

voted to establish an Elections Contest Board to investigate the residency controversy. The names of the nine members of the board were drawn randomly from the senate's membership. As it happened, five of the names selected were Democrats, and four were Republicans.

The board issued its findings on January 7. A majority of five—all Democrats—concluded that Stephenson did not meet the state's residency requirement and that Woodward was the correct winner. The panel's minority report was split, with three Republican members finding that Stephenson met the legal requirements and should be entitled to the seat. The other Republican on the board agreed with the Democrats that Stephenson should not be seated but argued that a special election should be held to fill the vacant seat.

Later that same day, the full senate voted, almost entirely along party lines, to accept the minority report recommendation to seat Stephenson. (Stephenson's father did not vote.) Before the vote, Senate President Williams argued that the body had the right to determine the qualifications of its members, even if it did so arbitrarily. Williams went so far as to assert that although the state constitution requires senators to be at least 30 years old, a majority could seat a 23-year old, "If 20 people in this body voted that someone was 30 years old, no court in the land could overturn that." Immediately after the vote, Stephenson was sworn into office. Afterward, the Democratic floor leader vented his anger, saying, "I refuse to participate in what I believe to be the greatest single act of pure, raw, ugly politics as I have ever seen take place in our Capitol."

The senate's decision, however, failed to settle the matter. Woodward went back to court, and a week after Stephenson took office, the Franklin Circuit Court issued a temporary injunction preventing the new senator from exercising the powers of her office. It took six months for the court to render its final decision on the case. On June 1, the Franklin Circuit Court found that Stephenson did not meet the constitutional standard for residency and declared her ineligible to serve in the senate. The court also held that it did not have the power to force the senate to seat Woodward.

Now it was Stephenson's turn to pursue the matter in the courts. She, along with Senate President Williams, appealed the decision to the state supreme court. On December 22 the Supreme Court of Kentucky handed down its verdict, upholding the decision reached by the Franklin Circuit Court. By a five-to-two vote, the Court rejected the argument that the state constitution left the matter of member qualifications to the legislature to determine. The court reasoned that they had jurisdiction because:

> Stephenson's and Williams' arguments are predicated on the fundamentally flawed belief that Stephenson was actually a member of the Senate. . . . A Senator-elect only becomes a member of the Senate when

his or her term commences "upon the first day of January of the year succeeding [the] election." Ky. Const. Sec 30. . . . Here, though, when the Jefferson Circuit Court rendered its order finding that Stephenson was not a bona fide candidate and therefore ineligible to appear on the ballot, she lost all rights to that office. This determination was made on November 22, 2004—before Stephenson had taken the oath of office, before she had been sworn in as a State Senator, and before the term of office which she sought commenced on January 1, 2005.

Although the Supreme Court refused to allow Stephenson to take office, it also refused to seat Woodward because she had failed to get the most votes in the election.

In early January 2006, Senate President Williams signed a proclamation setting February 14 as the date for the special election to fill the vacant 37th district seat. When the election was held, neither Stephenson's nor Woodward's name was on the ballot. The Democratic candidate, a state representative who had resigned to run in the special election, won.

Later in 2006, Dana Seum Stephenson ran for a seat in the Kentucky House of Representatives. The constitution only requires House candidates to be residents of the state for two years, a standard that Stephenson noted she met. She lost the election.

Sources: Elizabeth J. Beardsley, "218 Set Sights on Legislature," Louisville Courier-Journal, February 1, 2006; Mark R. Chellgren, "Stephenson Seated in Senate, Republican Threatens Resignation in Protest," Associated Press State & Local Wire, January 7, 2005; Mark R. Chellgren, Divided High Court Rules Stephenson Cannot Serve in Senate," Associated Press State & Local Wire, December 22, 2005; Joseph Gerth, "Judge Reverses Election for State Senate," Louisville Courier-Journal, November 23, 2004; Joseph Gerth, "Stephenson Ruled Out as Senator," Louisville Courier-Journal, June 2, 2005; Tom Loftus, "Stephenson Asks Senate to Name Her the Winner," Louisville Courier-Journal, December 8, 2004; Bruce Schreiner, "Democrat Wins Leftover Election for Kentucky Senate Seat," Associated Press State & Local Wire, February 15, 2006; Stephenson v. Woodward, et al. 182 S.W. 3d 162 (Ky., 2005).

In most states, the winner of the primary election is determined by a plurality rule—the candidate with the most votes wins. Often in primary elections in the states, there is only one candidate, and the decision rule is therefore moot. And, of course, if only two candidates get votes, then plurality is the same as majority. But about a dozen states, almost all of them Southern states, use a run-off primary system if no candidate wins a majority in the primary.[7] In this system, if no candidate received a majority in the primary election, then the top two vote getters face each other in a "run-off primary" that is usually held just a few weeks after the original primary. Because only two candidates are now involved, the winner is assured of receiving a majority of the votes cast. From the point of view of the candidates, run-off primaries have several implications. Obviously, it means an extension of the

TABLE 2-3   2006 REPUBLICAN PRIMARY AND RUN-OFF ELECTION, OKLAHOMA
HOUSE DISTRICT 41 JULY 25, 2006: REPUBLICAN PRIMARY

CANDIDATE	VOTES	PERCENT
Jeff Davis	1,628	39.2
John Enns	943	22.7
Tim Vanover	842	20.3
Arthur Reed	510	12.3
Paul Denny, Jr.	233	5.6

Total votes = 4,156

AUGUST 22, 2006: REPUBLICAN RUN-OFF PRIMARY

CANDIDATE	VOTES	PERCENT
John Enns	2,323	58.3
Jeff Davis	1,660	41.7

Total votes = 3,983

campaign—and additional costs are sure to be incurred. Second, a run-off system may favor more moderate (or at least less controversial) candidates.

The top vote getter in the first primary usually wins the run-off, but not always—in fact, he or she loses about 30 percent of the time. Such was the case for Jeff Davis, the owner of several auto repair shops in north central Oklahoma. In July 2006, Davis ran in the Republican primary for House District 41. In a five-way race he received a clear plurality of the 4,156 votes (Table 2-3). John Enns, a rancher from Enid, was a distant second; indeed, in the primary, Davis received almost twice as many votes as runner-up Enns.

But in the run-off election four weeks later, Davis was soundly defeated, garnering less than 42 percent of the vote to Enns' 58 percent (of the 3,983 votes cast). Note that fewer people voted in the run-off than in the original primary, a typical outcome. Although there are usually numerous contests to vote for in the original primary election, in the run-off, there typically is just one contest, and some citizens do not make the effort to vote in the run-off because of this or because their preferred candidate is no longer running. We can infer that, for whatever reason, most of the voters in the District 41 race who originally chose Vanover, Reed, or Denny voted for Enns instead of Davis in the run-off. Enns went on to overwhelm his Democratic opponent 71 to 29 percent in the general election. For Jeff Davis, the electoral rules clearly mattered; the Oklahoma run-off rule almost certainly cost him a seat in the Oklahoma House of Representatives.

Another important issue involves voter eligibility. The basic question here is who can participate in a party's primary election? Slightly over half of the states have "closed" primaries, meaning only registered party members are allowed to vote in the primary. Other states have "open" primaries, wherein party registration is not a requirement. In these open primaries, it is possible for independents or even members of an opposing party to vote in the primary.

The type of primary may favor certain candidates—at least the political parties seem to think so. An example involves members of the Idaho Republican Party. Idaho has had open primaries for many decades. But in 2008, some of the more conservative elements of the Republican Party sued the state of Idaho to require the GOP to establish a closed primary. Their presumption was that moderate independents and even some Democrats vote regularly in the Republican primary, causing more moderate candidates to be nominated.[8] There is some research showing that closed primaries do indeed lead to more "extreme" candidates (on the right in Republican primaries and on the left in Democratic ones) winning, but the evidence is limited at this point.[9]

TIMING OF PRIMARY ELECTION

Although increasingly more states are moving their presidential primary elections earlier in the year (a process known as "frontloading"), many of these states retain a later date for the primary election for state offices. In 2006, the primary calendar was scattered from May (10 states), June (13 states), July (two states), and August (nine states) to September (13 states). There are, of course, implications based on the timing of the primary. For potential candidates, earlier primaries mean they must decide at an earlier date if they are going to run or not. An earlier primary also means they must develop a campaign organization and begin fundraising sooner than some might prefer. For voters, an early primary means a longer campaign season. For the political parties, early primaries push forward the candidate recruitment process. In contrast, very late primaries (e.g., those in September) mean the parties must be extremely well-organized because there is only about six to eight weeks between the primary and the general election. As soon as the primary is over, the party must be prepared to offer assistance to the primary winners.

REDISTRICTING PRACTICES

Every 10 years, after a new federal census is taken, states must redraw their legislative district lines to realign electoral boundaries with shifting populations. They must do this because of the "one person, one vote" principle; because we rely largely on SMDs in this country, "one person, one vote" means that districts must have equal populations. Most people understand this. But there are three things about the process that many people do not realize: the state government is responsible for drawing the congressional district lines within that state in addition to state legislative lines, the process for drawing these lines is not the same in all states, and the criteria for drawing the lines is different for congressional and state legislative districts (although the state is responsible for drawing both).

Each state determines the process for drawing state legislative and congressional district lines within that state. For most states, the procedure is to have the state legislature create the districts through statutory law, which of course means the plan must be approved by a legislative majority in both chambers and by the governor. If one party controls both chambers and the governor's office, they are likely to draw the new district lines in such a way as to facilitate the election of more members of that party. Drawing lines to favor a specific group or individual is known as a "gerrymander." There are several types of gerrymanders, but the most common is a partisan gerrymander. According to data from one redistricting analyst, 24 of 26 states with unified government in the last redistricting cycle produced a plan that favored the majority party.[10] But if divided government exists—if one party controls the legislature and the other party controls the executive branch or if one party controls the state senate but the other party is a majority in the lower house—then each party can check the other. This does not mean gerrymandering is unlikely to occur; it just means the nature of the gerrymander will be different—in this case, being one in which incumbents (regardless of party) are more likely to be protected.[11]

In at least 14 states, the redistricting process is currently outside the immediate control of the legislature. With the passage of Proposition 11 in November 2008, California is the most recent addition.[12] Most of these states use an independent redistricting commission to draw the district lines. This does not necessarily make the process less political. As one redistricting analyst notes, "Reformers often mistakenly assume that commissions will be less partisan than legislatures when conducting redistricting but that depends largely on the design of the board or commission."[13] Each of the commissions works in a somewhat different way, depending on how commissioners are selected in a particular state and whether the legislature has the opportunity to veto or modify the commission plan. The use of redistricting commissions is especially popular in the West, where, in addition to California, they are used by Alaska, Arizona, Colorado, Hawaii, Idaho, Montana, and Washington.

The most unusual redistricting process is Iowa's. There the drawing of district lines is done by nonpartisan state legislative staff, and they must follow very specific criteria, developing district maps "without any political or election data including the addresses of incumbents."[14] The legislature can pass or reject the first redistricting plan submitted by the nonpartisan staff, but it cannot amend it. If the first plan is rejected, the nonpartisan staff produces a second plan, which the legislature can again only vote up or down. If that plan is rejected, a third set of districts is produced by the nonpartisan staff. The legislature can amend that plan only after they first reject it. In the three rounds of redistricting since this process was instituted in 1981, the legislature has never gotten to the point where it has amended a plan. In some ways, this is surprising because the Iowa process often results in very dramatic changes. After the 2001 redistricting, for example, 64 of the 150 Iowa legislators wound up in districts with at least one other incumbent, forcing many of them to retire from the legislature, move to an unoccupied district, or face a competitive election.[15]

Proposals to reduce or remove partisanship from the redistricting process have surfaced in most states that still allow the legislature to draw its own lines. The likelihood of a majority party giving up the chance to enhance its future electoral prospects through drawing favorable lines is, however, very small. As a member of the Republican majority in the Virginia House of Delegates confessed during a debate over a Democratic proposal to adopt an independent redistricting scheme, "I'm going to tell the gentlelady from Fairfax that when I get in [the] minority, I will support her bill."[16]

CASE LAW AND STATE REDISTRICTING

The standards for drawing state legislative district lines are somewhat different from those used for congressional districts. The biggest difference is in what passes for "one person, one vote." Recall that the courts interpret the phrase "one person, one vote" to mean that each district must have the same population as the next district—that is, districts within a state must be equipopulous.[17] But just how close to "equal population" must a plan be? For congressional districts within a state, the answer is extremely close. As a leading congressional text notes, "The Supreme Court has adopted rigid mathematical equality as the underlying standard."[18] Thus, each congressional district within a state must have almost exactly the same number of people. In contrast, the courts have been a bit more flexible when it comes to state legislative districts. The difference is that the interpretation of "equal representation" for congressional districts stems from Article I, Section 2 of the U.S. Constitution, but for state legislative districts, the relevant constitutional sources are the 14th and 15th Amendments to the U.S. Constitution and appropriate sections of the state constitutions.

The key state legislative redistricting case is *Reynolds v. Sims*, which was decided by the U.S. Supreme Court in 1964.[19] The 1960s was a time of major policy shifts by the Court in regard to redistricting and representation. And the *Reynolds* case is especially important for states. The decision forced a number of states to abandon the practice of apportioning their senates by county. (A few states in New England had to give up apportioning their lower houses by cities and towns.) At the congressional level, of course, the allocation of seats in the House of Representatives is by state population, as directed by Article I, Section 2 of the U.S. Constitution. The allocation of seats in the U.S. Senate, however, is not by population but by political jurisdiction—that is, by state. Each state is allocated two senators (Article I, Section 3). Thus, Wyoming (with a population of 515,000) has the same representation in the U.S. Senate as California (with a population of 37 million). There are both symbolic and political purposes to this equal allocation; it reflects the fact that all states are equal in the federal system of government. Many states, when devising allocation principles for their own legislatures, followed similar reasoning. They determined that districts should be allocated by population for the lower chambers and by political subdivision for the upper chamber; in most states, this political subdivision was the county. There would be one state senator from each county, regardless of population. In 1960 in Florida, for example, one senate district (Dade County) had a population of 935,000, and another had a population of 9,543. Each county had the same representation, but one county had 98 times more people! The U.S. Supreme Court largely ended this practice with their decision in *Reynolds v. Sims*.

The court did recognize, however, that many state constitutions required counties or other jurisdictions (e.g., New England towns and municipalities elsewhere) to remain intact when drawing legislative district lines. To facilitate these *state* constitutional stipulations, the U.S. Supreme Court permits some latitude in population deviation in the drawing of state legislative lines. Essentially, the courts have ruled a population deviation (from the district with the smallest population to the district with the largest population) under 10 percent to be acceptable. And on occasion, the courts have even accepted somewhat larger deviations if the state can justify such variances.

There are two important points here. First, the redistricting agents (state legislatures or commissions) have a bit more latitude in drawing state legislative districts than congressional districts, and this often permits states to draw lines that keep political subdivisions such as counties, townships, or municipalities intact rather than being split among several districts. Second, redistricting agents understand quite well that deviations under 10 percent are far more likely to be accepted by the courts than deviations over 10 percent. Most states take advantage of this knowledge; in the last redistricting cycle, 19 states approved plans with population deviations under 9 percent, and 28 states devised state house districting plans with deviations between 9 and 10 percent.[20] Only three states created plans that exceeded the 10 percent variation. By comparison, no state submitted a plan for its *congressional* districts with variances as great as even one percent.

There are several other important considerations in redistricting. One is the issue of racial gerrymandering. The way district lines get drawn did not become an important issue for the federal courts until the 1960s, and one of the main reasons the courts finally did become involved was because of racial discrimination in the way some states drew the district lines for state legislatures.

Many of the early cases centered on the fact that states were diluting the voting strength of minorities. One of the ways this was done was by creating

MMDs in urban areas. A 1973 Texas case, *White v. Regester*, is typical.[21] In San Antonio (Bexar County), where a sizeable Hispanic population resided, and in Dallas (Dallas County), where a significant black population lived, the creation of SMDs would likely result in the election of some Hispanic and black legislators. But by using county-wide MMDs in each county, the majority of white voters could control the election. In a series of similar cases in the late 1960s and 1970s, the U.S. Supreme Court discouraged the use of MMDs (without declaring them unconstitutional per se). Likewise, the Court was sensitive to other forms of racial gerrymandering. The long-term result was the elimination of many electoral practices that diluted the voting strength of minorities and, over the course of the last quarter of the twentieth century, facilitated an increase in the number of minorities—especially African Americans in the South—serving in state legislatures.

CAMPAIGN FINANCE LAWS

Several years ago, Congress passed what was hailed as a "sweeping" campaign finance law known as the Bipartisan Campaign Finance Reform Act (BCRA), perhaps better known as the "McCain-Feingold" Act after the two principal sponsors of the law. BCRA received a lot of media attention and did represent something of a change in the existing system. But for the most part, BCRA affected congressional campaigns far more than it affected state races. The reason is that each state has its own state campaign finance system, which is defined in state statutes and state constitutions. Granted, all states must comply with some rules and standards established by the U.S. Supreme Court, but most of the elective offices in the United States are more influenced by state laws than BCRA. And these state laws exhibit some major differences from one state to another.

Campaign finance laws differ among the states in three ways: disclosure requirements, rules for contributing to campaigns, and rules for campaign spending. Disclosure is the reporting of campaign finance activity, including who contributed and how much, how much was spent, and what it was spent on. All states have some disclosure requirements, but they vary in terms of the level of specificity and how often reports must be filed.[22] For example, Colorado and Wisconsin require all contributions over $20 to be itemized and identified by source; other states set this threshold at $50, and still others at $100. Some states require individual contributors to report their occupation; others do not.

Much greater differences exist in the laws concerning who can contribute and how much. Some states ban direct contributions from corporations or unions; others allow them. There are very big differences among the states in regard to how much money an individual or political action committee can contribute to a state legislative campaign. The range varies from $160 in Montana to $1,000 in Michigan to no limit at all in Alabama. Consequently, in

Alabama, a single individual could legally contribute $10 million to a candidate for the Alabama House of Representatives! Lower limits appear to encourage more candidates to run for the legislature.[23]

The U.S. Supreme Court views campaign spending as facilitating political speech and therefore has consistently ruled that limits on campaign spending are a violation of the First Amendment guarantee of freedom of speech.[24] Therefore, any limitations to spending must be *voluntarily* agreed to by candidates. What could possibly induce a candidate in a campaign for state legislative office to voluntarily limit campaign expenditures to some predetermined level set by the state? A few states offer candidates "free" money to run their campaigns if the candidates agree not to spend more than a specific amount. The inducement, therefore, is being relieved of the burden of raising campaign funds; if a candidate voluntarily agrees to the spending limit, he or she does not have to spend time "dialing for dollars" and holding fundraising events. For many candidates, this is an attractive inducement, indeed—the overwhelming majority of candidates report that fundraising is the most distasteful aspect of running for office.[25] At this point, only a few states offer this sort of public financing in exchange for accepting spending limits.

The most extensive public financing programs, known as "clean elections," exist in Arizona and Maine. (Connecticut began its program in 2008). In these states, candidates become eligible for public funds if they agree to limit spending to a specified amount and demonstrate their viability as a candidate by raising a modest amount of "seed money" in small donations. For example, candidates for the Maine House of Representatives must gather donations of $5 from 150 donors; then they are eligible to receive about $4,400 for the general election campaign (and an additional $1,500 if they have an opponent in the primary election). But by accepting these public funds, the candidate agrees not to spend more than these funds on his or her campaign. Thus, for the 2006 electoral cycle, "clean election" candidates for the Maine House of Representatives were limited to about $6,000 in spending.[26] In Arizona, where the population of each House district is much larger than in Maine, the spending limit is higher (about $29,000 for the 2006 cycle).[27] Violating these spending limits can have dire consequences. In 2006, Arizona Representative David Burnell Smith became the first legislator in the country to be removed from office for having overspent campaign limits.[28]

It is important to remember, however, that candidates do not have to accept the public funds; such candidates are not subject to the expenditure limits that are a condition of acceptance of public funds. These "traditional" candidates are free to spend as much money as they want (or can afford). Most legislative candidates in both states now accept the public funds, but the participation is decidedly higher in Maine, where more than 80 percent of the candidates "ran clean," than in Arizona, where just under 60 percent of the candidates accepted public funds.

Clean elections impact state legislative campaigns in intriguing ways. Some of the effects are as anticipated. Since instituting clean elections, Arizona and Maine have seen modest increases in the competitiveness of their state legislative campaigns.[29] Other consequences were unanticipated. Female candidates, for example, are more likely to accept public funding than are male candidates.[30] Campaigns are also altered by clean election rules. They depress overall campaign activity levels and push the bulk of spending into the final days before the election.[31]

TERM LIMITS

A final law that varies by state and affects the nature of elections is the limit on how many terms a legislator can serve. For most states, there is no limit; as long as an individual can continue to win elections, he or she can serve indefinitely. But currently 15 states impose term limitations. Term limits in the states that have them, however, vary in regard to the specifics. As Table 1-3 shows, the differences basically revolve around the number of terms one may serve and whether those term limits are lifetime bans or simply consecutive terms. For example, Louisiana and Nevada have 12-year limits in each house, and Arkansas, California and Michigan have more stringent limits of six years in the lower chamber and eight years in the upper chamber. Both Ohio and Missouri have eight-year limits in each chamber, but Missouri's is a *lifetime* limit and Ohio's is simply a consecutive term limit. In Ohio, a termed-out legislator is eligible to run again after sitting out for four years. From the standpoint of elections, term limits have several implications. The most obvious is that because incumbents are eventually forced out, there is likely to be higher turnover in legislatures with term limits. Another implication is that there will be more open-seat elections (those in which there is no incumbent), which tend to be more competitive than races involving incumbents.

In term-limited states, the decision to "stay or go" is eventually made for the legislator—he or she no longer has the option to stay. Nicole Parra, the California Assemblywoman discussed at the beginning of this chapter, is an example; she was term limited out of her Assembly seat in 2008. Now that the 30th Assembly District was an open seat, Republican Danny Gilmore (who had lost to Parra in both 2004 and 2006) ran again. This time he won.

THE CANDIDATES

A few years ago, in a book about running for state legislature, we wrote:

> No greater commitment to participation in the political process can be made than to stand for election. Most Americans give little thought to what is

involved in running for elective office. Unappreciated is the tremendous personal cost in money, time, and emotion involved in seeking public office.[32]

Running for state legislature is a more daunting task than most realize. In fact, between 35 and 40 percent of all state legislative seats nationwide are uncontested—that is, only one major party candidate runs, so that person is automatically elected.[33] In some states, the figure is considerably higher. In 2006, more than 70 percent of the legislative races in Arkansas, Georgia, Massachusetts, and South Carolina were not contested by one of the major parties.[34]

Why is it so hard to get people to run for the state legislature? Being a candidate for office requires a great deal of time and energy, often more than some aspiring politicians realize. A physician running for the Missouri state senate in 2008, for example, dropped out before the primary, explaining, "It was mostly the demands on my time. Trying to run two businesses—my work is somewhat unpredictable. All these things I could have known before hand, but I didn't realize how much work [running for office] was."[35] Psychologically, there is the reality that all of the effort might be for naught; as one observer notes, "You have to be strong enough personally that you can risk being rejected."[36] A veteran state lawmaker concurs, saying, "I don't like running for reelection every two years. It feels very much like a personal judgment. . . . I know it makes my stomach turn somersaults; I get anxious about it. Is this person going to vote for me? Did this person vote for me? Are you still going to vote for me?"[37] And there are potential financial costs associated with possibly winning office that might not pay very much. As an Iowa state senator involved in recruiting others to run observed, "It's a huge commitment financially and on your family. So there's not a huge line of people—not even a small line of people who are interested in giving up four months of the year to serve."[38]

CANDIDATE TYPE

When analyzing candidacies and campaigns, political scientists distinguish between three types of candidates: incumbents, challengers, and open-seat contestants. The incumbent is the current office holder. For the most part, incumbents enjoy substantial advantages in the American electoral system, and this is no less true of state legislative incumbents. In a typical year, state legislative incumbents win reelection about 90 to 95 percent of the time when they run.[39]

Challengers are candidates who run against incumbents. Because incumbents win so often, it is often difficult to find a challenger to compete against an incumbent. Almost all of the uncontested races mentioned earlier occur in situations when no challenger can be found to run against an incumbent. However, there are circumstances in which a candidate can pose a serious challenge to—and sometimes defeat—an incumbent. This is most likely to occur under one of the following circumstances:

1. **The race is in a marginal district.** A "marginal" district is a competitive one—one in which the voters' party preferences are split fairly evenly between the two major parties or one that contains a large number of independent voters. A "safe" district is one where members of one party almost always win. Thus, a Democratic challenger in a safe Republican district would find it almost impossible to win. But in a marginal district, such a challenger might have a chance.
2. **Redistricting has occurred since the last election.** When the lines are redrawn, even long-time incumbents sometimes find they may lose. Mainly, this is because the redrawing of the lines means there will be some new voters in the district who might identify with the other political party or who may simply be unfamiliar with the incumbent.
3. **The incumbent has issues.** "Issues" could be policy based. The incumbent may have voted on an important issue in a way that has alienated a sufficient number of voters so that reelection is in doubt. For example, any incumbent in Wyoming who votes for stricter gun control is likely to have stiff competition in the next election. But more often, "issues" in this context refers to personal issues such as ethical lapses or legal troubles. When these personal issues become public, even entrenched incumbents may lose.

The final type of candidate is an open-seat contestant. By definition, an open seat means there is no incumbent in the race. By eliminating the incumbency advantage, open-seat races are usually much more competitive than races involving incumbents. In open-seat races, both major parties usually run competent, qualified candidates. And because the race is likely to be closely contested, the campaign likely will be more expensive.

It is probably obvious that the recruitment patterns are different for the three types of candidates. Incumbents do not really have to be recruited at all; they have run before and won, and now they have the advantages of name recognition, political contacts, and campaign contributors as well as a track record of electoral success. Recruiting challengers is usually much more difficult and often involves appealing to someone's sense of party loyalty to run even though the chances of winning are minimal. Open-seat races, because they typically offer candidates a better chance of winning, involve a more intense recruitment process.

RECRUITMENT AGENTS

At one time, political parties controlled the recruitment of candidates. Party "bosses" determined who would run, when they would run, and for what office they would run. The party nomination was simply a matter of the party elite determining who would be the candidate. All of this began to change about a century ago with the advent of the Progressive Era. Several reforms of the Progressive period were aimed at weakening the control of political parties, but in regard to recruitment, the most important of these was the creation of the primary election system (discussed earlier in this chapter). Essentially, the primary election weakened the ability of party bosses to completely control the nomination process by allowing voters to choose the nominee. This is not to say that parties are no longer important in the recruitment process. Indeed, in recent years, the two major parties in various guises have become more active in recruiting candidates, especially in situations where control of the legislature may be at stake. But we are a long way from the pre-Progressive period when parties ruled the process. There are other recruitment agents as well; in particular, interest groups may be active in seeking out potential candidates. Community groups and religious organizations sometimes play a role.

A survey of non-incumbent candidates for state legislatures found that various party organizations were the most likely recruitment agents but that numerous other possible agents were also involved.[40] According to the survey, the most active recruitment agent is the local party organization; 45 percent of the candidates said they had been approached and encouraged to run by the local party committee. It is, ultimately, the responsibility of the local party committee or chair to fill out the slate of candidates for the party in an election in the area. Often, this means finding someone who is willing to be a "sacrificial lamb" when there is a seemingly invulnerable incumbent from the other party. This is evident when we break down the survey results by candidate type: 56 percent of the candidates who ran as challengers against an incumbent say they were approached and encouraged to run compared with only 39 percent of those running for an open seat. Whereas open-seat candidates are more likely to come forth on their own ("self-starters"), challengers against incumbents are more likely to have to be encouraged or persuaded to run.

State party officials and state legislative leaders are more likely to become involved in recruitment when the parties are closely divided in the legislature. Under these circumstances, legislative leaders or state party leaders determine which districts and races they think are winnable. These "targeted" races are the ones in which the party leaders are most likely to be involved, both in terms of recruiting "quality" candidates and in terms of providing campaign support to those they get to enter the race.

Although interest groups and other associations (e.g., religious organizations) are not as prevalent as parties in the recruitment process, they are sometimes important. This is most likely when such groups are closely allied with a particular party, such as labor unions (Democratic Party) or evangelical churches (Republican Party).

SELF-STARTERS

Some candidates do not need to be recruited; they recruit themselves. In the survey mentioned above, we asked non-incumbent candidates to describe the circumstances surrounding their decision to run. We asked them, "Whose idea was it to run for the legislature?" The responses to this question are given in Table 2-4. Almost one-third of the candidates were self-starters. About one-fifth had to be persuaded, and the rest (the largest group) were thinking about running when they received encouragement from others. As one might expect, self-starters are more likely to run for open seats, while those who must be persuaded are often recruited to run as challengers against incumbents. These figures do not include incumbents, who (by definition) are already in office. It is fair to say that, after they have been elected for the first time, almost all incumbents are self-starters in subsequent elections. They do not need to be recruited; the general assumption is they will run again. This is truer in some states than others, however, as we shall see when we discuss turnover.

THE RECRUITMENT OF WOMEN AND MINORITIES

As is true in most legislatures around the world, women and minorities in state legislatures are underrepresented relative to their proportion of the population. Nationwide, almost 24 percent of the all state legislators are women, although women comprise about 51 percent of the population. The percentages for minorities are about 8 percent African American (13 percent of the population nationwide), 3 percent Hispanic (14 percent nationally), and less than 1 percent Asian American (4 percent nationally). As one would expect and as we will show in Chapter 3, the percentage of legislators with a racial or ethnic minority heritage is highly variable by region and state, largely because the racial and ethnic mix varies by region and state. For example, more than 25 percent of Mississippi legislators are African American,

TABLE 2-4   "WHOSE IDEA WAS IT TO RUN FOR THE LEGISLATURE?" (IN PERCENT)

"WHICH OF THE FOLLOWING STATEMENTSS MOST ACCURATELY DESCRIBES YOUR DECISION TO RUN FOR LEGISLATIVE OFFICE?"	(N = 987)
Self-starters: *"It was entirely my idea."*	32.1
Encouraged: *"I had already thought about it when someone else encouraged me to run."*	46.6
Persuaded: *"I had not seriously thought about it until someone else suggested it."*	21.3

Source: State Legislative Candidate Survey conducted by the authors in 1998 and 2002.

more than 35 percent of the New Mexico legislators are Latino, and almost half of the Hawaii legislators are Asian-American, largely because each of these groups makes up a significant proportion of the population in these states.[41] This does not, however, explain the variation in female state legislators across the states.

Women are a majority of the population in every state except Alaska, but in 2009, the proportion of female state legislators ranged from 8.8 percent (South Carolina) to 38.3 percent (Vermont).[42] The reasons for this disparity are many, including differences in political culture; partisan strength (female legislators are more likely to be Democrats); and the apparent reluctance, even today, of party elites in some states to actively recruit women as legislative candidates.[43]

Several scholars point out that there is a gender gap between the parties in state legislatures.[44] A greater number of Democratic state legislators are women. Moreover, the gap is widening, as Figure 2-1 shows. In 1981, there were about 500 Democratic and about 400 Republican female state legislators. But because Republicans at the time were a distinct minority in most state legislatures, women actually constituted a larger proportion of Republican state legislators. Over the next generation, more women from both parties were elected to the legislatures, but the increase was much greater among Democrats than Republicans. For Republican women, the high point was 1994, the year that Republicans swept into office in many state legislatures as well Congress. Since then, the number of female Republican state legislators has actually declined.[45] Meanwhile, the number of women counted among the Democratic state legislative ranks continues to grow.

FIGURE 2-1   NUMBER OF WOMEN STATE LEGISLATORS BY PARTY

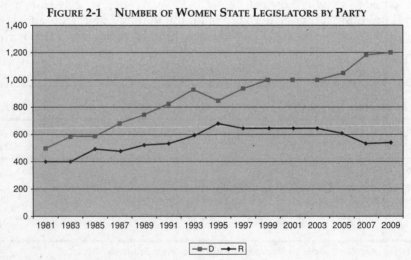

Source: Center for American Women and Politics.

TABLE 2-5   "WHOSE IDEA WAS IT TO RUN?" BY CANDIDATE GENDER (IN PERCENT)

"WHICH OF THE FOLLOWING STATEMENTS MOST ACCURATELY DESCRIBES YOUR DECISION TO RUN FOR LEGISLATIVE OFFICE?"	MEN ($N = 776$)	WOMEN ($N = 211$)
Self-starters: *"It was entirely my idea."*	36.5	16.1[a]
Encouraged: *"I had already thought about it when someone else encouraged me to run."*	46.5	49.8
Persuaded: *"I had not seriously thought about it until someone else suggested it."*	17.0	34.1[a]

Source: State Legislative Candidate Survey, 1998 and 2002.
[a]The difference between responses of men and women is significant at $P < .01$ for the chi-square test.

As of 2009, there were 1,201 female Democratic legislators and about 536 female Republican legislators. Because there were almost as many Republican state legislators as Democratic ones, this means that Republican women make up a much smaller percentage (16 percent) of their party in the state legislature than women make up of Democrats in the state legislatures (30 percent).

Ample evidence shows that women, as a group, are less likely to "self-start" as candidates—that is, they are less likely to decide on their own to run for office and more likely have to be recruited to run.[46] The first female speaker of the Ohio House, for example, notes of women, "They're harder to recruit. They're harder to convince to run."[47] Evidence of this gender difference appears in Table 2-5, again using the candidate survey discussed previously. Although more than 36 percent of male candidates were self-starters, only 16 percent of female candidates fell into this category.

For this reason, efforts by the political parties to recruit women appear to be especially crucial.[48] Further evidence from the candidate survey given in Table 2-6 demonstrates this point. Candidates were asked if they had been approached by any recruitment agents and urged to run before entering the race. In *every instance*, a higher proportion of women than men indicated they were approached and urged to run. In almost half the cases, the differences are statistically significant. For example, women (24 percent) were more likely than men (16 percent) to indicate they were recruited to run by members of a service organization (e.g., the Kiwanis).

Most importantly, female candidates were much more likely to say they were contacted and encouraged to run by state or local political elites. In particular, they were much more likely to indicate that they were recruited by state party officials or state legislative leaders. This indicates a crucial role for party elites. When women become candidates, they often point to the role of the party in their recruitment. And given the data in Figure 2-1, the Democratic Party appears to be making a more concerted effort to recruit women these days than are the Republicans.

TABLE 2-6   THE PREVALENCE OF RECRUITMENT AGENTS FOR MALE AND
FEMALE STATE LEGISLATIVE CANDIDATES[a]

RECRUITMENT AGENTS	MEN ($N = 834$)	WOMEN ($N = 230$)
Family members	29.7	37.8[b]
Coworkers	19.5	23.9
Service organization	15.5	24.3[c]
Church members	13.1	13.5
Neighbors	24.1	27.8
Interest groups	12.6	13.9
Local party officials	42.9	47.8
State party officials	27.3	39.1[c]
Local elected officials	31.3	38.7[b]
Legislative leaders	31.2	44.3[d]
Other	7.0	7.4

Source: State Legislative Candidate Survey, 1998 and 2002.
[a]Question: "Before you announced your candidacy, were you approached and encouraged to run for office by any of the following?"
[b]*$P < .05$ significance level between responses of men and women (chi-square test)
[c]$P = .01$.
[d]$P < .001$.

HOW CAMPAIGNS ARE RUN

Like many things about state legislatures, there is a wide variety of practices in campaigning. As noted at the beginning of this chapter, legislative campaigns in some states, such as California, are every bit as professional, sophisticated, and expensive as congressional campaigns. Such races rely on professional consultants using the latest polling, advertising, and fundraising techniques. These races, usually found in districts with large populations and known as *wholesale* campaigns, rely heavily on mass communication techniques such as television to reach potential voters.

In contrast, legislative campaigns in states with small population districts still rely on face-to-face, door-to-door retail campaigns that are designed to win over potential voters one at a time. Such campaigns are limited operations, involving the candidate and a few volunteers. Generally speaking, such campaigns are more likely in races for the lower chamber because, in most states, House districts have half or fewer people than Senate districts (recall from Tables 1-4 and 1-5 that the median population of state House districts is about 40,000; the median for state Senate districts is 110,000). Another important factor is the competitiveness of the district; less money is spent campaigning for safe seats.

Other factors also affect campaign spending. As mentioned earlier in the chapter, the campaign finance laws vary by state; it is possible to raise relatively large amounts of money from a small group of wealthy donors in some states where contribution limits are generous.[49]

Because of these and other factors, it is difficult to settle on the cost of a "typical" campaign. The most recent comparative data for state legislative campaigns are from the 2005 to 2006 electoral cycle.[50] The National Institute on Money in State Politics reports that the average amount raised by general election House candidates was $63,484 and the average amount raised by Senate candidates was $135,272.[51] However, these figures grossly distort the situation for the "typical" candidate because a handful of extremely expensive campaigns greatly inflate the average. Our own rough estimate is that a competitive race (i.e., a race in which both candidates have a reasonable chance of winning) in most states is likely to cost around $30,000 in a House district and $75,000 to $100,000 in a Senate race.[52]

One study a few years ago found that:

> The dividing line between professional and amateur campaigns is at the $50,000 spending level: many of the candidates above it run media and research-driven campaigns that utilize paid consultants and sophisticated vote-getting techniques; the vast majority of those below it run volunteer-driven grassroots campaigns.[53]

Using the $50,000 figure as a benchmark, we can assume that whereas most state House candidates run races oriented toward retail campaigns with a mostly volunteer organization, most Senate races run somewhat more wholesale, professional campaigns.

The most common campaign techniques found in state legislative races are direct mail and literature drops, billboards and yard signs, and "doorbelling."[54] As we stated elsewhere, "State legislative races tend to be fought doorstep-to-doorstep and mailbox-by-mailbox."[55] In districts with fewer numbers of voters, knocking on doors can be an effective campaign tactic, although it is also fraught with some peril, as Politics Under the Domes 2-2 notes.

Even relatively low-budget campaigns these days make use of direct mail advertising. Compared with the cost of television advertising, it is an inexpensive way to reach potential voters, even if the candidate hires a mail consultant. A survey in three Southern states a few years ago found that more than 80 percent of state legislative candidates used direct mail and almost 30 percent of those candidates sent out at least seven different mailings.[56]

In a few states, legislative candidates make use of television ads to reach voters. The data in Table 2-1 indicate that California Assembly candidate Nicole Parra spent almost $600,000 on television ads. But for most candidates, television is simply too expensive and too inefficient.[57]

> Consider, for example, the situation of a candidate running for the Missouri House of Representatives from a district in the Kansas City area. The Kansas City television market covers over two million people. Because the market

The Art and Science of Doorbelling

Retail politics rules in most state legislative elections. Candidates typically find mass media to be too expensive and too inefficient to meet their campaigning needs. Instead, they introduce themselves to the electorate by knocking on doors.

"Doorbelling" tends to be pursued by candidates in legislative districts with smaller constituencies, where they have a good chance to meet and greet a large percentage of voters. For example, in Maine, a state with small districts, "door-to-door campaigning is common, and most party organizers insist, essential . . . they place a premium on face-to-face meetings." Ringing doorbells and talking with people can be an effective and economical way to campaign. But even in very large districts doorbelling can be important. A candidate for the Texas state Senate commented, "I'm competing against TV, radio, and the demands of work life. The best way to get through to (voters) is by knocking on their doors." Validation for that proposition was given by one of the people who answered the Texas candidate's knock. The potential voter exclaimed, "There's nothing like the person-to-person contact. Coming out in [rainy and cold] weather like this shows me he really cares." Indeed, such personal interactions can have long-term payoffs for a candidate. Several years after the fact, one Seattle-area voter happily recalled the time when his state senator knocked on his door and "came in and we watched, like, half of a Mariners game together."

But retail politics of this sort can have drawbacks. One faced by many candidates is simply the fear of meeting strangers. A Vermont legislator confessed that during her first run for the legislature, she was so scared of knocking on doors that she had to practice her spiel on a friend before screwing up the courage to take to the streets. Other problems are physical, such as the plight of one California candidate who "knocked on 11,000 doors, met 7,000 voters and walked so many miles that he must now wear a knee brace" or an Indiana candidate who, in boasting about the large number of doors he had knocked, on stated, "I've got the blisters and the worn-out shoes to prove it." Some doorbelling pain is inflicted by others; a West Virginia candidate complained that her reward for doorbelling was that "I got bit by a dog Friday and I got bit by a dog Saturday." And, of course, such unstructured meetings can backfire, as they did for a young state house candidate in Iowa: "I was out knocking on doors during the election, and I asked a woman—I thought I knew her, and I knew she was fixing to have a baby, so I asked her when the baby was due. It turns out she had it four months ago." The candidate ruefully noted, "You should never say things like that, especially if you're trying to get people to vote for you." Perhaps it is no surprise that in this case doorbelling did not work; the candidate lost the election.

Although there are pitfalls to doorbelling, both politicians and voters benefit from it in ways that neither of them may fully appreciate. As a political science professor who lost a close race for the Minnesota House of Representatives later reflected, "As a door-knocking candidate, you are forced every day to meet people whose political views differ from your own. At every door you may have to answer a critic or rethink your views. And the same goes for the voters themselves."

Sources: T. A. Badger, "Texas Candidates Go Door-to-Door," Yahoo! News, March 3, 2002; Andrew Garber, "1 State Senator, 2 Months, 99 Bills, " *Seattle Times*, March 3, 2007; Charleston *Gazette*, "Legislative Hopefuls Struggle to Get Attention," November 6, 2000; John Fritze, "Voter Rolls Are Rising as Turnout Declines," *Indianapolis Star*, 9 October 2000; Kathleen Murphy, "Vermont House Speaker: 'I'm Not Slick'," Stateline.org, 25 April 2005; Francis X. Quinn, "Democrats Foresee Big House Win," *Kennebec Journal*, September 30, 2002; James H. Read, "Doorknocking is Democracy," *St. Cloud Times*, September 17, 2008; Nicole Riehl, "Aide to U.S. Senator Juggles Politics and College," Cedar Rapids *Gazette*, January 29, 2005; Nancy Vogel, "Candidate's Millions Go Toward Entry-Level Job," *Los Angeles Times*, October 26, 2004.

has the potential to reach so many viewers, the cost of advertising time is relatively high. Each state legislative house district in Missouri contains fewer than fifty thousand people. To buy time on a Kansas City television station means that an extraordinary majority of the viewers (over 95 percent) are not in the candidate's legislative district. . . . For the candidate, spending money on television advertising would be extraordinarily inefficient.[58]

Such inefficiency exists anywhere there is a large media market but relatively small population legislative districts (house races in Connecticut, Georgia, Maryland, Minnesota, Tennessee, and Virginia are all examples).

If the stakes are sufficiently high and the race is extremely tight, however, candidates and political parties have little choice but to spend money even if in inefficient ways. The 2007 election for control of the Virginia Senate is a case in point. Because the entire Virginia senate is elected for four-year terms (and in odd-numbered years), the November 2007 election was the last election before the next redistricting cycle. Both parties dearly wanted a majority so they could draw the district maps after the 2010 census. Because the stakes were so high and because the most competitive races for control of the chamber happen to be in Northern Virginia, "where TV advertising rates are among the nation's highest," numerous candidates each spent more than $1 million on their campaigns.[59] In one race, the two candidates raised $3.4 million between them—for a *state* senate race in Virginia. A race in a neighboring district garnered $3.2 million for the two candidates. Much of the money went toward buying television time in the Washington, D.C. market, meaning viewers in that city and in neighboring Maryland—people who had no tie to or direct stake in the elections—were also exposed to the ads.

In some instances, cable television is a reasonable alternative. Cable audiences are more narrowly segmented (e.g., "Bass Fishing for Beginners"); therefore, the advertising rates are generally much lower than for network television. Moreover, precisely because the audiences are segmented, the candidate can target specific types of people, similar to direct mail. Even with cable, however, it is usually the case that much of the audience lives outside the district or—even worse—lives in the district but does not vote. The advantage of direct mail is that candidates (or their mail specialists) can use lists of registered voters to communicate with the individuals who are likely to participate. Similar to cable television, radio has the advantage of being inexpensive with segmented listening audiences, but—also similar to cable—there is no guarantee that listeners are in the candidates' district or will turn out to cast a ballot.

In many legislative districts, traditional campaign techniques still reign. These include building name recognition through yard signs, billboards, newspaper ads, campaign brochures, and the face-to-face contact achieved through going door-to-door and attending local events. Take, for example, a description of a typical state legislative campaign in suburban Oklahoma City:

> Every day and evening, throughout the spring and summer, he rang doorbells and shook hands, trying to make contact with voters and get his name out. He . . . spent weeks analyzing the district traffic patterns before purchasing billboards. [He] made use of reliable political data to target neighborhoods, blocks, and houses for door-to-door efforts.[60]

Another candidate, a 24-year-old running (successfully, as it turned out) in the Atlanta, Georgia area, summed up the campaign experience in this way,

> This campaign was all about name recognition. . . . There are just too many races in this area to get any real ink . . . every candidate had some form of equity to run on—money, connections, experience. My equity was time. . . . Being twenty-four helped a lot. At nine p.m. I can still be running from house to house; these other guys just can't do this, not in a hot Georgia summer.[61]

This same candidate made heavy use of phone banks, saying, "[We] sent up a phone bank of volunteers . . . working to call people and talk about the campaign. . . . We must have made two thousand calls."[62] "Retail politics" is an apt description for most state legislative contests.

The rapid expansion of personal communication technologies that facilitate social networking (Twitter, Facebook, etc.) means that candidates are adapting their campaign tactics to take advantage of these instruments for campaign purposes. The number of state legislative campaigns with websites, for example, grows dramatically with every electoral cycle. Social networking is an inexpensive way to reach potential voters, and many state legislative candidates quickly will adapt to the new technology.

TURNOVER, PARTY COMPETITION, AND ELECTIONS

One of the more dramatic changes that occurred in state legislatures in the past century is the decline in turnover. "Turnover" refers to the percentage of new members coming in to legislative house. A very high turnover rate means there are many inexperienced lawmakers and a greater likelihood that the legislature is not an independent force in the policymaking arena; a very low turnover means there is almost no "new blood" infused into the institution. Neither of these situations is particularly attractive from an organizational point of view. The preferred situation is one in which there is enough turnover to ensure competition between parties and viewpoints and to facilitate new ideas but not so much turnover that the legislature has no "institutional memory" or ability to act as a co-equal branch in a system of separation of powers.

Historically, there has been a clear decline in the average turnover in state legislatures (Figure 2-2). In the 1930s, for example, turnover in every electoral cycle averaged more than 50 percent in state senates and almost 60 percent in state houses. This represents an extremely high turnover; it means that on average, half of senators and three of every five house members had not served in the previous session. But over the next five decades, there was a

FIGURE 2-2   AVERAGE TURNOVER BY DECADE

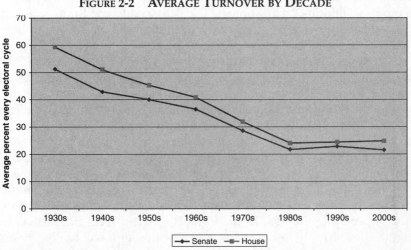

Data source: Moncrief, Neimi, and Powell, "Time, Term Limits, and Turnover." *Legislative Studies Quarterly* 29 (2004), Tables 1-2 and updated by authors.

steady decrease in turnover rates. By the end of the 1980s, turnover averaged 22 percent in senates and 24 percent in lower houses. And remember, these are averages for all states; some states were experiencing much lower turnover rates by this time. For example, the California Senate averaged 11 percent turnover and the Assembly (House) averaged 16 percent— extremely low rates comparable to those in Congress. Turnover in each chamber of the Arkansas, Delaware, Illinois, New York, and Pennsylvania legislatures averaged 15 percent or less for each electoral cycle in the decade.

The decline in turnover was brought about by several variables. First, and perhaps most importantly, many state legislatures had become more professionalized in the 1970s—which, as we will examine in greater depth in Chapter 3, means longer legislative sessions, better member pay, and more staff and other resources. The job became more demanding, but it also became more attractive for many legislators, and the incentive to stay increased. Second, electoral competition declined in many states (or, to be more precise, in many districts in these states). More and more seats became "safe" for one or the other parties, and fewer incumbents were defeated. These two variables—a greater incentive for incumbents to stay and a greater electoral advantage for incumbents when they sought reelection— help explain the decline in turnover. One recent study found that the median reelection rate for incumbents in state legislatures has been over 90 percent since 1992, and in several electoral cycles, the median was over 95 percent.[63]

TERM LIMITS AND TURNOVER

In the 1990s, a movement to limit the number of terms a legislator could serve swept across many states. The early phase of the term limit movement was two pronged: limiting terms for state legislative seats and limiting terms for congressional seats. The strategy of the term-limit advocates was to include both these offices (federal and state) in a "grass-roots" movement. The limitation on congressional terms was struck down by the U.S. Supreme Court in 1995, leaving the proponents to push for term limits at the state level.[64]

It was obvious that legislators were not likely to place limits on themselves, so the term-limit proponents took the fight to the states that allowed the public to make laws through the initiative process. The initiative is a form of "direct democracy" that allows the placement of a policy issue on the ballot for voters to approve or reject. This type of policymaking is provided for in 24 states. The particulars of the initiative process vary somewhat among the states that permit its use. But the key thing is that term limit proponents recognized that they had a much better chance of establishing term limits by pursuing the idea in the initiative states. Term limitations were introduced in virtually all of the initiative states and eventually passed in 21 states. In four of these states (Massachusetts, Oregon, Washington, and Wyoming), term limits (or the language in the ballot proposals proposing

FIGURE 2-3   TURNOVER IN STATES WITH AND WITHOUT TERM LIMITS

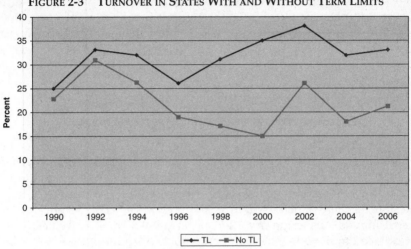

them) were struck down as a violation of the state constitution. (The state supreme courts in the other 17 states with term limits found no such violations in their state constitution). Term limits were repealed by legislative action in two other states, Idaho and Utah. Thus, 15 states currently limit the number of terms a legislator can serve.

Supporters of term limits attribute many positive consequences to term limits. Most of these consequences are reviewed in other chapters; here we focus on the effect of term limits on turnover. And there is no doubt that term limits have increased turnover. Figure 2-2 shows that turnover rates have flattened out in the past two decades. But the figures show turnover rates for all states combined. If we separate the term-limited states from the non-term-limited states, a different picture emerges, as Figure 2-3 reveals. Turnover in states without term limits continued to decline from 1992 throughout the remainder of the decade and reached its nadir at 15 percent in 2000 (and remember, 15 percent is the *average* for all states without term limits; some states experienced even lower turnover). The trend turns up in 2002 as expected because that was a redistricting year, and turnover rates almost always are highest in the "2" year of a decade because new districting plans go into effect. True to form, turnover then plunged back down to 18 percent in 2004. In 2006, turnover actually increased slightly (to about 21 percent), largely because of the substantial electoral tide that swept out many Republican incumbents nationally and in state legislatures.

The turnover rates in term-limited states show a different trend. By 1998 (when term limits were beginning to go into effect in many states), turnover rates began to climb, peaking at 38 percent in 2002. Since then, they have dropped slightly, to around 33 percent in 2006. Note the "turnover gap" between term-limited states and states without term limits. The gap is narrow (almost nonexistent) in the early years in the graph, but as states begin to adopt and implement term limits throughout the decade, the gap between term-limited states and non-term limited states emerges. The gap represents a difference of 12 to 20 percentage points, depending on the specific year. But clearly it is a significant difference and one that is directly tied to the implementation of term limits.[65]

COMPETITIVE VERSUS NONCOMPETITIVE STATES

Looking at the country as a whole, for many years, there were a lot more Democratic state legislators than Republican state legislators. This was due, in part, to the Democratic "Solid South." But over the past generation, the number of Democratic state legislators decreased but the number of Republican state legislators increased. In 1994, the GOP gained 472 state legislative seats nationwide, ushering in a 12-year period of virtual parity between the parties (see Figure 2-4). The Democrats picked up more than 300 seats in 2006 and another 100 seats in 2008, opening a modest lead in the margin of seats held. Nonetheless, the battle for state legislative seats across the country has been extremely heated now for some time.

But the closeness of the overall distribution of seats between the parties masks substantial differences in specific states. In some states, one party dominates most elections, which usually translates into a lopsided majority for that party in the legislature. These are often referred to as "one-party" states. In other states, however, the contest for control of the legislature is much closer, with each major party having a chance for majority status.

FIGURE 2-4   PARTISAN DISTRIBUTION OF STATE LEGISLATORS, ALL STATES

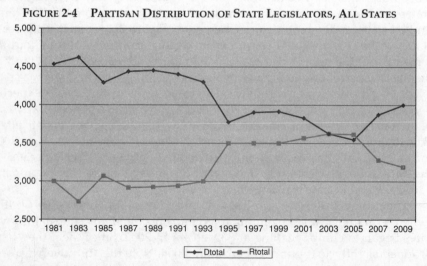

Source: National Conference of State Legislatures.

But even in these states, not all legislative districts are competitive. It may be, for example, that 40 percent of the seats are "safe Democratic," 40 percent are "safe Republican," and only the remaining 20 percent are truly competitive. But the competitive 20 percent of the seats determine which party will control the legislature. Consequently, both parties (and other interests) invest a lot of money in the campaigns for these "targeted" seats.

Before the 2006 election, Republicans controlled 20 state legislatures, Democrats controlled 19, and 10 were split (Republicans held a majority in one chamber, and Democrats held a majority in the other chamber).[66] But the elections of 2006 and 2008 produced a swing in favor of Democrats. The election in 2006 resulted in an unusually large partisan shift that greatly benefited the Democrats. The outcome was such that by 2007, there were 23 state legislatures controlled by Democrats, 16 controlled by Republicans, and 10 in which control was split. Across the states, Democrats picked up more than 300 seats previously held by Republicans. This was the largest electoral shift since the Republican surge in 1994, which resulted in 20 state legislative houses moving from Democratic to Republican control. Partisan swings of this magnitude are rare in American politics. The 2008 election saw the Democrats pick up about another 100 seats across the country, as well as several additional chambers. By 2009, Democrats controlled both chambers in 27 states compared with 14 for Republicans. Eight states were divided (with one chamber controlled by each party).

But for our purposes, the issue is not simply which party controls the legislative chamber; it is also about the degree of control. In some states, one party is firmly in control because it holds a substantial majority of seats (e.g., Republicans hold more than 70 percent of all seats in the Idaho and Utah legislatures, and Democrats hold more than 70 percent of all seats in the Arkansas, Hawaii, Maryland, and Michigan legislatures).[67] But in other states, the difference between majority and minority status is razor thin. As of 2009, there were 23 Democrats and 27 Republicans in the Montana Senate and 50 Democrats and 50 Republicans in the Montana House. In that same year, there were at least 17 (of 98) houses in which a shift of just three seats from one party to the other would change party control of the house.[68] These chambers are "marginal" in that either party has a chance to win control in any given election. Oregon and Tennessee are examples of states where state legislative control is usually marginal and thus campaigns are extremely competitive (and potentially expensive) in most electoral cycles.

THE EFFECT OF REGION

The electoral fortunes of the two parties are not the same everywhere. Some states are traditionally Democratic strongholds (e.g., Massachusetts), some are traditionally Republican havens (e.g., Kansas), and some change over time. In the past generation, the biggest shift of partisan strength is in the Southern states. For generations, the Democrats controlled Southern state legislatures

TABLE 2-7   CHANGING PARTISAN COMPOSITION IN FIVE SOUTHERN STATES
(DEMOCRATS–REPUBLICANS)

		1967	1977	1987	1997	2007
Alabama	Senate	34–1	34–0	30–5	22–13	23–12
	House	105–0	103–2	89–16	71–34	62–43
Louisiana	Senate	39–0	38–1	34–5	25–14	24–15
	House	98–4	101–4	87–15	78–27	63–41
Mississippi	Senate	51–1	50–2	45–7	34–18	25–27
	House	120–2	117–3	113–9	84–36	74–47
South Carolina	Senate	44–6	43–3	36–10	25–21	20–26
	House	107–17	111–12	92–32	52–71	51–73
Texas	Senate	30–1	27–4	25–6	14–17	11–20
	House	147–3	131–19	94–56	82–68	69–81

Sources: Data for 1967 to 1997 are from the Council of State Governments, *Book of the States,* various years. Data for 2007 are from National Conference of State Legislatures, "Partisan Composition of State Legislatures" (http://www.ncsl.org/programs/legismgt/statevote/partycomptable2007.htm).

consistently and with huge majorities. Indeed, one analyst reports that "many state manuals from this period did not bother to record the party of state legislators because the idea that legislators might not be Democrats simply did not occur to the authors in this era. . . ."[69] The Democratic Party dominance was so great in some Southern states that in some years, there were no Republicans at all in the legislature. For example, in 1967, all 105 members of the Alabama House and all 39 Louisiana senators were Democrats (see Table 2-7).

By the 1960s, Republicans made inroads in Southern states in presidential elections and subsequently in governor's races and U.S. Senate races. Beginning with the Reagan presidency, there was a steady increase in the number and proportion of GOP state legislators in Southern states, but only since the dramatic GOP sweep of 1994 have we witnessed Republican legislative majorities in some Southern chambers.[70] In Table 2-7, for example, note this partisan shift in the South Carolina and Texas legislatures. Today, about half of the Southern state legislatures are controlled by the Republican Party. Even in the Southern states where the Democrats still have a majority of the seats, the size of that majority is much smaller than it used to be; these states are now only marginally Democratic (e.g., see Alabama and Louisiana in Table 2-7). Of the Southern state legislatures, only Arkansas's can still be considered safely Democratic.

The rise of the Republican Party in the South is a dramatic event that obscures the fact that other regions have experienced significant partisan shifts as well.[71] The Intermountain West became solidly Republican over this same time period.[72] The Pacific Coast states and many of the Northeastern states shifted in the opposite direction—from Republican to Democratic states.[73]

In other words, the relative strength of the two major parties shifts over time in different regions of the country. By focusing on the national scene only, these state legislative shifts—like underground tectonic plates—often go unnoticed. There are important implications to these regional and temporal shifts. The most obvious one is policy change. But a second one is that recruitment patterns shift as well. As a party gains in strength, it is better able to attract quality candidates to run because such candidates realize they have a chance of winning. And, ultimately, these regional shifts begin to appear in the congressional parties as well.

Earlier we noted the trend of a growing partisan gap for female state legislators; women make up a much higher proportion of Democratic state legislative parties than of Republican ones. But there are some regional differences in the gender gap as well.[74] The gap is especially wide in the West: 38 percent of the region's Democratic lawmakers are women, but fewer than 18 percent of the Republicans are women, a gap of more than 20 points.[75]

CONCLUSION

In some ways, electoral trends in the state legislatures reflect congressional trends. When incumbents run, they win more than 90 percent of the time and usually by a substantial vote margin. And, overall, competition between the parties is vigorous; over the past dozen years, neither party has held more than 56 percent of the state legislative seats nationwide.

But a closer look reveals that many differences exist at the state level. First, although there is relative parity between the parties nationwide, there are a number of states in which one party tends to dominate elections. Second, term limits alter the electoral dynamic in 15 states by putting a time limit on incumbency. Third, the recruitment of women and minorities varies greatly in different states and in different regions of the country. Finally, the nature of campaigning is highly variable. In some states where districts are large and electoral stakes are high, campaigns may indeed look a lot like congressional campaigns. But in other states—indeed, in most states—legislative campaigns are still relatively inexpensive, involving voluntary organizations and retail politics.

ENDNOTES

1. Parra was barred from running for the seat in 2008 because of California's term limit law, which prevents anyone from serving more than six years in the California Assembly. Her opponent in both 2004 and 2006, Republican Danny Gilmore, won the open seat in 2008 in a closely contested race. Everett McLeod, running unopposed, was reelected in the 11th District in Maine.

2. Gary Cox and Scott Morgenstern, "The Incumbency Advantage in Multimember Districts: Evidence From the U.S. States," *Legislative Studies Quarterly* 20 (1995): 329–349.
3. James M. Snyder, Jr. and Michiko Ueda, "Do Multimember Districts Lead to Free-Riding?" *Legislative Studies Quarterly* 32 (2007): 649–679.
4. See Peverill Squire and Keith E. Hamm, *101 Chambers: Congress, State Legislatures, and the Future of Legislative Studies* (Columbus, OH: Ohio State University Press, 2005), 49–54.
5. Although there is no filing fee in Illinois, candidates are required to submit petitions with valid signatures of registered voters in support of the candidate. For the state senate, the figure is 1,000 signatures.
6. On the impact of filing fees on state legislative elections, see Thomas Stratmann, "Ballot Access Restrictions and Candidate Entry in Elections," *European Journal of Political Economy* 21 (2005): 59–71.
7. Richard L. Engstrom and Richard N. Engstrom, "The Majority Vote Rule and Runoff Primaries in the United States," *Electoral Studies* 27 (2008): 407–416.
8. Phil Davidson, "GOP Reverses Course," *Idaho Falls Post Register*, June 15, 2008; Jim Fisher, "The Republican Lawsuit: Here Come the Crazies," *Lewiston Morning Tribune*, April 15, 2008.
9. Elisabeth Gerber and Rebecca Morton, "Primary Election Systems and Representation," *Journal of Law, Economic & Organizations* 14 (1998): 302–328. Although the authors find "strong support for the hypothesis that U.S. representatives from states with closed primaries take more extreme policy positions," it is important to note that the study is based on congressional roll call voting. We are unaware of any study that examines this issue at the state legislative level.
10. Michael P. MacDonald, "A Comparative Analysis of Redistricting Institutions in the United States, 2001–2002," *State Politics and Policy Quarterly* 4 (2004): 371–395. See Table 3 for MacDonald's assessment of redistricting outcome in each state.
11. According to the data in Table 3 of MacDonald, "A Comparative Analysis of Redistricting Institutions," 18 states produced redistricting plans that protected incumbents, regardless of party affiliation.
12. The actual number depends on one's interpretation of "outside the immediate control of the legislature"; at this writing, 12 states use commissions, plus the unusual case of Iowa, described in the text. But there are other procedures as well, such as in Maryland, where the governor submits a plan to which the legislature responds. See MacDonald, "A Comparative Analysis of Redistricting Institutions" or the National Conference of State Legislatures' (NCSL's) website (http://www.ncsl.org/programs/legismgt/redistrict/com&alter.htm) for a discussion of the specifics in each state.
13. Tim Storey, "Redistricting Commissions and Alternatives to the Legislature Conducting Redistricting." NCSL's website, accessed July 23, 2007 (http://www.ncsl.org/programs/legismgt/redistrict/com&alter.htm).
14. See the NCSL's website (http://www.ncsl.org/programs/legismgt/redistrict/com&alter.htm). For a detailed description of the Iowa process, see http://www.legis.state.ia.us/Central/LSB/Guides/redist.htm and Peverill Squire, "Iowa and the Political Consequences of Playing Redistricting Straight," in *Redistricting in the New Millenium*, ed. Peter F. Galderisi (Lanham, MD: Lexington Books, 2005).
15. Lynn Okamoto, "Redistricting Gives Legislators Opportunities, Tough Choices," *Des Moines Register*, June 21, 2001.
16. Tyler Whitley, "Redistricting Bill Stopped in House," *Richmond Times-Dispatch*, January 13, 2007.
17. This assumes we are dealing with SMDs only. MMDs must have the same population *per seat* as SMDs. Thus, if an SMD in a state has 25,000 population, a three-person MMD in the same state should have a population of 75,000.
18. Roger Davidson and Walter Oleszek, *Congress and Its Members*, 10th ed. (Washington, DC: CQ Press, 2006), 46.
19. *Reynolds v. Sims*, 377 U.S. 533 (1964).
20. Because the Nebraska unicameral does not have a house of representatives, we used the Nebraska senate figures.
21. *White v. Regester*, 412 U.S. 755 (1973).
22. See The NCSL's website for a good summary of information about campaign finance rules in each state (http://www.ncsl.org/programs/legismgt/about/campfin.htm).

23. Keith E. Hamm and Robert E. Hogan, "Campaign Finance Laws and Candidacy Decisions in State Legislative Elections," *Political Research Quarterly* 61 (2008): 458–467.
24. *Buckley v. Valeo,* 424 U.S. 1 (1976).
25. Gary Moncrief, Peverill Squire, and Malcolm Jewell. *Who Runs for the Legislature?* (Upper Saddle River, NJ: Prentice-Hall, 2001), 83.
26. These figures assume contested elections in both the primary and the general elections. For candidates for the Maine senate, where the districts are much bigger, the 2006 spending limit was about $28,000. The figures cited here are from a memo titled "An Invitation to Comment on Maine Clean Election Act Issues," dated June 26, 2007, from the Commission on Governmental Ethics and Election Practices, State of Maine.
27. The Arizona figures are from Allison Hayward, "*Campaign Promises: A Six-Year Review of Arizona's Experiment with Taxpayer-financed Campaigns.*, Goldwater Institute, Policy Report No. 209; March 28, 2006, 3.
28. Paul Davenport, "Court: Ouster of Lawmakers not Limited to Impeachment, Recall," *Arizona Republic*, May 3, 2006; Christian Palmer, "Supreme Court Orders David Burnell Smith to Vacate Office," *Arizona Capitol Times*, January 27, 2006.
29. Timothy Werner and Kenneth R. Mayer, "Public Election Funding, Competition, and Candidate Gender," *PS: Political Science & Politics* 40 (2007): 661–667.
30. Werner and Mayer, "Public Election Funding, Competition, and Candidate Gender," 666.
31. Michael Miller, "Gaming Arizona: Public Money and Shifting Candidate Strategies," PS: *Political Science & Politics* 41 (2008): 527–532.
32. Moncrief, Squire, and Jewell, *Who Runs for the Legislature?*, 4.
33. Peverill Squire, "Uncontested Seats in State Legislative Elections," *Legislative Studies Quarterly* 25 (2000): 131–146; see also Erin Madigan, "Scores of Statehouse Candidates Lack Challengers," Stateline.org, October 29, 2004; and John McGlennon and Cory Kaufman, "Expanding the Playing Field," *Report from the Thomas Jefferson Program in Public Policy*, Williamsburg, VA: The College of William & Mary, 2007.
34. McGlennon and Kaufman, "Expanding the Playing Field," 2.
35. Jason Rosenbaum, "Candidate for Graham's Seat Changes Mind," *Columbia Daily Tribune*, May 19, 2008.
36. Grant Reeher, *First Person Political: Legislative Life and the Meaning of Public Service* (New York: NYU Press, 2006), 94.
37. Reeher, *First Person Political*, 95.
38. James Q. Lynch, "New Districts Create More Interest," *Iowa City Gazette*, July 10, 2001.
39. Thomas M. Carsey, Richard G. Niemi, William D. Berry, Lynda W. Powell, and James M. Snyder, Jr., "State Legislative Elections, 1967–2003: Announcing the Completion of a Cleaned and Updated Dataset," *State Politics and Policy Quarterly* 8 (2008): 430–443.
40. The survey is of non-incumbent legislative candidates and was conducted by the authors in 1998 and 2002. Overall, more than 1,000 candidates in 11 states responded. Details on the methodology appear in Moncrief, Squire, and Jewell, *Who Runs for the Legislature?*, which includes data from the first (1998) survey.
41. See Table 3-4 for numbers on African American and Latino legislators. Estimates in 2005 were that 41 percent of Hawaii's legislature is Asian American (with another 9 percent Pacific Islander).
42. Center for American Women and Politics, Eagleton Institute of Politics, Rutgers University, "Fact Sheet: Women in State Legislatures 2008" (December 2008).
43. See Kira Sanbonmatsu, *Where Women Run: Gender and Party in American States* (Ann Arbor, MI: University of Michigan Press, 2006). Also see Richard Fox and Jennifer Lawless, "Entering the Arena? Gender and the Decision to Run for Office," *American Journal of Political Science* 48 (2004): 264–280; David Niven, *The Missing Majority: The Recruitment of Women as State Legislative Candidates* (Westport, CT: Praeger, 1998); and Moncrief, Squire and Jewell, *Who Runs for the Legislature?*, especially Chapter 4.
44. See, for example, Kira Sanbonmatsu, *Where Women Run*, and Laurel Elder, "The Partisan Gap Among Female State Legislators," unpublished manuscript, 2008.
45. In 1995, there were 673 female GOP state legislators; by 2009, the figure was 536, a loss of 147 Republican women (a 22 percent decrease). During the same period, the number of female Democratic state legislators grew from 843 to 1,201, an increase of 358, or 42 percent. These data are from the Center for American Women and Politics.

46. See, for example, Susan Carroll, *Women as Candidates in American Politics*, 2nd ed. (Blooming-ton, IN: Indiana University Press, 1994); Moncrief, Squire and Jewell, *Who Runs for the Legislature?*; and Fox and Lawless, "Entering the Arena?"

47. Peter Slevin, "After Adopting Term Limits, States Lose Female Legislators," *Washington Post*, April 22, 2007.

48. Sanbonmatsu, *Where Women Run*.

49. For a more complete discussion of the effect of campaign finance laws, see Hamm and Hogan, "Campaign Finance Laws and Candidacy Decisions in State Legislative Elections."

50. National Institute on Money in State Politics, "State Elections Overview 2006," March 2008.

51. National Institute on Money in State Politics, "State Elections Overview 2006," 6.

52. We arrive at these figures in the following way: The National Institute on Money in State Politics states that the 2005 to 2006 median figure for fundraising for legislative candidates was $20,493 for House and $47,546 for Senate candidates. Median figures are usually preferable to the mean (average) figures because of the highly distorting effect of a few hyperexpensive races. See Joel A. Thompson and Gary F. Moncrief, *Campaign Finance in State Legislative Elections* (Washington, DC: CQ Press, 1998), 45. However, competitive races are also more expensive than races that are simply contested. Comparing median figures in contested and competitive races in the study reported by Thompson and Moncrief indicates that the latter are often 20 to 50 percent more expensive, depending on the state (see Thompson and Moncrief, Table 3-2). In a few states, the median spending in competitive races was twice that in contested races.

53. Ron Faucheux and Paul Herrnson, "See How They Run: State Legislative Candidates," *Campaigns and Elections* (August 1999): 25.

54. This discussion of campaign techniques is based, in part, on Gary Moncrief and Peverill Squire, "State House and Local Office Campaigns," in *Guide to Political Campaigns in America*, Paul Herrnson, ed. (Washington, DC: CQ Press, 2005).

55. Moncrief, Squire, and Jewell, *Who Runs for the Legislature?*, 77.

56. Jonathan Smith, "Professionalization of State Legislative Campaigns in South Carolina, North Carolina and Georgia," paper presented at the annual meeting of the Southern Political Science Association; Atlanta, Georgia; November 2001. Also see Robert Hogan, "Voter Contact Techniques in State Legislative Campaigns: The Prevalence of Mass Media Advertising." *Legislative Studies Quarterly* 22 (1997): 551–571 and Owen Abbe and Paul S. Herrnson, "Campaign Professionalism in State Legislative Elections," *State Politics and Policy Quarterly* 3 (2003): 223–245.

57. Hogan, "Voter Contact Techniques in State Legislative Campaigns."

58. Moncrief, Squire, and Jewell, *Who Runs for the Legislature?*, 76.

59. Bob Lewis, "Legislative Candidates Raised $67.2 Million," *Washington Times*, December 9, 2007.

60. Ronald Keith Gaddie, *Born to Run: Origins of the Political Career* (Lanhan, MD: Rowman & Littlefield), 35.

61. Gaddie, *Born to Run*, 7.

62. Gaddie, *Born to Run*, 8.

63. Richard Niemi, Lynda Powell, William Berry, Thomas Carsey, and James Snyder, Jr., "Competition in State Legislative Elections," in *The Marketplace of Democracy*, Michael P. McDonald and John Samples, eds. (Washington, DC: Brookings Institution and Cato Press, 2006), 56. By "median," the authors refer to the incumbency rate in the median state.

64. *U.S. Term Limits v. Thornton*, 514 U.S. 779 (1995).

65. For a more detailed analysis and explanation of the effect of term limits on turnover, see Gary F. Moncrief, Richard G. Niemi, and Lynda W. Powell, "Time, Term Limits and Turnover: Trends in Membership Stability in U.S. State Legislatures," *Legislative Studies Quarterly* 29 (2004): 357–381.

66. The figures total 49 because the Nebraska legislature is nonpartisan.

67. These figures are based on data from the National Conference of State Legislatures as of January 2009.

68. Because Nebraska is both unicameral and nonpartisan, 98 state legislative chambers are under consideration in the partisan analysis.

69. David Lublin, *The Republican South* (Princeton, NJ: Princeton University Press, 2004), 47.

70. Lublin, *The Republican South*, 48–49. See especially his Table 2.1, 49. See also Terrel L. Rhodes, *Republicans in the South: Voting for the State House, Voting for the White House* (Westport, CT: Praeger, 2000), 79–89.
71. Charles Bullock III, Donna Hoffman, and Ronald Keith Gaddie, "Regional Variations in the Realignment of American Politics, 1944–2004," *Social Science Quarterly* 87 (2006): 494–512.
72. Eric R.A.N. Smith and Peverill Squire, "State and National Politics in the Mountain West," in *The Politics of Realignment*, Peter F. Galderisi, Michael S. Lyons, Randy T. Simmons, and John G. Francis, eds. (Boulder, CO: Westview, 1987), 44–45.
73. Bullock, Hoffman, and Gaddie, "Regional Variations in the Realignment of American Politics," 513–517.
74. On regional differences, see Laurel Elder, "The Partisan Gap Among Female State Legislators" (unpublished manuscript, 2008).
75. These figures were calculated by the authors using data from the Center for American Women and Politics before the 2008 election.

THE CHANGING JOB OF STATE LEGISLATOR

Wyoming senate district 8 is represented by a Democrat, Floyd A. Esquibel of Cheyenne. California senate district 8 is represented by a Democrat, Leland Yee of San Francisco. Although both Esquibel and Yee are state senators and perform the same job, the conditions of their legislative service contrast dramatically.

Senator Esquibel serves in an organization in which members view themselves as citizen-legislators. The Wyoming legislature meets for only 60 days over a two-year period—40 days in odd-numbered years, and 20 days in even-numbered years, with the latter meeting limited to budget issues. For his legislative service, Senator Esquibel receives a per diem—a daily payment—of $150 for each day the legislature is in session. Assuming the legislature meets for the full 60 days it is allowed to meet over two years, that means Esquibel and his colleagues got paid $9,000 biennially, or $4,500 a year. This modest sum is supplemented by an $85 a day per diem to cover living expenses during the session and for travel days for legislators living outside of the capital, Cheyenne. The per diem is, however, vouchered, meaning Wyoming legislators must document their expenses to receive the payment. As a resident of Cheyenne, Esquibel is not entitled to the per diem. The low pay and limited time demands mean that no member of the Wyoming legislature considers him- or herself a full-time legislator. Senator Esquibel, for example, lists his occupation as "attorney."[1]

Very little in the way of staff assistance or facilities is provided to Senator Esquibel. According to the *Citizen's Guide to the Wyoming Legislature*:

> [L]egislators in Wyoming do not have individual staff. . . . Except for a few officers of the House and Senate, members of the legislature are not provided offices in the Capitol nor do they maintain full-time offices in their districts. While in session, the "office" of a typical Wyoming legislator consists of the legislator's desk on the floor of the House or Senate and one or two file cabinet drawers in a committee meeting room. Except for the

relatively short periods of time they meet each year in Cheyenne for the annual legislative session, Wyoming legislators can be contacted at home or at
their places of business.[2]

Senator Yee's working conditions are remarkably different. Service in the
California state legislature is considered a full-time position, much like the
U.S. Congress. Over a two-year period, the legislature is in session about 240
days. Senator Yee and his colleagues are paid $116,208 a year.[3] In addition, Cal-
ifornia legislators are entitled to a $173 unvouchered per diem—meaning they
do not have to produce receipts to get the payment—for each day the legislature is in session. They also receive other perks, among them a government-
leased vehicle for their use in either Sacramento or back in their district.[4]

Senator Yee also enjoys impressive staff assistance and facilities. He has
an office in the capitol, with seven staff members: a chief of staff, a communications director, two legislative aides, an assistant consultant, an executive
assistant, and an office aide. In addition, the senator has two district offices,
one in San Francisco and the other in San Mateo, which between them have
seven more staff members: a district director, an office manager, and five
field representatives. Staff members not only help the senator with his legislative business but also manage his media and constituent relations.[5]

As the comparison of conditions in the California and Wyoming legislatures suggests, legislative service differs across the states. In this chapter, we
will investigate what the job of state legislator is like in different settings.
The concept of "legislative professionalization" will be examined, allowing
us to explore differences across the 50 state legislatures in member pay, the
time demands of service, and staff and facilities. We will look at who serves
in the legislature, how long they serve, and what their service entails. We
will conclude with an examination of the different legislative career opportunity structures found in the states.

LEGISLATIVE PROFESSIONALIZATION

"Legislative professionalization" is a concept that assesses the capacity of
both legislators and legislatures to generate and digest information in the
policymaking process. Professional legislatures, such as the U.S. Congress,
are those with unlimited legislative sessions, superior staff resources, and
salaries sufficient to allow the members to pursue service as their full-time
occupation. Thus, more professional legislators and legislatures are better
equipped to play a more active role in policymaking than are their less well-
equipped counterparts. Professionalization has been found to influence a
wide range of legislative behaviors, from the adoption of particular internal
rules and procedures to specific policy outputs. A number of different measures of legislative professionalization have been devised over time, but they

TABLE 3-1 IMPLICATIONS OF PROFESSIONALIZATION
FOR LEGISLATORS AND LEGISLATURES

PROFESSIONALIZATION COMPONENT	IMPLICATIONS FOR LEGISLATORS	IMPLICATIONS FOR LEGISLATURE
Salary and benefits	• Increased incentive to serve, leading to longer tenure • Increased ability to focus efforts on legislative activities	• Lead to members with longer tenures, creating a more experienced body • Attract better-qualified members
Time demands of service	• Reduced opportunities to pursue other employment and increased need for higher salary to compensate for lost income • Increased opportunity to master legislative skills	• More time for policy development • More time for policy deliberation
Staff and resources	• Increased ability to influence policymaking process • Increased job satisfaction • Enhanced reelection prospects	• Make legislature a more serious policymaking competitor with the executive

Source: Adapted from Peverill Squire, "Measuring Legislative Professionalism: The Squire Index Revisited," *State Politics and Policy Quarterly* 7 (2007):213.

all revolve around member salary, time devoted to legislative activities, and staff support.[6]

The theoretical implications of professionalization for legislators and legislatures are presented in Table 3-1. As we might expect, as legislative salaries increase, legislators have greater incentive to continue service in the legislature. But increasing pay has an additional, less appreciated, impact on legislators: it also allows them to focus their energies on their legislative responsibilities rather than having to juggle them with the demands of other occupations.

The implications of legislative time demands condition the impact of legislative pay on member behavior. On the one hand, when limited demands are made by legislative service, as in Wyoming, legislators do not need much salary to compensate for their time. Indeed, when legislatures meet for only a month or so, members may not have to sacrifice much time (and income) from their regular jobs to serve. On the other hand, when a legislature meets year round, as in California, legislators must be paid enough to support themselves and their families to compensate them for forgoing income from outside occupations. Thus, at the extremes of time demands, the implications of its relationship with salary are straightforward. But in the mid-range of time demands, where legislatures meet for several months each year, calculations get more complicated. In these states, the point at which financial incentives are sufficient to compensate for lost income is not clear.

Legislative time demands also have a second implication for legislators. The more days that a legislature meets each year, the better legislators come to understand the complexities of the legislative process. Thus, longer sessions give members a better chance to master arcane rules, procedures, and norms.

The level of staff resources in a legislature has several clear-cut implications for legislators. First, more staff leads to better informed legislators, which allows members to exert greater influence in the policymaking process. Second, as legislators enjoy making greater impact on policymaking, their job satisfaction likely increases.[7] Finally, more staff improves member reelection prospects by enhancing their ability to provide constituent services.

The institutional implications of legislative professionalization are generally straightforward. First, higher salaries allow legislators to devote more time and energy to lawmaking without the distraction of another occupation and thus can lead to longer serving and therefore more informed and effective legislators.[8] Second, higher salaries are likely to attract better-qualified legislators in terms of academic credentials, occupational status, and the like. Third, meeting for more days each year gives legislators more time to develop legislative proposals and more time to deliberate on them, thereby improving the quality of legislative output.[9] Fourth, increased staff resources make the legislature a more equal partner with the executive branch in policymaking.[10]

Thus, the components of legislative professionalization have slightly different implications for legislators than for the institutions in which they serve. But it is also clear that these components in combination constitute something that is not captured by each of them individually. Conceptually, professional legislators are not just longer serving; they are also better equipped as policymakers for reasons beyond their longevity. And professional legislatures are stronger competitors in the policymaking process for more reasons than just their being composed of veteran members.

WHAT DIFFERENCE DOES PROFESSIONALIZATION MAKE?

Legislative professionalization influences legislator behavior and legislative output in many important ways. As we would expect, membership turnover declines as professionalism levels increase and members enjoy greater electoral security.[11] Legislators in more professional legislatures have more contact with their constituents, are more attentive to their concerns, and are more representative of their views than are their counterparts in less-professional legislatures.[12] Legislative efficiency—the percentage of bills passed and the number of bills enacted per legislative day—goes up with professionalization level.[13] The inclination to reform government personnel practices also increases with legislative professionalization, as does the willingness to adopt increasingly complex and technical regulatory policies and income tax systems, stronger environmental programs, and more novel policies; to allow local governments to adopt anti-smoking ordinances; and to increase the number of economic enterprise zones in a state.[14] More professionalized legislatures also are better able to mediate policy disputes, thereby reducing the motivation for interest groups to turn to citizen initiatives in the states that allow them.[15]

PROFESSIONALIZATION LEVELS IN CURRENT STATE LEGISLATURES

The state legislative professionalization movement began in earnest in the 1960s, in large part because of the efforts of California Assembly Speaker Jesse Unruh, who pushed the California legislature to professionalize, and the Citizens Conference on State Legislatures, which later took the reform movement nationwide.[16] Over the next decade or so, many state legislatures greatly improved member pay, extended legislative sessions, and improved staff resources. But the drive to professionalize leveled off in the 1980s. Since then, a few legislatures have continued to professionalize, but most others only held their ground or even regressed a bit.[17]

How do professionalization levels currently compare across the 50 state legislatures? The most recent comparison is presented in Table 3-2. This widely used measure compares a state legislature with the U.S. Congress on the three dimensions of professionalization: member pay, legislative days in session, and staff resources.[18] A score of "1" indicates that a state legislature perfectly resembles Congress in terms of professionalization, and a score of "0" indicates a complete lack of resemblance.

As the median and mean scores for the 50 state legislatures suggest, most state legislatures are only faintly similar to Congress in terms of professionalization. There is, however, considerable variation in legislative professionalization across the states. A handful of legislatures, most notably California and New York, might be considered professional along the lines of the U.S. Congress. In contrast, another somewhat larger handful of legislatures, those from Maine at 0.089 to New Hampshire at 0.027, have almost nothing in common with either Congress or California and are considered "citizen legislatures." Most state legislatures, however, share at least some characteristics with their more professionally blessed counterparts.

EXAMINING THE COMPONENTS OF PROFESSIONALIZATION: SALARY AND BENEFITS

One reason legislative professionalization levels vary across the states is the salaries they pay their legislators. Most states offer an annual salary, but seven states pay a daily salary, Vermont pays a weekly salary, and New Mexico does

TABLE 3-2   State Legislative Professionalism—2003 (from Highest to Lowest)

State	2003 Rank	2003 Score[a]
California	1	0.626
New York	2	0.481
Wisconsin	3	0.439
Massachusetts	4	0.385
Michigan	5	0.342
Pennsylvania	6	0.339
Ohio	7	0.304
Illinois	8	0.261
New Jersey	9	0.244
Arizona	10	0.232
Alaska	11	0.227
Hawaii	12	0.225
Florida	13	0.223
Colorado	14	0.202
Texas	15	0.199
North Carolina	16	0.198
Washington	17	0.197
Maryland	18	0.194
Connecticut	19	0.190
Oklahoma	20	0.187
Missouri	21	0.174
Iowa	22	0.170
Minnesota	23	0.169
Nebraska	24	0.162
Oregon	25	0.159
Delaware	26	0.148
Kentucky	27	0.148
Vermont	28	0.144
Idaho	29	0.138
Nevada	30	0.138
Rhode Island	31	0.133
Virginia	32	0.131
Louisiana	33	0.129
Kansas	34	0.125
West Virginia	35	0.125
South Carolina	36	0.124
Georgia	37	0.116
Tennessee	38	0.116
New Mexico	39	0.109
Mississippi	40	0.107

(Continued)

TABLE 3-2   (CONTINUED)

STATE	2003 RANK	2003 SCORE[a]
Arkansas	41	0.106
Indiana	42	0.102
Maine	43	0.089
Montana	44	0.076
Alabama	45	0.071
Utah	46	0.065
South Dakota	47	0.064
Wyoming	48	0.054
North Dakota	49	0.051
New Hampshire	50	0.027
Mean score		0.184
Median score		0.154

Source: Adapted from Peverill Squire, "Measuring Legislative Professionalism: The Squire Index Revisited," *State Politics and Policy Quarterly* 7 (2007):213.

[a]A state legislature's professionalism score is based on its member pay, number of days in session, and staff per member, all compared with those characteristics in Congress during the same year.

not pay any salary at all. As shown in Table 3-3, in 2007, the annual salary state legislators got paid varied dramatically, from $116,208 a year in California to $100 in New Hampshire to, of course, no salary in New Mexico. Note that in every state legislature, except for Virginia, members of both houses are paid the same sum. In Virginia, the difference between the two houses stems from a 1992 decision by the House of Delegates to reduce their salaries by 2 percent in sympathy for a 2 percent pay cut imposed on state employees. The Senate chose not to follow suit, and the pay between the two houses has differed ever since.[19]

Overall, state legislative salaries are not impressive, with a median of only $17,640. Lawmakers are paid more than the state's median household income in only seven states. Indeed, in many states, the legislative salary is well below the average household income. Salaries paid to legislators in a majority of states have actually lost ground to inflation over the past three decades.[20] Thus, service in most state legislatures across the country is not financially enticing. This is not true elsewhere. American state legislative salaries pale in broader comparison; state and provincial legislators in Australia, Canada, and Germany—all federal systems—make considerably more than their U.S. counterparts.[21]

The official legislative salary is, however, somewhat deceptive. Most states offer state legislators payments to cover expenses, usually called a "per diem." Some of these expenses require submission of vouchers documenting the incurred costs. North Dakota legislators, for example, are given

TABLE 3-3   STATE LEGISLATIVE SALARIES AS OF DECEMBER 2007
(FROM HIGHEST TO LOWEST)

STATE	LEGISLATIVE SALARY	ESTIMATED LEGISLATIVE SALARY WITH UNVOUCHERED EXPENSES INCLUDED[a]	MEDIAN HOUSEHOLD INCOME IN STATE, 2005–2006
California	$116,208[b]	$135,405	$54,385
Michigan	$79,650	$91,650	$48,043
New York	$79,500	$89,380	$48,472
Pennsylvania	$73,613	$82,966	$48,148
Ohio	$58,934	No per diem	$45,776
Massachusetts	$58,237	$68,337	$56,592
Illinois	$57,619	$64,400	$49,328
New Jersey	$49,000	No per diem	$66,752
Wisconsin	$47,413	$51,857	$48,903
Maryland	$43,500	$53,593	$63,082
Delaware	$42,000	No per diem	$52,676
Oklahoma	$38,400	$46,452	$38,859
Washington	$36,311	$41,582	$53,515
Hawaii	$35,900	$48,620	$61,005
Missouri	$31,351	$37,370	$44,487
Minnesota	$31,141	$41,701 (S) $39,611 (H)	$56,102
Florida	$30,996	$36,414	$45,038
Colorado	$30,000	$38,514	$53,900
Connecticut	$28,000	No per diem	$60,551
Iowa	$25,000	$37,390	$48,075
Alaska	$24,012	$40,520	$57,071
Arizona	$24,000	$28,200	$46,693
Oregon	$18,408	$25,762	$46,349
Tennessee	$18,123	$36,932	$40,696
Virginia	$18,000 (S) $17,640 (H)	$23,530 (S) $22,973 (H)	$55,368
Georgia	$17,342	$23,311	$48,388
Louisiana	$16,800	$24,252	$37,472
Idaho	$16,116	$23,294	$45,919
Kentucky[c]	$15,797	$25,326	$38,694
West Virginia	$15,000	$19,945	$38,029
Arkansas	$14,765	$21,070	$37,458
North Carolina	$13,951	$31,893	$41,616
Vermont[c]	$13,217	$20,433	$52,174
Rhode Island	$13,089	No per diem	$52,421
Nebraska	$12,000	$19,425	$48,820
Indiana	$11,600	$24,431	$44,618

(Continued)

TABLE 3-3   (CONTINUED)

STATE	LEGISLATIVE SALARY	ESTIMATED LEGISLATIVE SALARY WITH UNVOUCHERED EXPENSES INCLUDED[a]	MEDIAN HOUSEHOLD INCOME IN STATE, 2005–2006
Maine[d]	$10,935	$13,665	$45,503
South Carolina	$10,400	$18,135	$40,583
Mississippi	$10,000	$18,281	$34,343
Kansas[c]	$7,462	$16,174	$44,478
Texas	$7,200	$16,930	$43,044
South Dakota	$6,000	$10,180	$44,996
Utah[c]	$5,850	$12,330	$55,619
North Dakota[c]	$4,940	$4,940	$42,311
Montana[c]	$4,464	$9,797	$39,821
Wyoming[c]	$4,350	$6,815	$46,613
Nevada[c]	$4,137	$11,112	$51,036
Alabama[c]	$990	$31,560	$38,160
New Hampshire	$100	No per diem	$60,411
New Mexico	No Salary	$6,390	$40,126
Mean	$26,460	$34,307	$48,050
Median	$17,640	$26,881	$47,368

Sources: Salary data were calculated by the authors from National Conference of State Legislatures data, *The Book of the States* for various years, and legislative websites. Median household income data are from the U.S. Census Bureau, *Current Population Survey, 2005 to 2007, Annual Social and Economic Supplements.*

[a]Unvouchered expenses are considered to be payments that do not require receipts for actual incurred expenses and are calculated for the maximum regular session per diem provided.

[b]Salaries in bold are greater than the state's median household income. In May 2009, the California Citizens Compensation Committee decreed that the salary paid to the state's legislators will be cut by 18 percent to $95,291, starting in December, 2010.

[c]The legislature is paid on a daily or weekly basis. Annual salary is an estimate. In Nevada, the per diem is only paid for the first 60 days of the legislative session.

[d]Maine pays more for the longer session year than for the shorter session year. The pay for the two years calculated here was $12,615 (2007) and $9,254 (estimated for 2008).

$900 a month to cover lodging in Bismarck. But they have to submit receipts documenting their expenses; thus, as one representative noted, "In no case can you put money in your pocket."[22] In Nebraska, an outside auditing firm examines expense records from a random sample of lawmakers to make sure they are not pocketing any of the money.[23] Most state legislative expense payments, however, are provided without the submission of any documentation. But some of these expenses are real, even if legislators do not have to produce receipts to demonstrate them. As a Minnesota legislator observes, "There's a big difference between living expenses and salary."[24] But to the extent that the money does not cover incurred expenses, it can add to a state legislator's income. Thus, it is not easy to calculate the actual amount of money state legislators make. One estimate of state legislative salaries with unvouchered expenses included is given in the middle column of Table 3-3.

These estimates are probably conservative because they are calculated only for the regular legislative session. In many states, legislators are also entitled to collect per diems for other days when they are performing legislative business, such as serving on an interim committee, which would give them the opportunity to claim even more expense money.

Expense payments given to Tennessee state legislators provide an example of how this system works. Tennessee legislators were paid an annual salary of $18,123 in 2007. That sum was, however, supplemented by a per diem of $153 for each day the legislature met. Lawmakers were also entitled to $12,000 a year for home office expenses, money the IRS treats as income unless documentation of the expenses incurred is provided. A former legislator, however, admits, "Everyone I know spends that home office allowance on themselves."[25] Taking all of the money provided to Tennessee state legislators into account, one member observed: "It's really more accurate to say we make $30,000 than to say we make $18,000."[26] Indeed, in some states, the additional sums paid through expense payments greatly increase legislative salaries. In Alabama, almost all of the money legislators take home comes through expense payments, and their take-home pay is much higher than their $10 per day stipend would suggest. And, of course, the only pay New Mexico lawmakers get is their per diem.

Even in California, where legislators draw large salaries, a per diem of $173 a day is provided. (By state law, the per diem cannot be lower than the rate paid by the federal government to its employees traveling to Sacramento on official business.[27]) This expense money is paid seven days a week as long as the legislature is not out of session for more than three consecutive days. Perhaps not surprisingly, members of the legislature have devised ways of maintaining their per diems even when the legislative schedule might not otherwise allow for it because of holidays and the like. Consequently, "per diem sessions" (a short meeting held on Friday mornings) and "check-in sessions" (when formal floor sessions are not held but members "visit the Capitol long enough to sign their names—sometimes during brief stops while driving their cars through the Capitol garage") are arranged simply to meet the three-day requirement.[28] One report calculated that such maneuvers allow California lawmakers to increase their reported salaries by $30,000 a year. Moreover, because of favorable IRS treatment of state legislative per diem payments, that $30,000 sum is actually comparable to $50,000 in regular taxable income.[29]

State legislators in some states enjoy perks beyond per diems. Lawmakers in California, for example, may select a vehicle to use while in office; the state purchases the chosen vehicle and leases it to the lawmaker. In recent years, California legislators have used this program to get, among other vehicles, a $41,000 limited edition Mustang and a $57,000 Lexus hybrid SUV, for their own use.[30] Until recently, Pennsylvania state legislators enjoyed a similar perk, but in the wake of the pay raise fiasco discussed in Politics Under the Domes 3-1, they opted to pass rules limiting them to picking from a pool of less ostentatious state fleet cars.[31] More common benefits are of lesser monetary value but are still prized. Every Alabama state legislator, for instance, is given two tickets and a parking pass to the annual Iron Bowl football game between Auburn University and the University of Alabama.[32] A few state legislators enjoy more unusual benefits. Along with a select group of state officials, Texas lawmakers may purchase upscale furniture made by inmates working for the Texas Correctional Industries for well below what comparable products would sell to the general public.[33] Finally, some perks are more a matter of convenience than money. For instance, Virginia legislators are allowed to park illegally in Richmond during the legislative session.[34]

Still, even with expense payments included, state legislative pay in most states in not impressive. The median is only $26,881, and the pay in 16 states is less than $20,000 a year. How low is the pay in some legislatures? When state health insurance costs rose dramatically in early 2006, some Nebraska

POLITICS UNDER THE DOMES 3–1

The Pennsylvania Pay Raise Fiasco

Proposals to increase legislative pay almost always meet with public resistance. When legislators attempt to increase their salaries through underhanded means, voters can become outraged, as Pennsylvania lawmakers learned in 2005.

At the beginning of the 2005 legislative session, Pennsylvania senators and representatives made $69,647, more than their counterparts in every state but California, Michigan, and New York, and considerably more than the state's $45,941 median household income. Although Pennsylvania legislators had recently received cost-of-living-adjustments to their salary—an increase generously calculated using a Philadelphia area index (not one for Harrisburg, the state capital) and that had raised their pay by about $3,600 from the previous session—their base salary had not been changed since 1995.

Early in 2005, there were some rumblings from legislators about seeking a pay raise, but none of them publicly discussed the idea until June. At that point, Senate Democratic leader Robert Mellow began arguing in favor of a $10,000 salary increase, claiming, "A pay raise is warranted. People work very hard in this job. I work a full day Saturdays and a half day most Sundays. It's a seven-day-a-week job at this point." Bipartisan support for the idea surfaced. A House Republican said, "Do I deserve a raise? Sure do. And I'm not afraid to say it. I work very, very hard, like many of us do." Fearing a public backlash, however, some legislators were reluctant to support the proposal, leaving legislative observers to calculate the possibility of it happening to be "50-50 at best." Moreover, concerns were expressed that any pay raise attempt had to be handled properly and not, as Senate Democratic Leader Mellow noted, pushed through, "under the cover of darkness," as other raises had been in the past.

Thus, Pennsylvanians were understandably surprised when a just few weeks later, they opened their newspapers to learn, as *The Patriot-News* in Harrisburg put it, "While you were sleeping early yesterday, Pennsylvania lawmakers were making themselves richer." At 2:00 a.m. on July 7, a bill increasing legislative pay to $81,050—a 16 percent increase—had been brought up for a vote in the Pennsylvania House without any debate on it. The House immediately passed it, 119 to 79. The Pennsylvania Senate voted on the measure just 15 minutes later, backing it on a 27 to 23 vote. But not only had the legislators voted to boost their pay when they hoped nobody was looking; they also did it in a devious fashion. The state constitution requires an election to intervene between when a pay raise gets passed and when it gets received. To get around this prohibition, the bill the legislature passed provided the money for the raise not as salary but as an unvouchered expense. This would allow legislators to get their money right away without having to wait until after the next election and without providing any receipts documenting real expenses. The governor signed the pay raise bill the next day, supporting the legislators' efforts by observing, "This is for many of them their life's work, just like a mechanic in an auto repair shop has the right to hope for periodic raises."

Lawmakers understood they were taking a political risk by passing the measure. There were reports that two House Republicans nearly got into a fist fight when their caucus debated the raise. Leaders only brought the bill up for a vote when both party caucuses in both houses promised that 50 percent plus one of their members would vote in favor of it, a level of bipartisan support that would prevent the raise from being used as a partisan issue in the next election. With the bill's passage, certain party leaders were able to allow some of their more electorally vulnerable members to vote against it. A Democratic leader in the senate confessed, "There were some people that I as leader told not to vote for it." Likewise, a Republican senator admitted, "Leadership came to me and said: We don't expect you to do it." Senior legislators in secure districts, however, were expected to bite the bullet and back the raise, something not all of them felt comfortable doing. The penalty for not helping the leadership by casting the tough vote proved harsh. A few weeks after the raise passed, House Democratic leaders removed three committee chairs and 12 subcommittee chairs who had voted against it, replacing them with members who had voted as the leadership wanted. For the legislators involved in the shuffling, this action had important consequences beyond just the influence involved; committee and subcommittee chairs were entitled to an additional $4,050 in pay.

Although lawmakers knew the pay raise would be politically unpopular, they did not anticipate the level of public anger their actions would generate. Within days, unhappy citizens were agitating to get the

(Continued)

escind the measure and to get challengers to run against
porters in the next election. One activist, saying, "I'm
it what the Legislature does, but this time they truly did
cross the line," even started a campaign called Operation Clean Sweep
to provide support to legislative challengers who "sign a declaration
affirming their willingness, once elected, to repeal the raise. . . ."

Discontent with the pay raise was widespread. Talk radio shows
fielded a torrent of complaints: "I don't know how these legislators can
look the taxpayers or even the teachers in the eye and ask for any credi-
bility in their jobs." "I have not gotten a pay raise like this in the last two
or three years. In fact, I'm paying more for milk, I'm paying more for
gas. No one gives me a per diem to drive to work."

Legislative leaders, however, bet that voter anger would eventually subside. Public opinion surveys offered them some comfort. Although an October poll showed that the public held the legislature in
low esteem—only 26 percent of respondents approved of the way the
legislature was handling its job and 83 percent thought the pay raise
should be repealed or scaled back—almost two-thirds of voters admitted that they did not know if their state legislators had voted for the
salary increase. Perhaps even more importantly, only 37 percent said
they would vote against a legislator solely because of a vote in favor of
the pay raise.

Yet, contrary to the legislative leadership's expectations, resentment
over the pay raise continued to build. On September 26, 1,500 people
stood in the rain outside the statehouse in protest. Some carried signs
saying, "Public servants, not parasites," "Shame on you, pay-hike
hogs," and "Vote the bums out." A 25-foot-tall inflatable pig with the
label "Repeal the illegal legislative pay raise" hovered over the crowd.
A radio talk show host gave legislative leaders petitions opposing the
pay increase signed by 129,000 people. A Pottstown newspaper submitted 9,000 irate letters from its readers.

The pressure on legislators increased further when anti-pay raise
activists filed several court cases opposing the legislative action. And to
ratchet up things even more, the inflatable pig began a tour of the state.
Slowly, legislators began to back away from the raise. By the fall, more
than 25 of them had decided to give up the increase after first accepting
it. Still others donated their raises to charity.

The full legislature capitulated a few weeks later. On November 2,
after a brief debate during which one senator railed, "We need to re-
pent, repeal, and reform," the senate voted unanimously to rescind the
pay raise. Only a few hours later, the House also passed a repeal bill,
196 to 2. After the vote, a representative admitted, "Pressure mounted

in individual lawmakers' districts and they had to listen to the public."
A senator, noting that he received hundreds of letters from people in his
district complaining about the pay increase, acknowledged, "It showed
it has hit a nerve with voters. And I got the message."

A technical difference between the Senate and House versions of the
pay repeal measure, however, threatened to void the legislative action
and keep the raise in effect. But, as if legislators need any additional pressure to resolve the difference, they got another strong signal of public discontent from the results of the November 8 elections. No legislators were
on the ballot, but voters were asked whether to retain two state supreme
court justices. When the results were announced, one justice had barely
survived, and the other lost. This was notable because it was the first time
a Pennsylvania state supreme court justice had ever lost a retention election, and most observers blamed his loss on voter unhappiness with the
legislative pay raise scheme. Not surprisingly, less than a week later, the
House and Senate resolved their differences and finally rescinded the pay
raise. Only one legislator in either house, Representative Mike Veon, the
Democratic minority whip, voted against the repeal.

Legislators may have hoped that at this point that the political
storm would pass. Some things did return to normal. On December 1,
2005, legislators got their regularly scheduled cost of living increase,
bringing their salaries up to $72,187. But momentum for the anti-incum-
bent backlash continued unabated.

Efforts to recruit candidates to run against pay raise supporters
proved surprisingly successful. More than twice as many incumbents
faced primary challengers in 2006 compared with recent elections. More
than 80 non-incumbent candidates running for the legislature won the
endorsement of PACleanSweep (the renamed Operation Clean Sweep).
Rather than face a difficult reelection campaign, 30 legislators chose
to retire.

Retiring lawmakers may have made the correct calculation. The primary election saw an astonishing 17 incumbents defeated, among them
the Senate majority leader and the Senate president pro tem. They were
the first legislative leaders in the state to lose an election since 1964. In the
November general elections, seven more incumbents were swept from
office. Among the losers was House Minority Whip Mike Veon, the last
supporter of the pay raise, who lost despite running in a district where
his party enjoyed a massive voter registration advantage and against an
underfunded challenger.

In the end, the pay raise fiasco exacted a considerable toll. By the
end of 2006, 56 state legislators had retired or lost. Of the 56, 49 had initially voted in favor of the pay raise.

(Continued)

POLITICS UNDER THE DOMES 3-1 (CONTINUED)

Sources: Tom Barnes, "Dems Reward Pay Raise Backers," *Pittsburgh Post-Gazette,* July 29, 2005; Tom Barnes, "Pay Raise Anger Starts Boiling Over," *Pittsburgh Post-Gazette,* July 19, 2005; Tom Barnes, "State Senator Pushes for $10,000 Raise," *Pittsburgh Post-Gazette,* June 30, 2005; Mario F. Cattabiani, "Rendell Signs Pay-Raise into Law," *Philadelphia Inquirer,* November 16, 2005; *Philadelphia Inquirer,* March 8, 2006; Mario F. Cattabiani and Thomas Fitzgerald, "New Faces in Pa. Legislative Races," Mario F. Cattabiani and Alison Knezevich, "Lawmakers in Pa. could be 2d in pay," *Philadelphia Inquirer,* July 6, 2005; Mario F. Cattabiani and Amy Word, "Legislators Reverse Raise," *Philadelphia Inquirer,* November 3, 2005; Mario F. Cattabiani and Amy Worden, "Pay-Hike Death Warrant Signed," *Philadelphia Inquirer,* November 17, 2005; Debra Erdley, "Backlash Continues Against Pay Grab," *Pittsburgh Tribune Review,* November 12, 2006; Richard Fellinger, "Throng Vents at Capitol," *Lebanon Daily News,* September 27, 2005; John Grogan, "Protesters Ask: Where's Perzel," *Philadelphia Inquirer,* September 27, 2005; Jan Murphy, "Raise or Not, Lawmakers get Boost," *The Patriot-News,* August 18, 2005; Jan Murphy and Charles Thompson, "Lawmakers Boost Their Pay 16%," *The Patriot-News,* July 8, 2005; Jan Murphy and Charles Thompson, "Raises Put Lawmakers in Charitable State of Mind" *The Patriot-News,* August 25, 2005; Quinnipiac University Poll, "Rendell Approval Slips, But Challengers Don't Gain, Quinnipiac University Pennsylvania Poll Finds; Voters Say Lawmakers Should Repeal Their Pay Raise," October 5, 2005; Quinnipiac University Poll, "Pennsylvania Voters Have Little Confidence in Tax Fix, Quinnipiac University Poll Finds; Anti-Incumbent Feeling is Strong," December 8, 2005; Martha Raffaele, "Challengers Line Up to Unseat Legislators," *Centre Daily Times,* March 20, 2006; Reggie Sheffield, "Taxpayers Express Outrage at Raises," *The Patriot-News,* July 19, 2005; Sharon Smith, "The Race is On," *The Patriot-News,* March 8, 2006; Charles Thompson and Jan Murphy, "It's Payback," *The Patriot-News,* May 17, 2006; Mike Wereschagin, "Porcine Protest Crosses the State," *Pittsburg Tribune Review,* October 29, 2005; Amy Worden, "Pay-raise Opponents Stripped of Posts, *Philadelphia Inquirer,* July 28, 2005.

senators saw their entire paycheck consumed by the expense. One legislator even ended up paying the state $40 above his salary to cover his health insurance payment. He sheepishly admitted, "When I took the job I knew how much it paid. But I did have to do a little explaining to my wife."[35] Given the time many lawmakers devote to their job, the pay they get in some states is miniscule. According to a Utah state representative:

> Frankly, I, and most Utah State legislators take a substantial "hit" salary-wise to serve in the legislature. Many legislators stack-up "comp" time and use vacation days at their non-legislative places of employment just so they can take a leave-of-absence for 45 days (33 weekdays). Many, like myself, are self-employed. A hand-full of legislators are retired. And, yet another group subsist on their spouse's income.[36]

How are state legislative salaries determined? State constitutions explicitly set legislative salaries in at least four states: Alabama, New Hampshire, Rhode Island, and Texas. Alabama's pay of $10 per day was placed in that state's constitution by a 1947 amendment.[37] The absurdly low salary of $100 a year in New Hampshire was set by an 1889 amendment to the state constitution and has been left untouched ever since.[38] Texas established its salary more recently; in 1975, that state's voters approved a constitutional amendment increasing legislative salaries to $7,200.[39] Voters in Rhode Island amended their constitution in the mid-1990s to set member pay at $10,000 annually but provided for an automatic yearly cost of living adjustment tied to federal government inflation figures.[40]

Compensation commissions currently exist in 20 states.[41] Only in California, Oklahoma, and Washington, however, do commissions set legislative salaries without requiring the legislature to pass some judgment on the decision.[42] Thus, lawmakers in these states get raises while still being able to publicly protest them.[43] In other commission states, the legislature plays a part in setting their pay. The particular role, however, varies across the states in subtle but important ways. In West Virginia, the state legislature must take positive action to put the commission's pay proposal into effect. The legislature may reduce the proposed salary but not increase it. Thus, legislators have to vote in favor of any pay raise, putting them in the same political hot seat they would have occupied in the absence of a compensation commission. In contrast, in Michigan and Utah, the compensation commission's proposal goes into effect unless the legislature votes it down. Consequently, by taking no action—and not requiring legislators to go on record in support—pay raises in those state can be achieved without much political pain. Missouri recently changed its commission procedures to make it easier for raises to be implemented, discarding a process whereby legislators had to both approve a commission recommended pay raise and appropriate the money for it in favor of one in which the commission's recommendation automatically goes into effect unless it is rejected by a two-thirds majority in each house.[44] Only in Arizona do compensation commission recommendations get put before the voters. This, of course, puts a significant obstacle between legislators and any pay raise. In 2006, for example, the state commission's recommendation to increase legislative salaries to $36,000 from $24,000 was defeated at the polls. Two years later, the state's voters also overwhelmingly rejected a more modest proposal to raise salaries to $30,000.

The process by which pay raises are achieved matters because legislative salaries can be politically controversial. In states where legislators have control over setting their own salaries, their sense of political self-preservation inevitably conflicts with their financial self-interest. Publicly, lawmakers offer two main justifications for legislative pay raises. The first is that they work long and hard and deserve higher salaries:

- An Alabama state senator, a Democrat: "People look at this as a part-time job. It's not a part-time job, it's a full-time job."[45]
- An Alaska state representative, a Republican: "Legislators, from my experience, work their tails off."[46]
- The California Assembly speaker, a Democrat: "I don't think anybody needs to be apologetic about [a legislative pay raise]. I don't think anybody needs to turn it down. We work hard, and we put a lot of time into this job, and sometimes it's a thankless task."[47]

- An Oregon state representative, a Republican: "How many people would work for 1,283 bucks a month? I believe that the romantic ideal of the citizens' Legislature doesn't exist anymore. The Legislature is getting to be more and more of a full-time job."[48]
- A Pennsylvania state representative, a Democrat: "I put a lot of time into the job. For me it's a full-time job, even on Sundays. I respond to a lot of constituent letters, go to meetings and write legislation. I have a busy office."[49]

The second justification offered by legislators is that higher salaries are needed to allow a broader array of people to serve in the legislature:

- The West Virginia Speaker of the House, a Democrat: "If we don't [pass a salary increase], we'll end up with a Legislature of the super-wealthy, rather than a Legislature made up of people from all walks of life. It would be unfortunate if only the rich could serve in the Legislature."[50]
- The Kansas Speaker of the House, a Republican: "The Legislature shouldn't become the playground for the rich or the pastime of the retired. To have a truly representative democracy, we need working men and women to be able to serve in the Legislature."[51]
- A Nebraska senate senator: "We're missing the young people because they cannot afford to be here. We're missing different cultures because they cannot afford to be here."[52]
- The Maine House minority leader, a Democrat: "It has become harder and harder to recruit young people, recruit working people when legislators get paid an average of $10,000 a year. That's tough for some people."[53]
- A North Dakota state representative, a Republican: "I think when we make it a policy to underpay ourselves so we look good to the public, we limit this chamber to people of a certain amount of means. I don't think that's right."[54]

Supporting a legislative pay raise is, however, politically risky. As an Alabama representative recently complained, "I think a lot of people would rather give a dead cat a pay raise than a legislator."[55] Indeed, in states where voters have a direct say over legislative salaries, pay increases have proven to be very unpopular. For instance, in Nebraska, voters have approved only one pay increase for their lawmakers in the past 40 years (in 1988). Even where voters do not get to vote on pay raises, they can make their views known. In 2007, when Maine legislators, who make about $11,000 annually, proposed a modest pay increase of about $2,600 a year, they ignited a political firestorm. Mainers writing in response to a newspaper story on the proposal were universally opposed to the idea, and many were venomous in their comments:

- "Until they start working for us, I say no pay raise!"
- "You wanted in, live on what you get like the rest of us!!! This makes my blood BOIL!!! How dare they!!!"
- "Give me a break! What exactly have these folks done to deserve a raise?"
- "Add up all of the benefits the Legislators get and they're getting a darn good pay for the time they put in."

- "I say lets freeze the pay of our legislators . . . cut their travel and food expense . . . THEN THEY WILL SEE HOW THE REST OF US HAVE TO LIVE ON A DAILY BASIS."[56]

Not surprisingly, Maine legislators did not pursue the proposed pay raise.

Legislators fear they will pay a price at the polls if they vote in favor of a salary increase. In 2001, for example, a proposal to increase their meager pay came before the Kansas House of Representatives. Early in the vote, the electronic display in the House chamber showed the measure almost passing, 57 votes in favor to 63 votes opposed. But after it became clear that the pay increase would not garner the necessary majority to pass, a number of legislators changed their votes from "yes" to "no," and the final tally showed that the bill lost, 46 to 75. One vote switcher justified his change by claiming, "My support for that wasn't strong enough to keep me as a yes vote, so I had second thoughts and decided to switch." A colleague who supported the pay proposal commented, "I think they chickened out. If you had a secret ballot, that bill would have passed 125 to nothing. The fact is the members are running scared."[57]

An Indiana state representative pushing a pay raise in that legislature offered a similarly scathing assessment of his colleagues, noting, "Legislators, when it comes to their own pay, are gutless, just gutless. They're just afraid they won't get reelected."[58] Consequently, legislators have every incentive to concoct schemes to allow them to get pay raises without having to take political responsibility for them. In 2007, Indiana lawmakers passed legislation tying their salaries to those paid to the state judges. Starting in 2009, members of the Indiana legislature are paid 18 percent of the salary paid to a state judge. This Rube Goldberg–like plan works to the advantage of state legislators because increases in judicial salaries are linked to salary increases for state employees. So, when Indiana legislators make a politically easy vote to give state employees a raise, judicial salaries will automatically increase, and when judicial salaries go up, state legislators will also get paid more.[59] Such indirect pay raise mechanisms are not new. In Florida, state law provides that legislators get the same percentage salary increase as general state employees.[60] Even though Montana lawmakers are paid a per diem, the rate is tied to the wages given to state employees and to the daily allowances provided to state legislators in neighboring Idaho, North Dakota, South Dakota, and Wyoming.[61] A little-noticed constitutional amendment passed by Massachusetts voters in 1998 increases (and, theoretically, decreases) legislative pay every two years by the percentage change in the state's median household income.[62] The process in Rhode Island provides state lawmakers an automatic cost of living boost.

Not all of these indirect pay-raise plans sneak past the voters. In 2008, Louisiana legislators attempted to set their salary at 30 percent of the salary earned by members of Congress, which would have immediately increased their pay to $50,762 from $16,800 and have allowed that new figure to increase in the future without any effort on their part. Public outrage forced lawmakers to backtrack on the proposal, and they opted instead to increase their annual salary to $37,500 without any link to congressional pay. Future raises, however, were to be automatically tied to the federal Consumer Price Index. The lower salary figure still represented a substantial boost—and lawmakers' first pay raise in almost three decades. But after having promised legislators that he would let the measure become law, the governor buckled under to immense public pressure and vetoed it.[63]

In the end, how much does low pay matter to those pursuing legislative service? Unsurprisingly, it is important because it influences who serves and how long they serve. The low salary in Kansas, for example, caused one representative to resign so he could take a better paying position. He explained, "It's a simple matter of two jobs I love, one that pays and one that doesn't. It hurts a lot of us financially. Some make a real sacrifice to serve. I have to do what is best for my family."[64] Indeed, another Kansas lawmaker recently introduced a bill to increase legislative salaries to the federal poverty level.[65] Many state legislators note that taking time away from their regular occupation is expensive. A Utah representative complained, "It costs me a ton of money to serve."[66] An Iowa senator, for example, calculates that his law practice loses $500 every day the legislature is in session, a Texas senator estimates that she forgoes more than $40,000 in earnings as a pharmacist, and it costs a Nebraska senator up to $25,000 a year in additional labor costs to cover his absence from the specialty meat market he owns.[67] A Florida representative expressed what may be a widely shared sentiment among his colleagues around the country: "I wouldn't advise the average person to think about [legislative service] because it can put you at real financial risk. . . . I've been blessed to have this opportunity. I wouldn't trade it for the world. But I'm not sure that I could do it again."[68]

EXAMINING THE COMPONENTS OF PROFESSIONALIZATION: TIME DEMANDS

Similar to member pay, the time demands made by legislative service vary considerably across the states. Unlike the U.S. Congress, which meets annually for as many days as it wishes, state legislatures operate under two potential time limitations: how often they may meet and how long those meetings may last. Because the original state legislatures were seen as a vital check on gubernatorial power and because it was thought that regular sessions enhanced representation, they were required to meet annually.[69] But during the early decades of the nineteenth century, the public came to distrust state legislatures; consequently, annual sessions were replaced with biennial sessions because it was reasoned that meeting less often would give legislators less time to create mischief.[70] By the beginning of the twentieth century, only seven states still had annual sessions; the rest met biennially, except for Alabama, which met only once every four years.[71]

Over the course of the twentieth century, the trend was a return to annual sessions. By 1960, 19 states had annual sessions. The number of legislatures meeting annually continued to escalate over the next four decades, in large part in response to the professionalization revolution of the 1960s and 1970s. In 2008, Arkansas voters decided to allow their legislature to meet every year, leaving just five states with legislatures that only meet every two years—Montana, Nevada, North Dakota, Oregon, and Texas.[72] It is important to note, however, that annual sessions are not always created equal. Among the legislatures that meet every year, seven—Arkansas, Connecticut, Louisiana, Maine, New Mexico, North Carolina, and Wyoming—have one year out of every two during which the session is limited, with varying degrees of strictness, to budget matters. Moreover, although the trend toward annual meetings is widespread, it is not universal. Montana's 1972 constitution established annual sessions, but the state's voters passed a referendum two years later returning the legislature to biennial sessions. The voters reaffirmed their decision again in 1982 and 1988.[73]

Even as most states have moved to meeting annually, session lengths continue to be limited in a majority of legislatures. Currently, only 12 states do not place any limit on the length of the regular legislative session.[74] In 28 states, constitutional provisions establish the limits. For instance, the Wyoming Constitution limits the legislature to 40 legislative days in odd-numbered years and 20 legislative days in even-numbered years.[75] Session length limits in Alabama, Indiana, Maine, and South Carolina are imposed by law. Legislative rules limit the number of days in session in Arizona, California, and Massachusetts. Finally, indirect limits on legislator compensation, such as cut-off dates for per diems or mileage reimbursements, are used in three states—Iowa, New Hampshire, and Tennessee. In Iowa, for example, state legislators can no longer collect their per diem after 110 calendar days in session in odd-numbered years or 100 calendar days in even-numbered years. This gives them a financial incentive to finish their business on time.

Thus, the formal time demands made on state legislators by legislative sessions vary dramatically by state. The Utah state legislature, for example, is considered part-time and meets for fewer days than most state legislatures. The 2007 session started on January 15 and finished on February 28, covering 45 calendar days, the constitutional limit. Floor sessions were actually held on 33 days.[76] In contrast, the Wisconsin state legislature is considered a full-time body. The 73 days the Wisconsin legislature was scheduled to meet in floor sessions in 2007 might not seem particularly imposing. But those 73 days were distributed across nine months, meaning that legislators were in a position where the legislature commanded much of their time during the course of the year.[77] California state legislators are also considered full-time legislators. During the 2007 regular session, members of the Assembly met for 121 day over 272 calendar days, and members of the Senate met for 130 days.[78]

State legislators, however, spend more time on matters related to their legislative service than the number of days spent in session might suggest. A recent survey of legislators in all 50 states reveals the median state legislator sees his or her position as being two-thirds of a full-time job.[79] Not surprisingly, lawmakers in more professional legislatures report spending more time on the job than do their colleagues in less-professional bodies. But even in South Dakota—the legislature where members report spending the least amount of time on legislative matters—legislators still estimated that their efforts constituted more than one-third of a full-time position. This is in large part because, beyond their responsibilities associated with the legislative session, lawmakers report spending considerable amounts of time providing constituency services as well engaging in campaign-related activities.[80] Thus, as one South Dakota representative commented, "It's more like a second job, and it's a first job when you consider you're trying to do the people's business. I sure don't feel like it's a half-time job. It's a mammoth job."[81]

EXAMINING EACH OF THE COMPONENTS: STAFF AND FACILITIES

State legislatures started with almost nothing in the way of staff or facilities. Even by the middle of the twentieth century, most state legislators were provided very little assistance.[82] The professionalization revolution of the 1960s and 1970s produced dramatic changes in staff and facilities in most, but not all, state legislatures.[83] By 2009, almost every state legislative chamber provides professional and clerical staff to committees. Roughly half of the states provide members with year-round personal staff, but fewer than 10 provide district staff and offices.[84] Many state legislators are still without individual offices. Overall, some states, such as California, Florida, New York, and Texas, operate with staff and facilities comparable to those of the U.S. Congress. Many other states provide remarkably little in the way of assistance or facilities. Indeed, in a few states, legislators have little more than their desk, much like elementary school students.

WHO SERVES?

The stereotypical state legislator is a middle-aged white male lawyer. In reality, state legislators are drawn from a wide range of backgrounds. Indeed, over time, the ranks of state legislators have become increasingly diverse, better mirroring the societies they represent. The membership diversity of state legislatures in 2007 in terms of gender, race, and ethnicity is presented in Table 3-4.

WOMEN

The first women were elected to a state legislature in 1894, when three women were elected to the Colorado House of Representatives. By the time the first woman was elected to Congress in 1916, women had already served in the Arizona, Colorado, Idaho, Oregon, Utah, Washington, and Wyoming state legislatures.[85] The number of female lawmakers in the states grew over the course of the twentieth century, reaching more than 1,000 by 1985. In 2009, 1,751 women were state legislators, a figure representing 24 percent of all state legislative seats, the highest figure in American history.[86] Women held one-third or more of the seats in six states but fewer than 10 percent of the seats in South Carolina. Although women are still far from holding state legislative seats in proportion to their share of the population, those serving in state legislatures now hold many of the most powerful positions. In 2009, for example, women served as speakers of the house in California, Maine, Nevada, New Hampshire, and Oregon. Moreover, women now hold committee chairs in proportion to their numbers in state legislatures.[87]

AFRICAN AMERICANS

The first African American state legislator was elected in Vermont before the Civil War. Reconstruction saw the election of African American legislators in a number of states in the South, but no African Americans were elected again for decades after it ended. Indeed, the number of African Americans serving in state legislatures grew at a glacial pace through the first half of the twentieth century. Since then, their numbers have increased more rapidly.[88] By 2009, 628 African Americans held state legislative seats. They were, however, concentrated in a relatively small number of states: in 5 states, more than 20 percent of seats were held by African Americans, but in 20 states, they held at most 2 percent of seats.

Interestingly, African American women make up a larger percentage of all African American state legislators than white women make up of all white state legislators. There is no convincing explanation for this discrepancy.[89] Over time, African American state legislators have moved into leadership positions as their numbers have increased in a legislature, particularly in those chambers where the black caucus is an important part of a Democratic majority.[90] As their numbers have grown in legislative chambers and as they have moved into positions of power, African American legislators have gained influence in the state policymaking process.[91]

TABLE 3-4   STATE LEGISLATIVE MEMBERSHIP DIVERSITY, RANKED BY STATE, 2007

Rank	State	Number of African American Legislators	Percent of Total Seats	State	Number of Latino Legislators	Percent of Total Seats	State	Number of Women Legislators	Percent of Total Seats
1	MS	43	25	NM	44	39	VT	68	38
2	AL	34	24	CA	28	23	NH	152	36
3	GA	56	24	TX	36	20	CO	35	35
4	MD	42	22	AZ	17	19	MN	70	35
5	NY	44	21	FL	17	11	AZ	30	33
6	LA	29	20	NY	17	8	HI	25	33
7	SC	28	16	IL	11	6	WA	48	33
8	IL	29	16	CO	5	5	MD	61	32
9	FL	25	16	NJ	6	5	OR	28	31
10	NC	26	15	NV	3	5	DE	19	31
11	MI	19	13	CT	6	3	NM	34	30
12	VA	17	12	RI	3	3	NV	19	30
13	OH	16	12	KS	4	2	ME	56	30
14	AR	15	11	WY	2	2	KS	48	29
15	NV	7	11	MD	4	2	CA	34	28
16	TN	14	11	NE	1	2	CT	53	28
17	CT	19	10	WA	3	2	IL	48	27
18	NJ	11	9	MI	3	2	NC	44	26
19	TX	16	9	MA	4	2	MT	38	25
20	IN	13	9	UT	2	2	MA	49	25
21	PA	21	8	DE	1	2	NY	51	24
22	DE	5	8	MN	3	1	ID	25	24
23	CA	9	8	HI	1	1	WY	21	23
24	MO	12	6	GA	3	1	FL	37	23
25	WI	8	6	NC	2	1	IA	34	23

Rank	State		State		State		
26	KY	7	OR	1	WI	30	23
27	MA	9	ID	1	AK	13	22
28	OK	6	TN	1	NJ	26	22
29	KS	6	VA	1	AR	28	21
30	OR	3	IN	1	MI	29	20
31	CO	3	MT	1	GA	46	20
32	AZ	2	SC	1	RI	22	20
33	NE	1	MO	1	IN	29	19
34	WA	3	NH	2	MO	38	19
35	IA	3	PA	1	TX	35	19
36	NM	2	AL	0	NE	9	18
37	AK	1	AK	0	ND	25	18
38	RI	1	AR	0	LA	25	17
39	VT	1	IA	0	UT	18	17
40	MN	1	KY	0	SD	18	17
41	NH	1	LA	0	VA	24	17
42	HI	0	ME	0	OH	22	17
43	ID	0	MS	0	TN	22	17
44	ME	0	ND	0	PA	37	15
45	MT	0	OH	0	WV	19	14
46	ND	0	OK	0	MS	24	14
47	SD	0	SD	0	AL	18	13
48	UT	0	VT	0	OK	19	13
49	WV	0	WV	0	KY	17	12
50	WY	0	WI	0	SC	15	9
Mean		8		3		24	24
Median		6		1		23	23

Sources: Center for American Women and Politics, National Association of Latino Elected Officials, National Black Caucus of State Legislators, and National Conference of State Legislatures.

HISPANIC AMERICANS

As with African Americans, the number of Hispanic state legislators has only become noticeable in recent decades, although they have yet to achieve parity with their percentage of the population. In 2009, 242 Hispanic Americans held state legislative seats. Again, they tend to be found in a relatively small number of states. Indeed, no Hispanic Americans serve in 16 state legislatures. The largest percentage, 44 percent, is in New Mexico. This is not surprising because Hispanic Americans have long been integrated into that state's political culture. Even as far back as 1912, when the state was admitted to the union, more than 40 percent of the lower house and 20 percent of the state senate were Hispanic Americans.[92] The prominence of Hispanic Americans in the California and Texas state legislatures, however, is of much more recent vintage. The legislative success of Hispanic lawmakers varies considerably across state legislatures.[93] Where they constitute a larger block of members, Hispanic lawmakers have had success in influencing state policymaking.[94]

AMERICAN INDIANS

As of 2009, the National Caucus of Native American State Legislators, an organization open to "all Native American, Alaska Native and Native Hawaiian state legislators," had 80 members from 17 states. The largest number of American Indian state legislators was in Oklahoma, with 26 lawmakers.[95] In the Oklahoma Legislature, lawmakers were members of seven tribes: Cherokee, Chickasaw, Choctaw, Creek, Muscogee, Potawatomi, and Seminole.[96] Maine is the only state that has seats reserved specifically for representatives from Indian tribes, one for a member representing the Passamaquoddy and another for a representative of the Penobscot. Their status is similar to that of territorial representatives in the U.S. House of Representatives in that they have seating and speaking privileges and draw lawmaker salaries, but they cannot participate in floor votes.[97]

EXPLAINING THE NUMBER OF WOMEN AND MINORITY LEGISLATORS

What accounts for the differences in the diversity of state legislative memberships? In the past, legislative professionalization has demonstrated differing relationships with the percentage of women and African American state legislators. Two decades ago, women were found to be less likely to serve as legislative professionalization scores increased, but African American were more likely to serve as professionalization scores increased.[98] Are these same relationships still found today?

A series of simple ordinary least-squares regression equations to address this question are presented in Table 3-5. The regression equations examine the impact of professionalization on membership diversity while controlling for the effects of other independent variables that also are thought to be

TABLE 3-5 ORDINARY LEAST-SQUARES REGRESSION EXPLAINING PERCENT WOMEN
AND MINORITY LEGISLATORS IN STATE LEGISLATURES

VARIABLE	PERCENT WOMEN LEGISLATORS	PERCENT AFRICAN AMERICAN LEGISLATORS	PERCENT HISPANIC AMERICAN LEGISLATORS
Professionalization score	−5.043 (8.757)	10.437[c] (3.662)	−1.963 (3.987)
South	−4.518[a] (2.602)	0.697 (1.423)	0.184 (1.127)
Percent conservative population	−.355[a] (0.181)	−.042 (0.073)	−0.007 (0.078)
Percent African American population		0.703[d] (0.059)	
Percent Hispanic American population			0.698[d] (0.045)
Constant	37.530[d] (6.855)	−0.251 (2.734)	−2.233 (2.981)
N	50	50	50
Adjusted R^2	0.181	0.880	0.850

[a] $P < .10$
[c] $P < .01$
[d] $P < .001$, two-tailed tests.

important. We might, for example, hypothesize that for historical and cultural reasons, states in the South—considered to be the 11 states of the Confederacy—would be less likely to elect women, African Americans, and Hispanic Americans to their state legislatures than Northern states. We might also expect women and minorities to have a more difficult time getting elected in more conservative states than in more liberal states.[99] Finally, we also might anticipate that Hispanic and African American state legislators are more likely to be elected in states where those communities constitute a larger percentage of the population.[100]

The regression results reveal that there is no longer a statistically significant relationship between legislative professionalization and the percentage of women in the state legislature. Women are just as likely to serve in the most professional legislatures as in the least professional legislature. Southern states, however, have 5 percent fewer women state legislators than Northern states, and the most conservative state has 10 percent fewer women state legislators than the most liberal state. Both of these relationships are consistent with those found in earlier studies.

Professionalization, however, continues to exert a positive relationship with the percentage of African American state legislators. The coefficient suggests the most professional state legislature will have 6 percent more African American state legislators than the least professional legislature. Professionalization, however, has no relationship with the percentage of state legislators who are Hispanic Americans. The percentage of the population that is African American or Hispanic American, however, has by far the greatest statistical impact on the percentage of state legislators from those groups. The state with the largest African American population has 26 percent more African American state legislators than the state with the lowest percentage of African American residents. The state with the largest Hispanic American population has 30 percent more Hispanic American state legislators than the state with the lowest percentage of Hispanic American residents. Indeed, with community size controlled, neither region nor state conservatism exerts any statistical influence on the percentage of minority legislators.

DIVERSITY BY OTHER MEASURES

In recent years, state legislatures have become increasingly diverse in ways beyond gender, race, and ethnicity. The number of openly gay and lesbian state legislators, for example, has grown significantly in recent years. In 2009, there were 76 openly gay and lesbian state legislators, constituting approximately 1 percent of all state legislators nationally.[101] Gays and lesbians held seats in 30 state legislatures. As might be anticipated, larger numbers of gay and lesbian state legislators are found in bigger and more liberal states, such as California, Massachusetts, and New York. But gays and lesbians have been elected to office in conservative states as well; three, for example, served in the Utah state legislature in 2009. As more gays and lesbians are elected to a state legislature, more pro-gay rights legislation gets introduced and adopted. But at the same time, their service appears to generate a backlash; more anti-gay rights legislation also gets introduced and passed. On balance, however, electing more gay and lesbian state legislators produces more pro-gay rights laws.[102]

Another example of the increasing diversity of state legislatures is the number of foreign-born lawmakers. In 2006, 79 state legislators hailed from a total of 36 different foreign countries.[103] Foreign-born legislators are not concentrated in just a few states; instead, they serve in a wide range of legislatures. Among those holding office in 2009 were Margaret Craven, a Maine senator born in Ireland; Swati Dandekar, an Iowa senator born in India; Jean Jeudy, a New Hampshire representative born in Haiti; Mee Moua, a Minnesota senator born in Laos; Selim Noujaim, a Connecticut representative born in Lebanon; Juan Pichardo, a Rhode Island senator born in the Dominican Republic; Paull Shin, a Washington senator born in Korea, Herbert Vo, a Texas representative born in Vietnam; and Juan Zapata, a Florida representative born in Colombia. Most foreign-born state legislators came to the

United States as children or young adults, became established in their communities, and then committed themselves to public service. Many have taken a special interest in working to help assimilate immigrant communities in their districts and states.[104]

OCCUPATIONS

In the eighteenth and nineteenth centuries, farming was the dominant occupation of state legislators. But by the early twentieth century, lawyers started outnumbering farmers in state legislatures.[105] A study comparing occupational data across the twentieth century revealed that the percentage of state legislators who were lawyers actually declined during this period, although not dramatically. In 1909, 20 percent of state legislators were attorneys; by 1999, that figure had slipped to 15 percent. The percentage of farmers holding legislative office declined much more precipitously, to 7 percent in 1999 from 25 percent 90 years earlier. That decrease was consistent with the decrease in farmers as a percentage of the nation's population.[106] It is important to note, however, that state lawmakers come from a variety of occupations. Indeed, by 1999, a plurality of state legislators came not from law or agriculture but from business.

Table 3-6 presents the proportion of state legislators in selected states in 2007 holding one of four different occupations: legislator, attorney, farmer, or retired. Obviously, legislators hold occupations in addition to those listed in Table 3-6. A generic business category would likely include more legislators than the four presented, but such a category would mask the diversity of the jobs legislators perform. Some state legislators own small businesses, and others hold management positions in larger companies. Real estate agents, insurance agents, and funeral directors have traditionally served in state legislatures as a way of both performing public service and generating clients, and members of those occupations are still found in most legislatures today. Still others who might be categorized as being in "business" hold jobs not usually associated with lawmakers:

- An electrician in the Delaware House
- A locomotive engineer in the Ohio House
- An outdoor adventure guide in the Colorado House
- A wedding cake decorator in the North Dakota House
- A fire protection sprinkler fitter in the Missouri House
- A longshoreman in the Pennsylvania House
- A waitress in the Nevada Assembly
- A ski instructor in the Wyoming House
- A tire technician in the Iowa House
- A high school secretary in the Rhode Island House
- A UPS delivery driver in the West Virginia House
- A retired Major League Baseball umpire in the Tennessee House

TABLE 3-6   SELECTED STATE LEGISLATOR OCCUPATIONS, SELECTED STATES, 2007–2008
(IN PERCENT, RANKED FROM HIGHEST TO LOWEST SALARY)

STATE	LEGISLATIVE SALARY	PERCENTAGE CLAIMING			
		LEGISLATOR	ATTORNEY	FARMER, RANCHER, OR FISHING	RETIRED
Pennsylvania	$73,613	77	9	<1	<1
Ohio	$58,934	35	23	3	8
Massachusetts	$58,237	54	22	0	0
Illinois	$57,619	21	15	2	0
New Jersey	$49,000	26	23	0	0
Wisconsin	$47,413	38	11	6	0
Maryland	$43,500	15	20	1	3
Delaware	$42,000	24	3	0	5
Missouri	$31,351	1	13	10	10
Minnesota	$31,141	8	14	4	8
Florida	$30,996	4	23	4	5
Colorado	$30,000	9	16	3	15
Iowa	$25,000	6	8	18	13
Alaska	$24,012	2	12	3	22
Tennessee	$18,123	0	13	6	12
Georgia	$17,342	<1	13	3	6
Idaho	$16,116	0	9	17	21
Kentucky	$15,797	1	21	6	9
West Virginia	$15,000	0	15	1	13
Arkansas	$14,765	0	10	7	12
North Carolina	$13,951	3	19	2	28
Vermont	$13,217	1	8	5	18
Rhode Island	$13,089	0	26	1	10
Nebraska	$12,000	0	14	18	20
South Carolina	$10,400	6	20	1	8
Mississippi	$10,000	1	20	4	8
Kansas	$7,462	0	12	11	13
Texas	$7,200	2	28	4	5
South Dakota	$6,000	0	10	23	17
Utah	$5,850	0	9	5	8
North Dakota	$4,940	0	4	24	19
Wyoming	$4,350	0	11	10	17
Nevada	$4,137	0	11	8	16
Alabama	$990	0	12	1	11
New Mexico	No Salary	0	11	4	18

Source: Occupational data gathered by the authors from state legislative web pages and documents.
Occupations are self-identified by lawmakers.

The number of state legislators claiming full-time legislator as their occupation has increased substantially over time. Only three state legislative houses had any members who claimed full-time status in 1909. But by 1999, most legislative houses had at least some full-time legislators; a few had significant proportions. But, as Table 3-6 demonstrates, those claiming to be full-time lawmakers are much more likely to be found in more professionalized legislatures than in less professionalized bodies. Moreover, it is likely that the numbers in Table 3-6 actually underestimate the number of full-time legislators in several of the more professionalized bodies. Observers believe many lawmakers in more professionalized legislatures are really full-time legislators, but they fear admitting it publicly because of the possible negative electoral repercussions of being labeled a career politician.[107] Outside of the more professional legislatures, very few, if any, members claim to make their living from public office.

Lawyers still enjoy a prominent role in state legislatures; in large part, they develop skills that lend themselves to success in the legislative process.[108] The percentage of lawyers in the 35 states presented in Table 3-6 fluctuates between a low of 3 percent in Delaware (where no attorneys have served in some sessions) to a high of 28 percent in Texas.[109] (Keep in mind that some of those claiming "legislator" as their occupation are also lawyers.) The percentage of legislators who are in farming or ranching is strongly related to agriculture's role in a state's economy. Thus, farmers and ranchers are found in much greater numbers in South Dakota and North Dakota than in Massachusetts or New Jersey. Finally, much larger percentages of those who are retired are found in lower salary state legislatures, notably Idaho, Nebraska, and North Carolina. It is not surprising that service in those bodies is attractive to retired people because they usually have other means of income and flexible schedules.

Until 2008, legislators in New Jersey enjoyed an occupational opportunity denied their counterparts in most other states. Garden State lawmakers were allowed to concurrently hold both their legislative seat and a local or county office, an outcome that would be considered a felony in Indiana. A law passed in 2007 prohibited dual office holding for New Jersey state legislators, but it allowed those currently holding two offices to continue to do so.[110] Consequently, in 2008, 19 members of the legislature simultaneously served as mayor, city council member, or county freeholder (county supervisor in much of the rest of the country). These legislators often tout their position in Trenton to their voters in local elections back home. As one mayor running for office noted, "It's become very clear to me that mayors who advocate for their cities in the state Assembly and Senate are very successful at protecting the interests of their cities."[111] The potential conflict of interest (or opportunity for a salary double dip) did not appear to trouble Garden State voters until recently.

Finally, there is another occupation that gets almost no attention but that potentially impinges on the ability of legislators to perform their duties. Although active duty military officers are not allowed to hold elective office, those serving in the National Guard or reserves may do so. In 2007, 68 state legislators served concurrently in the reserves or the guard. Of these, 23 had been deployed outside of the country for more than 30 days at some point during their time in the legislature.[112] In 2008, for example, Ohio state Senator John Boccieri, a Democrat from New Middletown was a major in the Air Force Reserves, where he piloted C-130 cargo planes. Over the previous few years, Senator Boccieri had been called away from his legislative duties five times: once to Germany and four times to Afghanistan and Iraq. His absence from the legislature, however, did not cause him any political difficulties. Indeed, in 2006, he ran for election unopposed, and two years later he was elected to the U.S. House of Representatives.

THE JOB OF STATE LEGISLATOR

Most state legislators do not serve in legislatures that meet year round. Yet, as noted by the time study discussed above, although they are thought to be performing a part-time job, their legislative tasks consume a great deal of their time. This forces them to juggle their legislative responsibilities with demands from their regular occupation and families.

Thus, during the legislative session, life for a legislator can be very hectic, as the weblog of Alabama representative Cam Ward reveals:

Monday: Usually up early to get into work at my real job. . . . Pack clothes for the week in Montgomery. Lay in bed and read legislation before going to sleep sometime after midnight.

Tuesday: Get up around 6:30 am to help get my daughter off to school. Go to office and get some work done on economic development job first. Then leave for Montgomery. . . . First meeting is at 11:00 am with House GOP Steering Committee. . . . Meeting ends a little after noon. Since I have about 15 minutes before next meeting I usually eat a Power Bar for lunch before going to my Rules Committee meeting at 12:30. Session begins at 1:00 pm. While listening to debates I usually read bills coming up the next to be voted on while returning e-mails from the House floor. In the course of the day I get an average maybe 10–15 calls to return. . . . In between all of this I get prepared for my own bill to come up for a vote by lobbying other members in the chamber. . . . Session usually ends around 5:30 p.m. . . . Then I typically have a couple of receptions to go to before we finally get to dinner around 7:00 p.m. After dinner, around 9:30 p.m. I go back to the hotel to check in for the night and then read bills and return e-mails for a couple of hours before going to bed.

Wednesday: This is the day we spend in our committees. I try to get to the State House by 8:00 a.m. so I can have my bills in order for the day. . . . First committee of the day for me is the Judiciary Committee. . . . We usually meet for about 3 hours. I usually have some of my bills in other committees at this same time so I rush up from the basement where Judiciary meets to the 6th floor and present my bills in front of other committees. . . . As soon as I am done I go back to the basement and finish up the Judiciary Committee meeting. At noon I go to the House GOP Caucus meeting where we usually talk about what will be going on in the House for the rest of the week. . . . At 1:30 p.m. I go to Education Policy Committee and get out by 2:30 p.m. I then go back to my office where I return calls, speak with student groups visiting the capitol and handle constituent issues. I go back to the hotel around 5:00 p.m. and make phone calls and work for my economic development job until 6:30 p.m. and then go to dinner . . . I get back to my room at about 9:30 p.m. where I respond to e-mails and read the news clips for the day.

Thursday: After breakfast I go to the State House where I return phone calls to constituents for about an hour and a half to two hours. Then at 9:30 a.m. I [have] the Rules Committee meeting where the agenda for the House debate that day is set. At 10:00 a.m. I rush to get down on to the House floor for the beginning of the session. . . . Once on the House floor we debate bills until around noon when we adjourn for lunch. We go back into session at 1:15 p.m. and usually go until about 3:30 p.m. before adjourning. . . . On the drive home I return calls the entire way back to Alabaster. . . .

Friday: I spend as much time as possible working on my economic development work. . . .

Saturday: Usually 3 out of every 4 Saturdays each month I have an event on this day. I try to get up early and respond to mail that I have received throughout the week. Sometimes that can be an hour and a half long chore there. Then we all have breakfast before I head off to my [district] event.

Sunday: After church we come back home where I will work in the yard for a couple of hours, then go back to my office in the house to work for a couple of hours preparing for the week. I read legislative bills until about 4:00 p.m.[113]

Even when the legislature is not meeting, a legislator's time can be consumed by legislative commitments. Constituents make a number of demands on lawmakers, and lawmakers devote a great deal of time and effort to respond to them. A Michigan senator estimates that she spends 30 hours a week communicating with people in her district.[114] Staff can help with the workload. A senator in Hawaii claimed, "One day I tried to do all the responding [to constituents] myself. I started at 8 in the morning. I did not go to meetings, and I didn't go answer phone calls or respond to faxes. It took me until 8 in the evening almost to complete it all."[115] And the requests for assistance come year round, not just when the legislature is in session. A Nevada senator and pastor notes of members of his congregation: "They'll come out after services and say, 'Great sermon—and, by the way, my son's in jail and I'm wondering what you can do to help.'"[116]

Lawmakers are expected to play an active role in the communities they represent and to be seen by their constituents. A Louisiana representative advises, "You need to be visible, available, and accessible."[117] Accordingly, a Wisconsin representative admitted:"If there are two people [at an event in the district], I try to be there." Thus, one day he attended an arts and craft show in Melrose and a spaghetti dinner in Sparta. The next day, he went to a lumberjack breakfast in Sparta, a smelt fry in Millston, and another spaghetti dinner in Sparta. The representative joked, "In this job, you'd better like fish, pancakes, and chicken."[118] (Perhaps not surprisingly, a Florida Representative complained, "You've heard of the 'Freshman 15' you pick up at college? It's the same here [in the legislature]."[119]) Lawmakers in less professional legislatures are not exempt from similar time pressures. South Dakota legislators devote several weekends during the legislative sessions to "cracker barrels," sessions during which the legislators in a district solicit public input about the issues facing their constituents. Because many legislators have to drive long distances to get back home for their cracker barrels, these events represent a considerable time commitment. One South Dakota senator lamented, "We have no time for ourselves, but we really should get to the people."[120]

Serving in the legislature can take a toll on family life because most legislators do not take their spouse and children with them to the capital. Thus, many legislators spend several months apart from loved ones, and the burden for running the household and raising children falls heavily on the spouse. This can cause some pain and friction. During a floor debate on whether to call a special session of the legislature, a Utah state representative argued against it by reading a letter written to him by his seven-year-old daughter, "Dear Dad, I miss you so much. I wish you got voted off, because I want you to stay home."[121] When Californians voted against extending term limits in 2008, thus ending Speaker Fabian Núñez's legislative career, his seven-year-old son shouted "Hooray, hooray." When his father asked him, "Why are you celebrating?" the son explained, "Now that you've lost, you get to spend more time with me."[122] The burden on female legislators who also are their family's primary caregiver may be particularly hard. An Iowa state representative noted with some irony that given her various responsibilities, "One minute I'm making laws, and the next minute I'm cleaning toilets."[123]

Lawmakers can find the juggling act required of them to be frustrating. Toward the end of a legislative session, an Iowa senator admitted, "I'm a perfectionist. I haven't done anything well for the past few months. I haven't spent enough time with my family or my law practice or on my legislative work."[124] Sometimes the pressure of public service gets to legislators. A Washington state senator, unhappy about having his integrity impugned by constituents, took to the Senate floor to rail about it. In an emotional outburst, he challenged his critics, saying, "I've had enough. If you don't like the way we do this job, you need to come down here and do it yourself."[125] At times, many of his colleagues across the country are apt to share the sentiment.

ETHICS

Most Americans do not think that state legislators rank particularly high in the political hierarchy. Yet state legislators make decisions that impact almost every aspect of daily life. Much rides on their votes; consequently, even lawmakers in the least professional bodies draw considerable attention from those with interests at stake before the legislature. Consequently, as a California senator admits, "It's a very seductive business. People want to be your friend. They shower you with gifts and meals and, while blowing smoke on your head, make you feel like you're the most wonderful person that ever stepped in the halls of Sacramento."[126] A similar assessment is offered by a Florida lawmaker: "There's this atmosphere of availability and perks. Freebie liquor. Freebie parties. Freebie food. It's almost like a temptation. You have to be strong-willed to be true."[127] Because of their power and the attention it generates, state legislators constantly confront ethical dilemmas.

Most of the ethical concerns raised about state lawmakers involve the appropriate use of their office. Part of the concern is triggered by the realities of service in states where lawmakers are not full-time legislators. This means lawmakers often have another occupation, which potentially poses a conflict of interest. Take, for example, two members of the Indiana House of Representatives: Bob Cherry and Terry Goodin. Cherry, a Republican, is director of Local Government Relations for the Indiana Farm Bureau and a farmer. Goodin, a Democrat, is the superintendent of the Crothersville Community Schools. Both are in positions where their support for various pieces of legislation—for example, tax policies that favor farmers or increased funding for public schools—could be construed as self-serving. Although they are conscious of the potential conflict, both men are comfortable that they make their decisions using appropriate criteria. Goodin states, "When I'm here, I'm a lawmaker representing all of my constituents."[128]

Despite such assurances, worries about potential conflicts still arise. South Carolina legislators who are also practicing lawyers, for example, bill clients for millions of dollars to appear on their behalf before state boards and commissions, government entities whose budgets and missions are overseen by the legislature. Good government groups, such as Common Cause, raise questions about the potential conflict, but lawmakers respond that tough disclose requirements prevent any malfeasance.[129] Other state legislators, however, speculate that stringent financial disclosure requirements may discourage people from running for office. In response to an attempt to force Oregon legislators to reveal their outside sources of income, a Republican state senator commented, "We can make this as difficult as possible for someone to serve in the legislature. If we say we're not going to trust anybody, we're not going to trust anybody."[130] Indeed, apprehensions about disclosure requirements appear to inhibit some potential state legislative candidates.[131]

Other ethical concerns are raised about the efforts of lobbyists to curry favor with legislators through free meals, trips, and gifts. State laws vary in how such lobbying efforts are treated. But even where rules are strict, they can be gotten around. In Iowa, for example, ethics rules prevent state legislators from accepting any gift of more than $3 in value. But those rules are waived for receptions and events where all 150 state legislators are invited. Consequently, in 2009, lobbyists spent almost $236,000 on some 90 receptions, many with open bars and lavish spreads of food.[132] In some states, regulations allow for other kinds of gifts. In recent years, South Carolina legislators were taken for cruises by lobbyists and given highly sought tickets to important college basketball games.[133] Generally, voters frown on such activities. A public opinion survey in Nevada found that 58 percent of Nevadans supported a ban on gifts to state lawmakers after it was revealed that 11 legislators had accepted free tickets to a Rolling Stones concert.[134] It is important to note that lobbyists engage in these activities to create goodwill with legislators. It is unlikely that votes are explicitly traded for tickets or the like.

Outright corruption, however, does occur, and some cases are blatant. In 2007, the speaker of the North Carolina House of Representatives pled guilty to bribery charges after he accepted $29,000 in cash from chiropractors to help pass legislation favorable to the profession.[135] Others cases are more subtle, such as that of a Colorado state senator who wrote to her state's Association of Realtors' political action committee, an organization that had previously opposed her election, requesting a payment of $1,400 in "reparations." She went on to tell them: "There are going to be some very important issues ahead of us. You have a choice. So do I."[136] Although the senator was forced to resign, a grand jury later declined to indict her.

Although the preceding cases were isolated acts by individual members, other incidents evidence more systemic and widespread corruption. Over the past quarter century, major scandals have enveloped several state legislatures. Known by colorful labels or FBI code names—AzScam (Arizona), Boptrot (Kentucky), Shrimp scam (California), and Operation Lost Trust (South Carolina)—these investigations resulted in a number of state legislators and others involved in the legislative process being convicted and sent to jail.[137] More recently, an undercover federal investigation called "Tennessee Waltz" resulted in five of that state's legislators being found guilty of bribery or extortion in requesting financial rewards to help pass legislation allowing a sham computer company created by the FBI to get state government contracts. In the past few years, the Alaska state legislature has also been roiled by bribery, extortion, and conspiracy charges. Among the three state legislators already convicted in this ongoing investigation is a former speaker of the house, who was secretly recorded telling an oil company executive that "I had to cheat, steal, beg, borrow and lie," to help defeat a tax provision opposed by the oil industry.[138] In return for his efforts, the lawmaker received $1,000 in cash, a check for $7,993, a public opinion survey conducted for his reelection campaign, and the promise of a high-paying job with a company. Another convicted legislator received between $2,100 to $2,600 in cash and a $3,000 summer job for his nephew.[139] The relatively small sums of money involved in these cases prompted an Alaskan humorist to sneer, "The fact of the matter is, we all want to bribe a politician. We all thought it'd take a Mercedes or a Porsche. Nobody knew you could buy a politician for the cost of a used riding lawn mower."[140]

Over time, such scandals have prompted state legislatures to adopt progressively tighter ethics laws. Consequently, state lawmakers operate under much more stringent regulations today than predecessors a generation or two ago.[141] Indeed, state legislators in 47 states now face more rigorous ethics rules than do members of Congress.[142] There is a pronounced relationship between legislative professionalization and ethics laws. The stringency of lobbying regulations and the vigor with which they are enforced increases with professionalization.[143] Similarly, more professional legislatures are more likely to adopt stricter campaign finance laws.[144]

LEGISLATIVE CAREERS AND LEGISLATURE CAREER OPPORTUNITY TYPES

As demonstrated in this chapter, state legislators operate in very different settings. This reality greatly influences their working experience. Given the different contexts in which state lawmakers operate, state legislatures offer members one of three possible legislative career opportunities. The particular career opportunity a legislature offers is dictated in part by the level of pay. As documented in Table 3-3, state legislatures vary widely in their salaries. Some of these positions pay well enough that members can contemplate service as their primary vocation. Most, however, do not compensate members well enough for them to forego their regular occupation. So based simply on the level of compensation offered, we would anticipate that some legislatures entice members to consider legislative service as their career but others do not.

Given the place of state legislatures in the American political hierarchy, there is a third potential career option. Some legislatures may be particularly well suited to serve their members as a springboard to higher political offices. That is, the current position is just a way station on the road to a more coveted elective post.

Thus, state legislatures offer their members one of three possible career opportunities. One is a *springboard legislature*, a body that gives members substantial electoral advancement opportunities. Among legislatures that do not offer members good prospects for moving up, some may be considered *career legislatures* because they offer members sufficient financial remuneration such that they can support themselves and their families from their legislative service. The other category is *dead-end legislatures*, bodies in which members cannot use to their service to advance politically and that pay so poorly that they cannot realistically be a member's primary source of income.[145]

Each of the 49 lower houses and the Nebraska Unicameral is categorized by its career type in Table 3-7. The line between career legislatures and dead-end legislature is drawn at $30,000; a salary of that figure or higher makes career service plausible. Determining whether a legislature qualifies as a springboard body is a bit more complicated. Advancement opportunities are calculated from two separate components. The first component is structural in nature: the number of higher elective offices (seats in the state senate and the U.S. House of Representatives) relative to the number of seats in the lower house. For instance, the 80 members of the California Assembly have 40 state senate seats and 53 U.S. House seats to which they can advance, a highly favorable ratio. In contrast, the 400 members of the New Hampshire House of Representatives have only 24 state senate seats and two U.S. House seats for which to shoot. Clearly, the odds of political advancement are not in their favor. The second component reflects whether, in fact, members of the lower house actually do advance to higher offices. Virtually all of the seats in the California state senate, for example, are held by former Assembly members, but almost none of the state senators in Idaho or New Mexico previously served in their state's lower house. The product of the ratio of higher seats to lower house seats and the percentage of higher seats held by former lower house members gives the advancement opportunity score. As we would expect, the score is very high for the California Assembly and very low for the New Hampshire House (and even lower for the Nebraska Unicameral).

The existence of term limits in 15 states influences the career opportunity categorization of most of their lower houses. By definition, term limits remove the possibility of service in legislative house from becoming a career. (An argument could be made that the more lenient limits in Louisiana and, perhaps, Nevada, leave open the possibility of becoming career bodies if either were to significantly increase its level of pay.) But term limits appear to have increased the number of states that fall into the springboard category. In states that have them, term limits have created something of a conveyor belt from the lower house to the state senate, with large numbers of former lower house members moving to the upper chamber as they get forced out of their current body (and as senate incumbents are forced out, creating open seats). Across the 14 term-limited states with bicameral legislatures, a mean of 69 percent of state senate seats are held by former lower house members; the mean for the 34 states without term limits is only 41 percent. Term limits have not, however, altered the career opportunity structure in every state in which they have been introduced. California, for example, was considered a springboard body even before voters forced members of the Assembly to leave after serving for only six years.[146]

STATE	SEATS IN LOWER HOUSE	SEATS IN UPPER HOUSE	SEATS IN U.S. HOUSE	TOTAL NUMBER OF HIGHER SEATS	RATIO OF HIGHER SEATS TO LOWER HOUSE SEATS	LOWER HOUSE ADVANCEMENT PROSPECT SCORE (SEAT PERCENT X RATIO)	LEGISLATURE CAREER TYPE
California[a]	80	40 (95)[b]	53 (38)	93 (62)	1.16	0.72	Springboard
Colorado	65	35 (71)	7 (86)	42 (74)	0.65	0.48	Springboard
Florida	120	40 (88)	25 (60)	65 (77)	0.54	0.42	Springboard
New Jersey	80	40 (68)	13 (46)	53 (62)	0.66	0.41	Springboard
Oregon	60	30 (73)	5 (60)	35 (71)	0.58	0.41	Springboard
Washington	98	49 (69)	9 (44)	58 (66)	0.59	0.39	Springboard
Arizona	60	30 (67)	8 (25)	38 (58)	0.63	0.37	Springboard
Michigan	110	38 (97)	15 (27)	53 (77)	0.48	0.36	Springboard
Montana	100	50 (70)	1 (100)	51 (71)	0.51	0.36	Springboard
Ohio	99	33 (79)	18 (44)	51 (67)	0.52	0.35	Springboard
Hawaii	51	25 (56)	2 (100)	27 (59)	0.53	0.31	Springboard

(Continued)

TABLE 3-7 (CONTINUED)

STATE	SEATS IN LOWER HOUSE	SEATS IN UPPER HOUSE	SEATS IN U.S. HOUSE	TOTAL NUMBER OF HIGHER SEATS	RATIO OF HIGHER SEATS TO LOWER HOUSE SEATS	LOWER HOUSE ADVANCEMENT PROSPECT SCORE (SEAT PERCENT X RATIO)	LEGISLATURE CAREER TYPE
Alaska	40	20 (55)	1 (100)	21 (57)	0.53	0.30	Springboard
Arkansas	100	35 (83)	4 (0)	39 (74)	0.39	0.29	Springboard
Nevada	42	21 (48)	3 (67)	24 (50)	0.57	0.29	Springboard
Wyoming	60	30 (53)	1 (100)	31 (55)	0.52	0.29	Springboard
Louisiana	105	39 (67)	7 (29)	46 (61)	0.44	0.27	Dead end
Wisconsin	99	33 (70)	8 (50)	41 (66)	0.41	0.27	Career
Illinois	118	59 (40)	19 (32)	78 (37)	0.66	0.24	Career
South Dakota	70	35 (49)	1 (0)	36 (47)	0.51	0.24	Dead end
Virginia	100	40 (48)	11 (45)	51 (47)	0.51	0.24	Dead end
Maryland	141	47 (57)	8 (25)	55 (53)	0.39	0.21	Career
Massachusetts	160	40 (68)	10 (50)	50 (66)	0.31	0.20	Career
New York	150	62 (26)	29 (41)	91 (31)	0.61	0.19	Career
Texas	150	31 (58)	32 (31)	63 (44)	0.42	0.19	Dead end

Utah	75	29 (45)	3 (33)	32 (44)	0.43	0.19	Dead end
Iowa	100	50 (36)	5 (0)	55 (33)	0.55	0.18	Dead end
Minnesota	134	67 (33)	8 (25)	75 (32)	0.56	0.18	Career
Delaware	41	21 (29)	1 (100)	22 (32)	0.54	0.17	Career
Missouri	163	34 (74)	9 (44)	43 (67)	0.26	0.17	Dead-end
Tennessee	99	33 (42)	9 (33)	42 (40)	0.42	0.17	Dead-end
Maine	151	35 (63)	2 (50)	37 (62)	0.25	0.16	Dead-end
Pennsylvania	203	50 (52)	19 (37)	69 (48)	0.34	0.16	Career
South Carolina	124	46 (39)	6 (33)	52 (38)	0.42	0.16	Dead end
Kentucky	100	38 (37)	6 (17)	44 (34)	0.44	0.15	Dead end
West Virginia	100	34 (33)	3 (33)	37 (38)	0.37	0.14	Dead end
Georgia	180	56 (30)	13 (38)	69 (33)	0.38	0.13	Dead end
Rhode Island	75	38 (21)	2 (100)	40 (25)	0.53	0.13	Dead end
Alabama	105	35 (31)	7 (29)	42 (31)	0.40	0.12	Dead end^c
Indiana	100	50 (22)	9 (22)	59 (22)	0.59	0.12	Dead end
North Carolina	120	50 (16)	13 (46)	63 (22)	0.53	0.12	Dead end

(Continued)

Table 3-7 (Continued)

State	Seats in Lower House	Seats in Upper House	Seats in U.S. House	Total Number of Higher Seats	Ratio of Higher Seats to Lower House Seats	Lower House Advancement Prospect Score (Seat Percent X Ratio)	Legislature Career Type
North Dakota	94	48 (21)	1 (100)	49 (23)	0.51	0.12	Dead end
Oklahoma	101	8 (17)	5 (80)	53 (23)	0.52	0.12	Dead end
Connecticut	151	36 (36)	5 (60)	41 (39)	0.27	0.11	Dead end
New Mexico	70	42 (14)	3 (33)	45 (16)	0.64	0.10	Dead end
Idaho	70	35 (14)	2 (100)	37 (19)	0.53	0.10	Dead end
Kansas	125	40 (30)	4 (0)	44 (27)	0.35	0.09	Dead end
Mississippi	122	52 (15)	4 (0)	56 (14)	0.42	0.06	Dead end
Vermont	150	30 (23)	1 (0)	31 (23)	0.21	0.05	Dead end
New Hampshire	400	24 (54)	2 (0)	26 (50)	0.07	0.04	Dead end
Nebraska	49	-	3 (33)	3 (33)	0.06	0.02	Dead end

Sources: Data collected by the authors from state legislature web pages and Project Vote Smart.

[a]States in italics have term limits.

[b]Numbers in parentheses are the percent of seats in category held by former members of the lower house.

[c]Given the great disparity in Alabama between salary and salary including unvouchered expenses, the legislature would be considered to be a career body if the latter criterion was used.

CONCLUSION

State legislators operate in a wide range of institutions. Some state legislatures are professionalized along the lines of Congress. Members in these bodies are able to devote themselves to legislative service and have staff and facilities to greatly assist them in their efforts. Other lawmakers serve in much less professionalized legislatures. They must juggle public service with the demands of their other occupations. Moreover, they have little in the way of staff to help them with their legislative work. Different kinds of people are attracted to service in different kinds of legislatures. Legislatures offer different career opportunities to their members based on the salaries and political advancement opportunities they offer.

What difference does career opportunity structure make for a legislature? Being a springboard body, for example, has important consequences for legislative organization and member behavior. Legislators in springboard bodies tend to be more responsive to constituents on policy preferences than are their counterparts in other sorts of legislatures.[147] Organizationally, members of springboard legislatures make different sorts of demands on their leaders than do members of career or dead-end legislatures.[148]

In the next chapter, we shift our focus to questions of legislative organization and structure, specifically the roles played by legislative parties, leadership, and standing committees. Each of these items will be assessed in the light of contrasting levels of legislative professionalization. We will also more fully investigate questions about the impact of career opportunity structures on legislative organization.

ENDNOTES

1. http://legisweb.state.wy.us/LegislatorSummary/LegDetail.aspx?LegID=1090.
2. Citizen's Guide to the Wyoming Legislature (http://legisweb.state.wy.us/leginfo/guide98.htm#citizen).
3. http://www.ncsl.org/default.aspx?tabid=14785. In May 2009, the California Citizens Compensation Committee decreed that the salary paid to the state's legislators will be cut by 18 percent to $95,291, starting in December, 2010.
4. Brian Joseph, "Lawmakers Capitalizing on Cars," Orange County Register, August 1, 2006.
5. This information was gleaned from the senator's web page (http://dist08.casen.govoffice.com).
6. Michael B. Berkman, "Former State Legislators in the U. S. House of Representatives: Institutional and Policy Mastery," Legislative Studies Quarterly 18 (1993): 77–104; William D. Berry, Michael B. Berkman, and Stuart Schneiderman, "Legislative Professionalism and Incumbent Reelection: The Development of Institutional Boundaries," American Political Science Review 94 (2002): 859–874; Ann O'M. Bowman and Richard C. Kearney, "Dimensions of State Government Capability," Western Political Quarterly 41 (1988): 341–362; John M. Carey, Richard G. Niemi, and Lynda W. Powell, "Incumbency and the Probability of Reelection in State Legislative Elections," Journal of Politics 62 (2000): 671–700; James D. King, "Changes in Professionalism in U.S. State Legislatures," Legislative Studies Quarterly 25 (2000): 327–343; Gary F. Moncrief, "Dimensions of the Concept of Professionalism in State Legislatures: A Research Note," State and Local Government Review 20 (1988): 128–132; Peverill Squire,

"Legislative Professionalization and Membership Diversity in State Legislatures," *Legislative Studies Quarterly* 17 (1992): 69–79; Peverill Squire, "Uncontested Seats in State Legislative Elections," *Legislative Studies Quarterly* 25 (2000): 131–146; Peverill Squire, "Measuring Legislative Professionalism: The Squire Index Revisited," *State Politics and Policy Quarterly* 7 (2007): 211–227.

7. See Wayne L. Francis, "Costs and Benefits of Legislative Service in the American States," *American Journal of Political Science* 29 (1985): 626–642.

8. Peverill Squire, "Career Opportunities and Membership Stability in Legislatures," *Legislative Studies Quarterly* 13 (1988): 65–82.

9. Alan Rosenthal, "State Legislative Development: Observations from Three Perspectives," *Legislative Studies Quarterly* 21 (1996): 169–198.

10. Rosenthal, "State Legislative Development," 171–172.

11. William D. Berry, Michael B. Berkman, and Stuart Schneiderman, "Legislative Professionalism and Incumbent Reelection: The Development of Institutional Boundaries," *American Political Science Review* 94 (2000): 859–874; Gary Moncrief, Richard G. Niemi, and Lynda W. Powell, "Time, Term Limits, and Turnover: Membership Stability in U.S. State Legislatures," *Legislative Studies Quarterly* 29 (2004): 357–381.

12. Cherie Maestas, "The Incentive to Listen: Progressive Ambition, Resources, and Opinion Monitoring among State Legislators," *Journal of Politics* 65 (2003): 439–456; Peverill Squire, "Professionalism and Public Opinion of State Legislatures," *Journal of Politics* 55 (1993): 479–491; and Gerald Wright, "Do Term Limits Affect Legislative Roll Call Voting? Representation, Polarization, and Participation," *State Politics and Policy Quarterly* 7: 256–280.

13. Peverill Squire, "Membership Turnover and the Efficient Processing of Legislation," *Legislative Studies Quarterly* 23 (1998): 23–32.

14. Sangjoon Ka and Paul Teske, "Ideology and Professionalism—Electricity Regulation and Deregulation Over Time in the American States," *American Politics Research* 30 (2002): 323–343; J. E. Kellough and S. C. Selden, "The Reinvention of Public Personnel Administration: An Analysis of the Diffusion of Personnel Management Reforms in the States," *Public Administration Review* 63 (2003): 165–176; Thad Kousser, *Term Limits and the Dismantling of State Legislative Professionalism* (New York: Cambridge University Press, 2005); Charles R. Shipan and Craig Volden, "Bottom-Up Federalism: The Diffusion of Anti-smoking Policies from U.S. Cities to States," *American Journal of Political Science* 50 (2006): 825–843; Joel Slemrod, "The Etiology of Tax Complexity: Evidence from U.S. State Income Tax Systems," *Public Finance Review* 33 (2005): 279–299; Robert C. Turner and Mark K. Cassell, "When Do States Pursue Targeted Economic Development Policies? The Adoption and Expansion of State Enterprise Zone Programs," *Social Science Quarterly* 88 (2007): 86–103; Neal D. Woods, "The Policy Consequences of Political Corruption: Evidence from State Environmental Programs," *Social Science Quarterly* 89 (2008): 258–271.

15. Frederick J. Boehmke, "Sources of Variation in the Frequency of Statewide Initiatives: The Role of Interest Group Populations," *Political Research Quarterly* 58 (2005): 565–575.

16. See Bill Boyarsky, *Big Daddy: Jesse Unruh and the Art of Power Politics* (Berkeley, CA: University of California Press, 2008), 163–172; Citizens Conference on State Legislatures, *State Legislatures: An Evaluation of Their Effectiveness* (New York: Praeger, 1971); Donald G. Herzberg, and Alan Rosenthal, *Strengthening the States: Essays on Legislative Reform* (Garden City, NY: Doubleday, 1971); Jesse Unruh, "Science in Law-Making," *National Civic Review* 54 (1965): 466–472; Alan Wyner, "Legislative Reform and Politics in California: What Happened, Why, and So What?" in *State Legislative Innovation*, ed. James A. Robinson (New York: Praeger, 1973).

17. Squire, "Measuring Legislative Professionalism: The Squire Index Revisited," and Peverill Squire, and Keith E. Hamm, *101 Chambers: Congress, State Legislatures, and the Future of Legislative Studies* (Columbus, OH: Ohio State University Press, 2005), Chapter 3.

18. A detailed explanation of how this measure is calculated can be found in Squire, "Measuring Legislative Professionalism: The Squire Index Revisited."

19. Tyler Whitley, "This is Not Something You Do for the Money," *Richmond Times-Dispatch*, February 11, 2007.

20. Jack Penchoff, "Legislative Pay Daze," *State News*, February 2007. The longitudinal salary study discussed in the article was conducted by the Council on State Governments.

21. Peverill Squire, "The State Wealth-Legislative Compensation Effect," *Canadian Journal of Political Science* 41 (2008): 1–18.

22. Tom Rafferty, "Informal Poll: Lawmakers Pay Part of Lodging," *Bismarck Tribune*, April 6, 2005.
23. Leslie Reed, "Legislators Reimbursed $490,202," *Omaha World-Herald*, July 1, 2007.
24. Conrad Defiebre, "State Legislators Get Healthy Expense Raises," Minneapolis *Star Tribune*, January 10, 2007.
25. Andy Sher, "Legislators' Annual Pay is $50,000 to $60,000," *Chattanooga Times Free Press*, April 22, 2007.
26. Sher, "Legislators' Annual Pay is $50,000 to $60,000."
27. Jim Sanders, "Lawmakers' Per Diem Goes Up—Retroactively," *Sacramento Bee* Capitol Alert, October 23, 2008.
28. Dan Walters, "Legislative Per Diem is Boondoggle," *Sacramento Bee*, July 9, 2007.
29. Walters, "Legislative Per Diem is Boondoggle." The favorable tax treatment can be found in the Internal Revenue Code, Title 26, Subtitle A, Chapter 1, Subchapter B, Part VI, Section 162 (h).
30. Joseph, "Lawmakers Capitalizing on Cars;" Kevin Yamamura and Jim Sanders, "Senate, Assembly Get Deals on Wheels," *Sacramento Bee*, December 19, 2002.
31. John M. R. Bull, "State Lawmakers' Car Leases $1.5 Million per Year," Pittsburgh *Post-Gazette*; Mario Cattabiani, "State House's New Rules," *Philadelphia Inquirer*, March 14, 2007.
32. Rick Harmon, "Rep. Holmes alleges AU ticket snub," *Montgomery Advertiser*, November 28, 2007.
33. *Houston Chronicle*, "Thrifty Lawmakers get Prison Bargains," February 8, 2006.
34. Wes Allison, "Infusion of Lawmakers/Perquisites, Parties on Assembly's Agenda," Richmond *Times-Dispatch*, January 13, 1999.
35. *Grand Island Independent*, "Senators Don't Get Paycheck Due to Higher Insurance Costs," February 1, 2006.
36. See the weblog of Utah Representative Craig A. Frank for September 24, 2006 (http://underthedome.org/?p=54).
37. Amendment 57 to the 1901 constitution.
38. See the New Hampshire Constitution, Part Second, article 15, as amended in 1889: "The presiding officers of both houses of the legislature, shall severally receive out of the state treasury as compensation in full for their services for the term elected the sum of $250, and all other members thereof, seasonably attending and not departing without license, the sum of $200."
39. See the Texas Constitution, Article 3, Section 24(a), "Members of the Legislature shall receive from the Public Treasury a salary of Six Hundred Dollars ($600) per month, unless a greater amount is recommended by the Texas Ethics Commission and approved by the voters of this State in which case the salary is that amount." The procedure involving the Ethics Commission recommendation followed by a public vote has never been used since it was placed in the constitution by the voters in 1991.
40. Rhode Island Constitution, Article 6, Section 3: "Commencing in January 1995, senators and representatives shall be compensated at an annual rate of ten thousand dollars ($10,000). Commencing in 1996, the rate of compensation shall be adjusted annually to reflect changes in the cost of living, as determined by the United States government, during a twelve (12) month period ending in the immediately preceding year."
41. These data are from *The Book of the States 2007* (Lexington, KY: Council of State Governments, 2007), 90–91.
42. Johanna Donlin, "Compensation Commissions," *Legisbrief* 7 (November/December 1999).
43. See, for example, Andrew Garber, "State Lawmakers Object, Get Raises Anyway," *Seattle Times*, May 20, 2003.
44. David C. Valentine, "Citizens' Commission on Compensation for Elected Officials," Missouri Legislative Academy, Report 16-2006, November 2006.
45. David White, "62% Raise Divides Area Legislators," *Birmingham News*, March 20, 2007.
46. Lisa Demer, "Politicos Agree to Big Raise," *Anchorage Daily News*, July 6, 2005.
47. Gary Delsohn, "Governor Rips Legislators Over Their Pay Raise," *Sacramento Bee*, May 26, 2005.
48. Steve Law, "Lawmakers Say Minority Ranks are Far Too Low," Salem *Statesman Journal*, February 12, 2004.
49. Tom Barnes, "State Senate, House Members Get 2.4% Pay Raise," *Pittsburgh Post-Gazette*, December 2, 2003.

50. Tom Searls, "House OKs $5,000 Raise," *Charleston Gazette*, February 27, 2008.
51. Roger Myers, "Jennison Backs Legislative Pay Raise," Topeka *Capital-Journal*, October 19, 2000.
52. Nate Jenkins, "Lawmakers Take Step Toward Asking for Pay Raise," Associated Press State & Local Wire, May 18, 2007.
53. Mal Leary, "Legislative Pay Hike Proposed in Augusta," *Bangor Daily News*, April 4, 2007.
54. Dale Wetzel, "Lawmakers Get Session Pay Raise," *Bismarck Tribune*, April 1, 2005.
55. Bob Johnson, "Lawmakers Blasted Over Pay Raise," *Montgomery Advertiser*, March 13, 2007.
56. Comments on the *Bangor Daily News* website, April 4, 2007, in response to Leary, "Legislative Pay Hike Proposed in Augusta."
57. Jim McLean, "House Votes Against Pay Increase," Topeka *Capital-Journal*, March 13, 2001.
58. Michele McNeil Solida, "159% Lawmaker Pay Hike Urged," *Indianapolis Star*, August 27, 2004.
59. Niki Kelly, "Daniels OKs Legislative Pay Raises," Fort Wayne *Journal Gazette*, April 25, 2007; Mary Beth Schneider, "Plan Doubles Lawmaker Pay, Ensures Raises," *Indianapolis Star*, February 21, 2007.
60. See Florida Statutes 2007, Title III, Chapter 11.13: "Compensation of members, (b) Effective July 1, 1986, and each July 1 thereafter, the annual salaries of members of the Senate and House of Representatives shall be adjusted by the average percentage increase in the salaries of state career service employees for the fiscal year just concluded. The Appropriations Committee of each house shall certify to the Office of Legislative Services the average percentage increase in the salaries of state career service employees before July 1 of each year. The Office of Legislative Services shall, as of July 1 of each year, determine the adjusted annual salaries as provided herein."
61. Montana Statutes of 2005, 5-2-301: "Compensation and expenses for members while in session. (1) Legislators are entitled to a salary commensurate to that of the daily rate of an entry grade 10 classified state employee in effect when the regular session of the legislature in which they serve is convened . . ." See also http://leg.mt.gov/css/For%20Legislators/compensation.asp.
62. David Abel, "Romney OK's Pay Increases for Lawmakers," *Boston Globe*, January 4, 2007; Rick Klein, "Legislative Pay Raise a Political Hot Potato," *Boston Globe*, December 26, 2002.
63. Ed Anderson, "20 Legislators Will Abstain from Pay Raise," New Orleans *Times-Picayune*, June 18, 2008; Sarah Chacko and Marsha Shuler, "Legislative Raises get Final Approval, Bill gets Just Enough Votes," *The Advocate*, June 17, 2008.
64. *Topeka Capital-Journal*, "Alldritt Expects to Resign House Seat," November 27, 2001.
65. Scott Rothschild, "State Lawmaker Seeks Raise in Pay—To Poverty Level," *Lawrence Journal-World*, April 20, 2007.
66. Lee Davidson and Bob Bernick, Jr., "Campaign Funds for Clothes, Nannies?" *Deseret Morning News*, April 9, 2007.
67. Jonathan Roos and Tim Higgins, "Gridlock," *Des Moines Register*, April 26, 2005; Leslie Reed, "Some State Senators Must Decide: Serve the Voters or Pay Bills?" *Omaha World-Herald*, December 9, 2007; Lisa Sandberg, "Sessions Upend Legislators' Lives," San Antonio *Express-News*, July 31, 2005.
68. Andrea Fanta, "Bill Would Raise Lawmaker Pay, But Plan Stalls in Election Year," *St. Petersburg Times*, April 9, 2006.
69. William J. Keefe, and Morris S. Ogul, *The American Legislative Process: Congress and the States*, 10th ed. (Upper Saddle River, NJ: Prentice Hall, 2001), 71; Belle Zeller, ed. *American State Legislatures* (New York: Crowell, 1954), 89.
70. James Bryce, *The American Commonwealth*, abridged and revised ed (New York: Macmillan, 1906), 337; Robert Luce, *Legislative Assemblies* (Boston: Houghton Mifflin, 1924), 129–130.
71. Alabama did not change to biennial sessions until 1939. See Alden J. Powell, "Constitutional Growth and Revision in the South," *Journal of Politics* 10 (1948): 354–384.
72. In 2008, however, Oregon began experimenting with holding an extended special session during the off-year as a possible prelude to a campaign to allow for annual sessions. See David Steves, "Lawmakers' Experiment," *The Register-Guard*, February 4, 2008.
73. Rosenthal, "State Legislative Development," 192.
74. These data are tabulated from *The Book of the States 2007 edition*, 76–79, and the National Conference of State Legislatures, "Legislative Sessions" (http://www.ncsl.org/Programs/Legman/about/sesslimits.htm).

75. See Article 3, Section 6.

76. These data were calculated by the authors from the Utah State Legislature, Legislative Calendar.

77. These data were calculated by the authors from the Wisconsin Legislature's, "2007-2008 Session Schedule at a Glance."

78. The data on the California Assembly are taken from the *Assembly Daily File* for September 11, 2007. The data on the California Senate are taken from the *Senate Daily File* for October 9, 2007.

79. Karl T. Kurtz, Gary Moncrief, Richard G. Niemi, and Lynda W. Powell, "Full-Time, Part-Time, and Real Time: Explaining State Legislators' Perceptions of Time on the Job," *State Politics and Policy Quarterly* 6 (2006): 322–338. A second, smaller, survey of legislators in five states reached a similar conclusion. See Alan Rosenthal, *Heavy Lifting: The Job of the American Legislature* (Washington, DC: CQ Press, 2004), 22.

80. Kurtz, Moncrief, Niemi, and Powell, "Full-Time, Part-Time, and Real Time."

81. *Black Hills Pioneer*, "South Dakota Lawmakers Say Duties Amount to Half-time Job," July 7, 2003.

82. Squire and Hamm, *101 Chambers*, 76–78.

83. Alan Rosenthal, *Legislative Life* (New York: Harper & Row, 1981), 206–207.

84. See *The Book of the States 2007 edition*, 124–127.

85. Elizabeth M. Cox, *Women, State and Territorial Legislatures, 1895–1995: A State-by-State Analysis, with Rosters of 6,000 Women* (Jefferson, NC: McFarland, 1996), 329.

86. These data are taken from the Center for American Women in Politics (http://www.rci.rutgers.edu/~cawp/Facts/Officeholders/stleg.pdf), as of December 2008.

87. R. Darcy, "Women in the State Legislative Power Structure: Committee Chairs," *Social Science Quarterly* 77 (1996): 888–911; Thomas H. Little, Dana Dunn, and Rebecca E. Dean, "A View from the Top: Gender Differences in Leadership Priorities among State Legislative Leaders," *Women and Politics* 22 (2001): 29–50; Donald E. Whistler and Mark C. Ellickson, "The Incorporation of Women in State Legislatures: A Description," *Women and Politics* 20 (1999): 81–97.

88. Squire and Hamm, *101 Chambers*, 138.

89. Becki Scola, "Women of Color in State Legislatures: Gender, Race, Ethnicity and Legislative Office Holding," *Journal of Women, Politics, & Policy* 28 (2006): 43–70.

90. Byron D'Andra Orey, L. Marvin Overby, and Christopher W. Larimer, "African-American Committee Chairs in U.S. State Legislatures," *Social Science Quarterly* 88 (2007): 619–639.

91. Kerry L. Haynie, *African American Legislators in the American States* (New York: Columbia University Press, 2001).

92. Jack E. Holmes, *Politics in New Mexico* (Albuquerque, NM: University of New Mexico Press, 1967), 230.

93. Kathleen A. Bratton, "The Behavior and Success of Latino State Legislators: Evidence from the States," *Social Science Quarterly* 87 (2006): 1136–1157.

94. Robert R. Preuhs, "Descriptive Representation as a Mechanism to Mitigate Policy Backlash," *Political Research Quarterly* 60 (2007): 277–292.

95. See National Caucus of Native American State Legislators (http://www.ncsl.org/?TabID=756&tabs=951,70,389#951).

96. These data are taken from the National Caucus of Native American State Legislators (http://www.ncsl.org/?TabID=756&tabs=951,70,389#951). See also Isaac Smith, "Tribal Membership in the 51th Oklahoma House of Representatives," Oklahoma House of Representatives, July 9, 2007 (http://www.okhouse.gov/Documents/TribalMembership.doc).

97. See A Brief History of Indian Legislative Representations (http://www.maine.gov/legis/lawlib/indianreps.htm).

98. Squire, "Legislative Professionalization and Membership Diversity in State Legislatures."

99. The state conservatism scores are taken from data for 2003 gathered by Erikson, Wright, and McIver (http://mypage.iu.edu/~wright1/).

100. These expectations are based on Squire, "Legislative Professionalization and Membership Diversity in State Legislatures."

101. These data were gathered by the authors from the Gay and Lesbian Leadership Institute (http://www.glli.org/out_officials/search).

102. Donald Haider-Markel, "Representation and Backlash: The Positive and Negative Influence of Descriptive Representation," *Legislative Studies Quarterly* 32 (2007): 107–133.

103. Ann Morse, "Oath of Citizenship to Oath of Office," *State Legislatures* (May 2006), 29–30.
104. Morse, "Oath of Citizenship to Oath of Office."
105. Squire and Hamm, *101 Chambers*, 131–133.
106. Squire and Hamm, *101 Chambers*, 134–135.
107. Beth Bazar, *State Legislators' Occupations: A Decade of Change* (Denver: National Conference of State Legislatures, 1987), 4; Alan Rosenthal, "The Legislative Institution: Transformed and at Risk," in *The State of the States*, ed. Carl E. Van Horn (Washington DC: CQ Press, 1989), 72.
108. David R. Derge, "The Lawyer as Decision-Maker in the American State Legislature," *Journal of Politics* 21 (1959): 408–433; David R. Derge, "The Lawyer in the Indiana General Assembly," *Midwest Journal of Political Science* 6 (1962): 19–53; Gerard Padró I. Miquel and James M. Snyder, Jr., "Legislative Effectiveness and Legislative Careers," *Legislative Studies Quarterly* 31 (2006): 347–381.
109. On the lack of attorneys serving in Delaware, see Bazar, *State Legislators' Occupations*, 33; and Squire and Hamm, *101 Chambers*, 131.
110. John Reitmeyer, "Must Choose Between Local, State Needs," (Bergen County) *The Record*, April 21, 2008; Trish G. Graber, "Change of Political Plans for Sweeney," (Easton, PA) *Express-Times*, April 3, 2008.
111. Mitch Lipka, "N.J. Legislators are Doing Double Duty," *Philadelphia Inquirer*, June 18, 2003.
112. K. Mark Takai, "An Analysis of State Legislators Who Also Currently Serve in the Military (National Guard or Reserve)," National Conference of State Legislatures, August 8, 2007.
113. Taken from the entries for March 11, 2007, "A Week in the Life, Part One," and March 10, 2007, "A Week in the Life, Part Two" (http://www.politicalparlor.net/wp/posts-from-the-legislature/page/8/).
114. Jane Carroll Andrade, "Keeping in Touch," *State Legislatures*, February 2006.
115. Andrade, "Keeping in Touch."
116. Tom Gorman, "Part-Time Legislature Suits Most Nevadans Just Fine," *Los Angeles Times*, February 5, 2001.
117. Andrade, "Keeping in Touch."
118. Stacy Forster, "Legislative Expenses Drive Up the Price of Government," Milwaukee *Journal Sentinel*, October 16, 2004.
119. J. Taylor Rushing, "Recovering Davis Files Film Bill," *Florida Times-Union*, March 11, 2007.
120. Elizabeth Pierce, "Legislators Give Up Weekends for Cracker Barrels," *Yankton Daily Press & Dakotan*, January 12, 2002.
121. Kirsten Stewart, "Extend Session for Two Weeks? Thanks but No Thanks, Legislators Decide," *Salt Lake Tribune*, January 31, 2003.
122. Jim Sanders, "Núñez's Young Son Applauds Loss," *Sacramento Bee* Capitol Alert, February 8, 2008.
123. Amie Van OverMeer, "Women Advised to be Candidates," *Des Moines Register*, October 7, 2001.
124. James Q. Lynch, "Freshman Legislators Learn Tough Lessons," *Cedar Rapids Gazette*, May 14, 2001.
125. Chris McGann, "Legislature: We've Had an Awful Session," *Seattle Post-Intelligencer*, April 14, 2005.
126. Aurelio Rojas, "Illness under Control, Firebaugh Fights Back," *Sacramento Bee*, March 29, 2004.
127. Cara Buckley, "Tallahassee Politicking Hasn't Shed Frat-House Reputation," *Miami Herald*, May 5, 2005.
128. Michele McNeil Solida and Jennifer Wagner, "Lawmakers' Job Conflicts are Obscured, Defended," *Indianapolis Star*, January 22, 2002.
129. Jeff Stensland, "Potential Conflicts of Interest Rife in S.C.," Columbia *The State*, July 3, 2005.
130. Janie Har and Dave Hogan, "Bill Aims to Reveal Legislators' Outside Income," *The Oregonian*, February 21, 2007.
131. Beth A. Rosenson, "The Impact of Ethics Laws on Legislative Recruitment and the Occupational Composition of State Legislatures," *Political Research Quarterly* 59 (2006): 619–627.
132. Chase Davis, "Interest-Group Tab for Legislative Receptions Nears $236,000," *Des Moines Register*, May 14, 2009.

133. Aaron Gould Shenin, "S.C. Legislators Wined and Dined," Columbia *The State*, July 3, 2005.

134. Ed Vogel, "Poll: Public Disapproves of Lawmaker Gifts," *Las Vegas Review-Journal*, April 11, 2006.

135. Christopher A. Cooper, "The People's Branch," in *The New Politics of North Carolina*, ed. Christopher A. Cooper and H. Gibbs Knotts (Chapel Hill, NC: University of North Carolina Press, 2008), 152–153; Dan Kane, Lynn Bonner, and Barbara Barrett, "Speaker Says New Rules Will Open Process," Charlotte *News & Observer*, March 1, 2007.

136. Chris Frates, "Senator Recall, DA Probe Afoot," *Denver Post*, March 7, 2006.

137. See Alan Rosenthal, *The Decline of Representative Democracy* (Washington, DC: CQ Press, 1998), 92–93.

138. Lisa Demer, Don Hunter, and Sabra Ayres, "Kohring also Charged with Bribery, Extortion," *Anchorage Daily News*, May 4, 2007.

139. See the Anchorage Daily News web summary of the investigation, David Hulen and Rich Mauer, "The Alaska Political Corruption Investigation," October 29, 2007 (http://community.adn.com/adn/node/112569).

140. Karl Vick, "I'll Sell My Soul to the Devil," *Washington Post*, November 12, 2007.

141. See Beth A. Rosenson, *The Shadowlands of Conduct* (Washington, DC: Georgetown University Press, 2005).

142. Leah Rush and David Jimenez, "States Outpace Congress in Upgrading Lobbying Laws," The Center for Public Integrity, March 1, 2006 (http://projects.publicintegrity.org/hiredguns/report.aspx?aid=781).

143. Cynthia Opheim, "Explaining the Differences in State Lobby Regulation," *Western Political Quarterly* 44 (1991): 405–421.

144. Christopher Witko, "Explaining Increases in the Stringency of State Campaign Finance Regulation, 1993–2002," *State Politics and Policy Quarterly* 7 (2007): 369–393.

145. Squire, "Career Opportunities and Membership Stability in Legislatures," and Peverill Squire, "Member Career Opportunities and the Internal Organization of Legislatures," *Journal of Politics* 50 (1988): 726–744.

146. Squire, "Career Opportunities and Membership Stability in Legislatures," and Squire, "Member Career Opportunities and the Internal Organization of Legislatures."

147. Cherie Maestas, "Professional Legislatures and Ambitious Politicians: Policy Responsiveness of State Institutions," *Legislative Studies Quarterly* 25 (2000): 663–690.

148. Richard A. Clucas, "Principal-Agent Theory and the Power of State House Speakers," *Legislative Studies Quarterly* 26 (2001): 319–338; and Squire, "Career Opportunities and Membership Stability in Legislatures."

CHAPTER 4

LEGISLATIVE ORGANIZATION ACROSS THE STATES

In 2008, William McCoy served as the speaker of the Mississippi House of Representatives. That same year, James Amann served as the speaker of the Connecticut House of Representatives. Both leaders were granted similar formal powers. Both, for example, exercised the authority to appoint members and chairs for almost all of the committees in their chambers.[1] But the similarities in their positions were superficial because the organizations they oversaw are remarkably different.

Speaker McCoy enjoyed an unusual position compared with his counterparts in other states. Except for a speaker pro tempore, there are no other party leaders in the Mississippi House. Indeed, the speaker is chosen by the entire House membership, not by a party caucus.[2] The lack of party organization is a remnant of the time when, as noted in Chapter 2, only Democrats held seats in the Mississippi House. In the absence of a two-party system, there was no need for the development of elaborate party leadership structures.[3] In contrast, in Connecticut, where Republicans and Democrats have long competed on relatively even terms, the House is organized around party. It has an elaborate leadership structure. Speaker Amann was joined in the majority party leadership by a majority leader, four deputy speakers of the house, an assistant deputy speaker of the house, six deputy majority leaders, a party caucus chair, a deputy party caucus chair, a majority whip-at-large, a deputy majority whip-at-large, three deputy majority whips, seven assistant majority whips, and 18 assistant majority leaders. Another 22 representatives held positions in the minority party leadership structure.

Committees were also organized very differently in the two houses. In Mississippi, the legislative workload in the House was divided among 44 standing committees. The Connecticut House has evolved a very different committee system. In 2008, it employed 23 standing committees and four select committees. In addition, all of these committees were joint committees, meaning that members of the House and the state Senate serve on them together.

It is worth pointing out that neither the Connecticut House nor the Mississippi House was organized in the same fashion as the U.S. House of Representatives. Indeed, examination of the organizational features of the 99 state legislative chambers reveals that none of them exactly mirrors its federal counterpart. Moreover, although state legislative houses share some notable organizational similarities, they each typically have a few distinctive features. Thus, state legislatures are not smaller or simpler versions of Congress or of each other. They have evolved a wide range of organizational structures, all of which influence the process by which they make decisions and the policies they produce.

In this chapter, we examine the roles legislative parties, leadership, and standing committees play in state legislatures. Each constitutes an important and distinct part of the legislative system, yet they are intertwined. Parties are the main organizational vehicle for the legislature. Committees do much of the legislative work. Leadership makes the various parts of the process function together. Collectively, parties, leaders, and committees structure how legislatures make decisions.

LEGISLATIVE PARTIES

In one way or another, political parties organize every state legislature, except for Nebraska, which is nonpartisan. As a now classic text observed: "In most two-party legislatures, the presiding officer is selected by the majority party caucus, the members of which will normally unite behind that choice in balloting on the floor of the house or senate."[4] Leaders are chosen in an organizational session usually held in December, after the election but before the convening of the legislature in regular session. If there are several people in the majority party caucus seeking the position of, say, speaker of the House, there will be a vote in the caucus to choose the party's nominee. The nominee must then be approved by the entire membership of the House. Obviously, the normal process is for all the members of the majority party to vote for the majority party nominee, and thus that person becomes speaker. Although that is what happens most of the time, the past 30 years has witnessed the occasional formation of bipartisan coalitions to elect state legislative leaders, something that does not happen in Congress. Chambers in Alaska, California, Connecticut, Illinois, Massachusetts, Montana, New Mexico, North Carolina, Pennsylvania, Tennessee, Vermont, and Washington have experienced one or more such coalitions.[5] In the closely divided Tennessee Senate, for example, Democratic Speaker John Wilder was reelected in 2005 only when two Republicans defected from their party's candidate and voted for him. Wilder lost the position in 2007 when a Democrat jumped ship to vote for the Republican candidate.[6] In 2009, the 49 Tennessee House Democrats joined with Kent Williams, a renegade second-term

Republican representative, to make him speaker on a 50 to 49 vote, frustrating the desires of the rest of the Republicans who thought they held the majority. Williams' victory was accompanied by "loud booing" and shouts of "traitor," "sell-out," and "Judas" from the public gallery.[7]

Why would some members of the majority party vote against their own party's nominee, throwing in with the minority party nominee? This is a risky maneuver because if it is unsuccessful, these "turncoats" are likely to be punished. They will be given the less desirable committee assignments, and any bills they introduce are likely to be buried by the leadership. They may be kicked out of their own party caucus, as Tennessee Speaker Williams was by the Republicans after he was elected with Democratic votes. (Williams took to officially labeling himself a "Carter County Republican" in honor of his home county.) Unhappy leaders might even encourage a challenger to them in the next primary election.

Such "revolts" by some members of the majority may be the result of ideological factions with strong issue differences. But the more typical situation is one in which deep dissatisfaction with the actions and conduct of an incumbent leader leads disaffected party members to seek an accommodation with the opposition party. In the Missouri House in 2008, for example, although they were members of the majority, a group of unhappy Republicans approached the Democratic minority leader to investigate the chances they might combine forces to overthrow the speaker. The minority leader observed that the majority had "some serious problems of sticking together, and their major priorities aren't going to pass . . . there's some discontent within the [GOP] caucus."[8]

Some of the bipartisan coalitions that form last over a full session or two; others are, in the words of a Connecticut representative, only "one-day dates."[9] And some of the coalitions make for very odd bedfellows. In 1981, Republican votes elevated Willie Brown, a very liberal African American from San Francisco, to the speakership of the California Assembly. Brown went on to become the bane of California Republicans; indeed, the term limits movement in California was partly pursued by the GOP as a means of dislodging Brown from the speakership that their votes had originally made possible.[10]

Although party is the main organizing device in state legislatures, party competition is not a constant; at different points in time, many states have been dominated by a single party. As noted in Chapter 2, as recently as the early 1960s, there were *no* Republican state legislators in Alabama, Arkansas, Georgia, Louisiana, Mississippi, South Carolina, and Texas, and there were only a handful in Florida, Maryland, New Mexico, North Carolina, Oklahoma, Tennessee, and Virginia. Over the course of the next 40 years, the situation changed, in some states dramatically.[11] By the beginning of the 2000s, both parties were represented in every legislature, although each party had a few chambers in which it enjoyed very large majorities. The

process of moving from a one- to a two-party house has important consequences for legislative organization, with partisan structures such as
caucuses developing only after the minority party size reaches roughly one-
third of the seats in a chamber. At that point, voting also becomes organized
by partisanship rather than by factional allegiances.[12]

Parties in state legislative chambers differ from those in Congress and
among each other in several additional ways. They vary in the power exercised by party caucuses. In some legislative chambers, party caucuses are
powerful, even to the point of making votes binding on certain important
issues, as in the New Mexico and Oklahoma legislatures.[13] But in other
state legislative chambers, caucuses are very weak or even essentially nonexistent. The importance of party caucuses also varies over time. As many as
one-quarter of the strong-party caucuses in the 1950s were not considered
powerful by the 1980s.[14] In Colorado, for example, caucus decisions used to
be binding on member floor votes. But in 1988, Colorado voters passed the
GAVEL (Give a Vote to Every Legislator) amendment outlawing the practice.[15] The importance of party caucuses appears to be a function of the size
and the degree of party competition in the chamber. The more evenly
matched the parties and the smaller the chamber, the greater the importance
of caucuses.[16]

Parties also vary in the power and influence exercised by legislative
campaign committees.[17] In some states, party campaign committees controlled by the legislative leadership are responsible for raising the bulk of the
money members spend on their reelection efforts. In New York, for example,
legislative candidates get almost no money from their state party organizations. Instead, legislative campaign committees raise substantial sums for
their election efforts. These committees also help recruit candidates to run
for the legislature.[18] In other states, campaign fundraising falls almost exclusively on the members themselves. Overall, the power and influence parties
have to affect the ability of their members to achieve their policy or career
goals vary substantially across states and over time.

LEGISLATIVE LEADERSHIP

Legislatures are created as egalitarian institutions, with each legislator exercising a single, equally weighted vote. State constitutions provide for minimal leadership, typically a speaker in the lower house and a president in the
upper house. Over time, however, most state legislatures have evolved
much more elaborate leadership structures, with floor leaders and a host of
whips, deputies, and assistants. Such leadership structures arise because of
the need to try to organize the preferences of legislators and to coordinate
their efforts to reach decisions. But because of the reality that legislators are
created equal, being a legislative leader is challenging. A former speaker of

the North Carolina House likens trying to lead lawmakers to "pushing a wheelbarrow full of frogs."[19]

Unlike legislators, legislative leaders are not created the same. Some enjoy far more power than others. One reason they differ is the leadership structure in which they operate. Where there are fewer leadership positions, more power can be concentrated in the top leader's hands. As suggested by the comparison between the Connecticut and Mississippi houses that opened this chapter, leadership structures vary greatly across state legislatures.[20] Among the lower houses, Louisiana and Mississippi have just two leaders: a speaker and a speaker pro tempore. The other extreme is anchored by the Connecticut House, which has 62 leadership posts. Regardless of the number of leadership posts, as Table 4-1 shows, the top leader in every lower house is called the "speaker."

State senate leadership structures also vary in size and, at the top, they are more complicated and confusing than those found in lower houses. Formally, the lieutenant governor is the president of the senate in 26 states, holding a position in most of them that is similar to that of the vice president in the U.S. Senate. In the other 24 state senates, the president is elected by the membership. To further confuse matters, in both Tennessee and West Virginia, the senate elects one of its own members to serve simultaneously as the leader of the chamber—called the "speaker" in Tennessee and the "president" in West Virginia—and as lieutenant governor. Moreover, although the members of the Nebraska Unicameral are referred to as "senator," they are,

TABLE 4-1   THE TOP LEADER IN STATE LEGISLATIVE HOUSES, 2007–2008

LEGISLATIVE LEADER TITLE	UPPER HOUSE[a]	LOWER HOUSE
Lieutenant governor/ president	AL, GA, MS, NV, PA, SD, TX, WA, *WV*	
President	AK, AZ, CO, FL, HI, IL, IA, KS, KY, LA, ME, MD, MA, MN, MT, NH, NJ, ND, OH, OR, UT, WI, WY	
President pro tempore	AR, CA, CT, DE, ID, IN, MI, MO, NM, NC, OK, RI, SC, VT, VA	
President/majority leader	NY	
Speaker/lieutenant governor	*TN*	
Speaker		All 49 lower houses
Speaker		NE Unicameral

Source: National Conference of State Legislatures, "2008 State Legislative Leadership," April 11, 2008 (http://www.ncsl.org/programs/leaders/Leaders08.htm).

[a]States in italics allow members of the senate to elect a senator to be president or speaker and to serve as lieutenant governor.

like in Tennessee, presided over by a speaker. The twist in New York is that the senate president also holds the title of majority leader.[21]

Looking across the 50 state senates, however, real leadership power is vested in the president or president pro tem in the vast majority of them. Thus, as Table 4-1 implies, although many lieutenant governors serve as senate president, they essentially perform a ceremonial role. Only a few, notably the lieutenant governors in Georgia and Texas, exercise significant power within their state senates.[22] But it is important to understand that these leadership powers are not chiseled in stone; they can be and occasionally are altered. As discussed in Politics Under the Domes 4-1, for example, the lieutenant governor in Alabama used to enjoy great power in the state senate, but the position lost much of its authority as the result of a partisan conflict in 1999.

POLITICS UNDER THE DOMES 4-1

The Battle over the Gavel in the Alabama State Senate

For almost the entire twentieth century, the Alabama state legislature was a one-party institution. Indeed, between 1922 and 1978, only a single Republican served in the state Senate, and for only a single term. Consequently, legislative rules and procedures evolved to meet the needs of the Democrats operating in a system without any opposition party. Thus, although the lieutenant governor is constitutionally mandated only to act as the state senate's presiding officer and allowed to vote only in the event of a tie, senate Democrats adopted rules over time that invested the office with considerable power. They came to allow the lieutenant governor to make all committee assignments, name all committee chairs, and control the flow of legislation to the floor. As long as the Democrats continued to control both the Senate and the lieutenant governor's office, this delegation of power made sense.

In the 1998 election, however, the GOP won the lieutenant governorship for the first time in 126 years. Although the Democrats took the governorship and appeared to enjoy a comfortable majority in the Senate, having a Republican as the lieutenant governor posed a potentially serious problem. The new lieutenant governor, Steve Windom, opposed many of the new governor's policy proposals, and given the traditional powers accorded to his position in the senate, he would be able to stop legislation he did not support dead in its tracks.

Senate Democrats anticipated this predicament and, exploiting a quirk in the political calendar, they moved quickly to diminish the lieutenant governor's legislative powers. During the state senate's

(Continued)

POLITICS UNDER THE DOMES 4-1 (CONTINUED)

organizational meeting on January 12, 1999, the Democrats voted to strip
the lieutenant governor of the powers to make committee assignments,
name committee chairs, and assign bills to committees. Instead, they assigned these responsibilities to the president pro tem, Lowell Barron, the
Democratic leader in the Senate. The Democrats were able to push
through these changes for two reasons. First, the organizational meeting
took place one week before the new governor and lieutenant governor
were inaugurated. That meant that the GOP lieutenant governor-elect,
Windom, could not preside over the Senate and use his position to block
the rules changes. Instead, the outgoing Democratic lieutenant governor,
Don Siegelman, wielded the gavel and was able to render parliamentary
decisions favorable to the majority party. Siegelman had every reason
to do so because he was the governor-elect whose policies the new
lieutenant governor was promising to block. Second, the Democrats had a
majority in the Senate, holding 23 seats to the GOP's 12 seats. That margin
should have guaranteed them complete control over the chamber. But five
Senate Democrats had been elected with considerable support from
groups aligned with the Republicans, and they all voted against the rules
changes, leaving the majority with a razor-thin 18 to 17 advantage. With
that single extra vote, however, the Democrats could still call the shots.

At least, that is what they thought. On March 2, the opening day of the
regular Senate session, one of the five renegade Democrats offered a proposal to restore the powers traditionally assigned to the lieutenant governor. Over the heated shouts and wild gesticulations of the 18 Democrats in
the majority, Lieutenant Governor Windom, finally having the chance to
act in his capacity as the chamber's presiding officer, dispensed with any
debate on the measure; refused to recognize any of the senators objecting
to his decision; called for a voice vote; and pounded his gavel, declaring
that the proposal passed unanimously. This Machiavellian maneuver triggered such an uproar in the chamber that a five-year-old girl observing the
action from the public gallery was frightened to tears.

When asked later that day about the disputed voice vote, Lieutenant Governor Windom claimed, "That's what I heard. You obviously
do it on what the chair hears and sees, and I heard a majority. The pre-
vailing side voted the loudest." In response, an exasperated President
Pro Tem Barron complained, "We never dreamed that a madman would
just begin gaveling through laws by himself with 18 of us voting no."

The majority Democrats decided that a boycott of the Senate was
their only effective counter to the GOP's power play. By staying away,
the majority would deny the Senate the constitutionally required
quorum, thus preventing any official legislative business from being
transacted. Such a boycott was a particularly potent weapon in

Alabama because the legislature is limited to meeting for a maximum of 30 days in odd-numbered years. Moreover, under state law, the legislature had to meet every day to determine whether a quorum was present, and each of those days counted toward the 30-day limit even if no business could be conducted. The only way to stop the automatic meeting of the Senate required that a majority of the senators vote to adopt a different schedule, which the 18 Democrats would only consent to do if Lieutenant Governor Windom first agreed in writing to allow the Senate clerk to count and record all votes. Windom, however, refused to make any such guarantee. Not surprisingly, the majority Democrats did not sufficiently trust the lieutenant governor to return to the chamber without an agreement in hand. A Democratic senator acknowledged, "Oh no. We don't trust him with the gavel. We certainly don't."

Animosity over the contested vote grew so great that the Senate Democrats took the issue to court. On March 9, a Montgomery County Circuit Court judge ruled in their favor, holding that the lieutenant governor had illegally misrepresented the tally. President Pro Tem Barron, however, admitted that the court decision would not ultimately resolve the dispute: "The courts can't make us be civil. They can't make us cooperate. We're trying, on our own, to reach that level of trust and comfort." Lieutenant Governor Windom immediately appealed the circuit court decision to the state supreme court, which suspended the circuit court judge's order pending its own review of the matter.

On March 11, after boycotting the Senate for eight days, the Democrats agreed to return to the chamber after a meeting between President Pro Tem Barron, Lieutenant Governor Window, Governor Siegelman, and House of Representatives Speaker Seth Hammett. The governor and speaker pushed to resolve the Senate quarrel because it threatened to bring both their legislative agendas to a grinding halt. Moreover, they feared that the battle was reflecting poorly on the state's public image. Little did they know, the worst was yet to come.

Senate decorum degenerated almost immediately after the Democrats returned to the chamber. An attempt to force a recorded vote on changes to the clerk's record of the disputed March 2 tally was rejected by Lieutenant Governor Windom, which caused Democratic Leader Barron to become apoplectic:

> Steve Windom, what you're doing, if you continue breaking the law, you're going to cause this body to get into chaos that you can't stop. With what you are doing, you can cause violence, and that would be the wrong thing. Do you want us to take you physically out of the chair? We don't intend to violate the law, we're above that. But that's obviously what you're trying to provoke us to do.

(Continued)

POLITICS UNDER THE DOMES 4-1 (CONTINUED)

Tempers ran hot enough that Senate security personnel called for additional officers, "Just in case. Just to be seen." The senate secretary, a veteran of many legislative sessions, was so appalled by the fiasco that he left his post and walked off the floor. Even after things cooled down a bit, Democratic leaders raised the prospect of pushing for Lieutenant Governor Windom's impeachment by the House. Finally, both sides of the conflict agreed to take a week off to allow mediators to seek a compromise and to prevent more legislative meeting days from being lost to the dispute.

The mediation effort was conducted by a former Democratic governor and a former GOP state senator. They engaged in shuttle diplomacy, going back and forth between the warring parties for more than a week. In the end, however, they concluded that their efforts were futile, and they gave up in frustration.

Seeking to force a resolution to the seemingly endless conflict before it completely stymied his legislative agenda, Governor Siegelman called the Senate into a special session on March 26. Although hopes were high that the unusual action would produce a quick compromise, negotiations again broke down on March 28, and tempers flared anew after Lieutenant Governor Windom announced the creation of six new committees controlled by his Senate allies to review all legislation. The Democrats became particularly agitated after Windom refused to allow a vote on a motion to force him to vacate the chair for 15 days. One Democratic senator took to the floor to remark to his colleagues: "This stupidity of this Senate has gotten everybody on edge. People I've spoken to for years, up here today, I was ready to slug one of them." A Republican senator similarly lamented, "We are down here acting like children, and I'm ashamed. I'm embarrassed. I feel I'm working with a bunch of undignified, unruly people. This is not a street fight. We are grown men and women. We don't need to be shouting at each other."

Relations between the parties degenerated to the point that Lieutenant Governor Windom felt that he could not leave the podium, fearing that if he vacated his chair for even a moment the Democratic majority would take command of the chamber and reverse all of his previous decisions. Speaking to reporters by phone from his chair during the marathon 12-hour March 28 session, Windom confessed that he even had to discreetly relieve himself behind the podium, "I've had to use a cup up here, a jug. . . . This is the most demeaning thing to any constitutional officers that I've heard of, when I can't even leave the chair."

The lieutenant governor's humiliating confession quickly became a media sensation. The ensuing embarrassment to the institution and the people serving in it finally prompted the warring senators to reach a negotiated settlement. As one Democratic senator admitted, after the jug story broke, "We had to come to terms." The talks took all of Monday, March 29. When the compromise was announced, both parties thought it was critical to pass the proposed rules changes immediately before the carefully assembled package could unravel. Consequently, the Senate unanimously adopted the new rules at 3:50 A.M. on Tuesday, March 30.

The compromise was just that; both sides walked away with some, but not all, of what they wanted. The Democratic majority was given control over the legislative agenda, although Lieutenant Governor Windom and his allies were assured that one-third of the bills brought to the floor would be measures they were pushing. Committees that reviewed budget bills were to be equally divided, with seven members from each faction, but members of the Democratic majority would be the chairs. Other committees would have eight members from the Democratic majority, one of whom would be the chair, and seven members from among Lieutenant Governor Windom's allies. Each side would be allowed to name its committee members. Bills would be assigned to committees by Lieutenant Governor Windom, but if President Pro Tem Barron disagreed with an assignment, the decision would be made by the Senate Rules Committee, which the Democratic majority controlled.

After the battle was over and the smoke had cleared, the Senate actually managed to function reasonably well. In the end, Governor Siegelman was able to get most of his legislative agenda passed. Politically, however, neither Governor Siegelman nor Lieutenant Governor Windom fared well in the aftermath of the dispute. Windom lost badly in the 2002 GOP gubernatorial primary, and a few months later, Alabama voters turned out Governor Siegelman in the general election. Lowell Barron fared much better. He served as Senate President Pro Tem for eight years, several of which he spent frustrating a Republican governor's legislative agenda.

Sources: Dana Beyerle, "Mitchem Elected President Pro Tem of the Senate," *Tuscaloosa News*, January 10, 2007; David Firestone, "In Alabama, Senate Ends Bitter Rift Over Leader," *The New York Times*, March 31, 1999; Buster Kantrow, "Deal Ends Political Row That Tied Alabama Senate in Knots," Stateline.org, April 6, 1999; Kevin Sack, "Tug-of-War Over Power Roils Senate in Alabama," *The New York Times*, March 4, 1999; David White, "Boycott Shuts Down Senate," *Birmingham News*, March 4, 1999; David White, "Distrust Keeps Senate in Limbo," *Birmingham News*, March 11, 1999; David White, "New Rules Reduce Windom's Authority," *Birmingham News*, March 31, 1999; David White, "Senate Adjourns to Allow Cool-off," *Birmingham News*, March 12, 1999; David White, "Senate Erupts into Renewed Chaos Senate Talks Dissolve into Chaos," *Birmingham News*, March 29, 1999; David White, "Senate Frozen for 4th Straight Day," *Birmingham News*, March 8, 1999; David White, "Senators to Learn if New Rules Will Work," *Birmingham News*, April 6, 1999; David White, "Siegelman Wins Praise for Session," *Birmingham News*, June 13, 1999.

As in the lower houses, the size of senate leadership structures varies substantially. In Louisiana, Mississippi, and Texas, only a president pro tem supplements the president. In Nebraska, the speaker serves with just an Executive Board chair. Other senates operate with far more leaders. The Connecticut senate has 36 leadership positions—a president pro tempore, a majority leader, a chief deputy president pro tempore, four deputy presidents pro tempore, a chief deputy majority leader, five deputy majority leaders, a deputy caucus leader, two assistant presidents pro tempore, a chief assistant majority leader, an assistant majority leader, a majority whip, three deputy majority whips, two assistant majority whips, a minority leader, a minority leader pro tempore, two chief deputy minority leaders, six deputy minority leaders, and two assistant minority leaders. What makes this structure particularly noteworthy is that the 36 positions are spread across a 36-member body, meaning every Connecticut senator holds a leadership title.

State legislative leadership positions also vary in tenure. Longer leadership tenures are considered important because they are thought to increase the power wielded by leaders, especially relative to the executive.[23] As can be seen in Table 4-2, speaker careers in the lower houses have generally gotten gradually longer since 1901.[24] But several different patterns emerge across the states. In Pennsylvania and Wisconsin (both among the more professional legislatures in the country over the twentieth century), the increase in leadership tenure has been slight because even during the earliest periods, leaders in these two states served at least two terms or occasionally even three terms.[25] Similar patterns are seen in Minnesota and Rhode Island. In Georgia, Mississippi, and South Carolina (one-party states for much of the past century), longer speakership tenures emerged very early on and quickly became the norm. Because of this, each of these lower houses has had considerably fewer speakers over the past century than almost any of the other lower houses. The predominant pattern in the states, however, which is evident to varying degrees in Connecticut, Iowa, Kansas, Maryland, Oregon, Tennessee, Texas, Vermont, Washington, and West Virginia, is a decided increase in speakership tenure only in the past two to three decades, coinciding with professionalization efforts in many of these states.

The remaining four states—California, Michigan, Missouri, and South Dakota—all instituted term limits in the 1990s. Consequently, each state has potentially truncated a trend toward longer leadership service. In California, for example, no speaker served in successive sessions until C.C. Young did between 1913 and 1919.[26] Longer tenures became the norm from that point on, with Willie Brown establishing the record, serving as speaker from 1981 to 1995. With the introduction of term limits, of course, a California Assembly career can only be six years at most, and consequently recent speakers have held the post for only two to four years. As speaker-elect Karen Bass noted the day before she took over in the Assembly in 2008, "My speakership will be like all the other ones post–Willie Brown: short."[27] Indeed, in the

TABLE 4-2   THE INCREASING SPEAKERSHIP TERM, 1901–2008, SELECTED STATES (RANKED BY FEWEST SPEAKERS TO MOST SPEAKERS)

YEARS IN COMPLETED SPEAKERSHIP TERMS, 1901 TO THE PRESENT SPEAKERSHIP NUMBER[a]

STATE	1	2	3	4	5	6	7	8	9	10	11	12	13	14	15	16	17	18	19	20	21	22	23	24	25	26	27	28	29	30	31	32	33	34	35	36	37	38	39	40	41	42	43	44	45	46	47
MS	4	4	4	4	4	8	1	4	4	22	10	12	16																																		
GA	3	4	4	4	4	6	4	4	4	4	2	4	8	4	4	4	7	28	2																												
SC	2	4	4	4	3	2	2	6	2	6	2	2	9	2	2	2	6	5	7	11																											
RI	2	3	1	4	1	1	2	4	1	3	4	6	4	2	2	23	1	4	6	1	4	8	4	9																							
MD	1	1	2	2	2	2	4	4	2	1	3	2	2	4	2	2	2	4	5	3	4	8	4	1	6	4	5	8	6	9																	
MO	4	2	2	2	2	2	2	2	4	2	2	2	2	2	2	4	2	4	2	4	2	4	2	6	6	4	4	15	5	2	2[a]																
TN	2	2	2	2	2	2	2	2	2	2	2	2	2	2	2	2	2	2	4	2	2	2	4	10	4	2	2	2	14	4	18																
MN	2	2	2	2	2	2	2	2	4	6	2	2	2	2	10	6	4	4	8	4	6	2	6	1	1	4	2	1	6	3	4	2	8														
WV	2	2	2	2	2	2	2	2	2	2	2	2	2	2	2	2	2	2	4	2	4	2	4	4	4	2	6	6	2	10	10																
CA	2	2	2	2	2	2	6	4	6	1	2	2	2	1	3	4	6	2	2	3	8	6	6	6	15	1	1	1	3	2	2	4															
MI	3	2	2	2	2	4	2	1	2	4	2	2	2	4	2	2	8	4	4	2	2	2	2	2	6	8	6	4	2	4	2	2	4	2													
WI	4	2	2	4	2	4	4	1	2	2	2	2	2	2	6	4	4	2	2	2	2	2	2	2	4	2	4	2	3	2	2	1	5	4													
WA	2	2	2	2	4	2	2	2	2	2	2	2	2	2	2	4	2	2	2	2	2	2	2	2	2	8	2	2	2	4	4	2	6	2	8												
TX	2	2	2	2	1	2	2	2	2	2	2	2	2	2	2	2	2	2	2	2	2	4	2	4	2	4	4	2	3	4	4	2	2	8	10	10											
VT	2	4	4	4	2	4	1	4	2	2	2	2	2	2	2	2	2	4	2	2	2	2	2	2	2	2	4	2	2	4	2	4	2	6	4	10	6	4									
CT	2	2	2	2	2	2	2	2	2	2	2	2	2	2	2	2	2	2	2	2	2	2	2	2	2	2	2	3	2	2	2	2	4	4	4	2	2	2	4	6	6						
PA	2	4	2	4	3	2	2	2	2	2	2	2	2	2	2	2	1	2	2	2	2	2	2	2	2	2	2	2	2	4	2	2	2	2	2	6	1	2	2	8	4						
IA	2	2	3	2	2	2	2	2	2	2	2	4	2	1	1	2	2	2	2	2	2	2	2	2	2	2	2	2	2	2	2	2	2	2	4	2	1	8	2	2	5	3	4				
KS	2	2	2	2	2	2	2	2	2	2	2	2	2	2	2	2	2	2	2	2	2	2	2	2	2	2	2	2	2	2	2	2	2	4	4	2	4	4	2	2	4	4	2	2			
OR	2	2	2	2	2	2	2	2	2	2	2	2	2	2	2	2	2	2	2	2	2	2	2	2	2	2	2	2	2	2	2	2	2	2	2	6	4	2	6	6	2	2	4	2	2		
SD	4	4	2	2	2	2	2	2	2	2	2	2	2	2	2	2	2	2	2	2	2	2	2	2	2	2	2	2	2	2	2	2	2	2	2	2	2	2	2	2	2	2	2	2	2	2[a]	4[a]

Sources: Data gathered by the authors from state legislative web pages.

[a]Shaded areas show speakership term lengths after term limits took effect in a state. Every speaker was counted as having served at least one full year.

first 13 years after the end of Brown's long tenure, the Assembly had nine different speakers. Similarly, lower houses in both Michigan and Missouri have witnessed shorter speakership tenures since the imposition of term limits than was the case before they were put in place. But term limits do not necessarily change things in every legislature. In South Dakota, speakers rarely served for even four years even before term limits; thus, the adoption of term limits has not altered speakership careers there at all.

Why have speakers in most legislatures served for longer in recent decades? It is, of course, likely that professionalization, which encourages members to serve longer, has done the same for their leaders. But it is also the case that speakers have come to serve for more years because of reforms elsewhere in the political system that have had implications for legislative leaders' political career ambitions. Most notably, laws allowing governors to serve longer in office impeded political advancement opportunities for legislative leaders by forcing them to wait longer for the opportunity to move up the electoral ladder.[28] In North Carolina, for example, voter approval in 1977 of a constitutional amendment removing the one-term limit on governors convinced members of the lower house to allow their speaker to serve for more than two years.[29] Lengthening the gubernatorial term appears to have increased legislative leadership tenures in several other states, among them Texas and Louisiana.[30] A third variable explaining longer leadership service is the appearance in the legislatures of a politician with unusual political skills, allowing him or her to challenge the existence of a one- or two-term tradition. An example of such a politician is Don Avenson, who served as speaker of the Iowa House from 1983 to 1991. Avenson shattered the state's traditional two-term speakership limit through the sheer force of his personality and political ambition.

Generally, top legislative leaders gain their positions after a considerable apprenticeship, allowing them to gain valuable experience before taking the levers of power. As one former leader reflected, "Because of my long apprenticeship, I knew how to change the things that were wrong or unfair when I became the Speaker. And I knew how to listen."[31] Speakers of the house in all 49 lower houses in 2008 are listed in Table 4-3, along with the year they were first elected to the house and the year they first assumed the speakership. More than half of the speakers had served in the legislature for at least 10 years before gaining the top post, 10 had been in office at least 20 years, and two had been in office for more than 30 years. The mean across all 49 speakers is an impressive 12.2 years of previous experience. There is, however, an important difference in experience levels to be noted. The existence of term limits caps the amount of service any legislator can gain before becoming speaker. Even including Nevada—which in 2008 had yet to term limit out any members—speakers in term-limited houses had an apprenticeship of only 5.0 years compared with 15.1 years for their counterparts in non-term-limited houses. The latter number is noteworthy; by comparison, the three most recent speakers of the U.S. House averaged 16.3 years of apprenticeship service.

TABLE 4-3   SPEAKERS OF THE HOUSE AND APPRENTICESHIPS, 2008
(RANKED BY APPRENTICESHIP YEARS, FROM MOST TO FEWEST)

STATE[a]	SPEAKER	FIRST YEAR IN HOUSE	SPEAKER TENURE	APPRENTICESHIP YEARS
TX	Tom Craddick	1969	2003–	34
IN	B. Patrick Bauer	1971	2003–2004, 2007–	32
NM	Ben Lujan	1975	2001	26
NC	Joe Hackney	1981	2007	26
MA	Salvatore DiMasi	1979	2004	25
PA	Dennis O'Brien[b]	1983	2007	24
MS	William McCoy	1981	2005	24
HI	Calvin Say	1977	1999	22
AL	Seth Hammett	1979	1999	20
NJ	Joseph Roberts	1987	2007	20
KY	Jody Richards	1977	1995	18
IA	Pat Murphy	1989	2007	18
NY	Sheldon Silver	1977	1994	17
KS	Melvin Neufield[b]	1991	2007	16
MD	Michael Busch	1987	2003	16
TN	James Naifeh	1975	1991	16
VA	William Howell	1988	2003	14
CT	James Amann	1991	2005	14
IL	Michael Madigan	1971	1983–1995, 1997–	12
NV	Barbara Buckley	1995	2007	12
ND	Jeff Delzer[b]	1995	2007	12
SC	Bobby Harrell	1993	2005	12
WI	Michael Huebsch	1995	2007	12
ID	Lawerence Denny[b]	1997	2007	10
NH	Terie Norelli	1997	2007	10
RI	William Murphy	1993	2003	10
UT	Greg Curtis	1995	2005	10
OK	Chris Benge	1999	2008	9
GA	Glenn Richardson	1997	2005	8
MN	Margaret Kelliher	1999	2007	8
OR	Jeff Merkley	1999	2007	8
VT	Gaye Symington	1997	2005	8
FL	Marco Rubio	2000	2007	7
AK	John Harris	1999	2005	6
DE	Terry Spence	1981	1987	6
LA	Jim Tucker	2001	2007	6
ME	Glenn Cummings	2001	2007	6
WV	Richard Thompson[b]	2001	2007	6

(Continued)

TABLE 4-3   (CONTINUED)

STATE[a]	SPEAKER	YEAR ELECTED TO HOUSE	SPEAKER TENURE	APPRENTICESHIP YEARS
WY	Roy Cohee	1999	2005	6
WA	Frank Chopp	1995	Co-speaker 1999–2001, 2002	4
AR	Benny Petrus	2003	2007	4
CO	Andrew Romanoff	2001	2005	4
MO	Rod Jetton	2001	2005	4
MT	Scott Sales	2003	2007	4
OH	John Husted	2001	2005	4
SD	Thomas Deadrick	2003	2007	4
CA	Karen Bass	2005	2008	3
MI	Andy Dillon	2004	2007	3
AZ	James Weier[b]	2005	2005	0

Sources: Data gathered by authors from state legislative websites.

[a]States in italics have term limits, although in Nevada, no legislator had yet to be limited.

[b]Denny previously served in the lower house from 1991-1993; O'Brien from 1977–1981; Neufield from 1985–1989; Delzer in 1991; Thompson from 1981–1983; and Weier from 1995–2003 and also in the state senate from 2003–2005.

We can draw two important conclusions from these data. First, in general lower house speakers gain considerable experience before ascending to the top post. This is particularly the case in legislatures without term limits. It is noteworthy that extended apprenticeships hold even in less-professional legislatures, documenting that, at least at the highest leadership level, less-professional legislatures without term limits still benefit from experienced leadership. Second, term limits greatly reduce the apprenticeship period enjoyed by top legislative leaders. Indeed, the nine least experienced house speakers serving in 2008 were found in term-limited bodies, with several of them serving in some of the most professional legislatures.

How much power do legislative leaders really wield?[32] Typically, they have a number of formal powers at their disposal. As will be discussed below, top legislative leaders make the vast majority of committee assignments and usually name committee chairs. In a handful of state houses, the top leader even selects his or her floor leader. Top leaders who also serve as a chamber's presiding officer can use the gavel to their advantage, as shown in Politics Under the Domes 4-1. As will be discussed in Chapter 5, many leaders enjoy power over the referral of legislation to committees and over the flow of legislation to the floor. Both powers give a leader the chance to determine a bill's fate.[33] Finally, the authority to recognize speakers and make parliamentary rulings give a leader considerable opportunity to fashion debates and votes to his or her liking.

Legislative leaders use their powers in a "carrot and stick" fashion. The carrot is that leaders can greatly assist members by helping them get favorable committee assignments, progress up the legislative leadership ladder, and pass legislation. The stick is that members who fail to do the leadership's bidding can be punished in ways large and small, as discussed in Politics Under the Domes 4-2. Their powers give leaders leverage they can use to get their members to do their bidding without any explicit quid pro quo. A former California Assembly member, for example, recalls an incident that:

> involved a bill dealing with Continental Airlines taking over Western Airlines. I was opposed to the bill and was giving an impassioned speech . . . against the bill when [Speaker] Willie [Brown] walked by my desk and said, "Don't get too wound up, you're voting for this bill." I paused, looked at Willie and concluded, "Now that I have given you all the opponents' arguments, I am voting for this bill. I sat down and the bill passed."[34]

This lawmaker understood that it was in his long-term interest to vote the way the speaker wanted him to vote on this bill; he did not expect an immediate payoff.

POLITICS UNDER THE DOMES 4-2

Leadership Retribution in State Legislatures

Ralph Waldo Emerson allegedly advised a young Oliver Wendell Holmes that "when you strike at a king, you must kill him." Emerson was commenting on Holmes' feeble attempt to criticize the works of Plato, but his advice is apropos for any legislator who seeks to challenge legislative leaders. Deposed leaders pose little threat, but leaders who are only politically wounded—or even just irritated—can inflict plenty of pain and suffering on those who challenge them.

Failing to topple a legislative leader usually brings immediate and severe negative consequences to those made the attempt. In 2005, for example, several Republican members of the New York Assembly tried to overthrow their party's leader. After the coup failed, the leading insurgent, who had publicly characterized the leader as "wishy-washy," was removed as a deputy whip, losing not only the position but the $15,000 stipend that accompanied it. Most of the other rebels were similarly punished.

Occasionally, penalties for unsuccessfully challenging a leader are delayed. At the beginning of the 2005 legislative session, Alaska Representative Nancy Dahlstrom, a Republican, backed an unsuccessful attempt to forge a bipartisan coalition to challenge her party's candidate for speaker. She did not suffer any immediate retribution from the

(Continued)

POLITICS UNDER THE DOMES 4-2 (CONTINUED)

speaker, but after she failed to vote with her Republican colleagues on an important budget bill, he removed her as the chair of the House Economic Development, International Trade, and Tourism Committee; took away one of her staff members; and with his colleagues' consent, kicked her out of the party caucus. That action left Representative Dahlstrom to muse, "I think I am [now] a caucus of one." Her banishment, however, was not permanent. After Dahlstrom's district reelected her in 2006, the speaker and the GOP caucus relented and allowed her to return to the fold. She was even elected co-chair of the Armed Services Committee.

Punishing party members for failing to vote the way the leadership wants on an important vote is not uncommon. In 2008, for example, the GOP leader in the Minnesota House removed six of his caucus members from party leadership positions after they joined with Democrats to override the Republican governor's veto of a costly transportation measure. The leader further promised that his prodigal members would not receive campaign financial assistance from the caucus if they chose to run for reelection. But the leader said he would not go so far as to recruit candidates to run against the disloyal members. Not all aggrieved leaders are so generous. Texas House Speaker Tom Craddick barely survived an attempt by unhappy members of his own party to remove him in 2007. In GOP primary elections a year later, candidates backed by the speaker defeated several incumbents who had challenged the speaker, sufficiently solidifying his position so that others who had rebelled surrendered.

Taking away party positions or removing members from favored committee assignments does not exhaust the penalties legislative leaders can exact on recalcitrant lawmakers. Indeed, leaders can engage in remarkably petty behaviors. When a Republican member of the California Assembly continually irritated the Democratic majority during the 2007 session, the speaker took action against him. He ordered the GOP assembly member moved out of his capitol office to another room known as "the doghouse" that was only half the size. The next year, a Democrat who failed to provide the speaker a critical budget vote found herself not only booted out of her office but also out of the capitol altogether to an office building across the street where no other lawmaker was housed. Such punishment is not confined to California. A speaker of the Florida House of Representatives banished a member of a failed rebellion against him to a purgatory, "in the Capitol basement, shoehorned into an office so small his secretary set up her office in the hallway." A California Senate Majority Leader, however, may have plumbed new depths of petty punishments. When three of his caucus members attended the fund-raising dinner of a political group the leader did not support, he authorized that the locks on their capitol office doors be changed. Each of the locked-out senators had to first meet with the majority leader and make amends before getting a new key.

Sources: Elizabeth Benjamin, "Ax Falls as Would-Be Assembly Coup Crumbles," Albany Times Union, April 19, 2005; April Castro, "House Speaker Craddick Emerges Stronger After Elections," Houston Chronicle, April 20, 2008; Sean Cockerham, "Dahlstrom Cast Out of Majority Caucus," Anchorage Daily News, June 7, 2005; Laylan Copelin, "Legislative Session Ends," Austin American-Statesman, May 29, 2007; Don Davis and Scott Wente, "GOP Leader Punishes 6 Over Veto Vote," Bemidji Pioneer, February 27, 2008; Steven Harmon, "Senate Leader Flexes Muscle in Warning to Lawmakers," San Jose Mercury, March 13, 2007; Brian Joseph, "Spitzer Sent to 'the Doghouse,'" Orange County Register, May 11, 2007; E.J. Schultz, "Democratic Assemblywoman Banished from Capitol for Withholding Budget Vote," Sacramento Bee, August 19, 2008; Alisa Ulferts, "Ire from Top Not New for Senator," St. Petersburg Times, July 14, 2003.

But, as always, the authority accorded to leaders across state legislatures varies. A recent attempt to gauge the power of lower house speakers examined several different formal aspects of leadership authority, among them the ability to appoint other legislative leaders, committee chairs, and committee members, as well as the office's tenure potential and control over various resources and parliamentary procedures.[35] By this calculation, speakers in West Virginia, New Hampshire, and Arizona enjoy the greatest power, and those in Hawaii and Wyoming have the least ability to influence legislative action. Another assessment using this measure found that speakers in 44 states exercised greater power in their houses than U.S. House Speaker Dennis Hastert exercised during his tenure between 1999 and 2007.[36]

The power accorded to leaders varies by career opportunity type. In general, legislators in springboard legislatures invest less power in their leaders, preferring instead to have the ability to promote their own ambitions and agendas. Legislators in career and more professional bodies grant their leaders greater power.[37] Paradoxically, however, the process of professionalization may have actually worked to reduce leadership power from what it had been in the past as legislators with greater informational resources at their disposal opted to assert greater individual influence in the legislative process.[38] Perhaps not surprisingly, compared with their counterparts in other legislatures, "term-limited legislative leaders have less control over legislative members, the rules, and the agenda," only overcoming their lack of apprenticeship and the experience it produces if they possess strong leadership skills.[39]

In every legislature, however, the power leaders enjoy ultimately depends on the power a majority of members is willing to delegate to them. Thus, leaders often find that they must defer their own policy preferences to those of the members who put them in power. In 2005, for example, Connecticut House Speaker Amann strongly opposed civil unions for same-sex couples. But when he learned that a majority of the house favored such a bill, he allowed the measure to come to a vote despite his personal opposition.[40] Similarly, although Willie Brown was hailed as the "Ayatollah of the Assembly" during his long tenure as speaker in California, he stayed in the top post in large measure because he sublimated his policy preferences to those pursued by the members of his party caucus.[41] Leaders have to pick and choose when to exercise their power. The longest serving speaker in the history of the Idaho House, Bruce Newcomb, observed: "You only have so much political capital. One of the most important things to learn as a leader is to not waste your political capital on small matters or on fights you cannot win."[42] Thus, under most circumstances, leaders seek to facilitate the policy preferences of their members, or at least their supporters, rather than promoting their own preferences. As a former speaker of the Vermont House confessed, "I was captive to my caucus, and that, I believe, is a major reason I managed to serve five terms."[43]

COMMITTEES

Every state legislature operates with standing committees, bodies that exist from session to session and that have the power to recommend legislative proposals to the full house. Standing committees are mechanisms that allow legislatures to handle bills and other legislative matters efficiently by dividing the workload among lawmakers. Committees can be power centers in American legislatures because of the position they occupy in the legislative process. Legislation that is introduced is usually referred to a standing committee, and the decision that committee makes on whether or not to pass a bill or an amended version of it on to the full house may dictate the measure's ultimate fate. This is known as the gate-keeping power.

It might be assumed that the power of standing committees is universally great because of the considerable influence such bodies exercise in the U.S. House and Senate. In reality, the power of standing committees varies considerably, both across state legislative houses and over time within a house.[44] During the 1960s, for example, committees in the Illinois House favorably reported 81 percent of the bills referred to them and committees in the Senate favorably reported 83 percent of the bills referred to them, evidence of limited gate-keeping power. By the early 1980s committees in both houses were exercising considerably more gate-keeping authority, with house committees recommending only 46 percent of bills and senate committees recommending 65 percent of bills.[45] In California, committees in the Assembly and Senate recommended 76 percent of bills referred to them in the era just before the adoption of term limits and 83 percent after limits took effect, suggesting that committees lost gate-keeping power with the advent of term limits.[46] It is worth pointing out that, although their behavior shifted over time, committees in neither Illinois nor California can be said to exercise significant gate-keeping powers. Instead, the real gate-keepers in both legislatures are party leaders.

TABLE 4-4   STANDING COMMITTEES IN THE MARYLAND HOUSE OF DELEGATES
AND THE MISSISSIPPI HOUSE OF REPRESENTATIVES, 2007–2008

MARYLAND HOUSE OF DELEGATES (141 MEMBERS; 8 STANDING COMMITTEES)	MISSISSIPPI HOUSE OF REPRESENTATIVES (122 MEMBERS; 44 STANDING COMMITTEES)	
Appropriations	Agriculture	Juvenile Justice
Economic Matters	Apportionment and Elections	Labor
Environmental Matters	Appropriations	Legislative Budget Committee
Health & Government Operations	Banking and Financial Services	Legislative Reapportionment
Judiciary	Congressional Redistricting	Local and Private Legislation
Rules & Executive Nominations	Conservation and Water Resources	Management
Ways & Means	Constitution	Marine Resources
Consent Calendars	Corrections	Medicaid
	County Affairs	Military Affairs
	Education	Municipalities
	Enrolled Bills	Oil, Gas, and Other Minerals
	Ethics	Performance Evaluation and Expenditure Review (PEER)
	Executive Contingent Fund	Public Health and Human Services
	Fees and Salaries of Public Officers	Public Property
	Forestry	Public Utilities
	Gaming	Rules
	Insurance	State Library
	Interstate Cooperation	Tourism
	Investigate State Offices	Transportation
	Judiciary A	Universities and Colleges
	Judiciary B	Ways and Means
	Judiciary En Banc	Wildlife, Fisheries, and Parks

Sources: State legislative websites. Only standing committees were counted in each chamber; select committees were omitted.

There also are notable differences in standing committee structures across state legislatures. One important difference is revealed in Table 4-4. Although the 99 state legislative houses handle roughly the same set of policy decisions, they can divide up the workload in very different ways.

The Maryland House of Delegates, for example, has 141 members but uses only eight standing committees. All but one of the standing committees has subcommittees. Delegates typically have only one standing committee assignment and serve on a single subcommittee. The Judiciary Committee, for example, has 22 members. Each committee member serves on one of the committee's five subcommittees. In contrast, the Mississippi House, with 122 members, divides up its work very differently. It has 44 standing committees, some with subcommittees. Among the standing committees are three judiciary committees: Judiciary A, with 25 members; Judiciary B, with 25 members; and Judiciary En Banc, which, as the name suggests, incorporates all 50 members from Judiciary A and Judiciary B. In addition, there is a separate Juvenile Justice Committee. Members of the Mississippi House typically serve on between four to six standing committees.

An altogether different standing committee system from that found in most state legislatures and Congress developed in Connecticut, Maine, and Massachusetts. Legislatures in those states rely almost exclusively on joint standing committees. Members from each house serve on the same committee, with a co-chair from each house. In practice, joint committees greatly reduce the need for conference committees to reconcile legislative differences between the two chambers, thus arguably making the legislative process more efficient.[47] With joint committees, however, the distinction between separate houses is blurred to some extent, raising questions about the rationale for their independent existence. Vermont is said to have abandoned joint committees in 1917 because they were thought to invalidate bicameral principles.[48] Having separate committee systems in each house increases the number of obstacles that interests must overcome to get legislation passed and therefore arguably increases the power and resources each house enjoys.[49]

There are two questions about how standing committees are composed in state legislatures that merit special attention. First, does the majority party stack committees with a greater percentage of its members than their representation in the chamber would warrant, as happens in the U.S. House with the powerful Rules and Ways and Means committees? In general, state legislatures usually follow proportional representation rules, although stacking of committees does occur with some frequency. One examination of legislative rules in the late 1990s revealed that in 25 of 91 houses, an explicit rule mandated proportional representation, and in another 45 houses, the practice was usually followed even though it was not formally required.[50] Another study focusing on rules in the 1977–1978 and 1989–1990 legislative sessions reported similar results.[51] In Alaska, for example, Uniform Rule 1(e) states: "On each standing committee the minority is entitled to the number of seats that is proportional to the number of minority members compared to the total house membership or to one seat, whichever is greater." The Alaska rules include a table giving the minimum number of minority party members on a committee given the size of the committee and the size of the minority party membership.[52] Committee stacking is more likely to occur when the majority party controls a chamber by only a slim margin.[53] Moreover, it typically happens on committees that the majority wants to ensure it controls, such as rules committees that manage the legislative process and budget committees that determine how the government raises and spends money. In the Alabama House of Representatives in 2007, for example, Republicans were the minority party, holding 40 percent of the seats. But they were given just five of the 15 seats, or 33 percent, on the three most powerful committees in the House: Rules, Education Appropriations, and Government Appropriations. One more Republican member on each committee would have brought the party up to parity, but according to the speaker, who made the party ratio decision, "To say that cutting one person from each of the three committees is wrong is unreasonable."[54]

From the majority leadership's perspective, stacking important committees so as to be able to dictate outcomes is a reasonable strategy. When the Republicans took control of the Georgia House of Representatives in 2005—the first time they had organized the chamber since 1870—they went well beyond simply stacking committees in their favor to produce the outcomes they wanted. They adopted a creative scheme to allow the majority party leadership to directly shape committee decisions. The rules were rewritten to give the speaker the right to appoint an unspecified number of "hawks," majority party members empowered to swoop in and participate as full voting members on any standing committee at any point in time.[55] Thus, by calling in the hawks (three of whom were ultimately appointed), the GOP leadership would be able to force a committee to make the decision it wanted even if several committee Republicans preferred to side with the Democrats on a bill or an amendment. Democrats were predictably outraged by the creation of the hawks, with the Democratic leader complaining, "It does away with representative government," adding with disgust, "There's some political whoring going on. . . ."[56] With considerable hyperbole, another Democrat cried, "I'd love to see what would happen if Iraq installed these rules. . . . The entire world would cry out against an oppressive dictatorship."[57] In fact, a somewhat similar position had previously been used in the North Carolina House of Representatives, where the majority party leaders and a designated legislator were considered "floater voters" and allowed to participate and vote on all committees.[58] Such blatant efforts to stack the deck in the majority's favor are, however, rare.

After party ratios are set, the question becomes who gets to serve on each committee. Committee assignments are handled in different ways in different legislative houses, as shown in Table 4-5. The vast majority of assignments are made by the top leader in the house—the speaker in the lower house and the president, president pro tem, or majority leader in the senate. There are, however, some notable variations. In six lower houses and 11 senates, a "committee on committees" gives out committee positions, although in several chambers, the top leader chairs the committee and greatly influences the assignments it makes. The committee on rules acts as a committee

TABLE 4-5 STANDING COMMITTEE AND CHAIR APPOINTMENT POWERS
IN STATE LEGISLATURES, 2007

APPOINTING AUTHORITY	SENATE COMMITTEE MEMBERS[a]	SENATE COMMITTEE CHAIR	LOWER HOUSE COMMITTEE MEMBERS	LOWER HOUSE COMMITTEE CHAIR
Speaker	TN	TN	AL, *AZ*, CA, CO, DE, FL, GA, ID, *IL*, IN, IA, KS, KY, LA, ME, MD, *MA*, MI, *MN*, MS, MO, MT, *NV*, NH, NM, NY, *OH*, OK, OR, RI, SC, SD, TN, TX (half), UT, VT, VA, WA, WV, *WI*, WY	AL, AZ, AR, CA, CO, DE, FL, GA, ID, IL, IN, IA, KS, KY, LA, ME, MD, MA, MI, MN, MS, MO, MT, NV, NH, NM, NY, OH, OK, OR, PA, RI, SC, SD, TN, TX, UT, VT, VA, WA, WV, WI, WY
President	AZ, FL, *HI*, *IL*, KY, LA, ME, MD, MA, MS, *NH*, *OH*, OR, RI, TX, UT, WA, WV, WY	AZ, FL, HI, IL, KY, LA, ME, MD, MA, MS, NH, OH, OR, RI, TX, UT, WV, WY		
President pro tempore	DE, ID, IN, *MO*, NY, OK, PA, SD	DE, ID, IN, MO, NY, OK, PA, SD		
Majority leader	CO, *IA*, MI, NV, WI	CO, IA, MI, MN, NV, ND, WI		ND
Committee on committees	AL, AK, CT, GA, MT, NE, NJ, NM, NC, ND, VT	AL, AK, CT, GA, MT, NJ, NM, NC, VT, WA	AK, CT, NJ, NC, ND, PA	AK, CT, NJ, NC
Committee on Rules	CA, KS, MN	CA, KS		
Chamber election	VA	NE, VA		
Use of a seniority rule	AR, SC	AR, SC	TX (half) MS (in part)	
Party caucuses			HI	HI
District caucus			AR	

Sources: State legislative web pages and Council on State Governments, *The Book of the States 2007* (Lexington, KY: Council on State Governments) 128–129.

[a]States in italics allow significant minority party input into committee assignment decisions.

on committees in three senates. Party caucuses make committee assignments in the Hawaii House, and caucuses organized around congressional districts do so in the Arkansas House.[59]

Rules allow the minority party a role in assigning its members to committees in about 40 percent of state legislative houses.[60] Some rules give complete power to the minority party. In Illinois, for example, "The Minority Leader shall appoint to all committees the members from the minority caucus and shall designate a Minority Spokesperson for each committee. . . ."[61] Rules in some other houses only require that the minority leader be consulted. For instance, in the Missouri House, "All standing . . . committees shall be appointed by the Speaker . . . except the minority members of each standing committee shall be appointed by the Minority Floor Leader, subject to the final approval of the Speaker."[62] Even where the appointing power is not bound to do so by the rules, they often follow the minority party leadership's assignment preferences for minority party members. But if they are not compelled to follow them, appointing powers can choose to ignore minority party wishes when it suits their needs. A political tiff erupted in the Arizona House in 2007 when the GOP elected speaker changed several committee assignments made by the Democratic leadership, placing four dissidents on their preferred committees in place of four other Democrats who had originally been given the slots. Most House Democrats were incensed by the action, intimating that their four colleagues must have cut a deal with the speaker to get the assignments they wanted. The minority whip warned, "I would watch every move these representatives make—every vote, every bill they introduce, every action on the committees they were just placed on—because they definitely owe the speaker something. And it definitely won't be anything good."[63] The speaker denied any quid pro quo, defending his decision by asserting, "That's nothing more than doing what's right, trying to make people happy, and I'm sorry that some people feel it was done wrong. But the people who were done wrong feel it was done right."[64]

Those with the power to make committee assignments operate under different constraints in different legislative houses. No limitations are placed on the appointing power's ability to make assignments in a majority of houses. For instance, the rule in the Michigan House states, "All standing committees shall be appointed by the Speaker, except where the House shall otherwise order."[65] Speakers are similarly unfettered in Iowa and New York.[66] In these chambers, the appointing authority is constrained only by his or her political calculations.

Some chambers, however, do limit the appointing power's freedom to make committee appointments by requiring other considerations to be taken into account. One such constraint is a reliance on member seniority, where members who have served longer have the opportunity to select the committees on which they serve. Assignment rules in most states do not mention seniority, but a few do.[67]

Seniority as an absolute rule is used only in the Arkansas and South Carolina senates. But the rule differs between these two chambers. In Arkansas, no senator automatically gets to keep a specific committee assignment from one session to the next.[68] That means that there are no committee property rights of the sort that exist in both houses of the U.S. Congress. Instead, during the organizational session held before the start of the new legislative session, senators determine their assignments using something like a draft, with the most senior member of the Senate regardless of party making the first selection. Each senator in order of seniority then chooses his or her first assignment until the member with the least seniority has made a selection.[69] After the first round is completed, the senators follow the same procedure to determine their second committee assignment.

The South Carolina Senate uses a different seniority rule. South Carolina senators enjoy limited committee property rights that usually allow them to keep their previous sessions' committee assignments if they so wish. Open committee slots are then filled by a roll call in order of seniority, with each senator allowed to select four unfilled committee slots. The second round of choices is then conducted in reverse order of seniority.[70]

More limited use of seniority is required by the rules in the Texas and Mississippi houses. In Texas, the speaker has the freedom to designate all the members of procedural standing committees (e.g., committees on calendars, rules, ethics) and to select half of the membership of substantive standing committees (except for the Appropriations Committee, which is filled through a different process). The other half of the membership of the substantive committees is filled through the use of seniority.[71] In the Mississippi House, appointments to the powerful Appropriations and Ways and Means committees are made on the basis of seniority within congressional district caucuses. The use of congressional district residence as an assignment criterion ensures that all regions of the state will be represented on the powerful committees.[72] Members who have served in the House for four or more years and who are not on either the Appropriations or the Ways and Means committees are entitled to get three of their top seven committee assignment preferences; less senior members who are not on either the Appropriations or the Ways and Means committees are entitled to two of their seven choices. This process gives some reward for seniority but leaves the speaker flexibility in making assignments.[73]

Other constraints beyond seniority exist in the assignment process in some legislative houses. In the Alabama House, the speaker appoints all committees and subcommittees, but according to the rules, he or she "shall proportion, as accurately as is reasonably possible, all committee appointments in a manner which is inclusive and reflects the racial diversity and gender of the members of the body and the political party affiliation of the members of the body."[74] In Minnesota, "A committee of the House must not have exclusive membership from one profession, occupation or vocation," so the agriculture committee cannot be composed entirely of farmers, the judiciary committee entirely of lawyers, or the education committee entirely of teachers.[75] In several houses, the appointing authority is specifically directed to take into account member desires, as in the California Assembly, where, "In appointing Members to serve on committees, the Speaker shall consider the preferences of the Members."[76] Indeed, across state legislatures, member preferences are typically honored by those who make committee assignments.[77] This is to be expected because, as already noted, leaders retain their office only with the consent of those they lead. Irritating too many members with unwanted committee assignments might put a leader's job at risk. Even with the best of intentions, however, there are a limited number of preferred committee slots, creating more demand than the appointing authority can satisfy. A former Vermont speaker who "enjoyed" absolute assignment power admitted, "I really disliked making committee assignments. It seemed no matter what I did, I couldn't avoid having thirty or more members furious at me because they had been 'dumped' into committees on which they didn't want to serve."[78]

When allowed flexibility by the rules, appointing authorities can use committee assignments to settle political scores. After a Massachusetts representative voted in favor of imposing a limit on the number of terms a speaker could serve, the speaker sought revenge by taking away her coveted seat on a committee overseeing the insurance industry and placing her instead on a committee overseeing legislative administration. According to the representative, the demotion was to "a committee she said she never cared to know too much about, until reading a description of it in an in-house booklet [the day she was appointed]."[79] Representatives who backed the speaker on the term limit matter were, of course, rewarded with plum assignments.[80]

Given the latitude that appointing authorities typically enjoy in the committee appointment process, it would be easy to envision the creation of committees that are politically or ideologically unrepresentative of the larger house membership. In fact, most committees in state legislatures are representatives of their parent house.[81] This suggests that committees are intended to provide the chamber with information and issue expertise rather than being designed to skew policies away from what the chamber's median legislator would accept. The few state legislative committees that do not reflect the preferences of the larger chamber are likely to emerge in houses where committee assignment rules give considerable weight to member choices, member seniority is taken into account, or member committee property rights are observed. Representative committees are encouraged by rules that require parties to be proportionally represented and that give the minority party greater say on their members' committee assignments.[82]

Compared with the committee appointment process, fewer rules control the designation of committee chairs. As documented in Table 4-4, committee chairs are usually determined by the top leader. In most state legislative houses, as in both houses of Congress, committee chairs are reserved for majority party members. Obviously, when a bipartisan coalition takes control of a house, members from both parties are usually named to top committee posts. But in a handful of state legislative chambers, minority party members are traditionally named to lead a few committees even in the absence of a bipartisan coalition. In the Texas House, for example, about 25 percent of committee chairs were given to minority party Democrats in 2007.[83] And once in a while, the partisan monopoly is broken even in bodies without any history of bipartisanship. In the New York Senate in 2007, a Democrat was given a committee chair by the staunchly Republican majority leader.[84] Giving the minority party some committee chairs can, of course, buy the appointing power more friends and their goodwill.

Unlike in Congress, where both houses still largely observe an unwritten seniority rule that the majority party member with the longest consecutive service on a committee automatically becomes its chair, seniority dictates who takes control of committees in very few state legislative chambers. Explicit seniority rules are used in the Arkansas and South Carolina senates. But only the South Carolina Senate operates with a rule that is similar to those found in the two houses of Congress.[85] In the Arkansas Senate, the most senior member of the majority party on a committee becomes its chair, but seniority is measured by service in the full body, not on the committee, so conceivably a senator could chair a committee without every having served on it before.[86]

Seniority is listed as a criterion for becoming a standing committee chair in a few other state legislative houses. In the Pennsylvania House, for example, committee chairs are drawn from the most senior members of the majority party.[87] The speaker, however, gets to select which committee a senior member who is entitled to such a position gets. Consequently, as one Pennsylvania observer notes, "Seniority guarantees you a committee chairmanship but not necessarily a good one."[88] The Illinois House uses a slightly different seniority rule: "No member may be appointed to serve as a Chairperson, Minority Spokesperson, or Co-Chairperson of any committee unless the member is serving in at least his or her third term as a member of the General Assembly."[89] With this rule, a member must have a minimal level of experience to be eligible to serve as a committee chair. But it is the speaker's prerogative as to whether a veteran member who qualifies gets to be a chair and which committee that member is appointed to head.

Not surprisingly, the appointing authority can use the power to name chairs as a way to reward friends and punish enemies. After the unsuccessful attempt to dethrone Texas House Speaker Tom Craddick in 2007, five of the members who backed the challenge lost their positions as committee chairs. The leader of the failed rebellion, who had been the chair of the powerful Appropriations Committee, not only lost the leadership of that committee, but he was also removed from it altogether. The rebels' replacements were, of course, supporters of the speaker.[90] Inflicting such punishment on rivals is standard behavior and has been engaged in by leaders as disparate as the Democratic speaker of the New York Assembly and the Republican speaker of the Kansas House of Representatives.[91]

CAREER OPPORTUNITY TYPES AND COMMITTEE MEMBERSHIP AND LEADERSHIP

As discussed in Chapter 3, a legislative house can offer its members only one of three different career opportunities. These different career types link up with the way legislative chambers are organized. Career legislatures, where members anticipate serving for many years, are bodies where seniority is apt to be valued. Consequently, committee leaders and members of the most powerful committees should be senior lawmakers. In contrast, springboard legislatures, where members look to use their current position as a quick route to higher office, should prize seniority much less. Thus, legislators with little seniority should gain access to positions of power much more quickly than they would in career bodies. Dead-end legislatures should fall between the extremes of career legislatures and springboard legislatures. Because dead-end legislatures offer little incentive to stay or little opportunity to move up, lawmakers may not serve in the body for very long. But members of dead-end houses may find it rational to invest power in more senior members who understand the legislative process and who are able to help less senior members achieve their legislative goals.[92]

In Table 4-6, we present seniority means and medians for 33 lower houses, standing committee chairs in those houses, and members of the most powerful committee in each house. As hypothesized, among legislatures without term limits, career bodies have the most senior memberships, committee chairs, and power committee memberships; springboard bodies have the least. Indeed, median seniority is roughly twice as high in career bodies as springboard bodies. And as anticipated, seniority levels in dead-end chambers fall in between the levels in career and springboard chambers. There is, however, considerable variation among dead-end bodies. Some, such as Tennessee and New Mexico, have very senior members as committee chairs and as members of the most powerful committee. Others—notably Utah and Wyoming—have very low member seniority means and medians in their positions of power. Overall, however, it is important to note that although dead-end houses do not approach the very impressive levels of seniority found in the lower houses in New York and Pennsylvania, the data do suggest that they are led by members with considerable experience, certainly far more than the typical member of such bodies.

The importance of this observation becomes apparent when contrasting seniority levels in dead-end bodies with those found in term-limited legislatures. The dead-end bodies are among the least professional legislatures in

TABLE 4-6 CAREER OPPORTUNITY TYPE AND SENIORITY IN SELECTED
LOWER HOUSES, 2007–2008

| | | MEAN AND MEDIAN YEARS OF SERVICE | | |
LEGISLATURE (SALARY)[a]	CAREER TYPE	FULL HOUSE	COMMITTEE CHAIRS	POWER COMMITTEE MEMBERS[b]
New York ($79,500)	Career	9.5	16.9	19.2
		6.0	14.5	19.0
Pennsylvania ($73,613)	Career	9.4	21.6	20.1
		6.0	22.0	22.0
Massachusetts ($58,237)	Career	8.3	12.9	14.8
		8.0	12.0	14.0
Illinois ($57,619)	Career	8.5	8.8	23.2
		6.0	6.0	26.0
Wisconsin ($47,413)	Career	7.4	7.6	8.5
		4.0	6.0	7.0
Maryland ($43,500)	Career	6.8	18.3	16.0
		4.0	12.0	12.0
Delaware ($42,000)	Career	7.8	12.3	12.0
		4.0	12.0	10.0
Minnesota ($31,141)	Career	5.9	13.1	12.2
		4.0	9.0	10.0
Iowa ($25,000)	Dead end	5.8	6.4	6.5
		4.0	4.0	4.0
Tennessee ($18,123)	Dead end	8.1	16.5	16.6
		4.0	12.0	14.0
Georgia ($17,342)	Dead end	7.3	11.7	10.9
		4.0	10.0	8.0
Idaho ($16,116)	Dead end	4.6	10.9	8.1
		3.0	10.0	6.0
Kentucky ($15,797)	Dead end	8.1	13.9	13.4
		6.0	12.0	12.0
West Virginia ($15,000)	Dead end	5.8	7.6	9.4
		5.5	6.0	7.0
Vermont ($13,217)	Dead end	4.8	12.7	7.5
		4.0	10.0	6.0
Rhode Island ($13,089)	Dead end	8.4	12.5	9.1
		8.0	12.0	8.0
Kansas ($7,462)	Dead end	5.5	9.3	6.7
		4.0	10.0	6.0
Texas ($7,200)	Dead end	7.7	10.9	6.3
		6.0	10.5	6.0
New Mexico ($6,390)	Dead end	7.7	15.2	10.7
		6.0	14.0	8.0
Utah ($5,850)	Dead end	4.2	5.7	5.8
		4.0	5.5	4.5
North Dakota ($4,940)	Dead end	7.9	13.7	11.3
		6.5	14.0	10.0

TABLE 4-6   (CONTINUED)

| | | MEAN AND MEDIAN YEARS OF SERVICE | | |
LEGISLATURE (SALARY)[a]	CAREER TYPE	FULL HOUSE	COMMITTEE CHAIRS	POWER COMMITTEE MEMBERS[b]
Alabama ($990)	*Dead end[c]*	*8.8*	*13.1*	*13.3*
		8.0	*12.0*	*12.0*
New Hampshire ($100)	Dead end	4.0	8.3	6.7
		2.0	8.0	4.0
New Jersey ($49,000)	Springboard	5.7	8.4	7.2
		4.5	6.0	10.0
Washington ($36,311)	Springboard	5.6	9.2	5.8
		4.0	8.0	4.0
Alaska ($24,012)	Springboard	3.7	3.7	4.6
		4.0	4.0	8.0
Wyoming ($4,350)	Springboard	3.9	8.0	7.5
		4.0	8.0	8.0
Nevada[d] ($4,137)	Springboard	5.4	8.8	8.4
		4.0	8.0	6.0
California ($116,208)	Term limits	1.7	1.7	1.7
	Springboard	2.0	2.0	1.0
Michigan ($79,650)	Term limits	2.2	2.3	2.2
	Springboard	2.0	2.0	2.0
Ohio ($58,934)	Term limits	2.9	4.6	3.4
	Springboard	2.0	6.0	4.0
Arkansas ($14,765)	Term limits	1.9	3.2	2.3
	Springboard	2.0	4.0	2.0
Missouri ($31,351)	Term limits	3.0	4.4	3.0
	Dead end	4.0	4.0	3.0
Career legislatures means		8.0	13.9	15.8
Dead-end legislatures means		6.6	11.2	9.5
Springboard legislatures means		4.9	7.6	6.7
Term limits legislatures means		2.3	3.2	2.5

Sources: Data gathered by the authors from legislative web pages and Project Vote Smart. http://www.votesmart.org/official_five_categories.php?dist=bio.php.

[a]The top entry in each cell is the mean; the bottom number is the median. Seniority was calculated as consecutive years in the lower house. States in italics have four-year terms in the lower house, which likely inflates their seniority scores compared with states with two-year terms.

[b]The power committee examined was Appropriations in Georgia, Iowa, Kansas, Michigan, New Jersey, New Mexico, North Dakota, Texas, and Vermont; Calendar and Rules in Tennessee; Finance in Minnesota, New Hampshire, and Rhode Island; Finance and Appropriations in Ohio; Revenue and Finance in Delaware; Revenue and Taxation in Arkansas and Idaho; Rules in Alabama, Alaska, California, Illinois, Kentucky, Massachusetts, Missouri, New York, Pennsylvania, Utah, Washington, West Virginia, and Wisconsin; Rules and Executive Nominations in Maryland; Rules and Procedures in Wyoming; and Ways and Means in Nevada.

[c]Given the great disparity in Alabama between salary and salary including unvouchered expenses, the legislature would be considered to be a career body if the latter criterion was used.

[d]Although Nevada has term limits, no member is term limited out of office until the 2010 election. In the future, Nevada will likely be considered a term-limited, dead-end legislature.

the country, while several of the term-limited legislatures are among the most professional bodies. Yet the experience level of committee chairs in the lower houses of California, Michigan, and Ohio pales in comparison with the seniority of their counterparts in New Mexico, North Dakota, and New Hampshire. Even if the basis of comparison is shifted to legislative days from legislative years—a calculation that would greatly advantage the highly professional legislatures with their year-round sessions—their leaders are, at best, only as experienced as the leaders in many of the least professional legislatures. Given these numbers, it is not surprising that a study on the impact of term limits in the Michigan House found that after their imposition, "Committee chairs appear to be less . . . skilled at managing conflict and have less substantive policy expertise."[93] Indeed, committees in term-limited legislatures have been so weakened by their lack of experienced members that they have lost power to the executive branch and may even fail to provide the sort of informational expertise they were intended to generate for the legislature.[94]

Experience matters because the legislative process is, as will be documented in Chapter 5, complicated. The issues involved in public policymaking are complex. New legislators face a substantial learning curve in educating themselves about byzantine rules, procedures, and issues.[95] According to a first-term member of the Florida House "This is billed as a part-time job, but it's a full-time job getting adjusted to it."[96] Indeed, the adjustment period can be overwhelming. A Washington representative admitted, "My first term I spent looking at the ceiling, admiring the architecture."[97] Many new lawmakers must learn the realities of the legislative process. A first-year member of the Iowa House confessed, "Initially, I was disappointed when I learned that floor debate is not where the decisions are made."[98] Another new Iowa House member concurred, observing, "It's not like your high school textbook on how a bill gets passed. You might as well toss that out the window. I had this idea about these big, grand debates. . . . But already I'm learning that a lot of it goes on outside the chamber, out of the public eye. Some issues are decided before they come to the floor."[99]

Part of the legislative socialization process occurs through hazing. Many of these acts are silly, such as the note purportedly from the governor handed to a new member of the Mississippi Senate. The message claimed that the governor had a close friend who was interested in the lawmaker's first bill and asked him "to call a Mr. L.E. Fant" to sidestep problems that might lead to a veto. The phone number was, of course, for the Jackson city zoo, and veteran legislators had a good laugh at their new colleague's expense.[100] A more common form of this rite of passage is to give a new legislator a difficult time on the initial bill he or she brings to the floor. In the Georgia and Iowa senates, for example, first-term lawmakers find themselves having to answer detailed questions and taking some ribbing about their measures from colleagues.[101] In the Colorado Senate, first-term senators are shocked when their maiden bill fails to pass on the floor despite their strenuous and seemingly successful efforts to build support for it. They later learn that their fellow senators voted down their measure as a prank. The bills pass after they are reintroduced.[102]

Such hazing may serve a purpose by reminding new members that they serve as just one member of a larger body that requires agreement among a majority or more to accomplish anything. In recent years, legislatures have become much more aware of the need to formally socialize and educate their new members; consequently, many of them have instituted formal orientation and training sessions.[103] During these meetings, veteran lawmakers share their experiences as a way to bring their newer colleagues up to speed.[104] A speaker of the California Assembly, for example, advised his new colleagues, "Keep your mouths shut. Don't get out there and offer your opinion on every issue. Listen. Do your homework and do it again."[105] The Rhode Island Senate majority leader cautioned his new members to be humble in their efforts because "You are going to be amazed to find that not everyone agrees with you."[106] Given these harsh realities, a Maryland senator reasons: "If you can walk away after your first year getting a good grasp of the issues that are before your committee, and developing good relationships with your colleagues and other involved in the legislative process, I would call that a very successful year."[107] A New Jersey state senator observed with only slight exaggeration, becoming a good legislator takes time: "You don't do it in your first four or five years. In your first three years, you're lucky to know where the bathroom is."[108]

WHERE ARE DECISIONS MADE IN STATE LEGISLATURES?

Ultimately, who are the most powerful decision makers in a state legislative house—standing committees, party caucuses, or legislative leaders? In the 1981 legislative session, state legislators were surveyed and asked to identify the most important decision-making entities in their chambers. Committees were thought to be an important decision-making center in 81 of the 99 legislative chambers. In only three states (California, Illinois, and New Jersey) were committees deemed to be unimportant in both chambers. Committees shared power with the leadership, the party caucus, or both in almost two-thirds of the houses. Committees, however, hold dominant power in only about 15 percent of state legislative chambers. Another study found that the locus of power within a legislature can change over time.[109] Certainly, this is likely to be the case for committees in legislatures that have adopted term limits.[110]

CONCLUSION

Parties, leaders, and committees are central to the functioning of every state legislature, as they are in the U.S. Congress. But the particular configuration of each and the relationships among them differ across legislative chambers. In some houses, leaders dominate; in others, committees make the important decisions; and in still others, power is vested in party caucuses. Moreover, party, leadership, and committee structures and the powers they exercise can change over time. Understanding how parties, leaders, and committees are constituted and how they interact is critical to understanding how a legislative house as an organization operates. It is the context in which legislative decision making occurs, and (as we will point out in subsequent chapters) the context is critical. Comprehending how the mix works in one legislative chamber, however, may provide only limited insight into the operations of other legislatures. For one thing, the division of seats between the parties may make a difference; in chambers where only one or two seats separates the majority from the minority party, leadership is likely to exert more control. The key thing to understand is that the relative power of leaders and committees is just that—relative. Circumstances change, legislators and leaders come and go, and norms such as seniority may erode or strengthen over time.

In the next chapter, we will see how the relationships among leaders, committees, and the rank-and-file members of the parties help define the legislative process. Again, just as there are substantial differences across state legislatures in the roles played by parties, leaders, and committees, the rules under which legislation is considered also vary significantly. The complexity of the legislative process emphasizes the importance of the structures and players discussed in this chapter, each of which is invested with power as a means to help the legislature make decisions.

ENDNOTES

1. For Connecticut, see Connecticut General Assembly Office of the House Clerk: House Rules (http://www.cga.ct.gov/hco/houserules.htm). For Mississippi, see Mississippi Legislature: House Rules (http://billstatus.ls.state.ms.us/htms/h_rules.pdf).
2. See Douglas G. Feig, "The State Legislature: Representative of the People or the Powerful?" in *Mississippi Government and Politics: Modernizers versus Traditionalists*, ed. Dale Krane and Stephen Shaffer (Lincoln, NE: University of Nebraska Press, 1992), 121.
3. Feig, "The State Legislature: Representative of the People or the Powerful?" 121.
4. Malcolm E. Jewell and Samuel C. Patterson, *The Legislative Process in the United States*, 4th ed (New York: Random House, 1986), 119.
5. See Mario Cattabiani, Angela Couloumbis, and Amy Worden, "Gavel Passes from Perzel," Philadelphia *Inquirer*, January 3, 2007; Mike Denison, "Big Skies, Big Leaders," *State Legislatures* 31 (2005), 46–50; Jessica Fender, "Wilder's Ouster Spells End of Era," *The Tennessean*, January 10, 2007; Karen Hansen, "Are Coalitions Really on the Rise?" *State Legislatures* 15 (1989): 11–12; Jewell and Patterson, *The Legislative Process in the United States*, 155–156; and Alan Rosenthal, *The Decline of Representative Democracy: Process, Participation, and Power in State Legislatures* (Washington, DC: CQ Press, 1998), 248.

6. Theo Emery, "In the Tennessee Senate, a Historic Shift of Power," *The New York Times*, January 27, 2007.

7. Tom Humphrey, "Williams Elected as House Speaker," *Knoxville News Sentinel*, January 14, 2009.

8. Sarah D. Wire, "Some House Members Call for the Removal of Speaker," *Columbia Missourian*, May 14, 2008.

9. Michele Jacklin, "Conservative Democrats are Victorious in Connecticut House," *State Legislatures* 15 (1989): 13–15.

10. See James Richardson, *Willie Brown* (Berkeley, University of California Press, 1996), 261–271, 358. See also Thad Kousser, *Term Limits and the Dismantling of State Legislative Professionalism* (New York: Cambridge University Press, 2005), 33.

11. Nancy Martorano, Bruce Anderson, and Keith E. Hamm, "A Transforming South: Exploring Patterns of State House Contestation," *American Review of Politics* (2000):21:179–200.

12. Keith E. Hamm and Robert Harmel, "Legislative Party Development and the Speaker System: The Case of the Texas House," *Journal of Politics* 55 (1993): 1140–1151; Robert Harmel, "Minority Partisanship in One-Party Predominant Legislatures: A Five-State Study," *Journal of Politics* 48 (1986): 729–740; Robert Harmel and Keith E. Hamm, "Development of a Party Role in a No-Party Legislature." *Western Political Quarterly* 39 (1986): 79–92.

13. Rosenthal, *The Decline of Representative Democracy*, 281.

14. Keith E. Hamm and Ronald D. Hedlund, "Political Parties in State Legislatures," in *The Encyclopedia of the American Legislative System*, ed. Joel J. Silbey (New York: Scribner's, 1994), 968.

15. John A. Straayer, *The Colorado General Assembly*, 2nd ed. (Boulder, CO: University Press of Colorado, 2000), 142, 231; Rosenthal, *The Decline of Representative Democracy*, 77.

16. Wayne L. Francis, *The Legislative Committee Game: A Comparative Analysis of 50 States* (Columbus, OH: Ohio State University Press, 1989), 45.

17. Anthony Gierzynski, *Legislative Party Campaign Committees in the American States* (Lexington, KY: The University Press of Kentucky, 1992), 48–50; Cindy Simon Rosenthal, "New Party or Campaign Bank Account? Explaining the Rise of State Legislative Campaign Committees," *Legislative Studies Quarterly* 20 (1995): 249–268; Daniel M. Shea, *Transforming Democracy: Legislative Campaign Committees and Political Parties* (Albany, NY: State University of New York Press, 1995).

18. Jeffrey M. Stonecash and Amy Widestrom, "Political Parties and Elections," in *Governing New York State*, 5th ed., ed. Robert F. Pecorella and Jeffrey M. Stonecash (Albany, NY: State University Press of New York, 2006), 65.

19. Scott Mooneyham, "House May Limit Length of Session," *Charlotte Observer*, September 3, 2002.

20. The following data are drawn from Council of State Governments, *The Book of the States 2007 edition* (Lexington, KY: Council of State Governments), 86–89 and state legislative web pages.

21. There were negotiations to split control of the two positions in late 2008, but ultimately the decision was made to give both titles to the new Democratic leader. See Danny Hakim, "Democrats Reach Pact to Lead the Senate," *The New York Times*, January 6, 2009. During the summer of 2009 an attempted coup left control of the chamber tied between Democrats and Republicans. The Republicans, who claimed to be in charge of the Senate, operated with a separate president and majority leader. Once the Democrats regained control they also operated with a separate temporary president and majority leader.

22. Gary M. Halter, *Government & Politics of Texas* (Madison, WI: Brown & Benchmark, 1997), 104–105; Rosenthal, *The Decline of Representative Democracy*, 248.

23. Jewell and Patterson, *The Legislative Process in the United States*, 119.

24. On this point, see Peverill Squire, "Changing State Legislative Leadership Careers," in *Changing Patterns in State Legislative Careers*, ed. Gary F. Moncrief and Joel A. Thompson (Ann Arbor, MI: University of Michigan Press, 1992), 180–185. See also Patricia K. Freeman, "A Comparative Analysis of Speaker Career Patterns in U. S. State Legislatures," *Legislative Studies Quarterly* 20 (1995): 365–376.

25. On professionalization over time see Peverill Squire, "Professionalization of Legislatures in the United States over the 20th Century," paper prepared for the 20th International Political Science Association World Congress, Fukuoka, Japan. July 9–13, 2006.

26. James D. Driscoll, *California's Legislature* (Sacramento, CA: Center for California Studies, 1986), 199–200.
27. Shane Goldmacher, "For Bass, Budget gets Top Billing," *Capitol Alert*, May 12, 2008 (http://www.sacbee.com/static/weblogs/capitolalertlatest/012494.html).
28. Jewell and Patterson, *The Legislative Process in the United States*, 119.
29. Thad L. Beyle, "Political Change in North Carolina: A Legislative Coup D'Etat," *Comparative State Politics Newsletter* 10 (1989): 4.
30. Malcolm E. Jewell, "Survey on Selection of State Legislative Leaders," *Comparative State Politics Newsletter* 1 (1980): 10.
31. Tom Loftus, *The Art of Legislative Politics*, (Washington, DC: CQ Press, 1994), 59.
32. Rosenthal, *The Decline of Representative Democracy*, 254–260.
33. On bill referrals see Peverill Squire and Keith E. Hamm, *101 Chambers: Congress, State Legislatures and the Future of Legislative Studies* (Columbus, OH; Ohio State University Press, 2005), 120.
34. Steve Wiegand, "Assembly Civility is a bit Fleeting," *Sacramento Bee*, December 7, 2006.
35. Richard A. Clucas, "Principal-Agent Theory and the Power of State House Speakers," *Legislative Studies Quarterly* 26 (2001): 319–338.
36. Squire and Hamm, *101 Chambers: Congress, State Legislatures and the Future of Legislative Studies*, 101–103.
37. Clucas, "Principal-Agent Theory and the Power of State House Speakers"; Richard A. Clucas, "Legislative Professionalism and the Power of State House Leaders," *State Politics and Policy Quarterly* 7 (2007): 1–19.
38. Gary F. Moncrief, Joel A. Thompson, and Karl T. Kurtz, "The Old Statehouse, It Ain't What It Used to Be," *Legislative Studies Quarterly* 21 (1996): 57–72; William Pound, "State Legislative Careers: Twenty-Five Years of Reform," in *Changing Patterns in State Legislative Careers*, ed. Gary F. Moncrief and Joel A. Thompson (Ann Arbor, MI: University of Michigan Press, 1992), 20–21.
39. Thomas H. Little and Rick Farmer, "Legislative Leadership," in *Institutional Change in American Politics: The Case of Term Limits*, ed. Karl T. Kurtz, Bruce Cain, and Richard G. Niemi (Ann Arbor, MI: University of Michigan Press, 2007), 71.
40. Mark Paziokas, "House Speaker Talks the Talk," *Hartford Courant*, May 4, 2005.
41. Richard A. Clucas, *The Speaker's Electoral Connection: Willie Brown and the California Assembly* (Berkeley, CA: Institute of Governmental Studies), 19–27.
42. Former Idaho House Speaker Bruce Newcomb, quoted at "Behind the Scenes in the Idaho Legislature," a workshop conducted by Carl Bianchi, Gary Moncrief, and Bruce Newcomb, Boise State University, February 2, 2008.
43. Ralph G. Wright, *Inside the Statehouse: Lessons from the Speaker* (Washington, DC: CQ Press, 2005), 89.
44. Keith E. Hamm, Ronald D. Hedlund, and Nancy Martorano, "Measuring State Legislative Committee Power: Change and Chamber Differences in the 20th Century," *State Politics and Policy Quarterly* 6 (2006): 88–111.
45. Jack R. Van Der Slik and Kent D. Redfield, *Lawmaking in Illinois* (Springfield, IL: Office of Public Affairs Communication, 1986), 139.
46. See Bruce E. Cain and Thad Kousser, *Adapting to Term Limits: Recent Experiences and New Directions* (San Francisco, CA: Public Policy Institute of California, 2004), 31–32.
47. See Matthew C. Moen, Kenneth T. Palmer, and Richard J. Powell, *Changing Members: The Maine Legislature in the Era of Term Limits*, (Lanham, MD: Lexington Books, 2005), 94; Belle Zeller, ed., *American State Legislatures* (New York: Crowell, 1954), 260.
48. Robert Luce, *Legislative Procedure* (Boston: Houghton Mifflin, 1922), 137.
49. Tim Groseclose and David C. King, "Committee Theories Reconsidered," in *Congress Reconsidered*, 7th ed., ed. Lawrence C. Dodd and Bruce I. Oppenheimer (Washington, DC: CQ Press, 2001), 207–208.
50. American Society of Legislative Clerks and Secretaries in cooperation with the National Conference of State Legislatures, *Inside the Legislative Process* (Denver, CO: National Conference of State Legislatures, 1998), 4–4.
51. Ronald D. Hedlund and Keith E. Hamm, "Political Parties as Vehicles for Organizing U.S. State Legislative Committees," *Legislative Studies Quarterly* 21 (1996): 383–408.
52. See Legislative Affairs Agency, "Alaska State Legislature Uniform Rules," as amended 2004, xi and 1.

53. Ronald D. Hedlund, Kevin Coombs, Nancy Martorano, and Keith E. Hamm, "Partisan Stacking on Legislative Committees," *Legislative Studies Quarterly*, 35 (2009): 175-191.
54. Bob Johnson, "Hubbard Ousted from Key Budget Committee," *Mobile Register,* January 11, 2007.
55. See Georgia House of Representatives, "Rules, Ethics, and Decorum of the House of Representatives," Rule 11.8.
56. Jim Tharpe, Nancy Badertscher, and Sonji Jacobs, "Legislature '05: Republicans Write Rules; New GOP Majority Locks in Power as Democratic Unity Noticeably Erodes," *Atlanta Journal-Constitution,* January 11, 2005.
57. Brian Basinger and Brandon Larrabee, "Session so Far Gets Mixed Marks," *Augusta Chronicle,* February 19, 2005.
58. Tom Baxter and Jim Galloway, "Legislature 2005: Democrat Denied Ceremonial Role," *Atlanta Journal-Constitution,* January 13, 2005.
59. See Hawaii House of Representatives, "Rules of the House of Representatives, State of Hawaii, The Twenty-Fourth State Legislature, 2008," Rule 11.2 (1); Arkansas House of Representatives, "House Rules as Amended by HR 1031 of 2007," Rule 52. (a) (1).
60. American Society of Legislative Clerks and Secretaries, *Inside the Legislative Process,* 4.8.
61. Illinois House of Representatives, "Rules of the House of the State of Illinois Ninety Fifth General Assembly," Rule 5 (b).
62. Missouri House of Representatives, "Rules of the House of Representatives, 94th General Assembly, adopted January 18, 2007," Rule 22.
63. Jim Small, "Disaffected Democrats Split Over Committee Assignments," *Arizona Capitol Times,* January 19, 2007.
64. Small, "Disaffected Democrats Split Over Committee Assignments."
65. Michigan House of Representatives, "Standing Rules of the House of Representatives in Accordance with the Michigan Constitution, Article IV, Section 16," House Resolution No. 291, adopted February 28, 2008, Rule 33.
66. See Iowa House of Representatives, House Resolution 5, Division V, Rule 46; New York State Assembly, "Rules of the Assembly of the State of New York 2007–2008," Section 1. c. 3.
67. Nancy Martorano, Keith E. Hamm, and Ronald D. Hedlund, "Examining Committee Structures, Procedures, and Powers in U.S. State Legislatures," paper presented at the 2000 Annual Meeting of the Midwest Political Science Association.
68. State of Arkansas, "Parliamentary Manual of the Senate, Eighty-Sixth General Assembly," rule 7.01 (b) (4).
69. State of Arkansas, "Parliamentary Manual of the Senate, Eighty-Sixth General Assembly," rule 7.01 (b) (2). According to rule 7.05 (a), seniority is defined as the "continuous, uninterrupted senatorial service of the Senator."
70. See South Carolina Senate, "Rules of the Senate, 2005 Final," January 11, 2005, Rule 19 (D). The only proviso is that each senator must select either the Finance Committee or the Judiciary Committee on the first round.
71. "Each member of the house, in order of seniority, may designate three committees on which he or she desires to serve, listed in order of preference. The member is entitled to become a member of the committee of his or her highest preference on which there remains a vacant seniority position," Texas House of Representatives, "Rules and Precedents of the Texas House, 80th Legislature, 2007," Rule 4, Chapter A, Section 2 (2). Seniority is defined as cumulative years of service in the House in Rule 4, Chapter A, Section 2 (3).
72. The House actually uses six out-of-date U.S. House districts from the 1990s; the state lost a seat in the 2000 reapportionment, reducing it to five U.S. House districts.
73. Mississippi Legislature, "House Rules," Rule 60.
74. Alabama House of Representatives, "Rules of the House of Representatives of Alabama," Rule 63. Note that "Political party affiliation and racial diversity should be considered in instances where at least ten members of the body are affiliated with a political party or are members of the same race."
75. Minnesota House of Representatives, "Permanent Rules of the House," adopted March 1, 2007, Article VI, 6.02.
76. California State Assembly, "Standing Rules of the Assembly 2007-08 Regular Session," Rule 12.
77. Ronald D. Hedlund, "Entering the Committee System: State Committee Assignments," *Western Political Quarterly* 42 (1989): 597–625; Ronald Hedlund, "Accommodating Member Requests in Committee Assignments: Individual-Level Explanations," in *Changing Pat-*

terns in State Legislative Careers, ed. Gary F. Moncrief and Joel A. Thompson (Ann Arbor, MI: University of Michigan Press, 1992); and Ronald D. Hedlund and Samuel C. Patterson, "The Electoral Antecedents of State Legislative Committee Assignments," *Legislative Studies Quarterly* 17 (1992): 539–559.

78. Wright, *Inside the Statehouse*, 105.

79. Tina Cassidy, "Term Limits Backers Moved from Key Panels," *Boston Globe*, January 30, 2001.

80. Karen E. Crummy, "Finneran Allies Get Choice Posts: Speaker Reportedly Raps Renegade Rep," *Boston Herald*, January 30, 2001.

81. See James Coleman Battista, "Re-examining Legislative Committee Representativeness in the States," *State Politics and Policy Quarterly* 4 (2004): 161–180; L. Marvin Overby and Thomas A. Kazee, "Outlying Committees in the Statehouse: An Examination of the Prevalence of Committee Outliers in State Legislatures," *Journal of Politics* 62 (2000): 701–728; L. Marvin Overby, Thomas A. Kazee, and David W. Prince, "Committee Outliers in State Legislatures," *Legislative Studies Quarterly* 29 (2004): 81–107; David W. Prince, and L. Marvin Overby, "Legislative Organization Theory and Committee Preference Outliers in State Senates," *State Politics and Policy Quarterly*, (2005): 68–87.

82. Jesse Richman, "Uncertainty and the Prevalence of Committee Outliers," *Legislative Studies Quarterly*, 33 (2008): 323–347.

83. W. Gardner Selby and David Rauf, "Craddick Stands by Panel Choices," *Austin American-Statesman*, January 30, 2007.

84. Michael Cooper, "Bruno Adds to Intrigue by Elevating a Democrat," *The New York Times*, March 1, 2007.

85. "In the selection of the Chairman of the Standing Committees, the senior member of the Committee from the majority party . . . in terms of seniority with the Committee, shall be the Chairman of the Standing Committee, " South Carolina Senate, "Rules of the Senate, 2005 Final," January 11, 2005, Rule 19 (E). To keep too much power from being concentrated in the hands of the most senior members, South Carolina senators are limited to chairing a single standing committee.

86. State of Arkansas, "Parliamentary Manual of the Senate, Eighty-Sixth General Assembly," rule 7.01 (b) (2) and rule 7.05 (a).

87. "The chair and minority chair of each standing committee except the Appropriations Committee shall be limited only to the members of the applicable caucus with the most seniority as members of their respective caucus. Whenever there are more caucus members with equal seniority than available chairs or minority chairs for that caucus, the selection of a chair or minority chair from among such caucus members shall be in the discretion of the appointing authority. The appointing authority may designate the standing committee to which the appointing authority shall appoint a member as chair or minority chair without regard to seniority," Pennsylvania House of Representatives, House Resolution 108, adopted March 13, 2007, amended by House Resolution 263 October 22, 2007, Rule 43.

88. Quoted in Karl Kurtz, "Term Limits for Committee Chairs?" The Thicket at State Legislatures, May 31, 2007 (http://ncsl.typepad.com/the_thicket/2007/05/term_limits_for.html#more).

89. Illinois House of Representatives, "Rules of the House of the State of Illinois Ninety Fifth General Assembly," Rule 10 (b).

90. Laylan Copelin, "Few Changes in Craddick's Panel Picks," *Austin-American Statesman*, January 27, 2007.

91. See, for example, Jim McLean, "Mays Names Heads of Committees," *Topeka Capital-Journal*, December 6, 2002; and Richard Pérez-Peña, "From Speaker of Assembly, Punishment and Rewards," *The New York Times*, January 9, 2001.

92. Peverill Squire, "Career Opportunities and Membership Stability in Legislatures," *Legislative Studies Quarterly* 13 (1988): 65-82; Peverill Squire, "Member Career Opportunities and the Internal Organization of Legislatures," *Journal of Politics* 50 (1988): 726–744; Peverill Squire, "The Theory of Legislative Institutionalization and the California Assembly," *Journal of Politics* 54 (1992): 1026–1054.

93. Marjorie Sarbaugh-Thompson, "Changing the Action: The Impact of Term Limits on Committees," paper presented at the Eighth Annual Conference on State Politics and State Policy, Philadelphia, Pennsylvania, May 2008.

94. Bruce Cain and Gerald Wright, "Committees," in *Institutional Change in American Politics: The Case of Term Limits*, ed. Karl T. Kurtz, Bruce Cain, and Richard G. Niemi (Ann Arbor, MI: University of Michigan Press, 2007), 87–89.
95. Charles G. Bell and Charles M. Price, *The First Term* (Beverly Hills, CA: Sage, 1975).
96. Steve Bousquet, "Freshmen Get First Taste of Life at Capitol," *St. Petersburg Times*, November 22, 2004.
97. Diane Brooks, "Politics, Personalities, Populism: Wide Range of Experience and Ideas in the 39th," *Seattle Times*, October 25, 2000.
98. James Q. Lynch, "Freshman Legislators Learn Tough Lessons," *Cedar Rapids Gazette*, May 14, 2001.
99. Mike Klein, "New Kid on the Block," *Des Moines Register*, January 26, 2003.
100. Andy Kanengiser, "Lawmaker Learns the Ropes," *The Clarion-Ledger*, March 19, 2004.
101. Mike Billips, "Staton Leads Legislature's Freshman Class," *Macon Telegraph*, April 4, 2005; Dan Gearino, "Freshman Legislators Make Themselves Heard," *Waterloo/Cedar Falls Courier*, May 15, 2005.
102. Trent Seibert, "Pettiness Takes Office at Capitol," *Denver Post*, February 5, 2001.
103. Alan Rosenthal, "Education and Training of Legislators," in *Institutional Change in American Politics: The Case of Term Limits*, ed. Karl T. Kurtz, Bruce Cain, and Richard G. Niemi (Ann Arbor, MI: University of Michigan Press, 2007).
104. See, for example, the discussion in William K. Muir, Jr., *Legislature: California's School for Politics* (Berkeley, CA: University of California Press, 1982), 120–137.
105. George Skelton, "First-Day Advice for Newcomers to the Legislature," *Los Angeles Times*, December 4, 2000.
106. Edward Fitzpatrick, "Getting Elected: The Easy Part," *Providence Journal*, December 6, 2000.
107. Sean R. Sedam, "Young and Focused: Garagiola is a Rising Star in the Senate," (Maryland) *The Gazette*, February 9, 2007.
108. Herb Jackson, "Voting Record Belies Kean's 'Independent' Claim," (Hackensack) *The Record*, October 2, 2006.
109. Hamm and Hedlund, "Political Parties in State Legislatures."
110. Cain and Wright, "Committees."

CHAPTER

5

THE LEGISLATIVE PROCESS
IN THE STATES

We have all encountered diagrams showing "how a bill gets passed." These diagrams usually just outline various steps in the formal process of getting a bill passed into law. Unfortunately, these presentations only take us so far in gaining a real understanding of the legislative process. At the outset, we need to recognize that diagrams of the formal process do not give the full picture. Indeed, they are usually presented in such a way that readers are left to infer that the process is straightforward and rational, almost sterile. In fact, that is a reasonably accurate description of the process that only some bills follow. But these are usually minor bills making technical adjustments to existing laws or bills on which there is overwhelming agreement. In most legislatures, these measures account for half—perhaps three-fourths—of all enactments. But for bills involving conflict and disagreement—that is, almost any legislation of political significance—the process involves many more twists and turns than the textbook diagrams suggest.

To put it another way, there is the *textbook* version of the process, and then there is the *contextual* version of the process. Both are necessary to gain a full understanding of how a legislature operates. The textbook version (which we explain in this chapter) details the formal steps in the process. These formal steps are part of the "rules of the game" that must be understood and mastered if we are to understand how bills are passed. But the rules do not exist in a vacuum.

The legislative game involves many players—legislators, staffers, the governor, administrators, lobbyists, and many others. The relationships between the multitude of players are largely what defines the context in which lawmaking occurs. And this is just as important to understand as are the rules. Do the leaders of the House and Senate get along? Is the governor liked and respected? Is Senator A still angry with Senator B? Is someone going to challenge Representative X in the next primary election? These and other issues provide the context in which the process plays out. We will discuss many of these contextual factors in Chapter 6.

In this chapter, we begin by examining the broad differences in rules and legislative procedures across the states. There, we discuss the different types of bills—and different procedural tracks—that are found in all legislatures. Next, we present the basic "textbook" version of the steps in the legislative process (recognizing that the contextual version is also important). Fourth, we discuss the dimension of time as it applies to state legislatures. Fifth, we explore the appropriations process as a special subset of legislative bill-making. We conclude this chapter with an initial look at some of the contextual factors that affect legislative decision making as a prelude to a more detailed discussion in Chapter 6.

VARIATION ACROSS THE STATES

The process by which a bill gets passed is not quite the same across the 50 state legislatures or even between chambers in the same legislature. Although the basic procedure and purpose of the process is roughly the same in all states, each legislature has some quirks or oddities that have developed over time and make its process at least a little distinctive. For example, in the South Dakota Legislature, a move to "defer the bill to the 41st Legislative Day" is a common motion. Because there are only 40 days in a legislative session in South Dakota, this motion effectively kills the bill. It is a particularly prevalent motion in standing committees; probably 30 to 40 percent of all bills sent to committees are deferred to the 41st legislative day, and thus no further action is taken on the bill.

Table 5-1 shows the number of bills introduced and the percentage passed in a recent two-year period. We include the bills in both regular sessions of the biennium and any special sessions that were called. We can make several observations about these data. First, there is a wide range in the number of bill introductions across the states, from 737 in Wyoming to more than 33,000 in New York. New York, however, is an extreme case, with more than twice as many bill introductions as the next most prolific state (New Jersey, with 13,856 introductions). But four other states (Illinois, Minnesota, Pennsylvania and Tennessee) have at least 8,000 introductions each. The median is about 3,300 bill introductions.

Given the thousands of bills introduced, for the most part, state legislatures pass relatively few of them. Only a dozen states passed more than 1,000 bills each (Arkansas ranked first at 2,364). A more appropriate measure is the *proportion* of bills passed, and as Figure 5-1 indicates, most legislatures are not easy marks in this regard. In almost three-quarters of the states, fewer than 30 percent of the bills that are introduced are passed by both chambers. Clearly, most bills die along the way.

This is not, however, the case everywhere. In a few states, most legislation that is introduced is passed; in 2005–2006, these states were Arkansas,

Table 5-1　Bill Introductions and Enactments, 2005–2006 Biennium[a]

State	Introduced in 2005	Introduced in 2006	Special Session (2005 and 2006)	Total Bills (2005–2006)	Total Bills Passed (2005–2006)	Percent Passed (2005–2006)
Alabama	1,237	1,432	240	2,909	557	19
Alaska	513	308	25	846	223	26
Arizona	1,311	1,453	5	2,769	729	26
Arkansas	3,176	0	75	3,251	2,364	73
California	2,892	1,853	38	4,783	1,361	28
Colorado	602	651	36	1,289	855	66
Connecticut	3,391	1,550	7	4,948	517	10
Delaware	546	392	0	938	437	47
Florida	3,139	2,096	64	5,299	1,058	20
Georgia	1,304	1,937	3	3,244	919	28
Hawaii	3,680	2,758	0	6,438	616	10
Idaho	642	737	1	1,380	874	63
Illinois	6,217	2,547	0	8,764	1,029	12
Indiana	859	834	0	1,693	439	26
Iowa	2,182	1,211	0	3,393	375	11
Kansas	853	774	29	1,656	429	26
Kentucky	741	1,012	4	1,757	383	22
Louisiana	1,243	2,149	157	3,549	1,429	40
Maine	1,693	658	0	2,351	814	35
Maryland	2,632	2,856	25	5,513	1,258	23
Massachusetts	5,400	N/A	0	5,400	671	12
Michigan	2,475	1,752	0	4,227	1,022	24
Minnesota	4,906	3,139	248	8,293	285	3
Mississippi	2,950	2,819	251	6,020	973	16
Missouri	1,528	1,879	10	3,417	458	13
Montana	1,441	0	9	1,450	697	48
Nebraska	763	500	0	1,263	334	26
Nevada	1,107	0	12	1,119	524	47
New Hampshire	907	1,029	1	1,937	627	32
New Jersey	7,342	6,430	84	13,856	820	6
New Mexico	2,182	1,623	0	3,805	532	14
New York	15,379	17,700	2	33,081	1,514	5
North Carolina	2,903	1,905	0	4,808	727	15
North Dakota	944	0	0	944	615	65
Ohio	709	403	0	1,112	198	18
Oklahoma	2,077	2,133	376	4,586	891	19
Oregon	2,957	0	5	2,962	848	29
Pennsylvania	3,423	4,450	229	8,102	462	6
Rhode Island	2,914	2,812	0	5,726	1,214	21

TABLE 5-1 (CONTINUED)

STATE	INTRODUCED IN 2005	INTRODUCED IN 2006	SPECIAL SESSION (2005 AND 2006)	TOTAL BILLS (2005–2006)	TOTAL BILLS PASSED (2005–2006)	PERCENT PASSED (2005–2006)
South Carolina	1,386	721	0	2107	386	18
South Dakota	491	458	0	949	554	58
Tennessee	4,837	3,330	36	8,203	1,099	13
Texas	5,484	0	415	5,899	1,403	24
Utah	592	663	33	1,288	704	55
Vermont	728	485	0	1,213	250	21
Virginia	2,181	2,346	127	4,654	1,996	43
Washington	2,460	929	0	3,389	678	20
West Virginia	2,116	2,105	85	4,306	688	16
Wisconsin	1,404	1,967	4	3,375	597	18
Wyoming	524	213	0	737	372	50
Total	123,363	88,999	2,636	214,998	38,805	18

Source: Council of State Governments (Lexington, KY); *The Book of the States, 2006 and 2007 editions*, Table 3.20.
[a]Figures are for bills only and do not include resolutions.

FIGURE 5-1 STATE LEGISLATURES AND THE PROPORTION OF BILLS PASSED, 2005–2006 SESSIONS

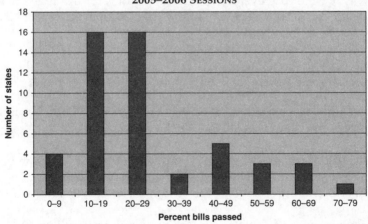

Colorado, Idaho, North Dakota, South Dakota, Utah, and Wyoming. With the exception of Colorado, these are all states with small populations and, except for Arkansas, they are all Northern Plains or Rocky Mountain states. But the reasons for the passage of such a high proportion of bills in these states are likely the results of specific rules and operating procedures rather than geography. For example, Colorado limits each legislator to five bill introductions per session—a rule that ensures that legislators will be very selective about what they introduce, focusing on only proposals they think are apt to pass.

In Idaho, bills are not automatically introduced; rather, they must be approved for printing by a standing committee. This process means that each year, 300 to 400 proposed bills are never printed and therefore never formally introduced. Some of these bills are simply held by the sponsor, but many are not introduced because the committee refuses to print the proposal. Thus, although Table 5-1 indicates that Idaho passed 63 percent of the *bills that were introduced*, the legislature actually passed a considerably lower percentage of the *total proposals that were drafted*. In other words, about 30 percent of the proposals were eliminated before they were formally introduced. Obviously, this gate-keeping function gives standing committees in Idaho extraordinary power.

State constitutions in North Dakota and South Dakota place strict limits on the number of days the legislature can meet (60 days total over a two-year period in North Dakota; 75 days total in South Dakota). Wyoming also has constitutional limits (60 days in a two-year session). Consequently, the high proportion of bills passed in these state legislatures does not necessarily reflect a permissive environment in which lawmakers are not vigilant; it is more likely the case that the rules and procedures keep legislators more focused on bills with a legitimate chance of passage.

This is not the case everywhere. In New York, for example, many bills that have no chance of passing are introduced. As one analysis of New York politics states:

> Many bills are introduced with no real legislative intent. . . . A bill that does not pass in one session must be reintroduced in the next or it will be dropped. A large proportion of those that fail will show up again. . . . One of the first functions of a legislator's staff at the beginning of the session is to dust off last year's bills for introduction.[1]

In Massachusetts, citizens have the right to write their own bills and petition their legislators to introduce the bills on their behalf.[2] This procedure inflates the number of bill introductions, the vast majority of which have almost no chance of passing.

At the extremes of Table 5-1 (either very high or very low levels of bill introductions), an inverse relationship generally exists between the number of bills introduced and the proportion passed. That is, all the states where large numbers of bills are introduced show low percentages of bill passage. Thus, the states with the highest number of introductions—New York (33,000 bills); New Jersey (almost 14,000); and Illinois, Minnesota, Pennsylvania, and Tennessee (all more than 8,000 bills) have enactment rates of 5 percent, 6 percent, 12 percent, 3 percent, 6 percent, and 13 percent, respectively. In contrast, states with few bill introductions tend to have much higher enactment rates; the exceptions are Alaska (846 bills introduced and only 26 percent of those passed both chambers) and Ohio (1,112 introductions and only 18 percent enacted).

But this inverse relationship between introductions and enactments appears to hold only in the extreme cases. For the rest of the states, other variables take primacy. These variables include the number of local bills (proposals that apply only to a specific locality and not statewide) introduced, the number of appropriation (budget) bills, unified or divided party control of the legislature, and whether carryover provisions exist. Each of these variables is discussed in this chapter.

In a few states, especially those with a "local act" system of local government chartering, a good deal of municipal, county, and other local jurisdiction business is conducted through the legislature. In Alabama, for example, the House of Representatives has eight standing committees that are each dedicated to local legislation for a specific county. Much of this legislation is noncontroversial, and as long as the legislators from the locality in question are supportive of the bill, it will pass without much dissent. In some states, such local legislation comprises a hefty amount of the workload—perhaps several hundred bills. For example, more than half the bills introduced in Alabama involve local government issues.[3]

The ways appropriation bills are handled vary by state. In some, such as California, Massachusetts, and Wisconsin, the entire state budget is typically handled in a single bill. In other states, each department or office is dealt with in a separate budget bill, so there may be more than 100 separate budget bills. Arkansas, for example, averages around 500 appropriations bills.[4] In most cases, the appropriations have been worked out in committee and between leadership in the two chambers before the bills are sent to the floor, so budget bills have a high degree of success on the floor. Thus, a state legislature in which the appropriations process is divided into scores or hundreds of bills is likely to have a higher overall "batting average" when it comes to determining the overall passage rate of bills.

Party control over the legislature matters as well. If the Republicans control one house and the Democrats the other, bills introduced in one house are more likely to die when they reach the other house. A good example is New York, where historically the Democrats have controlled the Assembly and routinely pass some bills knowing these bills will be killed in the Senate, where the Republicans (up until 2009) have the majority. The same procedure works in reverse—the Senate passes some bills knowing they have no chance of getting through the Assembly. But both parties can claim credit and make points with their partisan backers even though they realize the bills they pass have little or no chance of becoming law.

About half of the state legislatures make use of a "carryover provision" between the first and second years of the biennial legislative operation. This provision stipulates that a bill that was not passed in the first session stays alive in the second session. Thus, if a bill passed the Senate, was sent to the House, and was awaiting a committee hearing when the legislature adjourned, the bill would be picked up at the house committee stage when the legislature reconvened the next year. In other words, the bill would not have to be reintroduced in the first chamber and start all over. States with carryover provisions are likely to have a higher passage rate because the same bill does not have to be restarted.[5] Of course, if a general election has occurred between the sessions, then the bill must start anew because the legislature is not the same one that considered the bill previously.

Finally, it is worth noting that analyzing passage rates is just one aspect of the overall assessment of the legislative process. It is probably true that bills today are longer and more complicated than they used to be, a phenomenon often associated with congressional bills. Moreover, we know that some bills are much more important than others. And this leads us to the recognition that there are actually several different tracks that legislation may follow.

THE THREE TRACKS OF THE LEGISLATIVE PROCESS: BILLS THAT DIE, BILLS THAT FLY, AND BILLS THAT CRAWL

Many observers have sought to explain the legislative process by analogy. Making laws has been compared to sausage-making, the "torturous upriver runs of spawning fish," a casino with multiple games of chance, and the work of an improvisational jazz band, to name a few.[6]

Perhaps the legislative process is best described as at least three different processes, or tracks. These tracks correspond to different types of legislation. As indicated in Table 5-1 and Figure 5-1, most bills do not make it through the process to become law. They die, and they usually die in committee. These bills are like boxcars that are pulled off onto rail spurs, where they sit for the entire session.[7]

In contrast, of the bills that do pass, most do so with little or no opposition and encounter very little resistance. As Frank Smallwood, a political science professor and former state legislator, noted years ago, "It is important to realize that very few of these bills dealt with the creation of new statutory law from scratch. Instead, the overwhelming majority involved incremental amendments to existing state laws. . . ."[8] They are often referred to as "technical" or "housekeeping" bills, meaning they make only small changes in the current body of law. Take, for example, HB2021, a bill in Missouri "to appropriate money for supplemental purposes for the Department of Conservation, for the purchase of equipment, and for planning, expenses, and for capital improvements including but not limited to major additions and renovations, new structures, and land improvements or acquisitions, from the funds designated for the fiscal period ending June 30, 2008." A noncontroversial bill, it was introduced in the House of Representatives on January 8, 2008, passed the House on a 149 to 1 vote on January 22, was approved by the Senate on a 32 to 0 vote on January 28, and was signed into law by the governor on January 30.[9] These noncontroversial bills fly along the legislative tracks like express trains.

A much smaller but generally more significant group of bills are those on which legislators (and others) have differing opinions. These bills often involve important issues and represent a significant shift in thinking about policy options. In other words, they involve changing the status quo in a meaningful way. And that is precisely the problem for the bill's supporters. Changing the status quo means changing the relative benefits and costs for some group. There is a sort of natural inertia in the legislative process that must be overcome. Even what seems like a relatively simple matter can generate resistance. Take, for example, mandatory seat belt laws. Today, for most people, such laws seem to be a no-brainer. But when seat belt bills were first proposed, they encountered resistance from many quarters. Some citizens saw them as government invasion of privacy. Law enforcement agencies recognized that enforcement would be difficult and time-consuming. Other people were concerned about the nature of punishment for noncompliance— would it mean a fine? A suspension of the driver's license? A night in jail?[10]

Many bills involve much more controversial issues than seat belts. On such matters, there is enough resistance to change that it makes the crafting of significant public policy a difficult and artful endeavor. Here, there is no fast track, but rather a slow, winding route that seems always to be uphill, working against the inertia of the status quo. And, often, even if the train makes it to the final station, it will not be composed of quite the same set of cars that began the journey. Amendments are added and items deleted like boxcars being switched in an out in an effort to find the right combination to pull the bill through.

A special case of the bill that crawls is the budget. The way the budget is crafted is somewhat different from one state to another. A minority of states (20 of them) pass a two-year (biennial) budget, and the rest pass annual budgets.[11] In most states (e.g., Tennessee and Maryland), the governor plays the key role because the legislature is largely reacting to the parameters established in the executive budget. In other states (e.g., Idaho), the legislature takes on a significant independent role, largely ignoring the governor's budget proposal. Until recently, the practice in North Carolina was to ensure that all legislators (or at least all majority party legislators) could place a few local projects in the state budget—a sort of institutionalized pork barrel system.[12] As noted earlier, some states produce a single, massive appropriation bill—usually known as the "omnibus budget bill"—but in others, the budget is set through dozens of smaller appropriation bills (often a separate budget for each state agency). But regardless of the differences that exist, the budget process is the same in all states in one aspect: it is the one piece of legislation that must be passed. To put it simply, the state government (and often local governments such as school districts) cannot function without the funds appropriated through the budget bill (or bills). The appropriations function is such an integral part of the legislative process that, in many states, the legislature is likely to adjourn within days of passage of the budget. We have more to say about the budget process later in this chapter.

Most of the subsequent discussion in this chapter focuses on the third track—the legislative process as it applies to the bills on which there is some disagreement. This may be a relatively small subset of all bills, but these are almost always the ones that create interest, that affect some significant component of the population, and that have real consequences beyond "technical" or "housekeeping" matters. In terms of political significance, these are the bills that carry the freight.

STEPS IN THE LEGISLATIVE PROCESS

The legislative process is intended to be deliberative and slow. Several organizational and procedural features are specifically designed to promote this, including three readings rules, standing committee systems, reconsideration rules, and (except for in Nebraska) bicameralism. The process examined here is a generic model—a few of the stages vary from legislature to legislature.[13] This is true, for example, of the "three readings rules"—they do not necessarily appear at the same stage in all state legislatures. In fact, a few states (Maine, North Dakota, South Dakota) require only two readings, but the Nebraska unicameral requires four readings.[14]

INTRODUCTION AND FIRST READING

As discussed in Politics Under the Domes 5-1, the ideas for bills come from numerous sources. A few are outlined by the governor in the state-of-the-state address and are part of the governor's legislative package. Some are requested by administrative agencies. Many bill ideas come from interest groups. Some are suggested by constituents, and some come from the legislators themselves. Regardless of who develops the idea, a draft is eventually written. In some cases, an interest group may draw up an initial draft, or the legislator or his personal staff might create a proposal, but most of the time bills are drafted by staff attorneys who work for the legislature. In some states, the process is unusual. In Connecticut, legislators propose bills by writing a brief summary of their proposal's intent. Bills are only written in full statutory language at the request of legislative committees.[15] Regardless of who draws up the original version, it must be sponsored and introduced by a legislator.

POLITICS UNDER THE DOMES 5-1

"There Ought to Be a Law" or
Why Legislators Introduce Bills

As shown in Table 5-1, state legislators across the country introduced a total of 214,998 bills in 2005 and 2006. Where are the ideas for all those measures generated? And why are there so many of them, particularly given the slim odds that any will get enacted into law?

First, it is important to understand that state legislators do not concoct most, or even very many, of the policy proposals contained in the legislation they author. Rather than acting as policy innovators, state legislators typically act as policy entrepreneurs. They scan the political horizon looking for policy ideas that interest them. Second, legislators have many different motivations for introducing particular pieces of legislation. Because the motivations behind bills are many, there are many kinds of bills. Obviously, some bills, such as those involving appropriations, are routine matters the legislature must address every year or two. Other legislative proposals are developed by the executive branch to deal with administrative matters or local governments to address issues of interest to them. Still others are drafted by lobbyists to promote the interests of those they represent. But there are additional reasons why legislators introduce bills.

"There ought to be a law": Legislators, like the rest of American society, occasionally get exasperated by things. Unlike the rest of us, they are in a position where they can directly do something about it. Thus, a Rhode Island senator, irritated that Boston Red Sox players at a local event he attended were charging his young constituents large sums of money for autographs, introduced legislation providing that "no professional athlete or professional entertainer, film, corporation or other entity representing the entertainer or athlete shall charge a fee of any kind to any person under the age of 16 for an autograph." The bill proposed that violators face a $100 fine. An aggrieved Washington state senator filed a bill to require employers to pay to fly an employee business class for long distance business trips, explaining, "I got to thinking about the fact that my employer has to supply me with an ergonomically sound chair. But if they ask me to go to Washington, DC, they can stuff me in the back of the airplane. And I'm doing what they want." A Florida senator, stuck in a traffic jam and aggravated by rude drivers cutting in front of him, actually thought to himself, "There ought to be a law," and proceeded to write a bill to require police to issue $80 tickets to "me-first" drivers who cut in front of other drivers. All of these legislators

(Continued)

POLITICS UNDER THE DOMES 5-1 (CONTINUED)

saw things in their world that annoyed them and sought legislative solutions to correct them.

That's a good idea: Once in a while, lawmakers stumble across an idea that strikes them as worth pursuing legislatively. For example, when an Oregon senator met with a political science class at a community college in his district, the students pushed for a special tax break for working students. As one of the students recalled, the senator "liked the idea, got out his cell phone and called into legal counsel to have it drafted for us."

Constituent requests: Legislators often introduce bills that have been proposed by constituents. Recall that the Arkansas apostrophe bill discussed in Chapter 1 was introduced on behalf of a constituent. Indeed, a Wyoming representative admits, "Almost all of my legislation comes from constituent requests." In many cases, introducing a bill to make the constituent happy is all that matters to the legislator; getting the measure passed is beside the point. A Louisiana representative confessed that she sponsors constituent proposals "Even when I know or don't think it has a chance to pass, I do it because it's an obligation." Indeed, a staunchly anti-gay marriage Maine representative even introduced a pro-gay marriage bill because it was submitted by one of his constituents. There are, however, some risks for a legislator in introducing bills written by constituents. An Arizona representative thought a bill some of his constituents wrote and asked him to introduce would only protect people who carried concealed weapons without getting the required state permit from being charged with a crime. The representative "had no idea" the bill's language was so loose that it would allow any kind of weapon to be carried any place in the state until the flaw was embarrassingly pointed out by another legislator while the bill was being debated on the House floor.

Personal policy expertise and interests: As noted in Chapter 3, legislators come from a variety of occupational backgrounds. They often draw on their own life experiences for policy proposals. A member of the Alabama House, for example, acknowledged on his blog, "I am one of these horrible, lowlifes in our society commonly referred to as an attorney, so I often bring a number of these bills that I think will improve the criminal justice process."

Policy incubation: Legislators occasionally introduce a measure on an issue knowing that it is highly unlikely to resonant with their fellow legislators. Facing certain defeat, they still put the bill before the legislature simply to initiate a conversation on the policies promoted in it. Taking such a long-term perspective is known as "policy incubation." As an Iowa state senator acknowledged after proposing a bill allowing for doctor-assisted suicide, "My purpose is to start the dialogue. I have no illusions about its prospects for passage this year. . . ." A Georgia representative known for tackling controversial issues explained his perspective on policy incubation this way: "In molding opinion, it takes time, a lot of patience and the willingness to (introduce) a lot of bills. . . . It might not be until the third or fourth year that something germinates. . . ." The tendency to pursue an incubation strategy may be even more pronounced in term-limited legislatures as legislators approach the end of their time in office. A Missouri Representative observed: "The hope for many of these members is that they put all their ideas out there and that some day, somebody will take up their bill and run with it."

Policy fads: Legislative measures often diffuse from the state where they originated to other states, similar to a popular fad. After California adopted a law limiting the weight of textbooks in response to concerns about children having to carry heavy backpacks, legislators in other states picked up on the idea. The member of the New Jersey Assembly who authored that chamber's version of the bill admitted, "California tends to act first and this thing is going to move right across the country." The prediction was correct; a Massachusetts state representative subsequently introduced legislation along the same lines.

Media attention: Lawmakers sometimes introduce legislation as a way to get media attention for themselves. In 2008, the state of California was forecasted to have a $15.2 billion budget deficit. A Republican state senator introduced a measure to prevent state legislators from getting a pay raise in any year in which the state failed to balance its budget. The potential impact of the proposal was purely symbolic—it would have reduced state spending by only thousands of dollars, not the needed millions or billions—and it was voted down by senators from both parties. Indeed, a fellow Republican senator castigated the measure's author for the proposal, commenting, "Every time I've seen somebody [introduce a bill to block legislative salary increases], it's because they're looking for a headline." But the measure and its defeat did garner favorable media attention across the state for the senator who introduced it. And ultimately, the senator got the last laugh on his colleagues. Although his proposal failed to pass the legislature, the senator pushing it was able to get it on the ballot and in May 2009 California voters passed it by an overwhelming margin.

Cheap political points: Bills are occasionally written to score cheap and easy political points with voters. After Major League Baseball's Angels franchise decided to stop calling itself the "Anaheim Angels" in favor of the geographically challenged moniker the "Los Angeles Angels of Anaheim," the California Assembly member representing Anaheim quickly introduced the "Truth in Sports Advertising Act." The measure would have forced a professional sports team that played in one community but labeled itself as representing a different community to disclose its real geographic location in all advertising. It is likely that

(Continued)

POLITICS UNDER THE DOMES 5-1 (CONTINUED)

the Assembly member thought his constituents would appreciate his efforts to defend their city's honor.

Revenge: When a member of the Maryland House of Delegates from the suburbs of Washington, DC introduced a bill to ban black bear hunting, her colleagues in the far western reaches of the state were furious. To them, black bears were scary nuisances, and they did not appreciate a delegate from a part of the state that did not suffer from having their garbage cans violated telling them how the animals should be treated. In response, one of the western delegates proposed a bill to trap bears and release them around the rest of the state. The delegate knew his measure had no chance to pass, but he fumed, "I'm trying to make the point that the people who put bills in for someone else's area, they don't live with bears, they don't understand the situation. They think they are cuddly and cute with names like Fuzzy and Boo Boo."

Just because they can: Sometimes legislators introduce bills promoting unusual policies simply because they have the power to do so. For instance, a Washington state senator offered a bill to allow people to take their dogs into bars with them, reasoning, "I think dogs have a lot to offer. I think they actually take tensions out of situations."

Just to have some fun: In 2008, Missouri Senator Dan Clemens introduced Senate Bill No. 971, a measure to designate the Kansas Jayhawk as Missouri's official game bird. Senator Clemens, an alumnus of the University of Missouri, was poking fun at his alma mater's archrivals, the University of Kansas Jayhawks.

In the end, legislators see lawmaking as their main function. As a Washington state senator noted for introducing a large number of bills (among them the ones mentioned in this discussion) rationalized, "You get elected to legislate and introduce bills. What are you here for, to sit?"

Sources: Jill Carroll Andrade, "Keeping in Touch," *State Legislatures* (February 2006):29–31; *Athens Banner-Herald,* "Lawmakers Differ on Lawmaking: Active or Passive," February 17, 2002; Sam Dillon, "Heft of Students' Backpacks Turns Into Textbook Battle," *The New York Times,* December 24, 2002; Howard Fischer, "Bill Would Allow Guns in Schools, Anywhere," *Arizona Daily Star,* March 2, 2005; Andrew Garber, "1 State Senator, 2 Months, 99 Bills," *Seattle Times,* March 3, 2007; A.J. Higgins, "Legislators Proffer More than 2,100 Bills, *Bangor Daily News,* January 4, 2005; Debbie Howlett, "Legislators Target Road Rudeness," *USA Today,* May 4, 2004; *Iowa City Press-Citizen,* "Iowa Bill Would Legalize Doctor-Assisted Suicides," January 30, 1992; Legislative Press & Information Bureau, R.I. State House, "Charging Youngsters for Autographs May Be Fineable Offense," February 9, 2005; Tara McClain, "Students Press State for Tax Break," *Statesman Journal,* March 10, 2005; Representative Cam Ward, "Post from the Legislature," March 27, 2007 (http://www.politicalparlor.net/wp/2007/03/27/bills-for-the-week/); Jill Rosen, "Peeved Politicians Offer Up Payback," *Baltimore Sun,* March 27, 2006; Robert Sandler, "Mo. House Sets Record for Number of Bills Filed," *Columbia Missourian,* March 25, 2002; Bill Shaikin, "State Lawmaker Targets Angels," *Los Angeles Times,* February 22, 2005; "Kevin Yamamura," "Bid to Curb Legislative Raises Dies," *Sacramento Bee,* May 22, 2008.

Drafts become bills when they are "dropped" or "placed in the hopper"— that is, given to the clerk of the chamber, who assigns an identification number (e.g., H1000 for a House bill, S1000 for a Senate bill). The bill is then introduced and "read" for the first time. In reality, the bill is normally not read in its entirety. More likely, the bill number, sponsor, and bill title are read. The bill title is actually a synopsis of the bill and its intent, identifying the relevant aspect of the state code of laws. For example, the "Bicycle Safety" bill (S446) was introduced in the 2008 Florida session.[16] The bill is reprinted here as Figure 5-2. The title of the bill appears on lines 1 to 8 and indicates that the bill would amend section 316.2065 of the Florida Statutes, changing the safety standards for bicycle helmets and bicycle lighting equipment. The bill, if passed into law, would also define penalties for violations and create a process for warning bicyclists who are in violation of the new law without actually penalizing the offender for the first violation. All this information can be gleaned from the title of the bill.

REFERRAL TO STANDING COMMITTEE

For several reasons, the committee stage is a critical phase in the legislative process. Because so many bills are introduced, legislatures divide up the workload for reviewing them by creating a standing committee system. As discussed in Chapter 4, the organization of these committees is not the same from one state to another. But, generally, each chamber will have somewhere between 10 and 30 standing committees, most of which deal with a specific subject area (e.g., Business and Commerce Committee, Education Committee, Transportation Committee). In most state chambers, each legislator is assigned to about three committees, and each committee has perhaps 10 to 15 members. But there are real differences in how this works out in different states. For example, in the Missouri House of Representatives, there were 24 standing committees in 2008, supplemented by 20 special committees. On average, a representative sits on three standing committees and several special committees. In the Kentucky Senate that same year, there were 14 "session committees" (the name given standing committees in the Bluegrass State), and each senator serves on five to seven of these.

Because a different array of legislators sits on each committee, the ideological position and policy preferences of each committee may be different from those of other committees. They may also be different from the overall array of preferences of the chamber. Thus, it sometimes makes a difference which committee receives a particular bill. Although one committee might be predisposed to hold and kill a bill, another committee might choose to act favorably on the same measure. And although different committees have jurisdiction over different topics, it is not always clear to which committee a specific bill should be referred. In lower houses, the referral decision usually rests with the speaker. But, again, variations are seen across the states. In some houses, a

FIGURE 5-2   A BILL INTRODUCED IN THE FLORIDA SENATE

Florida Senate - 2008 (Reformatted) SB 446

39-00424-08 2008446__
Page 1 of 2
CODING: Words stricken are deletions; words underlined are additions

1 A bill to be entitled
2 An act relating to bicycle safety; amending s. 316.2065,
3 F.S.; revising safety standard requirements for bicycle
4 helmets that must be worn by certain riders and
5 passengers; providing for enforcement of requirements for
6 bicycle lighting equipment; providing penalties for
7 violations; providing for dismissal of the charge
following a first offense; providing an effective date. 89
10 Be It Enacted by the Legislature of the State of Florida:
11
12 Section 1. Paragraph (d) of subsection (3) and subsection
13 (8) of section 316.2065, Florida Statutes, are amended to read:
14 316.2065 Bicycle regulations.—
15 (3)
16 (d) A bicycle rider or passenger who is under 16 years of
17 age must wear a bicycle helmet that is properly fitted and is
18 fastened securely upon the passenger's head by a strap, and that
19 meets the federal safety standard for bicycle helmets, final
20 rule, 16 C.F.R. part 1203. Helmets purchased before October 1,
21 2008, and meeting standards of the American National Standards
22 Institute (ANSI Z 90.4 Bicycle Helmet Standards), the standards
23 of the Snell Memorial Foundation (1984 Standard for Protective
24 Headgear for Use in Bicycling), or any other nationally
25 recognized standards for bicycle helmets adopted by the
26 department may continue to be worn by riders or passengers until
27 January 1, 2012. As used in this subsection, the term "passenger"
28 includes a child who is riding in a trailer or semitrailer
29 attached to a bicycle.
30 (8) Every bicycle in use between sunset and sunrise shall
31 be equipped with a lamp on the front exhibiting a white light
32 visible from a distance of at least 500 feet to the front and a
33 lamp and reflector on the rear each exhibiting a red light
34 visible from a distance of 600 feet to the rear. A bicycle or its
35 rider may be equipped with lights or reflectors in addition to
36 those required by this section. Law enforcement officers may
37 issue a bicycle safety brochure and a verbal warning to a bicycle
38 rider who violates this subsection. A bicycle rider who violates
39 this subsection may be issued a citation by a law enforcement
40 officer and assessed a fine for a pedestrian violation, as
41 provided in s. 318.18. The court shall dismiss the charge against

FIGURE 5-2 (CONTINUED)

42 a bicycle rider for a first violation of this subsection upon
43 proof of purchase and installation of the proper lighting
44 equipment.
45 Section 2. This act shall take effect October 1, 2008.

Source: Florida legislative website, accessed March 27, 2008 at: http://www.myfloridahouse.gov/
Sections/Bills/billsdetail.aspx?BillId=37380&BillNumber=S1064&SessionId=57.

committee (a committee on committees or a rules committee) makes the referral. In the Virginia House of Delegates, the clerk makes the decision with direction from the speaker. In the Maine House of Representatives, the full membership votes on the initial referral.[17]

On occasion, the referral can be a critical decision that, quite literally, determines the fate of a bill. In 2005, for example, Washington House Speaker Frank Chopp referred a collective bargaining measure to the Rules Committee rather than the Appropriations Committee, which usually had jurisdiction over such bills. He did this because the chair of the Appropriations Committee had battled with the union involved in the legislation, and the speaker did not want the committee chair to be in a position to kill the bill.[18] Assignment powers can also be used to kill bills. Former Vermont Speaker Ralph Wright confessed that by the careful use of his referral power, "I sent my share of bills off to death row during my tenure."[19]

COMMITTEE HEARINGS

The most extensive review of a bill occurs in committee. It is important to note that that this is the *only* stage in the entire legislative process during which nonlegislators can speak publicly in the legislature on proposed legislation.[20] Only legislators may introduce bills, and only legislators may speak on the floor during debate. Thus, the committee stage is important because a variety of points of view from a wide array of individuals and groups can be entertained. Although private citizens or government officials may give some of the testimony, the reality is that much of the discussion is provided by interest group lobbyists. Lobbyists are an integral part of the legislative process, and this is especially true at the committee stage. Committee hearings are about providing information, and lobbyists are key purveyors of it.

The committee chair is a pivotal person at this stage. In most state legislatures, control over the hearing process is in the hands of the chair. The chair usually decides when (or even if) a bill will be heard. As one committee chair contends, "[P]art of the power and part of the responsibility and part of the privilege of being a committee chairman is to set the agenda."[21]

COMMITTEE ACTION AND SECOND READING

Assuming a bill receives a hearing and has been reviewed by the committee members, the committee may report it to the entire chamber ("to the floor") with one of several recommendations. What the committee chooses to do at this stage is usually critical to the success or failure of the bill. The most common committee actions at this stage are to table the bill (hold it in committee) or to issue a report to the floor recommending that the bill "do pass" (a favorable recommendation), "do not pass" (unfavorable recommendation), or be amended (change some aspect of the bill). There are other potential recommendations, but they are less common (e.g., return the bill to the sponsoring legislator, send it to floor without a recommendation, refer the bill to another committee, or substitute a bill with an entirely new one).

For the most part, legislators on the floor follow the recommendation of the committee report; because most legislators did not hear the testimony and discussion in committee, they use the committee recommendation as an informed "cue" for voting. In essence, it is a system based on trust and deference: the legislator trusts the members of the committees on which he or she does not sit to make the right decisions based on the information provided in the committee hearing, and therefore the legislator defers to his or her colleagues' recommendation.

There are, however, times when the system does not work in quite this way. On issues that attract a lot of attention and emotion (e.g., abortion, gay rights, taxes), legislators are as likely to trust their own ideological orientation or political "gut reaction" as they are to trust the committee report. It is also the case that on some issues, the party has come to a position in caucus, and legislators are expected to follow that position. Sometimes this means that the party leadership or caucus has taken a position while the committee had the bill under consideration. Under these circumstances, the committee decision may be a foregone conclusion, and much of the testimony is more for show than anything else. But these cases are the exception, not the rule.

The committee recommendation is, therefore, usually the determining factor. About 90 percent of the bills that receive a favorable recommendation from the committee will pass on the floor. In most states, an unfavorable recommendation ("do not pass") is a rarity; if the committee does not like the bill, they will simply hold it in committee. But there are a handful of states (e.g., Utah and New Hampshire) in which all bills are required to be reported to the floor.[22] In these states, a "do not pass" recommendation is a very common report because the committee does not have the option of holding the bill.

On some occasions, a majority of house members wish to pursue a bill, but the committee to which it was referred prefers to kill it. In a number of houses, a discharge procedure exists to pull such a bill out of the committee's grasp, allowing it to come to the floor. The rules governing discharge procedures vary. In some houses, the discharge motion requires only a simple majority; in other houses, an extraordinary majority is needed.[23]

In 2004, the Mississippi House voted along party lines to change the required vote for discharging a bill to two-thirds of those present and voting from the long-standing standard of a majority of those present and voting.[24] Although the discharge procedure had rarely been used, the majority Democrats feared the minority Republicans would use the lower threshold to successfully pull two controversial bills out of committee, thus prompting the majority's desire to increase the number of votes needed to invoke the procedure. After the vote changing the rule, the House Speaker defended the maneuver and the sanctity of the committee system, saying "The committee process is where we dig in and get the facts." A GOP representative countered with a dissenting view, complaining that with the new rule, "There are no voices outside the committees."[25]

In many states, the committee report is made when the bill is on the calendar for the second reading. Again, in most cases, the bill is actually only read by title. A day or two after this second reading and issuance of the committee report, the bill moves to third reading calendar.

THIRD READING, DEBATE, AND FLOOR VOTE

Again, the bill is read (again usually by title only), and legislators may then discuss and debate the merits of the bill on the floor before a roll-call vote. Although floor debate occasionally makes for high drama, the reality is that by this point, leadership, most legislators, and many lobbyists and other legislative observers know the outcome before the vote is even taken. Leaders poll members of their party, often in a caucus meeting, to find out how individual lawmakers intend to vote. Thus, there is little mystery about the likely outcome. In the New York Senate, for example, 7,109 bills were brought to the floor for a vote between 1997 and 2001. Not a single one was defeated.[26] Because leaders typically control which bills get brought up for a vote on the floor, they can choose to only call up measures that are going to pass. As the speaker of the Missouri House—another body where almost everything brought to a vote passes—noted, "There were several controversial issues where the votes just weren't there. They weren't even close. There's no use wasting the House's time if you don't have 82 (votes out of 163 members)."[27]

In most states, passage of a bill requires a simple majority of those present and voting. Thus, if the chamber has 90 members and five are not present or abstain from voting, the bill requires 43 votes for passage (50 percent +1 of 85 present and voting = 43). However, some chambers require a "real majority" of the entire membership, even if some are absent or not voting. A real majority of 90 members in this case would be 46. The practical implications of voting standards are two-fold. First, it is harder to pass legislation in a state using a "real majority" rule. Second, in a state with this rule, a legislator can help defeat a bill by simply "taking a walk." Under this rule, being absent has the same effect as voting no but avoids placing a legislator in the position of actually going on record as voting against the measure. Consequently, what appears to be a minor difference in rules—present and voting majority versus real majority—can lead to very large differences in outcomes and in legislators' behavior.

Given that in many legislative chambers, the majority party leadership only brings bills to the floor for a vote if they are confident that the measures will pass, the minority party often feels impotent. One tactic the minority party can pursue to gain some leverage is to deny the majority the required quorum to conduct official business, as discussed in Politics Under the Domes 5-2.

POLITICS UNDER THE DOMES 5-2

Fun with Quorums

Of all the complex rules governing legislative procedures, quorums may be the simplest to understand. Quorum rules specify how many legislators need to be present for official business to be transacted. The Missouri Constitution (Article III, Section 20), for example, states: "A majority of the elected members of each house shall constitute a quorum to do business." Most state legislatures operate under a similar majority provision. In Texas, however, the state constitution (Article 3, Section 10) imposes a more stringent requirement: "Two-thirds of each House shall constitute a quorum to do business." The difference between these two standards is meaningful. In a two-party system, when only a majority is required for a quorum, the minority party cannot exploit the rule to cause mischief. But when a super majority requirement exists, the minority party—assuming it is of sufficient size—can use the rule to its advantage.

An extreme example of how the quorum rule can be taken advantage of is provided by events in the Texas state legislature in 2003. Having taken control of both chambers for the first time in the legislature's modern history Republicans chose to flex their new political muscles by pushing through an unusual mid-decade redistricting plan. The new district lines were drawn to elect more Republicans (and therefore fewer Democrats) to office. Predictably, the Democrats vigorously objected to the GOP ploy. As the minority party, however, the Democrats' ability to prevent the redistricting plan from passing was limited; they were outnumbered and did not have the votes needed to block the measure if it came to a vote. But under the quorum rule in Texas, there were enough Democrats in each chamber to deny a quorum if they chose to withdraw from the process by absenting themselves. Simply leaving the House or Senate floor would not, however, be sufficient. In reference to the quorum rule, the Texas Constitution (Article 3, Section 10) allows that each chamber can "compel the attendance of absent members, in such manner and under such penalties as each House may provide." Thus, if enough Democrats failed to show up to deny a quorum, the Republicans could send law enforcement officials to find them and bring them to the chamber.

That is how events in Texas unfolded. The redistricting plan was first brought up for a vote in the state House of Representatives on May 12. With no other way to prevent the redistricting plan from passing, 53 Democrats failed to appear in the House chamber, thereby denying a quorum and preventing any official business from being conducted. The Republicans were incensed and ordered the Texas Department of Public Safety to locate the missing Democratic members and bring them back to vote. The Department of Public Safety put out a plea for public assistance in finding errant legislators, complete with a 1-800 phone number to call with information. State troopers and investigators joined the hunt. They found the AWOL lawmakers later that day—just across the state border in Ardmore, Oklahoma, beyond the jurisdiction of Texas state law enforcement. The legislators were happily ensconced at a Holiday Inn with a Denny's restaurant next door. The Democrats stayed there for five days, long enough for the redistricting measure to die—along with a number of other bills—because it failed to pass by a deadline specified in the House rules.

Although House Democrats managed to kill the redistricting proposal during the legislature's regular session, Governor Rick Perry, a Republican, called a special session of the state legislature to raise the issue again. This time, Democrats in the state Senate blocked GOP efforts. Texas state Senate rules required support from two-thirds of the membership to bring the redistricting bill up for consideration. That meant that Democrats only needed eleven votes in the 30-member body to block the proposal. As it happened, a dissident Republican senator joined with 10 Democrats to prevent the Senate from taking up the measure. After 30 days, the special session came to a close with no redistricting bill passed.

The governor and Republican legislators, however, did not give up. A second special session was immediately called. And this time around, the lieutenant governor, a Republican and the state Senate's presiding officer, intended to disregard the two-thirds rule, which would allow the GOP to pass the redistricting bill without interference. Senate Democrats anticipated the lieutenant governor's parliamentary maneuver, and

(Continued)

POLITICS UNDER THE DOMES 5-2 (CONTINUED)

even before the special session was called, they had decided to resort to their last option to block the plan from passing: following the example of their Democratic House colleagues, they, too, left the state to deny the required quorum. This time, the fleeing legislators took up residence in a Marriott Hotel in Albuquerque, New Mexico, and they prepared to stay for 30 days, the length of time the special session could meet. A Democratic state senator proclaimed, "This group is united in availing ourselves of the tool granted to us by our Texas Constitution to break a quorum of the Senate." Senate Republicans did everything they could think of to force the Democrats to return, including imposing fines and taking away cell phones and parking privileges. But the Democrats stayed put and again managed to prevent the redistricting bill from passing.

Undaunted by the failure of the first two special sessions, Governor Perry called a third special session. This time, Democratic unity dissolved when one of their members decided that it was futile to continue denying a quorum. With the senator's return from Albuquerque and promise to attend the third special session, his fellow Democrats were forced to give up the fight. When they came back to the Senate, the Democratic senators had their fines rescinded and lost privileges restored. And finally, after months of battling, the GOP redistricting plan was passed.

The events in Texas were unusual, but they were not unprecedented. Breaking quorums for political advantage has a long history in American legislatures, even going back to the colonial era. In recent years in Indiana, which like Texas has a two-thirds quorum requirement, both Republicans and Democrats have used the rule to their advantage when they have been in the minority, albeit without having to flee the state. Legislative rules usually work to the majority party's advantage. But some rules, like quorum rules, allow the minority party to gain some leverage in the legislative process.

Sources: Kevin Corcoran and Michele McNeil, "Dems Boycott All Day, Dooming 132 Bills," *Indianapolis Star*, March 2, 2005; Ken Herman, "AWOL Democrats Found," *Austin American-Statesman*, May 13, 2003; Ken Herman, "Democrats Boycotting Senate," *Austin American-Statesman*, July 29, 2003; Christy Hoppe and George Kuempel, "Runaway Texas Democrats Return with Victory in Hand," *Dallas Morning News*, May 17, 2003; Legislative Reference Library of Texas, "2003–2004 Congressional Redistricting Chronology," updated April 26, 2004; R.G. Ratcliffe, "11 Democrats Face Stiffer Penalties; GOP Votes to Revoke Parking, Cell Phone Privileges if Senators Don't Return," *Houston Chronicle*, August 16, 2003; Michele McNeil Solida, "Republicans Again Leave House Session," *Indianapolis Star*, February 27, 2004; Texas Department of Public Safety, "DPS Seeks Help from Public in Locating Missing Legislators," May 12, 2003.

Another possible strategy is to use a filibuster in chambers with rules that allow for it. A filibuster is an effort to slow down the legislative process to the point at which business comes to a standstill. It is a tactic used by an individual or minority of legislators when they object to a bill and do not have enough votes to otherwise prevent its passage. Although filibusters are usually only associated with the U.S. Senate, unlimited debate is allowed in roughly one-third of state legislative houses.[28] In some of the chambers that allow for unlimited debate, the rules make it easy to bring a filibuster to a stop; in others, it is more difficult to do.[29]

Typically, state legislators engage in filibusters only as a last resort. In 2007, for example, having failed to stop the bill or amend it to their satisfaction, Democrats, who were in the minority in the Missouri Senate, filibustered a GOP measure dealing with a novel mechanism to fund construction at the state's public universities. Operating as a tag team, the Democrats held the bill hostage to a filibuster during a 15-hour debate, starting at 8 p.m. on a Monday evening and ending at 11 a.m. the next morning. Although the filibuster successfully blocked the bill from coming to a vote in the short term, the Republican majority ultimately prevailed. They did so by employing a seldom used parliamentary procedure, one that had been invoked only nine times during the previous four decades. After the GOP broke the filibuster, they passed the bill—minus funding for two major projects scheduled to be built at the University of Missouri campus in Columbia, the district of the Democratic leader of the filibuster.[30]

Of course, not every filibuster is motivated by high-minded purposes. Personalities play a role in the legislative process. According to an Alabama representative,:

In fact one of the first bills this session was brought forward by Rep. Paul DeMarco (R) of Birmingham. It took nearly four hours to move this bill off of the floor of the House. Why? Because of—here it comes—a filibuster led by Rep. John Rogers (D) of Birmingham. Why did he filibuster a bill that was requiring mandatory ethics training for legislators? I quote Rep. Rogers-"Mr. DeMarco I will filibuster this bill because you filibustered one of my bills last year, so it is pay back time."[31]

While the classic filibuster involves one or more legislators commanding the floor by continuing to speak, there are other delaying tactics that may be used. One ploy is to make a motion that bills be read in their entirety rather than by title. Another is to propose dozens of amendments to a bill on the floor. In the Alabama legislature, the weapon of last resort is "Big Bertha," an insurance regulation bill that is over 1,000 pages long. Big Bertha was written decades ago specifically as a delaying tactic. It has been estimated that reading just the title of Big Bertha could take 24 hours.[32]

Even if a bill passes on the floor, that action may not settle the matter; the vote can be reconsidered within a specified time frame (usually 24 to 48 hours). Reconsideration is the legislative equivalent of "buyer's remorse"—the term for a buyer making a purchase and almost immediately regretting it. Consumer protection laws often allow for buyer's remorse and give the buyer a limited number of days to back out of the deal.

Reconsideration works the same way. If a bill is passed and then some legislators who voted for passage have second thoughts, they may call for a reconsideration of the bill the next day. Although rare, it does occasionally happen that a bill will pass, be reconsidered, and then fail. In 1999, for example, members of the New Hampshire House of Representatives made the politically difficult decision to vote in favor of a state income tax to finance a more equitable school funding program as ordered by their state court. But after the governor reconfirmed her threat to veto the measure, the House voted to reconsider the measure and then defeated it.[33]

Of course, the process can work the other way as well—a bill may fail, be reconsidered, and pass. In fact, the latter case is actually the more likely scenario, especially in a body with part-time legislators who are pressed for time toward the end of the session. It occasionally happens that the leadership has not clearly communicated that they favor a particular bill. If the rank-and-file members are unclear about a bill, they are likely to vote against it. If this happens, the majority party leadership may call for a brief recess, assemble the members of the party in caucus, and explain that the bill in question is a "good" bill and should pass. When the legislators reconvene on the floor, there will be a call for reconsideration, and the vote will be retaken.

SAME STEPS IN SECOND CHAMBER

There may be some differences in the legislative process between the two houses, but for the most part, the basic outlines are the same. This means a bill again has to undergo three separate readings, committee hearings, and action and, if the bill gets that far, a floor vote. Again, the committee stage is usually critical. It is often the case that a bill will pass the first chamber but not the second. It may be that the committee that receives the bill in the second chamber has very different policy preferences compared with the original committee. Perhaps only the committee chair in the second chamber is strongly opposed to the bill, but that alone is enough to keep it in committee if the chair refuses to hold hearings. It may be that the Republicans are the majority party in the House but the Democrats are the majority in the Senate. In other words, there are numerous ways in which the political context of one chamber may be different from the context of the other chamber. And this, of course, makes it harder to build the sort of coalition necessary to pass the bill in both chambers.

POTENTIAL CONFERENCE COMMITTEE

Even if a bill does pass in both chambers, it is possible that it does not pass with quite the same wording. To become law, it must pass both chambers in precisely the same form. Suppose, for example, the House passes a bill that lowers the drinking age law for all alcoholic beverages from 21 to 18 years of age. But when the bill goes to the Senate, it is amended, and now the bill stipulates that the drinking age law will be lowered from 21 to 19 years of age, and only for beer and wine (one would still have to be 21 years old to purchase "hard" liquor). Clearly, this is not the same bill that was passed by the House. So now what happens?

The typical procedure is that the original chamber votes on whether or not to accede to the changes made by the second chamber. If they do accept the changes, the bill is sent to the governor. If the original chamber does not accept the changes, a conference committee will ensue. A conference committee is ad hoc (in other words, it is unique to each such instance and is not a standing committee). The rules vary a bit from one state and chamber to another, but generally conference committees consist of about six to ten legislators (usually three to five from each chamber) appointed by the presiding officer or party leaders.[34] The task of the conference committee is to craft a compromise—a bill that both chambers will accept. If the chambers passed substantially different bills, then the conference committee has a great deal of policymaking discretion. As one expert explains, "Conference committees . . . are the least visible phase of the lawmaking process. And, although they may have a low profile, it is in conference committees that some of the most important action in the legislative game takes place."[35]

The conference report must be accepted by a floor vote in each chamber; otherwise, the bill is dead. Likewise, if the conference committee cannot agree on a report, the bill is dead. Clearly, conference committees can be an important and influential part of the process. But they are not used in every state. Some state legislatures, most notably New York, make very little of use of conference committees.[36] There, differences between the houses are typically resolved through negotiations between the leaders of the two bodies.[37] But in most other state legislatures "going to conference" is a very common procedure, so much so that conference committees are sometimes referred to as the "third chamber." In some states, they have an especially significant role in the budget process.

THE GOVERNOR'S DESK

When a bill is passed by both chambers (in the same exact form), it is sent to the governor. The governor may sign the measure into law or veto it. (On occasion, a governor will allow a measure to become law without his or her signature, as Vermont governor James Douglas did with a 2008 bill to allow farmers to grow hemp. A governor may take this course of action with a bill he or she does not like but does not want to veto.)[38] Vetoes are most likely to occur when the governor is affiliated with one party but the legislative majority is from the other party—a condition known as "divided government." If the governor does veto a bill, the legislature has the opportunity to pass the bill into law anyway through an override. Overriding a veto is not easy; in almost all states, it can only be done if an extraordinary majority (usually two-thirds) of the legislators in *each* chamber votes to do so. Only about 5 percent of vetoes are overridden.

The role of the governor in the legislative process, however, is often far greater than wielding the veto threat. Most significant legislation involves detailed negotiation between the governor and the legislative leadership. Some of this legislation is set forth as part of the governor's legislative agenda—problems the governor addresses in the state-of-the-state address at the beginning of the legislative session. We will discuss the governor's role in the legislative process in greater detail in Chapter 6.

LEGISLATIVE TIME

As we discussed in Chapter 3, most state legislatures only meet for a few months each year. For example, in 2008, the overwhelming majority of state legislatures were in session for four months or less.[39] There are numerous implications of this reality, but the most immediate is that part-time legislatures are under severe time pressures when they do meet. Legislators must deal with many issues, some complex and difficult, some minor and easy. It is human nature, apparently, to defer the complex and difficult issues. Indeed, part of this may be procrastination. But another part of it is that complex, difficult issues require more study, more negotiation, and more time to develop the compromises and coalitions that are necessary for passage. Therefore, many of the most critical issues do not get resolved until the end of the session, if they are resolved at all. This creates a legislative logjam as the end of the session draws near.[40] To help combat this problem, many state legislatures establish deadlines for bill introductions, committee reports (called "funnel days" in Iowa), and the transmitting of bills from one chamber to the other. Although bill deadlines help, there are always exceptions to them. Rules can be waived, and in many states, a few "privileged" committees do not have to abide by the deadlines; these are usually budget committees, state affairs committees, and rules or leadership committees.

Because of all of this, one astute observer of state legislatures notes that "Political time differs from ordinary approaches to time in that it is not linear."[41] What is meant by this is that actions have a different pace and different locus, and time has a different (ever-increasing) value as the legislative session moves from beginning to end. Generally, at the start of the session, the legislative pace is somewhat leisurely. Many events on the social calendar are scheduled early in a session. These gatherings are hosted by a wide variety of associations and interest groups, each trying to get a little "face time" with legislators outside of the capitol.

During the day, bills are being sent to committees, and committee chairs are scheduling hearings. Very little action occurs on the chamber floor at this time—largely because there are so few bills to discuss or on which to vote because the bills are all at the committee stage. As the session progresses and some bills begin to move from committee to the floor for discussion, possible amendment, and floor vote, legislators find their time increasingly divided between committee hearings, floor sessions, and perhaps caucus meetings as the leaders and the rank-and-file members discuss priorities and strategies. As committee deadlines pass and most of the standing committees suspend operations for the year, the floor action comes to dominate, punctuated by the occasional caucus meeting. Meanwhile, one or more conference committees are likely negotiating, behind closed doors, the bills that passed in both chambers but in different versions. Finally, in the waning days of the session, action shifts again, at least in many legislatures, to the behind-the-scenes negotiations between party leaders in both chambers and, often, the governor or his or her key staffers.

The end of the session is typically a hectic time, with bills moving rapidly from one chamber to the other, some of them being held back by the leadership as bargaining chips, the fate of individual legislators' pet bills hanging in the balance, negotiations on critical bills breaking down and resuming again, nerves fraying, and tempers flaring. Typically, however, most of the activity centers on those in leadership positions. Rank-and-file members are left out of the action until they are needed to vote. As the final days approached during a recent session of the Maine House, the speaker warned his members: "Bring plenty of reading material. Bring musical instruments if you want. We will be doing a lot of waiting around."[42] His prediction proved accurate. A reporter observed that bored lawmakers "snapped rubber bands across the room during a break while leadership huddled to work out last-minute details."[43] Such behavior is not confined to the Maine legislature. During final late night hours of the 2009 Missouri Senate session a Wiffle ball game was played in a capitol corridor while the chamber's leaders hashed out needed compromises.[44] Such antics are an accepted part of the process. In the Iowa Senate, a first-term member took to the floor during the last day of a session to complain, "Here we are supposed to be representing the people, and we're down here playing Solitaire while we're supposedly passing these significant pieces of legislation." The Senate leader, who was busy with negotiations, sloughed off the complaint, noting, "Freshmen [legislators] are always shocked by what goes on. Next year he won't even mention it. He'll probably be playing games."[45]

Unorthodox legislative maneuvers are occasionally used in the last few days to try and salvage dying legislative proposals. In California, the scheme used is called "gut and amend." A low-profile and noncontroversial measure is amended to incorporate a more controversial proposal in a last-ditch effort to pass it.[46] In Nevada, the final days of a session see the appearance of "Christmas trees" and "Leg-O-Matics." A Christmas tree is a bill in which an unpopular proposal is attached to a more popular one—like an ornament hung on a Christmas tree—in the hope that it will enhance the prospects for it to get enough votes to pass. In another tactic, when a bill is so reconfigured from its original intent that it is no longer recognizable—and now pushes a very different set of policies—it is thought to be reminiscent of a Veg-O-Matic, the kitchen tool of several decades ago that was used to "slice and dice" vegetables; hence the label "Leg-O-Matic" is attached to the greatly altered legislation.[47]

Perhaps not surprisingly, errors are made in the hectic rush of the last few days of the legislative session. A Florida senator admits, "There's no way, when you are passing 50 bills a day, that you can look at every word. There's just no way."[48] The most egregious mistake made in the waning hours of a recent legislative session occurred in Arizona. The House speaker brought up a bill to create a tax refund program intended to encourage the state's citizens to purchase cleaner burning fuel vehicles. Although lawmakers had not seen the bill before, because it was the speaker's measure, they assumed it was error free. But as one representative later confessed, "The bottom line is that we are asking questions as we are thumbing through bills we've never seen before."[49] Had lawmakers had the opportunity to review the measure more closely, they might have caught the mistake that extended the program to 1 percent of all vehicles in the state rather than 1 percent of all newly registered vehicles as the speaker had intended. The error was enormously expensive to the state; projected to cost only $3 million to $10 million, the program actually cost closer to $450 million before the mistake was fixed.[50]

Ultimately, during the final days or even hours, consensus begins to build among legislators and media alike that some particularly dicey legislation is the "going home bill"—meaning it is the key issue that needs to be resolved before the legislature can adjourn for the year ("sine die") and everyone can go home. It may be a transportation issue, a social issue, or a tax reform question. More often than not, it is the budget bill. But whatever the "going home bill" turns out to be that year, after it is resolved, the legislature will adjourn soon thereafter. No matter that there are still bills on the calendar; no matter that there are still important issues to address. They will keep until next year; it's time to go home. After all, in 40 or so of the states, the legislatures are part-time organizations with part-time pay, and the legislators need to get home to their families and jobs.

THE BUDGET PROCESS

Although other bills may wait until the following year, the one bill that the legislature must pass is the appropriations (budget) bill.[51] As one text notes, "[T]he budget bill is far more important than any other bill the legislature considers each year. In fact, the budget may be more important than all the other bills a legislature considers combined."[52]

One of the reasons for this, of course, is that almost all other bills have a price tag associated with them—they create programs or laws that must be administered by state agencies, or they authorize construction of roads, bridges, public university buildings, or other aspects of the physical infrastructure. All of these things cost money to administer or build. And most of that money is appropriated through the state budget process.

What makes this task especially difficult at the state level is that virtually all states require that expenditures be balanced by revenues. States can borrow money (bonding) for large-scale projects like highways or state university buildings, but they cannot do so in the manner that the federal government and the U.S. Congress do. Therefore, state legislatures are far more constrained by economic realities than is the federal government. And this means that governors and state legislatures must make hard choices about what to fund and what to forego. When the economy takes a downturn, these choices are especially difficult. By January 2009, for example, 38 states had budget shortfalls totaling at least $70 billion, forcing them to downsize their budget commitments, raise taxes, or dip into their "rainy day accounts."[53] One consequence of very tight budgets is that other issues, particularly new initiatives that require spending, get squeezed off the legislative agenda. Fiscal difficulties in 2009 meant, as a Maryland state Senator put it, "The budget is going to suck 99 percent of the oxygen out of the State House."[54]

Since the 1950s, as many legislatures became more professionalized, as discussed in Chapter 3, executive dominance of the budget process has lessened, and state legislatures have become more equal partners in setting priorities.[55] Indeed, longer legislative sessions give more professionalized legislatures the time they need to battle the executive over the budget.[56] Legislators also have increased institutional information resources devoted to the state budget. The Missouri state legislature, for example, created a legislative budget office director in 2007 so that legislators would have access to financial data developed and analyzed independently of the executive branch.[57] The fiscal policy expertise of California's Legislative Analyst's Office, established more than 65 years ago, has long been held in high regard by legislators of both parties.[58]

The legislative rules under which budgets are adopted are similar in most of the states. In 41 states, a simple majority is all that is required to pass the budget. Another six states use majority rules under most circumstances. In Illinois, for example, a majority vote is all that is needed up until June 1, after which date a three-fifths vote is required. This super-majority vote penalty, of course, gives the majority party ample incentive to get the budget passed on time. In three states, a super majority is required to pass the budget: a three-fourths vote in Arkansas and a two-thirds vote in both California and Rhode Island.[59] Assuming the minority party has enough members to surpass the required threshold—often an incorrect assumption in Arkansas—it can wield disproportionate power over how the state government spends money. In such a circumstance, the trick for the minority part is to act cohesively. But the majority party is motivated to try to peel off enough minority party legislators to give them the votes needed to pass the budget. In California, for example, the Democrats have dominated the legislature in recent years, but they have not had enough seats to force through the budget without some Republican votes. So they have had to seek out wavering GOP legislators who can be enticed to vote for it. They are usually able to get the votes they need by directing state money to fund projects in a few Republican districts. By giving the Democrats his vote on the budget, one Republican senator secured for his district a $25 million parkway, a $12 million library, a $10 million sports field, and $750,000 to renovate a local playhouse.[60] But if the minority party sticks together, as California GOP legislators did in 2008 and 2009, they can prevent the majority party from passing a budget without first making significant concessions to them.

Pork barrel spending—the appropriation of government money to fund local projects of dubious value—occurs in every legislature.[61] In New York, for example, the euphemism used is "member items," and it constitutes more than $200 million in spending annually. Each house gets an equal share of the largesse. In recent years, the money has gone to support, among other things, a state Museum of Cheese and 83 different Little League baseball associations.[62] Such money is given out to help members get reelected and to assist party leaders in getting support from their members. A member of the California Assembly admitted, "Pork is never allocated on the basis of need. It is always allocated on the basis of politics, and usually to buy votes."[63] Along these lines, an analysis of "member initiative spending" in the Illinois state legislature revealed that monies were directed toward electorally competitive districts, districts represented by legislative leaders, and districts represented by moderate members who were being wooed by legislative leaders.[64]

INFLUENCES ON LEGISLATIVE DECISION MAKING

Ultimately, individual legislators must decide how to vote on individual bills. As former Vermont legislator Frank Smallwood noted:

> No matter how complex the issue, no matter how much you know, or often don't know, the ultimate choice always boils down to a simple affirmation or rejection of the issue at hand. A roll-call can be very rough. It's the moment of truth. There is no place to hide, no luxury of equivocation or vacillation. Every perplexity, ambiguity and uncertainty must be frozen into one of two words: Yes, or No.[65]

It is true that the roll-call vote on final passage of a bill is a visible decision because almost all votes are recorded and published in the official journal of the legislative proceedings. A recorded vote is, therefore, evidence that may be used for or against the legislator in the next election campaign. Legislators are very sensitive to this reality and occasionally take votes in such a manner as to protect themselves from possible attack by a future political opponent.

For instance, when the Missouri Senate voted in 2008 on a controversial measure to allow lawmakers and other elected officials to invest in ethanol plants that receive financial incentives from the state, they did so by taking a head count vote—one that recorded only the final tally, not how each individual senator voted on the measure.[66] Democrats in the California Assembly took such subterfuge one step further that same year. When a bill to reduce the penalties for possessing crack cocaine failed to pass, the Democratic majority successfully moved to have the vote, on which many of them had voted in the affirmative, expunged from the official record. That action left no trace of a vote that might have haunted some lawmakers in the next election.[67]

But even when recorded floor votes are taken, it is also true that many decisions on how to vote on an issue are made earlier in the process as well—often in committee, frequently on floor amendments or procedural motions, and sometimes in party caucus. And there are other decisions to be made that do not require a vote at all—whether or not to introduce a proposal, for example. These decisions are generally not recorded but may be just as important—indeed, often more important—than the final roll-call vote. And sometimes, as Politics Under the Domes 5-3 demonstrates, the final vote is not a very accurate reflection of where a lawmaker actually stands on an issue.

POLITICS UNDER THE DOMES 5-3

"I Voted for that Bill Before I Voted Against It": Why Floor Votes Don't Necessarily Tell the Whole Story

In many cases, the only formal vote of record is the final floor vote on a bill, the vote that occurs after third reading, in response to the question, "Shall the bill pass?" But votes that occur before the final floor vote may be just as important. These votes occur in committee, on floor amendments, and on procedural motions. Consider the following hypothetical example involving House Bill 1 (HB1): "An Act to Create the Center for the Study of Legislatures at State University and to Fund the Center at $200,000 in an Annual Appropriation."

Representatives Smith and Jones are both from districts in Polsbytown, where State University is located. Representative Smith is a State University graduate and a strong advocate of the university. Representative Jones is a graduate of another school, Tech College, and privately is not very supportive of State University.

Both Representatives Smith and Jones serve on the House Appropriations Committee, the powerful budget-writing committee. When the appropriation request for the Center for the Study of Legislatures (known hereafter as "The Center") is before the committee, Representative Smith

(Continued)

POLITICS UNDER THE DOMES 5-3 (CONTINUED)

makes a motion to increase funding for The Center to $500,000. The motion is defeated seven to 13 (seven ayes and 13 nays) in committee, with Smith voting for the increase and Jones voting against it (see Table at end of box).

Another committee member makes a motion to fund the Center at $100,000. The motion carries with 11 ayes and nine nays, with both Smith voting against it (because it does not fund The Center at a high enough level) and Jones voting against it (because it provides too much funding). The bill is sent to the floor with a "do pass" recommendation.

On the floor, a representative from Jewell City (where A&M Institute is located) moves to amend the bill to fund The Center at $100. The motion carries, with Representative Smith voting against it and Representative Jones voting for it on a voice vote. The bill is amended, sent to engrossment, and reaches the third reading. On the roll-call vote on final passage on the floor, Smith votes against the bill, arguing that a $100 appropriation is tantamount to killing The Center. Jones votes for the bill. It passes, and The Center for the Study of Legislatures is established at State University with funding of $100.

In the subsequent electoral campaign, Smith's opponent notes that Smith voted against the bill creating The Center. Meanwhile, Jones' campaign brochure states, "I voted to create The Center at State University."

But who really supported The Center and State University?

TRACKING THE PROCEDURAL VOTES TO CREATE THE CENTER
FOR THE STUDY OF LEGISLATURES AT STATE UNIVERSITY

PROCEDURE	STATE UNIVERSITY'S POSITION	PROCEDURAL VOTE	SMITH'S POSITION	JONES' POSITION
Original bill introduced, funds The Center at $200,000	Favors	None	Supports The Center	Opposes The Center
Smith's motion in committee to increase funding of The Center to $500,000	Strongly favors	Fails 7–13	Yes	No
Motion in committee to reduce funding to $100,000	Opposes	Passes 11–9	No	No
Floor Amendment to reduce funding to $100	Strongly opposes	Passes on voice vote	No	Yes
Final roll-call vote on HB1, as amended to fund The Center at $100	Strongly opposes	Passes 51–49	No	Yes

The story of "how a bill gets passed" is the culmination of numerous decisions and influences. Among the most important influences are partisanship, party leadership, committee actions, legislative staff, constituency considerations, and lobbyists. The relative importance of these variables varies by legislature and chamber and over time; they shift with the political context at any given moment. A good illustration of this is a concept known as "conditional party government."[68] Parties often frame issues and structure legislative action so that partisanship becomes an immediate frame of reference for decision making.[69] Party leaders tend to be strongest when two conditions are met. The first condition is that the parties are polarized in ideological terms—Democrats are strongly liberal, Republicans are strongly conservative, and very few moderates appear in either legislative caucus. The second condition is that the two parties are competitive for control of the chamber (in other words, one party does not always dominate).

When these two conditions are met, the role of political parties (and especially the party leadership) in determining the outcome of legislation is substantial. On important bills with ideological or partisan significance, the majority party will tightly control the agenda, will likely instruct the committee chairs on which bills to prioritize, and will make every effort to assure that everyone votes the party line. Legislators, especially those in the majority party, will go along because leadership can help maximize the party's electoral chances and thus maintain the party's majority status.[70]

But these conditions are not met all the time. For one thing, there is variation from legislature to legislature regarding the ideological cohesion of each party and the ideological distance between the parties.[71] For example, research on a group of state legislatures in the 1990s found that whereas the two parties in the Connecticut and Iowa Houses were especially polarized along ideological lines, such polarization was virtually nonexistent in the Louisiana and Rhode Island Houses.[72]

Moreover, the parties are not equally competitive for chamber control in all states. Some legislatures are characterized by one-party dominance, and others are known for razor-thin majorities that shift back and forth between the parties from one election to another. For example, in 2008, the majority party held between 50 and 54 percent of the seats in 21 chambers. Montana was especially competitive; the Republicans held the house by one seat, and the Democrats held the senate by two seats. Party leaders are likely to be more influential in these circumstances.[73]

There are, however, many cases of strong one-party control in which one party held a super majority of seats. In 2008, Democrats controlled more than 70 percent of the seats in *both* chambers of the Arkansas, Hawaii, and Massachusetts legislatures, and Republicans held more than 70 percent of the seats in *both* chambers of the Idaho, Utah, and Wyoming legislatures.[74] In states where one party dominates, the locus for decision making is likely to shift away from leadership and party caucus and toward committees.[75]

But party alone may not dictate voting decisions. On highly salient issues, an important determinant of vote is constituency. More than 85 percent of all state legislators represent single-member districts, which require legislators to be sensitive to local policy preferences. This, of course, is because voters in the geographic district have the power to defeat a legislator in a subsequent election. As a noted political observer once put it, "The next election is what keeps representatives as constituency oriented as they are."[76] District population is, however, highly variable between chambers and especially between states, as detailed in Chapter 1. The smaller the district population, the more likely it is that the district is relatively homogeneous demographically, politically, and ideologically. The upshot of this fact for legislative decision making is that constituency preferences are clearer, for the most part, in smaller districts. Again, the key phrase here is "on salient issues." Most bills involve minor change to policy that has little effect on the day-to-day lives of a lawmaker's constituents. There simply is no constituent preference on these bills. But on major issues, legislators pay attention to district opinion.

Although it is clear that the constituency can influence the way lawmakers vote on bills, it is important to be clear which constituency is pressuring a member. The usual assumption is that members are worried about how a vote might be used against them by the other party in the next general election. But sometimes, the constituency that matters is the "primary constituency," the voters a lawmaker counts on to ensure renomination if a threat emerges from within his or her own party.[77] The primary constituency can greatly constrain a lawmaker's voting behavior on issues that deeply divide the major parties. For instance, during the California legislature's epic partisan battle over the state's 2009 budget, the speaker of the Assembly observed:

> One of the reasons why it's hard for my Republican colleagues to vote for revenue—more important than their tax pledge—is their next primary. If they vote for revenue, then they're going to be easily challenged in another primary. But the Democrats face the same thing: If we vote for deep, permanent cuts in health and human services, then we have to face our next primary, too.[78]

In this instance, California legislators appear to be more worried about upsetting voters in their next primary than upsetting voters in the next general election. To the extent that state legislative districts are uncompetitive between the major parties—a problem noted in Chapter 2—the primary constituency, not the district more generally, becomes central to lawmakers. This potentially pushes Democratic and Republican legislators further apart.

But most votes a lawmaker casts are not apt to become campaign fodder for a political opponent. The vast majority of votes a lawmaker makes fly under his or her constituency's political radar. What influences a member's voting behavior when it appears that the public is not watching? Voting with the legislator's party is, of course, important. Indeed, in many cases, party even trumps personal views.[79] Sometimes a lawmaker's personal characteristics matter. On highly salient religious issues, for example, a legislator's religion is an important predictor of his or her vote, particularly among those with conservative Protestant affiliations.[80] Personal relationships can also matter; whether a legislator likes or identifies with another member may influence how he or she votes on a bill.[81] Indeed, a lawmaker's votes can even be swayed by who he or she sits next to on the chamber floor.[82]

CONCLUSION

In this chapter, we have focused on the more formal dynamics of the legislative process. Rules, procedures, and calendars all play critical roles in the legislative process. But other forces matter as well. As we will discuss in Chapter 6, the governor is usually an important actor; interest groups typically play a substantial role throughout the legislative process; the bureaucracy is often involved; and in some states, even the voters can play lawmaker. These are some of the contextual factors that we mentioned at the outset of the chapter. As we shall see, the context differs across the states, and it differs by issues. The context can even shift within a state. Over time, the players change. New legislators are elected, as are new governors. Sometimes the goals of individual players change. New issues appear, and some old issues fade away, creating new political cleavages while erasing others. Consequently, political circumstances change, and the relationships among players change. In other words, even when the rules—the textbook version of the process—stays the same, the context is always shifting.

ENDNOTES

1. Edward Schneier and John Brian Murtaugh, *New York Politics* (Armonk, NY: M.E. Sharpe, 2001), 245–246.
2. Alan Rosenthal, *Heavy Lifting* (Washington, DC: CQ Politics, 2004), 60.
3. *Birmingham News*, "Let Local School Systems Set Their Own Schedules," April 12, 2008.
4. See National Conference of State Legislatures, "Average Number of Appropriations Bills," December 1997t (http://www.ncsl.org/programs/fiscal/lbptabls/lbpc3t2.htm).
5. Peverill Squire, "Membership Turnover and the Efficient Processing of Legislation." *Legislative Studies Quarterly* 23 (1998):23–32.
6. Alan Rosenthal discusses the sausage-making metaphor and why it is no longer appropriate in "The Legislature as Sausage Factory: It's About Time We Examine This Metaphor," *State Legislatures* (September 2001), 12–15. Spawning fish is from Frank Smallwood, *Free & Independent* (Brattleboro, VT: The Stephen Greene Press, 1976), 85. Casinos is from John Straayer, *The Colorado General Assembly*, 2nd ed. (Boulder, CO: University of Colorado Press, 2000), 7. The jazz band is from Burdett Loomis, *Time, Politics, and Policies* (Lawrence: University of Kansas Press, 1994), 172.
7. We are not the only legislative observers to use the "train analogy." See Alan Rosenthal, *The Engines of Democracy.* (Washington, DC: CQ Press, 2009).

8. Smallwood, *Free & Independent*, 81.
9. See Missouri House of Representatives, 94th General Assembly, 2nd Regular Session: Activity History for HB2021 (http://www.house.mo.gov/billtracking/bills081/action/aHB2021.htm).
10. See, for example, the discussion in John G. Van Laningham, "The Making of the 1986 Florida Safety Belt Law: Issues and Insight," *Florida State University Law Review* 14 (1986):685–717.
11. See the National Conference of State Legislatures, "Legislative Budget Procedures: Budget Framework," July 2007 (http://www.ncsl.org/programs/fiscal/lbptabls/lbpc2t1.htm).
12. Joel A. Thompson, "'Bringing Home the Bacon': The Politics of Pork Barrel in the North Carolina Legislature," *Legislative Studies Quarterly* 11(1986):91–108. Also see Joel Thompson and Gary Moncrief, "Pursuing the Pork in a State Legislature: A Research Note," *Legislative Studies Quarterly* 13 (1988):393–404.
13. The following discussion is based on Box 6-1 in Keith Hamm and Gary Moncrief, "Legislative Politics in the States," in Virginia Gray and Russell Hanson, eds., *Politics in the American States*, 9th ed., (Washington, DC: CQ Press, 2008).
14. Tommy Neal, *Lawmaking and the Legislative Process* (Phoenix, AZ: Oryx Press, 1996), 48–49.
15. See Joint Committee on Legislative Management, Office of Legislative Research, Connecticut General Assembly, *This is Your General Assembly*, 2007–2008. (http://www.cga.ct.gov/asp/Content/This_is_Your_General_Assembly.pdf).
16. In this instance, an identical bill (HB7) was introduced at about the same time in the House.
17. Peverill Squire and Keith E. Hamm, *101 Chambers: Congress, State Legislatures, and the Future of Legislative Studies* (Columbus, OH: Ohio State University Press, 2005), 120.
18. Chris McGann, "Speaker of the House Reroutes Union-Backed Bill," *Seattle Post-Intelligencer*, March 8, 2005.
19. Ralph G. Wright, *Inside the Statehouse* (Washington, D.C.: CQ Press, 2005), 109.
20. Neal, *Lawmaking and the Legislative Process*, 53–54.
21. Denton Darrington, longtime Chair of the Idaho Senate Judiciary Committee, as quoted in Heath Druzin, "As End of Session Nears, It's Fighting Time," *Idaho Statesman*, March 26, 2008.
22. Neal reports that 21 legislative chambers require all bills to be reported out. Neal (1996) op.cit.
23. Squire and Hamm, *101 Chambers*, 124–126.
24. See Mississippi House Resolution 39 as adopted by the House, March 3, 2004.
25. Andy Kanengiser, "Tort, Voter ID Bills Appear Dead," *The Clarion-Ledger*, March 4, 2004.
26. Jeremy M. Creelan and Laura M. Moultan, *The New York State Legislative Process: An Evaluation and Blueprint for Reform*, Brennan Center for Justice at NYU School of Law, 2004.
27. *Jefferson City News Tribune*, "Few Bills Defeated on Floor Votes," May 21, 2001.
28. Nancy Martorano, Keith E. Hamm, and Ronald D. Hedlund, "Examining Committee Structures, Procedures, and Powers in U.S. State Legislatures," paper presented at the 2000 Annual Meeting of the Midwest Political Science Association. See also Scott Matthew Cody, "The Causes and Consequences of Restrictive Rules of Debate in State Senates," (Ph.D. dissertation, University of Iowa, 2006).
29. Squire and Hamm, *101 Chambers*, 122–123.
30. Kavita Kumar, "UM Gets Caught in Political Crossfire," *St. Louis Post-Dispatch*, April 20, 2007; David A. Lieb, "Democrats Block Blunt's Higher Education Plan," *Jefferson City News Tribune*, March 14, 2007; Kit Wagar, "Missouri Senate Tradition at Stake," *Kansas City Star*, April 19, 2007; Kelly Wiese, "MOHELA All-Nighter Ends After 15 Hours," *St. Louis Post-Dispatch*, March 13, 2007.
31. Representative Cam Ward, "Posts from the Legislature," March 25, 2007 (http://www.politicalparlor.net/wp/2007/03/page/2/).
32. Matthew Korade, "Alabama Senate Ducks Out Early, House Bogs Down in Filibusters," *The Anniston Star*, February 8, 2002; "Proposed Board Stirs Controversy," *Opelika-Auburn News*, March 3, 2002; David White, "GOP Fights Democrats by Stalling Bills," *Birmingham News*, February 8, 2002.
33. Tiffany Danitz, "New Hampshire Not Alone in School Finance Headaches," Stateline.org, March 31, 1999.
34. Squire and Hamm, *101 Chambers*, 114
35. Tommy Neal, "Learning the Game: How the Legislative Process Works," Denver: National Conference of State Legislatures, 2005, 28.

36. Squire and Hamm, *101 Chambers*, 113–114.
37. Creelan, and Moultan, *The New York State Legislative Process*.
38. Peter Hirschfeld, "AG Rules Hemp Bill is Legal," *The Barre Montpelier Times Argus*, June 21, 2008.
39. Six states did not hold a regular legislative session in 2008. Of the remaining 44 states, at least 29 held sessions of no more than four months in duration. See NCSL, "2008 State Legislative Session Calendar" (http://www.ncsl.org/programs/legismgt/about/sess2008.htm).
40. Harvey J. Tucker, "Legislative Logjams: A Comparative State Analysis," *Western Political Quarterly* 38 (1987):432–446.
41. Burdett A. Loomis, *Time, Politics, and Policies*. (Lawrence, KS: University Press of Kansas, 1994), 7.
42. Susan M. Cover, "Lawmakers Face Music—Literally—as Term Draws to Close," *Kennebec Journal*, June 16, 2003.
43. Cover, "Lawmakers Face Music."
44. Terry Ganey, "Late-Night Senate Action on Economic Development Stalls," *Columbia Daily Tribune*, May 15, 2009.
45. Rod Boshart, "Game Over: Senators Urged to Stay Professional," Cedar Rapids *Gazette*, April 20, 2007.
46. Ed Fletcher, "Season of the Stealth Bill," *Sacramento Bee*, September 1, 2003.
47. Joe Schoenmann, "In Legislature's Final Days, It's Time for 'Christmas Trees,' and 'Leg-O-Matics,'" *Las Vegas Sun*, May 31, 2007.
48. Julie Hauserman, "Chaos Leaves Lawmakers Unsure What They Did," *St. Petersburg Times*, May 13, 2003.
49. Jim Carlton, "If You Paid Half Price For That New SUV, You Must Be in Arizona," *Wall Street Journal*, October 26, 2000.
50. Carlton, "If You Paid Half Price For That New SUV, You Must Be in Arizona."
51. Technically, some states do wait "until next year" to pass a budget because 20 states have a biennial budget cycle, meaning they pass a budget for a two-year period. The remaining 30 states have an annual budget cycle, so they must pass the appropriations bill(s) every year. But even in the biennial states, budget adjustments must usually be made in the "off-year" because the economy may have slowed or because unforeseen expenditures (e.g., natural disasters) occur.
52. Todd Donovan, Christopher Z. Mooney, and Daniel A. Smith, *State and Local Politics: Institutions and Reform* (Belmont, CA: Cengage Learning Wadsworth, 2009), 223.
53. These data are from the National Conference of State Legislatures, as of January 6, 2009 (http://www.ncsl.org/summit/budgetmap.htm).
54. John Wagner and Anita Kumar, "Budget Cuts are Focus for Md., Va.," *Washington Post*, January 11, 2009.
55. See Glenn Abney and Thomas P. Lauth, "The End of Executive Dominance in State Appropriations," *Public Administration Review* 58 (1998):388–394.
56. Thad Kousser and Justin H. Phillips, "Who Blinks First? Legislative Patience and Bargaining with Governors," *Legislative Studies Quarterly* 34 (2009):55–86.
57. "Legislators Create Own Budget Director," *Jefferson City News Tribune*, March 16, 2007.
58. Paul Sabatier and David Whiteman, "Legislative Decision Making and Substantive Policy Information: Models of Information Flow," *Legislative Studies Quarterly* 10 (1985):395–421.
59. These data are taken from National Conference of State Legislatures, "Supermajority Vote Requirements to Pass the Budget," *Legisbrief* 6 (1998).
60. Dan Morain, "Legislative 'Pork' Okd in Boom Leaves Bad Taste in Lean Times," *Los Angeles Times*, December 30, 2004.
61. See, for example, Thompson, "Bringing Home the Bacon," and Thompson and Moncrief, "Pursuing the Pork in a State Legislature."
62. Empire Center for New York State Policy, "A Peep-Hole into New York's Pork Barrel," April 3, 2006. See also Gerald Benjamin, "Reform in New York: The Budget, The Legislature, and the Governance Process," paper prepared for The Citizens Budget Commission Conference On 'Fixing New York State's Fiscal Practices,'" November 13–14, 2003.
63. Morain, "Legislative 'Pork' Okd in Boom Leaves Bad Taste in Lean Times."
64. Michael C. Herron and Brett A. Theodos, "Government Redistribution in the Shadow of Legislative Elections: A Study of the Illinois Member Initiative Grants Program," *Legislative Studies Quarterly*, 29 (2004):287–311.

65. Smallwood, *Free & Independent*, 91.
66. David A. Lieb, "Missouri Governor Candidate Steelman Calls Senators 'Cowards,'" *Jefferson City News Tribune*, May 15, 2008.
67. Jim Sanders, "Assembly Vote 'Disappears'," Sacramento Bee Capitol Alert, January 29, 2008 (http://www.sacbee.com/static/weblogs/capitolalertlatest/010261.html).
68. John Aldrich and James S. Coleman Battista. "Conditional Party Government in the States," *American Journal of Political Science* 46 (2002):164–172.
69. As Wright and Schaffner put it, parties serve as a "default cleavage" in the legislature. Gerald C. Wright and Brian F. Schaffner, "The Influence of Party: Evidence from the State Legislature," *American Political Science Review* 96 (2002): 367–379. For a discussion of the role of parties in organizing committees see Brian Schaffner, "Political Parties and the Representativeness of Legislative Committees," *Legislative Studies Quarterly* 32 (2007):475–497.
70. Richard Clucas, "Principle-Agent Theory and the Power of State House Speakers," *Legislative Studies Quarterly* 26 (2001):319–338.
71. William T. Bianco and Itai Sened, "Uncovering Evidence of Conditional Party Government," *American Political Science Review* 99 (2005):361–371.
72. Aldrich and Battista, "Conditional Party Government in the States."
73. Shannon Jenkins, "The Impact of Party and Ideology on Roll-Call Voting in State Legislatures," *Legislative Studies Quarterly* 31(2006):235–257.
74. The greatest margin was in the Massachusetts House, with 141 Democrats and only 19 Republicans. The majority party held a phenomenal 88 percent of the seats. The largest Republican margin was in Idaho, where the Republicans held 80 percent of the senate seats (28 Republicans; seven Democrats).
75. Wayne Francis, *The Legislative Committee Game: A Comparative Analysis of Fifty States* (Columbus, OH: Ohio State University Press, 1989).
76. Alan Rosenthal, *Heavy Lifting: The Job of the American Legislature* (Washington, DC: CQ Press, 2004), 49.
77. See the classic discussion in Richard F. Fenno, *Home Style: House Members in Their Districts* (Boston: Little, Brown, 1978), 18–24.
78. *Sacramento Bee Capitol Alert*, "AM Alert: 'Hope for the Best and Ignore the Obvious,'" November 20, 2008.
79. Jenkins, "The Impact of Party and Ideology on Roll-Call Voting in State Legislatures."
80. David Yamane and Elizabeth Oldmixon, "Religion in the Legislative Arena: Affiliation, Salience, Advocacy, and Public Policymaking," *Legislative Studies Quarterly* 31 (2006): 433–460.
81. Clayton D. Peoples, "Interlegislator Relations and Policy Making: A Sociological Study of Roll-Call Voting in a State Legislature," *Sociological Forum* 23 (2008):455–480. See also Eric Uslaner and Ronald Weber, *Patterns of Decision-Making in State Legislatures* (New York: Praeger, 1981), 33–41.
82. Seth E. Masket, "Where You Sit is Where You Stand: The Impact of Seating Proximity on Legislative Cue-Taking," *Quarterly Journal of Political Science* 3 (2008):301–311. See also Samuel C. Patterson, "Party Opposition in the Legislature: The Ecology of Legislative Institutionalization," *Polity* 4 (1972):344–366.

6

THE LEGISLATIVE CONTEXT

In Chapter 4, we discussed the structure and organization of the legislature, which represents the internal environment in which legislative decisions are made. In Chapter 5, we examined how those internal processes work through the formal rules. But legislators do not make decisions in a vacuum. Other political forces are at play as well.

For legislatures, outside pressures are especially important because they are supposed to be the "most representative" branch of government. These outside forces fall broadly into several types, among them are public opinion, interest groups, other state governmental institutions, federal government institutions, and fiscal constraints. All of these forces come into play, sometimes constraining what legislatures can do and sometimes virtually mandating what they must do.

PUBLIC OPINION, CONSTITUENCY, AND THE REPRESENTATIONAL ROLE

Public opinion is an amorphous concept. For the individual legislator, it may refer to the array of policy preferences held by people within his or her district. Or it may refer to policy preferences on a specific issue at the district or state level. On the one hand, these opinions may be largely unstructured, in which case the legislator may not be aware of the shape of public views unless they are documented in a survey. On the other hand, opinions may be clearly articulated in a structured form through interest group communications or via instruments of direct democracy such as the initiative or referendum.

Ample evidence shows that public opinion matters at the aggregate level in state legislatures. In other words, states with more liberal residents (as measured by public opinion polls) are the states with the more liberal policies (as implemented through the state legislature).[1] Generally, this relationship also is true at the micro-level. When district opinion is clearly discernible, a lawmaker is quite likely to vote consistent with that opinion. But there are important qualifications to this statement. First, the linkage between district opinion and a legislator's vote is not the same in all states.[2] Second, constituent opinion may not be clearly discernible on many bills. Third, the perception of who the "constituency" is may not be consistent from lawmaker to lawmaker or even from issue to issue.

REPRESENTATIONAL ROLES

Legislators are representatives of a larger body politic, and therefore public opinion is one of the dimensions considered in discussions of representation. This is usually framed in terms of *representational roles*—the way the individual lawmaker views his or her policy obligation to the constituency. The discussion is often presented in terms of two opposing points of view, generally referred to as the *delegate* theory of representation and the *trustee* theory of representation. The delegate theory contends that the proper role of the legislator is to take the same position on a vote as the majority of constituents would take. In effect, the legislator is the agent operating on behalf of the policy wishes of the principles (constituents) he or she represents. Thus, when the elected representative holds one position on an issue but the constituency holds a different view, the agent's responsibility is to follow the preferences of the district, not the lawmaker's own preference.

The other view is that the legislator should vote his or her conscience, regardless of constituent opinion. The view here is that the legislator was elected to consider each issue and vote on the basis of his or her own best judgment. This "trustee" role is often called the "Burkean model" because a particularly trenchant description of this role was provided by Edmund Burke.[3] This trustee role asserts that constituent opinion should be consulted and considered, but ultimately the legislator must make the decision he or she thinks is right regardless of its popularity.

An example of this representational dilemma occurred in Idaho in 2003. The previous year, the U.S. Supreme Court had voided the death penalty in Idaho and eight other states because their laws stipulated that judges rather than juries should decide the sentences in capital punishment cases.[4] The Supreme Court determined this process violated a defendant's constitutional right to trial by jury. In response, the Idaho legislature rewrote the state law to require that juries determine the sentence in capital punishment cases, thus addressing the constitutional concern. The bill to do this, S1001, was the first measure to reach the floor for a vote in the Idaho Senate in 2003. Consequently, it was the very first bill on which newly elected senators had to make a decision. For one rookie senator, Elliot Werk (D-Boise), it was an excruciating experience. Werk personally opposed capital punishment but was convinced that most of his constituents wanted the death penalty reinstated, saying, "My district has told me loud and clear that they are in favor of the death penalty."[5] The new lawmaker agonized over what he should do, spending a near-sleepless night grappling with the decision. The next morning, he went to the capitol and cast a vote to reinstate the death penalty, stating, "I'm not representing Elliot Werk in the Senate. I'm representing the people of District 17." The novice senator was clearly uncomfortable with the vote, but he felt strongly that the delegate role was the proper representational role to follow. In this case, constituent public opinion was the guiding force in Senator Werk's behavior.

Sitting next to Werk in the Senate was Marti Calabretta, a veteran Democratic legislator from northern Idaho. She voted against reinstatement of the death penalty, although she knew her constituents supported it. Senator Calabretta commented, "In this case, we have to lead our public. . . . I'll probably end up walking in every bar in the district and letting them yell at me."[6] Senator Calabretta demonstrated the trustee role of representation. Although she knew her constituents would not agree with her, she believed her conscience on this issue outweighed the district preference: "Bottom line, it's your vote."[7] As a long-time lawmaker, she also knew that her constituents might forgive her if she went home, explained her vote, and took the heat by "letting them yell at me."

The trustee–delegate conundrum is as old as representative democracy. The dilemma is especially problematic in legislatures where single-member districts are the rule because it focuses the representational relationship on a very specific geographic constituency and an individual lawmaker. As long-time Idaho Senator Denton Darrington (and the author of the bill reinstating the death penalty in Idaho) said about the representational role conflict on his bill, "It's one of the great questions of political thought: 'Do you vote your conscience or do you vote your district?' By the way, it's unanswerable."[8]

Although the representational role dilemma is a classic problem for political philosophers to mull, for legislators, it rarely presents itself with such clarity as in the death penalty case. This is true for at least three reasons. First, most bills simply do not create a dilemma for the legislator because the general public does not care enough about the issue to develop a strong preference. Recall from Chapter 5 that most bills are relatively minor, often technical, issues. These are bills about which the general public knows little and about which it has no strong opinion. There may be a specific interest group or two that cares about the measure, but the general public does not. A recent five-state study found that most legislators estimated that their constituents had an opinion on no more than 10 percent of the bills before the legislature.[9] In other words, legislators believed there was no constituent opinion on at least 90 percent of the legislation before them. Obviously, this belief gives each legislator a good deal of room to make his or her own decisions.

Second, even if an issue is a salient one and people in the district have strong opinions about the bill, there is no guarantee that everyone will share the same view. It is infrequently the case that constituent opinion is clearly and overwhelmingly on one side of an issue. The five-state study mentioned found that most legislators claimed that their constituency held a clear position on no more than 10 bills each year—not 10 percent of all bills, but 10 bills in total![10] That constitutes less than 1 percent of the measures introduced in most state legislatures.

Third, if constituent opinion is indeed strongly and clearly on one side of an issue, it is quite likely that the legislator shares the same view as the constituency. After all, the lawmaker is "of the district" and probably shares many of the same demographic, political, and ideological points of view as the rest of the community from which he or she was elected. Voters tend not to elect someone who is consistently out of step with them—at least they do not elect them more than once. For the most part, legislators think like the people in their district. Most of the time, therefore, legislators do not encounter the "representation dilemma" and consequently do not generally think in terms of "trustee" and "delegate." Indeed, one of the pioneers of state legislative research said of this role distinction:

> The more carefully we examine what legislators say about representation, the easier it is to understand the difficulties of predicting legislative behavior from stereotypes of trustees and delegates. In a sense, most legislators share a dual role orientation: they are both trustees and delegates.[11]

DIFFERENT VIEWS OF CONSTITUENCY

One of the considerations complicating the relationship between the representative and the constituency is that "constituency" can be a rather vague term. One would think it is pretty clear who the constituency is—the people who live within the district that elected the particular legislator. And indeed, every legislator can tell you with great precision the physical, geographic, and demographic parameters of his or her district. It is, in the words of one student of the subject, "the entity to which, from which, and within which the member travels."[12]

But, as was noted in a classic study of the relationship between U.S. Representatives and their districts, lawmakers often have some subset of members of the district in mind when they refer to their "constituency." This was characterized as a "nest of concentric circles," each a smaller group than the previous one.[13] The same concept applies to state legislators, as several in-depth studies of legislative representation show.[14] Thus, when legislators refer to their "constituency," they may in fact be referring to the entire geographic district, but sometimes a representative may mean "the people who voted for me in the general election," but at other times he or she might mean "the partisan core that votes for me in the primary election and actively supports me during the campaign." And occasionally, the lawmaker is really thinking of specific economic or organizational interests or of her "personal support group" of family, friends, and closest political allies.

In other words, "constituency" seems to be measured on a sliding scale. It is unlikely that legislators even recognize that they use the term in different ways in different contexts—it seems to be a subconscious shifting of the definition of the word, expanding and contracting depending on the issue at hand and perhaps depending on perceived electoral consequences. Often, therefore, it is not clear precisely to whom the legislator refers when he or she says, "My constituency is in favor of this bill." For the most part, then, constituent opinion is in the eye of the beholder. Or, to put it another way, constituent opinion depends on which constituency the eye is beholding.

We do not, however, wish to discount the importance of constituent opinion. In the rare instances in which the district has a clear and strong preference for a specific policy position, the legislator ignores it at his or her own peril. It does not happen often, but legislators have been recalled from office or defeated in the next regularly scheduled election on the basis of a specific vote. For the most part, politicians are risk-averse individuals, and they understand the implications of going against the district on an important issue. Take the case of the Idaho Senator Marti Calabretta, who voted against reinstatement of the death penalty, although she knew her constituents disagreed with her position. She was defeated in the next election.

PUBLIC OPINION, ORGANIZED INTERESTS, AND LOBBYING

Although it may be true that the general public has little knowledge or interest in most of the issues that come before the legislature, that does not mean that *no one* is paying attention. There are hundreds—if not thousands—of interest groups in a state, each of which may care deeply about what is going on in a particular policy area. And these groups make known their policy preferences to the legislators. In other words, there are segments of the public, often highly organized, that have very definite opinions about a proposed policy. Each of these groups seeks to communicate its position and influence the policy decisions. They do this in a variety of ways, but most important from the legislator's perspective are lobbying and election-related activities.

THE LOBBYISTS

For the most part, lobbyists today do not call themselves "lobbyists." In part, this is because the term has a pejorative air about it. It also is because a lot of people who are registered as lobbyists spend only a small amount of their time actually trying to persuade legislators to do their bidding. Such efforts are just one of the things they do as part of a larger job description, and they do not think of themselves primarily as lobbyists. For instance, the executive director of the Blueberry Growers' Association spends a lot less time with the legislature than with the state Department of Agriculture, the state Commerce Department, and marketing groups. Only occasionally will a bill impact blueberry farmers (perhaps a pesticide bill or tonnage limits for trucks on secondary roads), and at that point, the director will put on the lobbyist badge.

People in the lobbying business prefer to be called "public affairs specialist," "government relations director," "policy advocate," "legislative liaison," "legislative agent," or something similar. There are several varieties of lobbyists. Examine almost any secretary of state website of almost any state, and you can find a list of registered lobbyists, usually in alphabetical order, and the clients each represents. For example, under "E" in the 2008 Texas list of lobbyists, one will find the following individuals:

- David Emerick, vice president and director of State Government Relations, of HSBC North America, one of the largest banks and financial services companies in the United States. Mr. Emerick and his staff represent the interests of HSBC in the southwestern regional area covering Texas, Oklahoma, Utah, and Arizona.[15] This is a typical pattern for corporate lobbyists; they often work a regional circuit, following events in several state legislatures.
- Paul Emerson, a financial analyst for the Texas Association of Counties. Mr. Emerson is a former legislative staffer and budget analyst for the legislature. Although lobbying is not his primary responsibility, he is a registered lobbyist for the Counties' association because of his state budgeting expertise. It makes sense that many former legislative staffers wind up working as lobbyists; they have experience, they know the issues, and they have the contacts.
- Stacey Emick, who represents the Texas Right to Life organization. As the legislative director for the Texas chapter of Right to Life, this is the only organization for which she lobbies.
- C.M. English, Jr., who (like Emick) represents a single client, the United Transportation Union, a labor union. He is the legislative director for the union in Texas.
- Bryan Eppstein, founder of the Eppstein Group. One of the more powerful and better-known public affairs organizations in Texas, the Eppstein Group represents numerous clients. In 2008, Bryan Eppstein was a registered lobbyist for more than 20 different clients, including such diverse organizations as the American Cancer Society, Monsanto Corporation, the Texas Medical Association, the Fort Worth Police Officers Association and the Fort Worth Firefighters, Verizon, and First Cash Financial Services (a company that operates hundreds of pawnshops and cash advance stores). Bryan Eppstein is also a well-known political campaign consultant, mostly working for Texas Republicans, and has managed dozens of campaigns for state legislative candidates (as well as U.S. Senator Kay Bailey Hutchison's campaigns, among many others).

These five individuals, from Emerick to Eppstein, are all registered lobbyists in Texas, but the nature of what they do, and for whom they do it, is quite different. Most of these people are "in-house" lobbyists employed by one organization to do their lobbying.

As the legislative director for the Texas chapter of Right to Life, Stacey Emick represents a "single-issue" organization with a very specific agenda. C.M. English represents a union, and David Emerick a single company (HSBC). Although not "single-issue" lobbyists, English and Emerick each represent a single organization, and each is primarily concerned with the economic impact various bills before the legislature will have on their respective organizations.

Emerson also represents a single organization, the TAC. But as an organization of local government officials, the TAC must follow many bills before the Texas legislature. This is true of all sorts of local governments, and one will find a large contingent of lobbyists representing counties, cities, school districts, public utility districts, and numerous other local government entities. One authoritative source estimates that about 30 percent of all lobbyists are government lobbyists.[16]

In contrast, Eppstein represents many different organizations, associations, and corporations. He is a "contract lobbyist," what some people would call a "hired gun." His firm is what is known as a "full-service public affairs company," meaning that the firm lobbies, performs public relations services, and manages the campaigns of political candidates. Most lobbyists at the state level are in-house lobbyists, but states like California, Texas, and New York have many contract lobbyists—perhaps 15 to 25 percent, depending on the state.

Although they differ in focus, these are all conventional types of lobbyists in the sense that most fall into one of the categories discussed above (i.e., in-house corporate, single-issue, trade or union, local government, contract). But not all lobbyists are conventional. In Politics Under the Domes 6-1, another registered lobbyist in Texas who does not fit neatly into one of the other categories is introduced.

Interest groups and lobbyists are an important part of the legislative scene. There are more than 1,400 registered lobbyists in Texas, for example. New York has more than 5,000 registered lobbyists representing more than 3,000 organizations, associations, causes, and companies.[17] These are states with large populations; in smaller states, the number of registered lobbyists is often much lower. About 400 are registered in Arkansas, and 600 are registered in Oregon, for example.[18]

WHAT LOBBYISTS DO

For the most part, interest groups and their representatives (lobbyists) have a symbiotic relationship with legislators; lobbyists seek to be heard on behalf of their clients, and legislators seek information on the likely political and policy consequences of proposed laws. This information exchange goes on

POLITICS UNDER THE DOMES 6-1

Lobbying Outside the Box

The stereotypical lobbyist is a middle-aged white male lawyer who represents wealthy and powerful interests. There is, of course, a kernel of truth to this stereotype, and many successful lobbyists fit that profile. But not all influential lobbyists do. Meet, for example, Sputnik.

H.W. "Sputnik" Strain, characterizes himself as "a card-carrying Cherokee Indian, a senior citizen, and a disabled veteran." He goes by only the single name Sputnik, claiming "I sign my checks Sputnik; I have Sputnik on my credit card." He wears his hair in a Mohawk, has five earrings in his left ear, and has the word "FREE" tattooed across his forehead. He is in no way, shape, or form the stereotypical lobbyist. Yet he is very successful in persuading the Texas state legislature to do what he wants them to do.

Sputnik is the state chair of the Texas Motorcycle Rights Association II. As an activist, he was largely responsible for convincing the Texas legislature in 1997 to ease the state's motorcycle laws to allow riders over 21 years of age and who either have adequate medical insurance or who have gone through additional safety training to choose whether or not to wear a helmet rather than being required to do so. The state senator who authored the helmet law change admitted that he was not "gung ho" about the proposal when it was first brought to him. The bikers were, however, well organized and tenacious in pushing the measure, persuading the lawmaker to introduce it. The proposal faced long odds, but Sputnik proved to be a forceful lobbyist. The bill's author noted, "Everybody's talking, but here comes Sputnik. He makes his case in a succinct, intelligent manner, and people shut up and listen." Another state senator said, "[Sputnik] presented a very rational argument and addressed genuine safety concerns. Appearances can be deceiving for any of us." Even one of the bill's opponents lauded Sputnik, commenting, "I think he really is sincere when he comes to lobby us. . . ."

It took more than impressive presentational skills, however, to get the bill passed. Sputnik got other bikers to pack a Senate hearing on the helmet bill. And he wanted them to make a lasting impression. Rather than have his fellow motorcycle enthusiasts don suits and ties to sway lawmakers, Sputnik wanted "my people to go down there just like they ride. I want [legislators] to know bikers came to town." Sputnik also put in a considerable amount of his own time pushing the helmet law repeal; he missed very few days during the session even though he had a 421-mile roundtrip commute to Austin. In the end, legislators passed the motorcyclists' bill.

How did a group of bikers get what they wanted over the opposition of the medical community and others who favored helmet laws? In part, they won because they seized on a message of freedom and liberty, arguing in Sputnik's words, "It is not a case of wearing a helmet but rather a case of a few elected and appointed officials believing they have the power to refuse me my God-given right to make my own choices about my personal right. . . ." Such an appeal to personal freedom carried weight in Texas. But the motorcyclists also won because they were an intense and vocal group and likely to be single-issue voters. Rather than alienate the bikers—and risk not only losing their votes but also the possibility the anti-helmet community would find candidates to run for the legislature—legislators gave them what they wanted.

Since their victory in 1997, bikers have continued to press their agenda before the Texas state legislature, and Sputnik continues to represent them. Attempts to pass a mandatory helmet law have failed, largely because of the biker lobby. They have not always gotten what they want, but they have become a political force to reckon with. Indeed, when bikers rallied in Austin in January 2007, the state House of Representatives unanimously passed HR 88, a resolution that, among other things recognized that: "Together with their readiness to lend a helping hand, motorcycle enthusiasts embody the spirit of adventure, love of the outdoors, and passion for freedom that have long been associated with the Texan character; through their attention to the legislative process, those who have gathered in Austin this week are also demonstrating an admirable example of civic engagement. . . ." The resolution was sponsored by Representative Norma Chavez (D-El Paso), who rides a bike under the road name "Da Lady."

Sources: Kara Altenbaumer, "Biker Revs Up to Hit Helmet Law; Senators Respond to Fight for Repeal," *Houston Chronicle*, April 6, 1997; Claire Cummings, "Freedom is Driving Helmet Foes: Despite Rise in Deaths, Many Bikers Say Choice Needs to be Protected," *Dallas Morning News*, June 15, 2006; Jim Dallas, "Biker Caucus Teaches Democrats a Lesson," *Daily Texan*, June 21, 2002; Karen Lundegaard, "Risky Riders: Touting Freedom, Bikers Take Aim At Helmet Laws," *Wall Street Journal*, December 1, 2004; Anna M. Tinsley, "Helmet Debate Pits Safety Against Freedom," *Fort Worth Star-Telegram*, September 24, 2007. See also the TMRA2 discussion of Legislative Day 2007 (http://legislativeday.tmra2.org/).

constantly in and around the capitol—it happens informally in legislators' offices and the halls of the legislative building, and it happens more formally in committee hearings.[19] It occurs over dinner in the restaurants around the capital city, and it takes place over appetizers on paper plates at the numerous "Legislative Appreciation" gatherings, where each organization holds an open house to which all the state legislators are invited.

Good lobbyists know as much—and often, more—about what goes on in the legislature than many of the legislators do. As one book on lobbying at the state level notes, "Lobbyists have to know the legislative process in a particular state inside and out."[20] And this means both the formal process and the political context within that state. They spend extraordinary amounts of time reading bills, attending committee hearings, talking to legislative staff, talking to legislators, and talking to one another. They keep in contact with their clients. They often draft legislation, and they research arguments in support of their own bills and with which to defeat the bills they oppose. They form coalitions with other groups when it is in their interest to do so. In states where legislative staffing is limited (which, as Chapter 3 documented, is most states), when committees meet to discuss the relative merits of a piece of legislation, most of the testimony, pro and con, is provided by lobbyists. In short, next to the legislators, their staff, and perhaps a few members of the statehouse press corps, lobbyists (as a group) know more about the legislators and the legislative process than anyone else in the state.

Virtually all lobbyists engage in personal, face-to-face meetings with legislators and staff. One survey of lobbying techniques finds that 98 percent of registered lobbyists say they meet personally with state legislators; 97 percent say they meet personally with legislative staff.[21] The latter interaction is especially common in the more professionalized state legislatures.

A great deal of the "social lobby" that circulates around the legislative session is designed to give interest groups and their agents some "face time" in an informal setting. The most effective lobbyists spend long hours at the legislature, staying in contact, touching base, and being seen, even if they do not have much on the agenda that particular day or week. As one observer notes, "Lobbyists who simply show up in the Capitol on decision day, introduce themselves to harried lawmakers, and ask for consideration of their clients' positions don't accomplish much. Indeed, no smart lobbyist would even think of operating that way."[22]

The word often heard in this regard is "access." Lobbyists insist that the campaign contributions they make and the meals and drinks they buy for legislators do not buy votes, but they help guarantee access to the legislator when the lobbyist needs to discuss a bill. As one observer points out, "access" in this sense really means "access before others are given access"— a sort of preferential treatment.[23] Discussing the impact of campaign contributions, a Florida lawmaker admitted, "It does buy access. If somebody gives me a campaign contribution I'm going to remember it, and I'm going to remember who they are and when they come calling, I'm going to listen to them. It doesn't mean they've bought me. But they have bought access."[24] Legislators' time is limited, especially toward the end of the session. With multiple demands on their time, lawmakers must decide who to see first, whose e-mail to respond to now, whose telephone calls to return. A lobbyist who is better known to the legislator is likely to be higher on that list.

Lawmakers, however, come to understand the nature of their relationship with interest group representatives. Discussing lobbyists, a veteran Vermont senator warned his younger colleagues, "They play a role here. They are good people. They tend to be fun, they tend to be bright, but their loyalty is not to you. It's to the people who pay them."[25]

Testifying at committee hearings is also a prevalent activity; a study of California, South Carolina, and Wisconsin lobbyists found that 98 percent of them reported testifying at legislative hearings.[26] Some of this testimony may be persuasive, involving information new to the committee members. But the reality is that the more effective lobbyists have already had one-on-one conversations with the committee chair and other members of the committee as well as with committee staff (in states where such staff exists). In these instances, the committee testimony serves to reiterate and emphasize specific points and to provide a public record of the interest group's or lobbyist's position.

Meeting with legislators and staff and testifying before committees are direct lobbying techniques. But lobbyists also engage in indirect techniques, which are designed to activate individual citizens and interest group members in the process. Organizing letter-writing campaigns, rallies, telephone banks and issuing press releases are examples. Increasingly, lobbyists send a "legislative alert" to the interest group's members, urging the members to contact their legislator and providing e-mail addresses for all legislators. Generally, these are rather ineffective tools, but sometimes they work. Some types of groups are more likely to use these techniques than others.

Another type of interest group activity is more directly related to elections. Some interest groups publicly endorse candidates. Generally, these are single-issue groups (e.g., the Right to Life organization mentioned above) or groups that are closely allied with a specific party (e.g., labor unions and the Democratic Party; some evangelical church organizations and the Republican Party). Other groups (especially corporations) tend not to formally endorse candidates. And the many organizations of local government officials—such as the Texas Association of Counties—are prohibited by law from active electioneering.

INTEREST GROUPS AND CAMPAIGN FINANCING

Many groups that do not formally and publicly endorse candidates nonetheless let their preferences be known because they contribute money to the campaigns of specific candidates. In most states, interest groups do this through their political action committees (PACs), which are the legal entity through which campaign funds are collected and disbursed. Different states have very different campaign finance laws, however. As discussed in Chapter 2, some states limit how much PACs can contribute to a legislative candidate to just a few hundred dollars. In other states, there is no limit at all.

When it comes to giving campaign contributions, most interest groups and their PACS are risk averse. As with the social lobby, what interest groups generally want from their campaign donations is access. Incumbents are likely to get reelected, so most PAC money goes to incumbents. It is an uncommon thing for PAC money to actually buy a legislator's vote on a particular bill. But, as already noted, it likely does buy preferential access. As one noted scholar says, "Legislators tend to be inclined to listen a little more attentively to a group's substantive arguments if that group has contributed to their campaign."[27] When there is no incumbent—an open seat—it is not unusual for a PAC to give money to both candidates in the general election. It is a form of bet hedging and, remember, PACs are generally risk averse.

This is not true of all interest groups and PACs, however. Single-issue groups, groups with a strong ideological perspective, and groups that are generally allied with one political party are not bet hedgers. They tend to be "all in" for the candidates who share their ideological perspective or who support their single issue. For these groups, interest group activity is more about getting the "right people" elected than about lobbying in the traditional sense. For such interest groups and for groups closely allied with a specific party, the outcome of the election largely determines the groups' success in the upcoming legislature. Simply put, when the election results in a Democratic legislative majority, the lobbyist for the state educational association is likely to have a more successful legislative session. When the Republicans win a majority, the lobbyist for the Association of Commerce and Industry is likely to be successful.

A recent phenomenon is the increasing involvement of some interest groups in what are known as "independent expenditures." Rather than contributing directly to a candidate's campaign, some groups are more likely to simply run their own advertisements on behalf of or in opposition to a specific candidate. Again, groups that are most likely to engage in such activities are either single-issue groups or organizations that are traditionally allied with one political party.

Finally, some groups and their lobbyists have the luxury of "going public" and trying to create public policy through instruments of direct democracy. Not all groups—in fact, probably not many groups—have the organizational or financial resources to undertake this sort of effort. But some groups do, and they use this tactic with increasing regularity.

PUBLIC OPINION AND DIRECT DEMOCRACY

From a procedural point of view, one of the biggest differences between the federal and state governments is that the latter are far more likely to operate with one or more forms of "direct democracy." The three basic instruments of direct democracy are the recall election, the referendum, and the initiative.

They are used in varying degrees in the states but not at all at the federal level.[28] One or more of these instruments is available in 35 states, and 11 states have all three.[29] And each of these mechanisms has the potential to affect the way the legislature conducts its policymaking business.

THE RECALL

At the state level, the recall is the least common form of direct democracy. Eighteen states provide for the recall of state officials, but it is rarely used (the well-known case of the recall of California Governor Gray Davis in 2003 notwithstanding). In recent decades, there have only been a few cases of state legislators being recalled. In 1996, a Wisconsin state senator was recalled because of his vote in support of appropriating state funds to build a baseball stadium for the Milwaukee Brewers. In 1995, two California lawmakers— both Republicans—were recalled for their part in helping Democratic Speaker Willie Brown retain control of the Assembly. In 1983, two Michigan senators were recalled for voting for a tax increase, and in 1971, two Idaho legislators were recalled for supporting a legislative pay raise. An Oregon state representative was recalled for falsifying a campaign solicitation letter in 1985. Only the Oregon case involved unethical behavior; the other cases were political in nature and involved constituent anger over a specific legislative vote or issue.

Although few legislators have actually been recalled in recent years, it does appear that the threat of recall has increased. In 2008, a rather nasty episode erupted in California.[30] State Senate President Pro Tem Don Perata (D-Oakland) was so frustrated by a budget stalemate that lasted almost two months in 2007 that he encouraged a recall petition against one of the Republicans who refused to vote for the budget—a vote that presumably would have broken the impasse. The targeted senator, Jeff Denham (R-Modesto) also happened to represent one of the few electorally competitive senate districts in California—a seat that the Democrats had designs on winning. But after qualifying the recall for the ballot, Perata had second thoughts about this tactic and withdrew his support for the removal effort; Denham then easily retained his office in the June 2008 recall election.

That is not the only recent example of a threat to recall a legislator. In July 2007, the Michigan Taxpayers Alliance began holding seminars across the state to train its members about the recall process, just in case the legislature voted for a tax increase. Although no legislators were actually recalled, some saw this action as a pre-emptive strike. As one veteran observer of Michigan politics noted, "Make no doubt about it, threat of recall has a tremendous impact on the state Legislature, in both parties."[31]

Recall petitions were filed in June 2008 against Louisiana House Speaker Jim Tucker and three other representatives after lawmakers voted for a bill that would increase legislative salaries from $16,800 to more than $37,000.

Two of the legislators threatened with recall recanted—one asked the governor to veto the bill, and the other published a letter of apology to his constituents in a local newspaper.[32] Governor Jindal's veto of the legislation likely saved these lawmakers from facing recall campaigns."[33] Occasionally, legislators even face recall threats from both ends of the political spectrum at the same time. In January 2009 a California labor union official announced "that unions will consider recalling from office any state legislator who votes to roll back regulations as part of a budget compromise."[34] And by July of 2009 petitions were circulating in California to recall several Republican lawmakers who had voted for a tax increase as part of the effort to balance the state's budget.

THE POPULAR REFERENDUM

There are two types of referenda. The more common is the "legislative referendum," an instrument allowing (or requiring) the legislature to put a proposal before the public for a vote. In all states but Delaware, this method is used to amend the state constitution; it requires (in most states) a two-thirds approval in each legislative chamber after which the proposed amendment is referred to the public for a vote in the next regularly scheduled election.[35] Undoubtedly, this type of referendum, by amending the state constitution, can have a major impact on the policy options available to legislatures. The legislature has a direct role in this process because such amendments require legislative approval before they are submitted to the public. In other words, the legislature is partly responsible for amendments passed in this way because they submit the proposal to the public for vote.

This is not the case with the second type of referendum, usually called the "popular referendum." The popular referendum is a mechanism whereby voters can override legislative action.[36] It exists in 24 states. In these states, when the legislature passes a law, it is possible for the general public to, in essence, "veto" the legislative action. Pursuing this process requires the circulation of petitions to gather signatures of registered voters. If enough valid signatures are gathered, the offending law is placed on the ballot in the next election for the voters to accept or reject. Clearly, then, legislatures in states with the popular referendum instrument are subject to an additional level of scrutiny. In addition to the traditional checks and balances offered by the executive and judicial branches, the legislature must also pass "popular muster" in these states.

It is a fact, however, that few legislative statutes are overturned through the popular referendum process. But occasionally one is. A well-known instance occurred in 2006; the South Dakota legislature passed HB 1215, the most restrictive abortion law in the United States and did so by an overwhelming margin in both chambers with bipartisan support.[37] The highly restrictive law was aimed at providing a test case for the U.S. Supreme Court to determine if the current justices would reinterpret the basic abortion law in the United States. However, some South Dakota citizens, objecting to the new law and its stated purpose to challenge *Roe v. Wade*, organized a petition drive to turn the matter over to the voters through the popular referendum. The South Dakota popular referendum process gives opponents 90 days after the legislature adjourns to collect valid signatures equal to 5 percent of the total votes in the last gubernatorial election—a relatively low threshold to meet. The petitioners managed to more than double the required number of signatures, and the referendum was placed on the November general election ballot as "Referred Law 6." The campaign that followed was lengthy and expensive by South Dakota campaign standards, and it attracted the attention of national organizations on both sides of the abortion issue as well as the national press. The law, which had been passed overwhelmingly by the legislature, went down to defeat; with 56 percent of the South Dakota voters rejecting it. [38]

But not every referendum overturns the legislature's decision. In 2008, the Ohio legislature passed House Bill 545, placing restrictions on payday lenders. The restrictions included capping the annual percentage rate on payday loans at 28 percent.[39] The bill also placed limits on the amount of money a consumer could borrow and the number of times a consumer could use payday loan services each year. The payday loan industry was successful in getting the measure placed on the ballot but was unsuccessful in overturning it. The public approved the legislature's bill by a substantial margin (64 percent in favor of keeping the law to 36 percent against).

THE INITIATIVE

The most prevalent instrument of direct democracy, in terms of its effect on state legislatures, is the initiative. The initiative exists in 24 states, about half of which are in the West. There are several varieties of initiative. The most important distinction among them is whether the initiative can be used to amend the constitution (18 states) or only to make statutory law (six states). Basically, the direct initiative process allows the public to bypass the legislature altogether. By collecting the requisite number of signatures on petitions, the public can get a proposal placed on the ballot for vote. If a majority of voters approve, the proposal becomes law (or becomes part of the state constitution, depending on the type of initiative). Clearly, both types of initiative have the potential to weaken the policymaking independence of the legislature, but an initiative that can change the state constitution has the greater effect because it precludes further legislative action on the issue.[40] In contrast, the statutory initiative can be changed by the legislature by simply writing a new law. Although this is legally permissible, it may be politically difficult. After all, a majority of voters approved the plebiscite in the first place, and they are not likely to want the legislature to overturn their decision. But it is also the case that in writing laws and passing appropriations to implement voter initiatives, legislators can sometimes cleverly blunt the impact of voter initiatives.[41]

Some initiative states use the instrument more than others. The key is how difficult or easy it is to qualify proposals for the ballot. Consequently, states where it is relatively easy to get measures on the ballot (California, Colorado, North Dakota, and Oregon) find many more issues being decided by public vote than states where the standards for qualifying measures for the ballot are more difficult (Alaska, Mississippi, and Wyoming). Table 6-1 shows the average number of initiative measures on the ballot in each biennium between 1996 and 2005. We chose to use the biennium because most legislatures operate on two-year cycles. Over each two-year period, for example, the California legislature has witnessed an average of 15 propositions decided by the public. To be sure, not all these propositions pass; in fact, only between 30 and 40 percent of the measures put before the voters pass in a typical year. Nonetheless, it is clear that states where the initiative is a viable instrument of direct democracy operate in a different policy environment than the rest of the states. For one thing, many of these initiatives involve fiscal policy— either mandating spending on specific items (e.g., education) or placing limits on specific taxes. Such constraints may have long-term consequences for the ability of the legislature to balance the fiscal needs of the state. A number of other initiatives address social policy, and some evidence suggests that the

TABLE 6-1   AVERAGE NUMBER OF INITIATIVE MEASURES ON
STATE BALLOT PER BIENNIUM, 1996–2005

STATE	AVERAGE NUMBER OF QUALIFIED BALLOT INITIATIVES PER BIENNIUM
California	15.0
Oregon	13.2
Colorado	8.2
Washington	7.8
Arizona	5.8
Nevada	4.6
Alaska, Florida, Maine, Montana, South Dakota	3.0–3.8
Arkansas, Massachusetts, Michigan, Missouri, Ohio, Nebraska	2.0–2.8
Idaho, North Dakota	1.0–1.8
Mississippi, Oklahoma, Utah, Wyoming	0.2–0.8
Illinois	0

Source: Calculated by the authors from data available in Todd Donovan, Christopher Z. Mooney, and Michael A. Smith, *State and Local Politics: Institutions and Reform* (Belmont, CA: Wadsworth Cengage, 2009), Table 5-1.

policies in initiative states more closely represent the preferences of the general public.[42] Perhaps, then, it is not surprising that voters like the initiative. In California in 2008, for example, 37 percent of voters in a statewide survey expressed a great deal or a fair amount of confidence in their state elected officials to make public policy compared with 52 percent who had confidence in the voters making policy decisions though direct democracy.[43]

THE GOVERNOR AND THE LEGISLATURE

One of the most important contextual factors that affects the legislative session is the relationship between the governor and the legislature. The relationship depends on several variables, but key among them is party affiliation. When the governor and the legislative majority are of the same party (i.e., unified party government), the legislature is more likely to follow the governor's lead on the more important policy matters.[44] When the governor is from one party and the legislative majority is from the other party, divided government exists. In this circumstance, the legislative majority is far less likely to bend to the will of the chief executive and instead is more likely to exert its own policy preferences.

Governors enjoy something of a natural advantage in dealing with state legislatures.[45] As two political scientists point out, "Although governors are not members of the legislative branch, the tools of the office of governor and the political environment in the states encourage governors to take an active role."[46] There are a number of reasons for this. One is the electoral connection: the governor is elected statewide and can claim a statewide mandate, something no legislator can do. Another is the ability of the governor to command media interest—the office of the governor is the highest elected office in the state. Moreover, as one textbook on state politics notes, "Governors attract media attention for a variety of reasons but mainly because it is just easier to report and understand state government by focusing on the governor."[47] Finally, as the leader of the executive branch, governors enjoy an information advantage over legislators, who, except in the most professionalized legislatures, do not have comparable policy experts at their disposal.

SETTING THE AGENDA

In addition, some practices, either ritualized or mandated by the state constitution, give the governor the great advantage of "agenda setting." This is the process of defining the issues for public consideration—and especially for the legislature's deliberation. The primary tools in this process are the "state-of-the state address" and the "budget address," both of which are presented by the governor to the legislature at the beginning of the legislative session and are usually accompanied by considerable pomp, fanfare, and media coverage. These addresses are really about the governor telling the public and the legislature what he or she thinks are the critical issues for consideration, floating potential solutions to issues, and proposing budgets to pay for these and other state programs. In his 2008 state-of-the state address, for example, Maryland Governor Martin O'Malley "asked for the General Assembly's help in holding down university tuition, further restricting development in environmentally sensitive areas and developing a long-term plan for energy generation and conservation. And he pledged to place heightened focus on fighting violent crime."[48] It is unlikely that any governor will get his or her way on all the matters he or she offers as worthy of consideration. But what is important is that the governor has set the parameters of the public agenda, and the legislature winds up reacting to it. The governor does not set the entire agenda, of course—not by any means. Most of the bills the legislature will pass are minor or narrow in scope and have nothing to do with the governor's legislative program. But a legislature, even at its best, can only deal with a limited number of major issues in a given year. And the governor has a powerful role in defining which of those major issues should be considered in a particular year. And right or wrong, the media's end-of-session assessment of how the legislature performed is often based on how much of the governor's agenda was passed.

The governor is sometimes referred to, therefore, as the "chief legislator" and has some specific tools to help persuade, negotiate with, and cajole the legislature.[49] Some of these tools are constitutionally derived, and because state constitutions differ from one another, the specifics of these tools differ from state to state. Others are a matter of personal style and political circumstance and differ from one governor to another even in the same state.

BUDGETS

We have already mentioned the *agenda setting* power afforded to the governor by the state-of-the state address and the media limelight. The budget message is in the same vein but is an even more powerful tool for the governor in many states. Governors can emphasize their policy preferences through the budget they submit to the legislature. State budgets are incredibly detailed documents, and in most states, the governor has a much larger staff to sift through the budget items agency by agency than does the legislature. Legislatures always find some items to change in the governor's budget plan— cutting a little here, adding some favored projects there—but for the most part, the legislature is only in a position to react to the governor's design. And on the back end of this process, the governor has considerable veto power, which means he or she can cut favored legislative programs if lawmakers alter the budget plan too much.

There are, however a handful of states, perhaps 10 or 12, in which the legislature operates as a truly independent force in budgetary matters. Idaho is one such state; over the years, the legislature has developed its own Legislative

Budget Office, which is well staffed and highly respected and allows the Joint Finance and Appropriations Committee (the budget committee) access to independent budget analyses. Another is Colorado, where the legislature has a long history of budgetary independence, to the point that some governors have publicly complained about their lack of power over spending.[50]

VETO POWER

Given that both the federal and state governments adhere to a "separation of powers" of the executive, legislative, and judicial branches, perhaps the most obvious tool the governor has is the *veto*. As a legislative leader in Vermont advised his new colleagues, "With one pen [the governor] has as much power as all the rest of us."[51] Every governor enjoys some form of veto—North Carolina's was the last to get the veto power in 1996—but the specifics of the veto are not the same in every states—a point that is quite evident from case examined in Politics Under the Domes 6-2. The key point here is that the veto is powerful because it is usually very hard for the legislature to override it. In most states, a veto override requires an extraordinary majority (either a three-fifths or a two-thirds vote).[52] And this extraordinary majority must occur in both houses. It is no wonder that on average only about 5 percent of gubernatorial vetoes are overturned. Indeed, in New York, the legislature failed to override a single veto of the thousands issued between 1873 and 1976![53] (New York legislators were actually able to turn this apparent weakness to their advantage. They passed and took credit for measures that special interests had requested even though lawmakers knew they were poor public policy. Legislators could do this because they were confident that the governor would veto the measures and the vetoes would not be overridden.)[54]

In addition to the general veto, which is used to block an entire bill, 43 states permit their governors to exercise some variant of a *line-item veto* on budget bills. The line-item veto allows the governor to object to specific appropriations (or occasionally provisions) within a bill without vetoing the entire measure. Ostensibly, this power is granted as a way to ensure fiscal responsibility, although it appears that governors use it to shape spending to their partisan preferences as much as they use it to lower the overall budget.[55] In some states, it is easier for the legislature to override a line-item veto than to override the general veto; in others, it still requires an extraordinary majority. But in either case, the governor, by blocking or reducing an appropriation measure, calls attention to it and makes it more difficult for the legislature to reinstate the full amount. Because vetoes (either line-item or general) are so hard to override, the mere threat of the veto is often a sufficient incentive for the legislative leaders to negotiate with the governor before the legislation is passed.

Even when actually deployed, the veto can give the governor considerable leverage with legislators. When the Republican majority in the Idaho House of Representatives blocked the Republican governor's expensive transportation

POLITICS UNDER THE DOMES 6-2

Vanna White, Frankenstein, and the Partial Veto in Wisconsin

In 1930, Wisconsin voters amended their state constitution by adding the following language to Article V, section 10 (1) (b): "Appropriation bills may be approved in whole or in part by the governor, and the part approved shall become law." This sentence created the partial veto, a version of a line-item veto but without using the term "line-item." By creating a partial veto instead of a strict line-item veto, Wisconsin's governors have had, arguably, the most powerful veto exercised by any governor in the country—and a far stronger veto than the president enjoys.

Over the years, Wisconsin governors came to use their partial veto to not only strike out numbers they did not want, as most versions of a line-item veto would allow, but to also strike out sentences, words, and even individual letters. By the late 1980s, Governor Tommy Thompson was able to use the partial veto, which he called "a pair of scissors," to selectively isolate particular letters. In one instance, he reconfigured legislation stating that juveniles could only be held in detention for 48 hours to read instead that they could be held for 10 days. The power to excise individual letters in a bill became known as the "Vanna White" veto after the *Wheel of Fortune* letter turner of that name, and it generated considerable controversy. In 1990, Wisconsin voters passed a constitutional amendment holding that "in approving an appropriation bill in part, the governor may not create a new word by rejecting individual letters in the words of the enrolled bill."

The amendment limited the governor's partial veto power, but only by a little bit. The executive was still able to delete sentences, words, and numbers and to do so in such a way as to subvert the will of the legislature. Governor Jim Doyle, for example, took a 752-word section of the 2005 state budget bill and cut it to just 20 words. In doing so, he completely changed its meaning, transferring $427 million to the general fund from the monies allocated for the Department of Transportation, as this abridged version of the veto shows (the words and digits that remained are highlighted in gray):

...for the purposes of the 2007-09 biennial budget act, the department of transportation shall include recommended reductions to the ... 2007-09 fiscal biennium reflecting the transfer from this appropriation account to the appropriation account under section ... in each fiscal year of the 2007-09 fiscal biennium on general obligation bonds issued under section ... in fiscal year 2006-07 is not sufficient to fund passenger rail service, ... the committee may supplement the appropriation account under

~~section 20.395 (2) . . . of the statutes,~~ from ~~the appropriations under section . . . by an amount that would not cause~~ the transportation fund ~~to have a negative balance . . . VILLAGE OF OREGON STREETSCAPING PROJECT.~~ In the 2005-07 fiscal biennium, ~~from the appropriation under . . . the department of transportation shall award a grant under section . . . of the statutes of $484,000 to the village of Oregon in Dane County . . . CHIPPEWA COUNTY CROSSING AND RAMP. In the 2005-07 fiscal biennium, from the appropriation under section 20.395 . . . of the statutes, the department of transportation shall award a grant under section 85.026 . . . of the statutes of $80,000~~ to ~~Chippewa County . . .~~

Lawmakers complained vociferously about such "Frankenstein" vetoes, and a movement to further limit the governor's veto power was begun. A proposed constitutional amendment passed overwhelmingly in both houses of the legislature in 2007 and subsequently received editorial support from every newspaper in the state. Thus, when Wisconsin voters were asked in an April 2008 referendum election, "Shall section 10 (1) (c) of article V of the constitution be amended to prohibit the governor, in exercising his or her partial veto authority, from creating a new sentence by combining parts of two or more sentences of the enrolled bill?" it was not surprising that, although the language was arcane, the amendment passed by a wide margin.

The partial veto power was now even further constrained, but the governor's spokesperson noted, "He still has got a very strong veto power, and he'll continue to use that when things get too far out of line." Indeed, the governor could continue to veto sentences, words in sentences, and individual digits. Only a few weeks after the amendment passed, Governor Doyle used his remaining partial veto powers to refashion a $69 million budget cut passed by the legislature into a $270 million reduction. Lawmakers have taken to referring to this sort of action as a "Frankenstein Junior" veto. With the partial veto and some creativity, governors in Wisconsin can, in the view of state legislators, still create a legislative monster.

Is the partial veto a good thing or a bad thing? When he was serving as the state Attorney General in 1992, Doyle told state legislators contemplating ways to constrain the governor's veto power, "No one should be able to create new laws through the use of a veto." As governor in 2005, Doyle changed his tune, exclaiming "Thank God I have a veto." He reconciled the contradiction with his earlier position by admitting, "Let's just say I see the world differently from the position I am in now." Wisconsin governors like their veto power. Wisconsin lawmakers detest it.

Sources: David Callender, "Doyle Detects New Love: The Veto," *Capital Times*, August 6, 2005; Monica Davey, "Wisconsin Voters Excise Editing From Governor's Veto Power,"

(Continued)

POLITICS UNDER THE DOMES 6-2 (CONTINUED)

The New York Times, April 3, 2008; Ryan J. Foley, "Senator's Delay on 'Frankenstein' Veto Draws Newspaper's Wrath," *Milwaukee Journal-Sentinel*, May 8, 2007; Stacy Forster and Steven Walters, "Voters to Decide on Veto Power," *Milwaukee Journal-Sentinel*, January 15, 2008; Peggy Hurley, "The Governor's Veto Power: To What Extent Can the Governor Reject Legislation?" *Governing Wisconsin*, 5 (October 2005); Patrick Marley and Steven Walters, "Doyle Boosts Spending Cuts," *Milwaukee Journal-Sentinel*, May 17, 2008; Frederick B. Wade, "The Origin and Evolution of Partial Veto Power," *Wisconsin Lawyer*, 81 (March 2008); *Washington Post*, "Governor Resists Curbs on Veto Power," April 5, 1990; *Wisconsin State Journal*, "Vote 'Yes' to Ban Crazy Veto," March 29, 2008.

plan in 2005, the veto became an important tool for forcing the administration's package through to passage. As the final days of the legislative session approached, the governor called reporters into his office, took the first eight bills from a stack on his desk awaiting his signature, and vetoed each of them. After finishing, he warned the members of the House, "And I've got a whole lot of other bills I can take action on. It is time for us to have cooperation on the highway bill on behalf of the citizens of Idaho." The governor then made his threat explicit: "Every House bill that comes down here is veto fodder."[56] Representatives fumed over the heavy-handed action. The House Commerce Committee chair complained to reporters that the governor was "a petulant cry baby, and you can quote me. He's behaving like a spoiled child."[57] But in the end, faced with the potential loss of many of the bills they had worked hard to pass, the House majority caved to the governor's demands.[58]

This is not to suggest that governors always get their way when they break out the veto stamp. In 2008, the Minnesota legislature passed a gasoline tax increase to help pay for transportation and infrastructure needs. The governor, Tim Pawlenty, vetoed the bill. The legislature overrode the veto, with all members of the majority DFL party (Democratic Farm-Labor Party, the name of the Democratic Party in Minnesota) and a handful of Republicans voting for the override. Pressure to hold the party line was intense on both sides of the aisle, and as mentioned in Politics Under the Domes 4-2, several of the Republican "defectors" who voted for the override were removed from key committee positions as punishment for voting against the wishes of the governor and party leaders. Nonetheless, the veto was overridden. Up to that point, Governor Pawlenty had vetoed 36 bills, and none of them had been overturned. Indeed, in the past 70 years, only 14 of 447 gubernatorial vetoes in Minnesota had been successfully overridden—and 12 of those occurred during Jesse Ventura's four-year tenure as an Independence Party governor with almost no allies in the legislature.[59]

Although the rules governing line-item vetoes almost always give the governor the upper hand on the legislature, relations between the two institutions occasionally degenerate to the point where legislators ignore party and unite against the executive. In 2004, for example, a strong disagreement over spending priorities led the South Carolina House to take only 99 minutes to override 105 of 106 vetoes issued by Governor Mark Sanford. Instead of cutting $96 million from the budget as the governor wanted, the legislature agreed to cut only $250,000. The governor retaliated by carrying two live pigs into the House chamber and accusing the representatives of engaging in pork barrel spending.[60] The governor's antics did little to improve relations with the legislature. The next year, the legislature overrode 153 of his 163 vetoes.[61] The anger between the institutions lingered even longer. When discussing a proposal to increase capitol security in 2007, Governor Sanford joked, "I have yet to read ever about any terrorism attack on a state capitol, I just don't think it's a high priority target, although sometimes I would like it to be." Legislators were not amused by the jab.[62]

OTHER GUBERNATORIAL WEAPONS

Another tool at the disposal of some governors is the *special session*. Most legislatures meet for only part of the year. The legislature adjourns *sine die* (indefinitely) and is not scheduled to return until the next regular session the following year (or in the case of biennial legislatures, the next regular session two years hence). Occasionally, however, the legislature may be called back to the capitol for a special session—usually to deal with an emergency situation or to address some important issue that was left unresolved at adjournment of the regular session. In about half of the states, the governor has the authority to call the legislature into special session (in the other half, only legislative leaders have such authority). Because most state legislators are not full time but instead have "real jobs" outside their legislative duties, being called to special session is quite disruptive of their private lives. Although this is probably true of almost all legislators, it is especially the case for those who live great distances from the capitol and for those with small children.[63] As in the case with the veto power, the mere threat of a special session may provide the governor enough leverage to get the legislature to comply with gubernatorial priorities.

To varying degrees, governors have at least two more advantages: patronage and campaign assistance. Most governors have several hundred appointments to make to advisory or regulatory boards and commissions. As Morehouse and Jewell note, "Although some of these are more ceremonial than substantive, legislators covet them to prove their ability to reward friends."[64] Governors can also use their appointment powers to directly entice legislators. In 2006, for example, Indiana Governor Mitch Daniels, a Republican, offered one Democratic representative a $60,000 position on the state Worker's Compensation Board and another a $55,000 post on the Indiana Parole Board. (Although legislative Democrats expressed outraged, a Democratic governor had made similar offers to several GOP lawmakers a decade before.)[65] And the governor can offer (or withhold the offer) to go out of his way to support a legislator who is expecting a difficult reelection campaign. If the governor is especially popular, the offer to come to the district and give a campaign speech on behalf of the legislator is hard to refuse.

The point is that the governor has many tools; some provide positive incentives, some threaten negative consequences, and some define the playing field. The branches may be separate, but they are not necessarily equal, and in most states, the legislature finds that it is playing uphill.

What all this means is that on major policy issues, the governor is usually a key player in legislative negotiations. Much of this occurs behind the scenes, with the governor (or, more likely, key staff members from the governor's office) meeting with legislative leaders (and their key staffers) to hammer out legislation that is acceptable to both legislative chambers and the chief executive.

THE BUREAUCRACY

A considerable amount of the legislature's time is taken up with issues involving the state agencies—the bureaucracy. First, the legislature must appropriate money for the operation of state government. The budget process involves agency heads coming before the appropriations committees of the legislature to make their case for funds. The budget is the single largest issue before the legislature on an annual basis. Even if the governor takes the budgetary lead, the appropriations committees are deeply involved in the process.

Second, the agencies initiate some of the legislative proposals brought before the legislature each session. Some of these proposals are brought because the agencies seek the authority to do something differently than they have been doing it or see the need for a new program. Some of these proposals are developed because the agencies find that federal grant requirements or federal or state court action requires the agency to operate in a different manner, and therefore the agency seeks legislation to put them into compliance with the new order. In a typical legislative session, perhaps 10 to 20 percent of the bills introduced were done so at the behest of one or another state agency.

Third, the legislature depends on the bureaucracy to carry out the laws after they are enacted. Legislatures pass the laws, but they do not implement them. State (and local) agencies are the entities that determine how the laws will be put into effect. In 2008, for example, the Mississippi Legislature passed HB 509, amending Section 47-1-19 of the Mississippi Code. This section authorizes inmates in the state prisons or county jails to perform public service work for nonprofit charitable organizations under certain conditions. HB 509 adds the following sentence to the code: "In addition, it is lawful for a state, county or municipality to provide prisoners for public service work for churches according to criteria approved by the Department of Corrections."[66] This was a popular measure; it was approved unanimously in the Senate, passed by a vote of 114 to 3 in the House, and was signed into law by the governor. Very simply, the legislature is extending the set of "nonprofit charitable organizations" to include churches. But what, exactly, qualifies as a church? And what, specifically, are the sort of activities that qualify as "public service work?" The legislature does not say. But the bill does say "according to criteria approved by the Department of Corrections."

In other words, the legislature has set a basic policy and then left the precise manner in which the policy is to be carried out to the administering agency—in this case, the Mississippi Department of Corrections. The legislature is delegating some of its authority to the agency; the legislature is authorizing bureaucratic discretion over the matter of what sort of activities constitute "public service work" and over what sort of religious organization qualifies as a church. This is a very common practice; a legislature cannot write legislation so detailed that it covers every possible contingency that might arise. Instead, a legislature authorizes state or local agencies to fill in many of the details. Usually, agencies are required to develop rules and standards for how they intend to implement the law, and these rules and standards are then subject to review by the legislature.

Thus, the relationship between the bureaucracy and the legislature is a complex one. According to a former state legislator, from a lawmaker's perspective, "administrators variously are enemies, allies, whipping boys or behind-the-scenes resources."[67] But legislators and bureaucrats each need the other to make policy work. Legislatures give agencies both money (through the budget process) and authority (to implement the policy). Legislatures then seek to oversee the way the agencies carry out the policy mandate. This *oversight* function is a difficult one to perform because most state legislatures are part time and proper oversight is a time-consuming and staff-intensive exercise. Given that legislators see lawmaking and casework as their primary functions, there is not much incentive to engage in serious oversight. And it is a time-consuming undertaking that, absent a public scandal, offers little political reward for legislators who engage in it. Thus, oversight is an important institutional function that is usually pursued with very little enthusiasm by lawmakers. Most state legislatures have committees to review agency rules, and virtually all state legislatures hire auditing staff to review agency expenditures. But except for a few states, legislative oversight of the bureaucracy is thin. Moreover, the ability of state lawmakers to legislatively design bureaucracies in such a way as to produce the bureaucratic outcomes the legislature wants is limited.[68]

The fourth way that legislators and the bureaucracy interface is *casework*. Casework, or constituent service, involves legislators and their staffs seeking to solve problems for individual constituents. Many times, these problems involve a state or local agency, and legislators increasingly act as intermediaries between their constituents and the bureaucracy. More than 25 years ago, political scientist Malcolm Jewell recognized the growing role of constituent service for state legislators: "They have been rejected by the agency administering the benefits, or have been unable to get an answer, or have been referred from one agency to another. . . . In cases such as this, the legislator may be able to get action expedited, or a case reviewed. . . ."[69] Because each party has something of value to the other—the legislator can give the agency budgetary and programmatic support, and the agency can give the legislator assistance in solving constituent problems—they have every incentive to work closely together. But ultimately, the legislator holds the upper hand. As an Iowa legislator observed about her interactions with state bureaucrats, "You get more flies with sugar than vinegar. I usually start with kind[ness]. Death and mutilation come later."[70]

Lawmakers receive two distinct benefits from the provision of constituent services. One is a sense of satisfaction. As a legislator confessed, "I have a lot of personal reward from getting somebody's social security check or whatever. . . . I remember a grandmother calling me up once because her grandson needed drug rehabilitation—we got him into a clinic. So you get a lot of personal reward that way."[71] The second benefit is political. Constituents who see a legislator as trying to help them solve their problems are potential voters in the next election, and evidence suggests that lawmakers who emphasize casework are rewarded at the polls.[72] Not surprisingly, almost all state legislators today view constituent service as an essential part of their job as a representative.[73] One study of state legislators in five states found that almost three-quarters of lawmakers report they receive at least five requests for help from constituents each week. Almost 20 percent of legislators said they received at least 25 requests a week.[74] As state populations grow, bureaucracies to serve their needs grow as well, and unfortunately, so too do problems for state legislators to help solve. Casework puts state legislators in contact with state agencies on a daily basis.

THE COURTS

Given the American notion of separation of powers, we might expect only limited interaction between state courts and state legislatures. For the most part, each branch operates in its own sphere of influence with little direct interference from the other. State courts, for example, tend to shy away from involving themselves in internal legislative disputes.[75] Remember that in Politics Under the Domes 2-1, the Kentucky Supreme Court went to considerable lengths to argue that because the candidate at issue was not yet a member of the state Senate, the judges were not meddling in a Senate business. (Although a lower court did enter into the dispute over the gavel in the Alabama Senate discussed in Politics Under the Domes 4-1, the state Supreme Court suspended that order and never issued a decision of its own.)

The formal relationship between courts and legislatures varies across the states, and it mirrors the relationship between Congress and the federal courts in only a few states. In just 11 states, for example, the governor nominates judges and the senate confirms or approves them in a process similar to the one followed by the U.S. president and U.S. Senate. In Connecticut, the governor nominates and both houses appoint judges to the bench. In most other states, the legislature plays little or no role in naming judges. But in two states, South Carolina and Virginia, the governor plays no role, and the appointment of judges is left entirely up to the legislature.[76]

From a policy perspective, the state court of last resort (usually, but not always, called the Supreme Court) can negate laws passed by the legislature if the Court determines that such laws are a violation of the state constitution. Just how often this occurs, however, varies widely across the states and varies across time periods within a single state. For example, the state Supreme Court data project reports that between 1995 and 1998, the state supreme courts of Connecticut, Indiana, Maine, and Michigan did not overturn a single state statute.[77] In contrast, the state Supreme Courts in Missouri and Illinois are likely to hear numerous challenges to legislative statutes, and they invalidate almost one-quarter of those laws challenged.[78]

STATE COURTS AND POLICY MANDATES

Typically, the influence of state courts on legislation is subtle. Policies adopted by the legislature are often shaped by court decisions at the bill development stage, as lawmakers anticipate potential legal challenges to the proposed law.[79] But more direct policy clashes between the state legislature and the state courts do occasionally occur. In 2005, the Kansas Supreme Court found on state constitutional grounds that the legislature was illegally underfunding public education. As a remedy, the Court ordered the state legislature to increase spending on schools by at least $285 million annually. This education funding issue has arisen in most states, and in many of them, the state court has taken a position similar to that in Kansas, which mandates the state legislature to fund public education at a higher level.

Kansas Republicans, who held the majority in both houses, were outraged and railed about the "non-elected judiciary's willingness to usurp the will of the people."[80] Some GOP legislators argued that they should ignore the Court's decision. One said, "I believe the Legislature's duty is to disregard this unconstitutional and unpermissive order of the court."[81] Another Republican lawmaker suggested that the process by which Supreme Court justices get put on the bench be changed so as to require Senate confirmation, arguing that doing so would make it more likely that the Court and the legislature would move in synch.[82] Still another Republican legislator raised the possibility of impeaching the members of the Court.[83] A number of legislators, however, counseled restraint, with one saying, "I tend to be upset with the court, too, and you want to say 'stick it.' But I don't know what the ramifications of that would be. We could be in an even stickier situation than we are now."[84]

As the battle dragged on, legislators seized on opportunities to take swipes at the Supreme Court. The House, for example, cut $3.7 million from the Court's budget, which, of course, is under the legislature's control.[85] It took two years for the funding issue to be resolved to the Court's satisfaction. But, grudgingly, the legislature increased spending for the public schools. And in the end, although many legislators fulminated about the Court's actions, the judicial appointment process was not changed.[86] And Kansas was not alone in this game of tug-of-war. Similar turf battles between the legislature and the courts were played out in other states, including Vermont, New Hampshire, Ohio, and New Jersey. And, as the battle over gay marriage in Iowa discussed in Politics Under the Domes 6-3 shows, the courts often prevail.

POLITICS UNDER THE DOMES 6-3

The Courts, the Legislature, and Gay Marriage in Iowa

When Governor Terry Branstad signed House File 382 in 1998, Iowa joined the majority of states in adopting a Defense of Marriage Act (DOMA). That measure, which passed both houses of the state legislature by overwhelming majorities, made a simple but significant change in the state's marriage law, altering Iowa Code section 595.2(1) to read explicitly, "Only a marriage between a male and a female is valid."

In 2005, that provision was challenged by six gay and lesbian couples who had been denied marriage licenses by the Polk County recorder's office. Later that year, a judge in Polk County ruled that Iowa's DOMA violated the state's constitution on equal protection grounds. The judge's order, however, was stayed until the case could be heard by the state supreme court, meaning that the decision to allow gay marriage did not go into immediate effect. In early 2009, the Iowa Supreme Court handed down a unanimous decision upholding the earlier verdict. The court wrote that Iowa's law prohibiting gay marriage was unconstitutional because: "We are firmly convinced that the exclusion of gay and lesbian people from the institution of civil marriage does not substantially further any important governmental objective." Thus, gay marriages were legalized in Iowa.

One question that quickly arose in the wake of the Supreme Court's decision was how the legislature was going to respond. After all, a decade earlier, it had passed the DOMA by large margins. Opponents of gay marriage immediately vowed to push the legislature to pass a constitutional amendment banning the practice. There were, however, two major obstacles to their plan.

The first was Iowa's requirement that any proposed constitutional amendment has to be passed by two successive legislatures. In this case, it meant that if a proposed constitutional amendment prohibiting gay marriage passed both houses of the legislature during the 2009–2010 legislative session, the measure would still have to pass the legislature again in the 2011–2012 session before it could be put on the ballot for the voters to ultimately decide. The process, which is similar to ones found in 11 other states, is intended to make amending the state constitution a slow, deliberative, and laborious process. It made it so that even if the Iowa state legislature moved as fast as possible, the court's decision could not be overturned until 2012 at the earliest.

The second obstacle was political—the fact that the membership of the legislature in 2009 differed from the legislature's membership in 1998. In 1998, the GOP controlled the legislature, and their leaders controlled the policy agenda. In 2009, the Democrats had a majority in both chambers, and the House speaker and the Senate majority leader supported the court decision, issuing a press release saying, "When all is said and done, we believe the only lasting question about today's events will be why it took us so long." Without the support of the legislature's top leaders, gay marriage opponents faced an uphill battle to get their proposed amendment brought up for a vote in either chamber. Indeed, although the Senate majority leader said he would listen to his party's caucus, declaring, "I will leave the option for my members to make suggestions," he admitted, "but it is exceedingly unlikely I would call up a constitutional amendment." Even the House majority leader, who had publicly opposed gay marriage in the past, said, "My personal opinion is irrelevant at this stage," and he said that he would defer to the wishes of the majority of his caucus not to pursue a constitutional amendment.

The legislative calendar also conspired against the hopes of those pushing the gay marriage ban. The court decision was handed down in early April. The Iowa legislature, like many others, operates under a strict schedule that requires most pieces of legislation to progress through committee and floor votes by certain dates in order to stay alive. By early April, the committee hearing dates had already passed, meaning that opponents of gay marriage had to get the rules waived (or, in parliamentary terms, suspended) to get their measure brought up for consideration. This greatly complicated their efforts. But, as the House Republic Leader, a gay marriage opponent, commented, "The Legislature has a whole mass of rules and while you can use them sometimes to hide behind, sometimes they work to your advantage in other situations." Although it appeared that the rules were working against the proposed amendment, gay marriage opponents hoped they would be able to manipulate them in such a way as to force a vote.

(Continued)

POLITICS UNDER THE DOMES 6-3 (CONTINUED)

A week after the court's decision was handed down, gay marriage opponents in the legislature made their move. The House Republican leader asked that the House suspend its rules and allow the proposed constitutional amendment to bypass the committee process and be brought directly to the floor for immediate consideration. The Speaker ruled the request out of order on a small but important technicality. The rule that House Republican leaders wanted waived was a rule jointly adopted by the House and the Senate. As a joint rule, it could only be suspended if a request was first introduced in the House Rules and Administration Committee and they passed it. Even then, it would have to go to the full house for approval and be passed by a similar procedure in the Senate. In contrast, a request to suspend a House only rule could have been passed by a simple majority vote of the House. The nuances of legislative procedure were lost on the gay marriage opponents who had packed the House public gallery. They chanted, "Let us vote," as they left after the Speaker's ruling. The Speaker countered that the demonstration was attempt to govern by "mob rule."

Later that same day, gay marriage opponents took a second run at getting a vote on their proposed constitutional amendment. This time, they opted to offer an amendment to House File 811, a measure to fund the state's health and human services budget. They wanted to replace the budget language with the contents of the constitutional amendment, in essence hijacking the original bill for a very different purpose. The amendment failed on a nearly party-line vote, with two Democrats joining with the Republicans in the failed effort.

After losing twice on procedural moves, gay marriage opponents conceded defeat for the year. As a dejected Republican lawmaker noted, "It means the Supreme Court ruling stands today." Indeed, it appeared likely that Democrats would frustrate the efforts of gay marriage opponents again in 2010, pushing back any ballot measure until possibly 2014. Gay marriage opponents could only hope to use the issue to swing control of the legislature back in their direction in the 2010 elections.

Sources: Jason Clayworth, "Crowd at Capitol Pushes for Amendment Barring Gay Marriage," *Des Moines Register*, April 9, 2009; Jason Clayworth, "Marriage Measure Pushed to No Avail," *Des Moines Register*, April 10, 2009; Jason Clayworth, "McCarthy: My Stand on Gay Marriage is Irrelevant," *Des Moines Register*, April 6, 2009; Jeff Eckhoff, "Today's Ruling at a Glance," *Des Moines Register*, April 3, 2009; Jeff Eckhoff and Grant Schulte, "Unanimous Ruling: Iowa Marriage No Longer Limited to One Man, One Woman," *Des Moines Register*, April 3, 2009; Tony Leys, "Opponents Promise to Push for Amendment," *Des Moines Register*, April 3, 2009; Office of the Speaker, "Out of Order Ruling for HJR 6" (http://www.desmoinesregister.com/assets/pdf/D213247449.PDF). The legislative history of the Iowa DOMA measure can be found at http://www2.legis.state.ia.us/GA/77GA/Legislation/HF/00300/HF00382/Current.html.

STATE COURTS, DIRECT DEMOCRACY, AND POLICYMAKING

In states where "direct democracy" instruments are commonplace, the courts play an important role because they must often mediate between the legislature and the proponents of various initiatives. Some of these issues directly affect the legislature; term limits is an obvious example. Today 15 states have legislative term limits, but as noted in Chapter 1, at one time or another, 21 states passed term limits—19 of them through the initiative process. In four of those states—Massachusetts (1997), Washington (1998), Oregon (2002), and Wyoming (2004)—the Supreme Court of the state struck down term limits as a violation of some aspect of each state's constitution. But the Supreme Courts in each of the remaining 17 states upheld term limits, determining that there was no violation of the particular state constitution.[87] As discussed in an earlier section, tax and expenditure limits (TELs) are another example of an issue in which the interpretation taken by the state courts can have an important effect on legislature's independence, in this case in its ability to craft a state budget.

THE FISCAL FACTOR

As we discussed briefly in Chapter 5, state budgets are constrained in ways the federal budget is not. For example, all states but Vermont have a balanced-budget requirement, although just how that constraint is interpreted varies from one state to another.[88] About half of the states have laws (either statutory or constitutional) that place specific limits on revenue or spending (e.g., a law limiting the increase in spending per capita to the rate of inflation).[89] Furthermore, a dozen states (almost all of them states with the initiative process) require a super majority vote to raise taxes. Some of these require a popular vote—not just a vote by the legislators—to increase taxes. More than three-fourths of the states have restrictions on the type and amount of bonded indebtedness the state can undertake. What all this means is that state legislatures are much more limited than the national government in their options for setting fiscal policy and devising budgets. Essentially, and unlike the federal government, the states, for the most part, must live within their means. Setting a budget that is acceptable to a majority in each chamber and to the governor is, therefore, a difficult task. And in years of economic downturn, it can be a painful process for legislators. States are responsible, in whole or in part, for public education, higher education, health care, roads and highways, prisons, and a host of other public services and regulations. What can be cut? Do we raise taxes? Do we do both? Do we do neither? These are questions that legislators must decide, and they can be assured that some segment of the population will be unhappy with whatever decision they make.

With the economic downturn in early 2008, about a third of the state legislatures expected to cut programs or otherwise reduce spending. Nevada legislators were forced to impose a 4.5 percent across-the-board budget cut, affecting all agencies and programs, to bring the fiscal year 2008 budget into balance.[90] The Florida legislature cut $1 billion from the budget, including a $50 million reduction in the budget for the University of Florida, which then announced it expected to reduce undergraduate enrollment by 4,000 students.[91] As the economic decline accelerated, the fiscal news for the states worsened. By January 2009, with the national economy in full recession, all but a small handful of state legislatures anticipated adopting budgets for fiscal year 2010 that would be smaller than fiscal year 2009 budgets. Overall, states estimated a total shortfall between 2009 and 2011 over $200 billion.[92] Legislative sessions dragged on in many states as legislatures struggled to plug the gaping budget holes. The California Legislature was unable to reach agreement on a state budget package by the July 1 deadline and the state began issuing I.O.U.s.

Legislatures have devised a series of procedures to cope with the difficult process of setting budgets. Most importantly, most legislatures have come to rely heavily on one of two mechanisms for getting the budget set. One option is to defer most of the budget decisions to the relevant standing committees (usually called the Appropriations or Budget or Finance Committees). These committees do the lion's share of the work in putting together the budget, and the floor largely goes along with their recommendations. The other option is to give most of the budget-setting power to the party leadership in the two chambers, along with the governor. In New York, for example, it is widely understood that the governor, the Senate majority leader, and the Assembly speaker negotiate the final budget.

Many state legislatures also have specific deadlines for revenue projections, committee reports on the budget, and final passage. For most states, the fiscal year begins on July 1, so the budget must be approved before that date. But, of course, disagreements can keep budgets from getting passed on time. Of the 32 budgets in California between 1977–1978 and 2008–2009, for example, only 10 were passed on time.[93]

THE FEDERAL FACTOR

Obviously, state legislatures are greatly affected by the federal relationship. On some occasions, legislatures are constrained by federal actions; on other occasions, they are forced to act. U.S. Supreme Court (and other federal court) decisions, congressional statutes, executive orders issued by the president, and federal agency rulings can all influence state legislative policymaking.[94] The federal grant-in-aid program (fiscal federalism) is especially important in this regard because federal money to states is often tied to specific policy or program requirements.

Many laws passed by Congress have direct impacts on states and state legislatures. One recent example is the No Child Left Behind Act (NCLB), which was passed by Congress in 2001. The cornerstone of President Bush's education policy, the law requires all public schools receiving federal aid through Title I of the Elementary and Secondary Education Act—another law passed by Congress—to demonstrate competency and improvement in the delivery of education to students. About 70 percent of all public schools, and all states, are affected. The mechanism for demonstrating these qualities are a series of annual tests to be administered to students in grades 3 to 8 and at least once for high school students. State legislatures have to deal with the fiscal consequences of creating and implementing testing procedures.

Another example is the 2005 Real ID Act, which requires every state to adopt federal standards for the issuance of state driver's licenses. Many state legislators were upset with this act on two grounds. First, they saw it as federal intrusion into an area traditionally left to the states (as part of the state police powers). Second, it was clear from the outset that Congress was unlikely to provide sufficient funds to cover the costs of implementing the new standards. As far as the state legislators are concerned, this constitutes an unfunded mandate from the federal government—one that the states estimate will cost them as much as $11 billion. Unfunded mandates are especially pernicious to state legislators because they force lawmakers to either shift money from other programs or to raise taxes. Thus, state legislators think that they are often the ones who have to pay the political price for decisions made at the federal level.

The situation in which the national government creates policies that must be carried out by state governments is called "coercive federalism," and according to federalism scholars, it is a trend that accelerated during the administration of President George W. Bush.[95] In response, the states, and especially the state legislatures, are becoming more aggressive in fighting back against what they see as national government intrusion into state policy areas. The National Conference of State Legislatures, an organization that represents all state legislatures, has been very active in seeking to protect what they see as state prerogatives. So have individual state legislatures. The Utah legislature was the first (but not the last) to resist some of the requirements imposed by NCLB. Even greater opposition arose to the Real ID Act, and by 2007, bills opposing the federal law had been introduced in almost half the states.[96] In the case of Real ID, the federal government eventually backed off of its original proposal because of opposition from the states.[97] There are other examples, such as state legislative resistance to changes in the basic federal welfare law (Temporary Assistance for Needy Families). The point is that, as state legislatures have become more capable over time, they appear to be more assertive of their own state rights and less willing to comply with federal mandates.

It is not just congressional actions that affect state legislatures, of course. By far, most of the laws struck down by the U.S. Supreme Court are state laws, not congressional acts. Some—perhaps most—of the more momentous U.S. Supreme Court decisions have had sweeping effects on states and their legislatures. The reapportionment cases of the 1960s are an obvious example. Beginning with *Baker v. Carr*[98] and *Reynolds v. Sims*,[99] the U.S. Supreme Court rendered decisions that forced the states to reapportion state legislative seats to more closely approximate the "one person, one vote" principle. The long-term effect on legislatures was substantial, including increased representation of urban and suburban constituencies, which resulted in "a growing responsiveness in state legislatures to the problems and interests of cities and suburbs."[100]

A good illustration of how federal Court action influences state legislatures and policymaking is the reaction to the 2005 U.S. Supreme Court case of *Kelo v. New London*.[101] In this case, the Court asserted that a city had the authority to exert "eminent domain" (the taking of private property, generally for public good) even for a private economic development. Here, the U.S. Supreme Court essentially upheld the interpretation of the Connecticut State Supreme Court that Connecticut law allowed such taking. In response, 30 state legislatures passed new laws clarifying and limiting the use of eminent domain in their respective states within one year of the *Kelo* decision.

CONCLUSION

State lawmakers are more constrained in their legislative actions than are members of Congress. There are at least three reasons for this situation. First, congressional laws, executive orders, and federal court decisions may limit or require certain actions by the states and their policymakers, the state legislatures—although recently state legislators appear increasingly willing to resist such actions when they are viewed as unwarranted intrusions into state policymaking. Second, state legislators are bound by fiscal restrictions not found at the federal level. The most important of these, of course, is the requirement of a balanced budget. Almost all state legislatures must operate under such fiscal constraints; this is obviously not the case for Congress. The implications of this reality are immense; when it comes to budgeting, state legislatures are forced to be much more attuned to economic trends than is the case at the national level. Finally, many state legislatures must consider their actions in light of the existence of the instruments of direct democracy. In particular, the initiative process, the popular referendum, and the recall petition mean that state legislators are bound by popular opinion and constituent desires in ways that members of Congress need not be.

ENDNOTES

1. Robert S. Erickson, Gerald C. Wright, and John P. McIver, *Statehouse Democracy: Public Opinion and Policy in the American States* (New York: Cambridge University Press, 1993).
2. Gerald Wright, "Do Term Limits Affect Legislative Roll Call Voting? Representation, Polarization, and Participation," *State Politics and Policy Quarterly* 7:256–280; Gerald C. Wright and Jon Winburn, "Patterns of Constituency-Legislator Policy Congruence in the States," paper presented at the annual meeting of the State Politics and Policy Conference, Milwaukee, WI, 2002.
3. Edmund Burke was an eighteenth century British political philosopher and member of Parliament who argued for the trustee role in his famous "Speech to Electors at Bristol."
4. *Ring v. Arizona.* 536 U.S. 584 (2002).
5. The quotation and other information about this case is from Dan Popkey, "Legislator Laments His Own Vote Against Principles," first printed in the *Idaho Statesman*, reprinted by on the "Idaho Reports" website (http://www.idahoptv.org/idreports/2003/showEditorial.cfm?StoryID=7992).
6. Popkey, "Legislator Laments His Own Vote Against Principles."
7. Popkey, "Legislator Laments His Own Vote Against Principles."
8. Popkey, "Legislator Laments His Own Vote Against Principles."
9. Alan Rosenthal, *Heavy Lifting: The Job of the American Legislature* (Washington, DC: CQ Press, 2004), 40, Table 3-2.
10. Rosenthal, *Heavy Lifting*, 41, Table 3-3.
11. Malcolm Jewell, *Representation in State Legislatures* (Lexington, KY: University Press of Kentucky, 1982), 114.
12. Richard Fenno, *Home Style: House Members in Their Districts* (Boston: Little Brown, 1978), 1.
13. Fenno, *Home Style*. See especially Chapter 1, 1–29.
14. Jewell, *Representation in State Legislatures*, and Michael A. Smith, *Bringing Representation Home* (Columbia, MO: University of Missouri Press, 2003).
15. The discussion of Texas lobbyists is based on information from the Texas secretary of state's web page (http://www.ethics.state.tx.us/tedd/lobcon2008b.htm).
16. Anthony Nownes, Clive Thomas, and Ronald Hrebenar, "Interest Groups in the States," in Virginia Gray and Russell Hanson, eds. *Politics in the American States*, 9th ed. (Washington, DC: CQ Press, 2008), 111.
17. Nownes, Thomas, and Hrebenar, "Interest Groups in the States," 101.
18. Nownes, Thomas, and Hrebenar, "Interest Groups in the States."
19. Alan Rosenthal, *Heavy Lifting*, 108.
20. Alan Rosenthal, *The Third House: Lobbyists and Lobbying in the States*, 2nd ed. (Washington, DC: CQ Press, 2001), 83.
21. Nownes, Thomas, and Hrebenar, "Interest Groups in the States," 107.
22. John Straayer, *The Colorado General Assembly*, 2nd ed. (Boulder, CO: University Press of Colorado, 2000), 194–195.
23. Rosenthal, *The Third House*, 137.
24. *St. Petersburg Times*, "Rookie Content with Nibbling Start," March 8, 2005.
25. Wilson Ring, "New Lawmakers Told to Succeed They Must Work Together, be Humble," *Boston Globe*, November 30, 2000.
26. Anthony Nownes and Patricia Freeman, "Interest Group Activity in the States," *Journal of Politics* 60 (1998):86–112, 92.
27. Rosenthal, *The Third House*, 138.
28. Technically, one could argue that the process of amending the U.S. Constitution involves a referenda component because Article 5 stipulates that one of the two ways to amend the Constitution is to hold ratifying conventions in each state subsequent to approval of the proposed amendment by at least two-thirds of the members each of the house and senate. At least three-quarters of the state ratifying conventions would be required to approve of the measure. But the point is that a convention is not the same as a vote of the public—which is precisely what is required in a state referendum.
29. Todd Donovan, Christopher Z. Mooney, and Daniel A. Smith, *State and Local Politics: Institutions and Reform* (Belmont, CA: Wadsworth Cengage, 2009), 100–101.

30. The following account is based on newspaper accounts of the episode, including Aurelio Rojas, "Drive to Recall Denham Goes Beyond Budget Bad Blood with Perata," *Sacramento Bee*, April 15, 2008.

31. Steve Mitchell, quoted in Pete Nichols, "Tax Hike Opponents Lecture on Recall Rights," *The State News*, July 20, 2007.

32. Kevin McGill, "Recall Petitions Filed Against Legislators," Associated Press, June 25, 2008 (http://www.2theadvocate.com/news/21541549.html?showAll=y&c=y).

33. Steve Mitchell, quoted in Pete Nichols, "Tax Hike Opponents Lecture on Recall Rights," *The State News*, July 20, 2007.

34. Kevin Yamamura, "Legislators Threatened with Recall if Labor Safeguards Cut," Sacramento Bee, January 30, 2009)

35. In Delaware, constitutional amendments are not subject to referendum vote, but the legislature may, if it chooses, place statutes on the ballot for approval or rejection. For detail about the way the various instruments of direct democracy operate in the different states, see the Initiative and Referendum Institute website (http://www.iandrinstitute.org).

36. Shaun Bowler and Todd Donovan, "The Initiative Process," in Virginia Gray and Russell L. Hanson, eds., *Politics in the American States*, 9th ed. (Washington: CQ Press, 2008), 130. We cite 35 states here because we are focusing only on the recall, the initiative, and the specific type of referendum known as the "popular referendum." If we include the instrument of "legislative referendum" as well, then all 50 states have at least one instrument of direct democracy.

37. The bill passed the House 50 to 18 and the Senate 23 to 12 and was signed by the governor. Our discussion of this bill relies on several sources, including Monica Davey, "South Dakotans Reject Sweeping Abortion Ban," *The New York Times*, November 8, 2006; Dale Oesterle, "The South Dakota Referendum on Abortion: An Alternative to Court Review?" October 31, 2006 at the Ohio State University Moritz College of Law's website (http://moritzlaw.osu.edu/electionlaw/commentary/articles.php?ID=18); and "Abortion Ban Supporters at Odd with Constituencies" at the South Dakota Campaign for Healthy Families' website (http://www.sdhealthyfamily.org).

38. The issue played out again in 2008, when the restrictive abortion proposal was placed on the ballot through the initiative process. It was defeated again.

39. Matt Burns, "Payday Industry Launches Referendum to Overturn Law," *Business First of Columbus*, June 5, 2008. According to the article, the current maximum APR on such loans in Ohio is 391 percent.

40. Technically, this is not quite true because the legislature could always begin a new constitutional amendment to overturn the one passed by initiative. This would be political folly and not at all likely to happen.

41. Elisabeth R. Gerber, Arthur Lupia, Mathew D. McCubbins, and D. Roderick Kiewiet, *Stealing the Initiative: How State Government Responds to Direct Democracy* (Upper Saddle River, NJ: Prentice-Hall, 2001).

42. John Matusaka, *For the Many or the Few: The Initiative, Public Policy, and American Democracy* (Chicago: University of Chicago Press, 2004).

43. Mark Baldassare, Dean Bonner, Jennifer Paluch, and Sonja Petek, "Californians & their Government," *Public Policy Institute of California*, December 2008, 18.

44. On the other hand, just because the governor enjoys a partisan majority in the legislature does not necessarily mean he gets his way. For an example See Alan Ehrenhalt, "Butch's Battle," *Governing Magazine*, June 2009 (http://www.governing.com/node/1745/).

45. Alan Rosenthal, *Heavy Lifting*, 165–179.

46. Thad Beyle and Margaret Ferguson, "Governors and the Executive Branch," in Virginia Gray and Russell Hanson, eds. *Politics in the American States*, 9th ed. (Washington, DC: CQ Press, 2008), 215.

47. Donovan, Mooney, and Smith, *State and Local Politics*, 267.

48. John Wagner, "O'Malley's Address a Fiscal Reality Check: Governor's Agenda Includes Fighting Crime, Ending 'Fast Track to Foreclosure,'" *Washington Post*, January 24, 2008.

49. The notion of the governor as "chief legislator" dates back to the beginning of the twentieth century. See Leslie Lipson, "Influence of the Governor upon Legislation," *Annals of the American Academy of Political and Social Science* 195 (1938):72–78.

50. Straayer, *The Colorado General Assembly*, 214.

51. Ring, "New Lawmakers Told to Succeed They Must Work Together, be Humble."
52. Sarah McCally Morehouse and Malcolm E. Jewell, *State Politics, Parties and Policy*, 2nd ed. (Lanham, MD: Rowman & Littlefield, 2003), 179.
53. Joseph F. Zimmerman, *The Government and Politics of New York State* (New York: New York University Press, 1981), 200–204.
54. Eugene J. Gleason and Joseph Zimmerman, "The Strong Governorship: Status and Problems—New York," *Public Administration Review* 36 (1976):92–95.
55. Glenn Abney and Thomas P. Lauth, "The Line-Item Veto in the States: An Instrument for Fiscal Restraint or an Instrument of Partisanship?" *Public Administration Review* 45 (1985): 372–377; Thomas P. Lauth and Catherine C. Reese, "The Line-Item Veto in Georgia: Fiscal Restraint or Inter-Branch Politics?" *Public Budgeting & Finance* 26 (2006):1–19.
56. *Idaho Statesman*, "Governor Vetoes 8 Bills after Panel Blocks His Roads Plan," April 1, 2005.
57. *Idaho Statesman*, "Governor Vetoes 8 Bills after Panel Blocks His Roads Plan."
58. Dana Dugan, "House Committee Blinks on Roads Bill," *Idaho Mountain Express*, April 8, 2005.
59. The discussion of the Minnesota case is based on Mike Kaszuba and Mark Brunswick, "House, Senate Override a Pawlenty Veto for the First Time," *Minneapolis Star Tribune*, February 25, 2008.
60. Jeff Stensland, "Veto Overrides Prompt Scolding," *The State*, May 27, 2005.
61. Stensland, "Veto Overrides Prompt Scolding."
62. Tim Smith, "Sanford's Joke on Terrorism at Statehouse Draws Criticism," *The Greenville News*, October 10, 2007.
63. Lisa Sandberg, "Sessions Upend Legislators' Lives," San Antonio *Express-News*, July 31, 2005.
64. Morehouse and Jewell, *State Politics, Parties and Policy*, 188.
65. Mary Beth Schneider, "Job Offers to 2 Lawmakers Questionable, Dems Say," *Indianapolis Star*, March 2, 2006.
66. Mississippi HB 509 was accessed through the Mississippi State Legislative's website (http://billstatus.ls.state.ms.us/documents/2008/html/HB/0500-0599/HB0509SG.htm).
67. Mordecai Lee, "Political-Administrative Relations in State Government: A Legislative Perspective," *International Journal of Public Administration* 29 (2006):1021–1047.
68. Christopher Reenock and Sarah Poggione, "Agency Design as an Ongoing Tool of Bureaucratic Influence," *Legislative Studies Quarterly* 29 (2004):383–406.
69. Jewell, *Representation in State Legislatures*, 153.
70. Adam Belz, "Dying Lundby Recalls Political Career," Cedar Rapids *Gazette*, January 1, 2009.
71. Grant Reeher, *First Person Political* (New York: NYU Press, 2006), 63.
72. George Serra and Neil Pinney, "Casework, Issues and Voting in State Legislative Elections," *Journal of Legislative Studies* 10 (2004):32–46.
73. Patricia Freeman and Lillard Richardson, Jr., "Exploring Variation in Casework among State Legislators," *Legislative Studies Quarterly* 21 (1996):41–56; Karl Kurtz, Gary Moncrief, Richard Niemi, and Lynda Powell, "Full-Time, Part-Time and Real Time: Explaining State Legislators' Perceptions of Time on the Job," *State Politics and Policy Quarterly* 6 (2006):322–338; Gary Moncrief, Joel A. Thompson, and Karl T. Kurtz, "The Old Statehouse, It Ain't What it Used to Be," *Legislative Studies Quarterly* 21 (1996):57–72.
74. Rosenthal, *Heavy Lifting*, 27.
75. On this point, see Michael B. Miller "Comment: The Justiciability of Legislative Rules and the 'Political' Political Question Doctrine," *California Law Review* 78 (1990):1341–1374. See also the discussion Peverill Squire and Keith E. Hamm, *101 Chambers: Congress, State Legislatures and the Future of Legislative Studies* (Columbus, OH: Ohio State University Press, 2005), 157, note 38.
76. These data were gathered by the authors from American Judicature Society's webpage on judicial selection (http://www.judicialselection.us/).
77. Melinda Hall, "State Courts: Politics and the Judicial Process," in Virginia Gray and Russell Hanson, eds. *Politics in the American States*, 9th ed. (Washington, DC: CQ Press, 2008), 251.
78. Hall, "State Courts: Politics and the Judicial Process," 252.
79. Teena Wilhelm, "The Policymaking Role of State Supreme Courts in Education Policy," *Legislative Studies Quarterly* 32 (2007):309–333; Teena Wilhelm, "Strange Bedfellows," *American Politics Research* 37 (2009):3–29.
80. Chris Moon, "Lawmakers May Spurn Court," *Topeka Capitol-Journal*, June 8, 2005.

81. Moon, "Lawmakers May Spurn Court."
82. David Klepper, "Spoiling for a Fight in Kansas," *Kansas City Star*, June 8, 2005.
83. Klepper, "Spoiling for a Fight in Kansas."
84. Klepper, "Spoiling for a Fight in Kansas."
85. *Kansas City Star*, "Obstinacy, Pettiness Won't End Problems," March 22, 2006.
86. Scott Rothschild, "After 7 Years, Litigation is Dismissed," Lawrence *Journal-World*, July 29, 2006.
87. The Idaho and Utah legislatures repealed term limits on their own.
88. Robert Lowry, "Fiscal Policy in the American States," in Virginia Gray and Russell Hanson, eds. *Politics in the American States*, 9th ed. (Washington, DC: CQ Press, 2008), 293.
89. Lowry, "Fiscal Policy in the American States."
90. Pamela M. Prah, "23 States Face Budget Gaps in '09" (http://www.stateline.org/live/printable/story?contentID=304139).
91. Shannon Colavecchio-Van Sickler, "Deep cuts Hit UF at All Levels," *Tampa Bay Sun Times* (http://www.tampabay.com/news/education/college/article489664.ece).
92. Raymond Scheppach, "Federal stimulus dollars, state deficits—and federalism," June 12, 2009. Stateline.org (http://www.stateline.org/live/details/story?contentId=406430).
93. These data are from the California Department of Finance (http://www.dof.ca.gov/budgeting/budget_faqs/information/documents/CHART-p.pdf). The authors added the most recent budget to the count.
94. Larry Gerston, *American Federalism: A Concise Introduction.* (Armonk, NY: M.E. Sharpe, 2007), 94–98.
95. John Kincaid, "State-Federal relations: A Policy Tug of War," *The Book of the States*, vol. 39 (Lexington, KY: Council of State Governments, 2007); Dale Krane, "The Middle Tier in American Federalism: State Government Policy Activism During the Bush Administration." *Publius: The Journal of Federalism* 37 (2007):453–477.
96. Krane, "The Middle Tier in American Federalism," 457.
97. Spencer S. Hsu, "Administration Plans to Scale Back Real ID Law," *Washington Post*, June 14, 2009.
98. 369 U.S. 186 (1962).
99. 377 U.S. 533 (1964).
100. Ann Bowman and Richard Kearney, *State and Local Government*, 8th ed (Boston: Houghton Mifflin Co., 2008), 139.
101. 545 U.S 469 (2005).

ARE STATE LEGISLATURES REPRESENTATIVE INSTITUTIONS?

Over the preceding six chapters, we have documented that although state legislatures share some important characteristics with Congress and with each other, by and large they are a varied lot. Each state legislature enjoys a unique history and a distinctive configuration of organizational features. Electoral contexts also vary, as do the powers the governor enjoys, the roles interest groups play, and the ability of voters to enact legislation. But beyond appreciating their variety, can we offer any assessments of state legislatures as representative institutions? Do they perform the tasks expected of them by the people they represent and serve?

Evaluating the performance of state legislatures is a daunting task, and we have no simple and easy answers to offer. Instead, we will compile bits and pieces of evidence to try to reach a valid appraisal of the job they do. We will begin looking at how the public rates state legislatures and the information people have at their disposal to make those judgments. We then note the quandaries state legislators often face as they go about trying to represent their constituents. Ultimately, we conclude that state legislatures, even if flawed, are representative institutions.

WHAT DO ELECTION RESULTS TELL US ABOUT EVALUATIONS OF STATE LEGISLATIVE PERFORMANCE?

In a representative democracy, the ultimate assessment of legislative performance occurs at the ballot box. After all, that is where voters can reelect their representatives or replace them. Consequently, we might assume that if most incumbents get reelected, then the voters must be pleased with their performance in office. If lawmakers lose their reelection bids, then we might conclude that voters were dissatisfied.

TABLE 7-1   INCUMBENT REELECTION RATES BY STATE, 1990–2003

RANK	STATE	INCUMBENT REELECTION RATE (%)	RANK	STATE	INCUMBENT REELECTION RATE (%)
1	NY	98.1	26	MN	93.9
2	DE	97.6	27	NM	93.8
3	PA	97.6	28	AL	93.7
4	MI	97.4	29	MS	93.5
5	AR	96.9	30	TN	93.5
6	MA	96.7	31	ID	93.3
7	TX	96.6	32	OK	92.7
8	WI	96.2	33	MD	92.5
9	KY	95.8	34	IA	91.7
10	SC	95.8	35	NC	91.5
11	CA	95.7	36	UT	91.4
12	CT	95.5	37	AK	90.6
13	WY	95.5	38	WA	90.5
14	IL	95.4	39	ME	89.7
15	VA	95.4	40	VT	89.3
16	AZ	95.3	41	NH	89.1
17	IN	95.1	42	HI	89.0
18	OH	94.9	43	WV	89.0
19	FL	94.7	44	NE	88.5
20	OR	94.7	45	SD	88.5
21	RI	94.7	46	NV	88.1
22	GA	94.4	47	NJ	87.7
23	CO	94.1	48	MT	87.4
24	KS	94.1	49	ND	86.1
25	MO	94.1	50	LA	84.4

Source: Calculated by the authors from the data set, State Legislative Election Returns, 1967–2003, Thomas M. Carsey, William D. Berry, Richard G. Niemi, Lynda W. Powell, and James M Snyder, Release Version 5.

As we noted in Chapter 2, most state legislators are successful in their efforts to retain office. Data documenting that point are presented in Table 7-1 which gives the incumbent reelection rate by state for 1990–2003. The reelection rate across the states during this time period approaches 94 percent, meaning that 94 of every 100 state legislative incumbents who sought reelection were successful. This is, of course, a very impressive figure and is comparable to that for members of Congress over the same set of years.

The range of reelection rates across the states does not vary dramatically. At the upper end, more than 98 percent of incumbents running again won in New York. At the lower end, a bit over 84 percent of incumbents in Louisiana were reelected. Eyeballing the table confirms that, as we would expect, with only a few exceptions the more professionalized legislatures are grouped at the upper end of the table and the least professional legislatures congregate at the bottom.[1] This suggests, as noted in Chapter 3, that legislators in more professional legislatures are able to exploit the additional institutional resources they enjoy for their electoral benefit.

If incumbent reelection rates reflect voter satisfaction, then it must be concluded from the data in Table 7-1 that state legislatures are doing a very good job. That assessment, however, is too simplistic. A number of explanations beyond voter contentment might account for these impressive reelection rates. As noted in Chapter 2, for example, about one-third of all state legislative elections are uncontested by one of the major parties. In those districts, voters are not provided an alternative through which to express their possible dissatisfaction with the incumbent. We also noted that population distribution patterns and redistricting practices often conspire to make state legislative districts safe for one party, again dampening potential competition and limiting the utility of election results as a measure of voter contentment. Finally, the fact that incumbents have the ability to raise the financial resources they need to communicate with the voters while their challengers generally do not also makes any purported link between reelection rates and voter satisfaction suspect.

Ample evidence suggests that support expressed for an individual legislator does not necessarily translate into support for the institution in which the member serves. A 2005 survey in Pennsylvania, taken in the midst of the pay raise fiasco discussed in Politics Under the Domes 3-1, revealed that although only 30 percent of respondents approved of the job the state legislature was doing, 58 percent approved of their state senator and 61 percent approved of their state representative.[2] Perhaps even more telling are the results from a 2007 survey of 500 likely voters in Illinois. Respondents were asked: "Suppose you could vote to keep all of the state legislators in office or to kick them all out and start with an entirely new legislature. If the election were held today, how would you vote?" Only 19 percent would opt to keep the current legislature; 55 percent preferred to elect a whole new group of legislators.[3] This is a striking result and an indictment of an uncompetitive electoral process given the fact that, as Table 7-1 shows, an average of 95 percent of Illinois incumbents get reelected each election.

HOW HIGHLY DO CITIZENS RATE THEIR STATE LEGISLATURES?

It appears that people like their local legislators yet dislike their legislature. How do citizens rate the performance of their state legislative institutions? We offer three sets of data to address this question.

The first is a 1999 national survey that asked how much trust or confidence respondents had in a number of governmental institutions. The results

TABLE 7-2   TRUST OR CONFIDENCE IN GOVERNMENTAL INSTITUTIONS—1999

	AMOUNT OF TRUST OR CONFIDENCE (%)			
INSTITUTION	GREAT DEAL	SOME	ONLY A LITTLE	NONE
Local police	43	39	12	6
State governor	30	47	16	8
Public schools	26	49	20	5
Local courts	23	52	17	8
State legislature	18	58	17	7

Source: National Center for State Courts, "How the Public Views the State Courts," May 14, 1999.

are presented in Table 7-2.[4] People expressed less confidence in their state legislatures than in their local police, state governor, public schools, or local courts. Although this ranking might appear not to reflect well on the legislature, it is important to note that more than two-thirds of respondents had a great deal or some trust or confidence in the state legislature but less than one-third had only a little or no trust or confidence. Thus, on the whole, state legislatures fare reasonably well in terms of public trust or confidence.

The second set of data consists of surveys asked in 18 states in 2007. Respondents were asked some variant of a question about whether they approved or disapproved of the way their state legislature was handling its job. Approval and disapproval scores for each of the 18 states are given in Table 7-3. We also supply two other pieces of information: the difference between the approval and the disapproval scores and the professionalization score for each state. The latter is important because several studies have documented a negative relationship between professionalization and public opinion. That is, the more professional the legislature, the less people approve of it.[5]

A review of the scores in Table 7-3 confirms the negative relationship between professionalization levels and public approval. The lowest approval ratings are in the states with the most professionalized legislatures, and the highest approval ratings are in the states with the least professionalized legislatures. This finding is true even though we know that contact between representatives and the represented increases with professionalization, as does policy responsiveness.[6] Overall, in this comparison, Americans appear ambivalent about their state legislatures. The median approval score is 42 percent (the mean is 41 percent). Disapproval scores are just as high. It appears, then, that although people do not love their state legislature, they also do not appear to hate it.

Our final set of data examines public approval scores over two decades in two states: California and Mississippi. Although over this time span, the Democrats controlled the Mississippi legislature every year and the California legislature almost every year, these two states offer a significant contrast.

TABLE 7-3   STATE LEGISLATIVE PROFESSIONALIZATION AND
PUBLIC OPINION IN SELECTED STATES—2007

STATE	PROFESSIONALIZATION SCORE	APPROVAL OF LEGISLATURE (%)	DISAPPROVAL OF LEGISLATURE (%)	APPROVAL MINUS DISAPPROVAL
California	0.626	38	43	−5
New York	0.481	32	48	−16
Wisconsin	0.439	49	45	4
Pennsylvania	0.339	35	48	−13
Ohio	0.304	39	35	4
New Jersey	0.244	29	53	−24
Florida	0.223	37	41	−4
Colorado	0.202	41	36	5
North Carolina	0.198	14	45	−31
Washington	0.197	44	49	−5
Maryland	0.194	49	43	6
Connecticut	0.190	46	36	10
Minnesota	0.169	43	39	4
Kentucky	0.148	43	44	−1
Virginia	0.131	44	44	0
South Carolina	0.124	53	28	25
Tennessee	0.116	50	24	26
Utah	0.065	59	41	18

Sources: Alabama, Rasmussen Reports, "Alabama Survey of 500 Likely Voters," September 19, 2007; California, averaged from the Field Poll, March 2007, August 2007, October 2007, December 2007; Colorado, Karen E. Crummy, "Poll: Voters Leery of Sweeping Change," *Denver Post*, September 28, 2007; Connecticut, averaged from Quinnipiac University Poll, February 15, 2007, and May 9, 2007; Florida, averaged from Quinnipiac University Poll, July 19, 2007, September 11, 2007, and October 24, 2007; Kentucky, John Stamper, "Child Health Care is Voter Priority: Also Interest in Casino Vote, Teachers' Pay," *Lexington Herald-Leader*, October 30, 2007; Maryland, Washington Post Poll, October 18–22, 2007 (all voters numbers); Minnesota, Mark Brunswick, "Minnesota Poll: Approval of Pawlenty is Highest in Four Years, Minneapolis *Star Tribune*, October 3, 2007; New Hampshire, Lauren R. Dorgan, "Opinions on Unions, State House," *Concord Monitor*, July 14, 2007; New Jersey, averaged from Quinnipiac University Poll, July 9, 2007, September 25, 2007, and December 11, 2007; New York, averaged from Quinnipiac University Poll, April 4, 2007, June 19, 2007, July 31, 2007, and October 2, 2007; North Carolina, Public Policy Polling, "State Legislature Either Unknown or Unpopular: Dole Leads Potential Challengers," August 16, 2007; Ohio, averaged from Quinnipiac University Poll, March 21, 2007, May 15, 2007, July 11, 2007, September 5, 2007, and November 13, 2007; Pennsylvania, averaged from Quinnipiac University Poll, March 28, 2007, May 30, 2007, August 22, 2007, and November 7, 2008; South Carolina, Winthrop Poll, February 7–28, 2007; Tennessee, MTSU Poll, Spring 2007, Middle Tennessee State University; Utah; averaged from Utah Voter Poll, "Unweighted Results from the Utah Voter Poll, July 31–August 10, 2007," and "Results of the October 2007 Utah Voter Poll," Center for the Study of Elections and Democracy, Brigham Young University; Virginia, Washington Post Poll, October 4–8, 2007 (all voters numbers); Washington, Strategic Vision, October 5–7, 2007; Wisconsin, averaged from Badger Poll, University of Wisconsin Survey Center, University of Wisconsin Madison, June 2007 and December 2007.

As noted in Chapter 3, California is far and away the most professionalized legislature in the country, and Mississippi falls well down the list on that dimension. Yet, as can be seen in Figure 7-1, what is interesting about their approval scores over time is that they track each other remarkably well. Indeed, they correlate at 0.82 ($P < .01$). Moreover, the ebbs and flows of the approval scores seem to be easily explained. When economic times are good, as they were through the mid to late 1990s, approval scores moved higher. When the economy performed poorly, as it did in the early 1990s and again in the early part of the current decade, approval scores trended downward. This relationship might suggest that public evaluations of state legislative performance are tied to things such as the performance of the economy over which state legislators have little, if any, real control. And that might raise a question about the basis on which people render judgments on their state legislatures.

HOW MUCH DO PEOPLE KNOW ABOUT THEIR STATE LEGISLATURES AND LEGISLATORS?

Considerable evidence suggests that most people know very little about their state legislature or legislators. In 2006, for example, Utahns were asked in a survey if they could name their state senator or state representative.

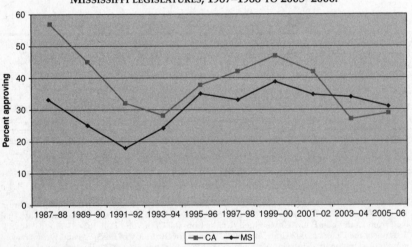

FIGURE 7-1 · PUBLIC APPROVAL OF THE CALIFORNIA AND MISSISSIPPI LEGISLATURES, 1987–1988 TO 2005–2006.

Source: California data are from Mark DiCamillo and Mervin Field, "Voters See State Budget Deficit as a Serious Matter. Small Plurality Thinks Taxes will have to be Raised. More Confidence in Governor than the Legislature in Resolving the Problem," The Field Poll, December 28, 2007; Mississippi data are from the Mississippi Poll conducted by the Survey Research Unit of the Social Science Research Center at Mississippi State University. The data are the average for polls taken over each two-year period. In Mississippi, excellent and good ratings are combined to calculate the approval score.

Only 17 percent could name both of their state legislators, and another 17 percent could name one of them. The remaining 66 percent of the respondents either were not certain of their legislators' names or admitted that they did not know them.[7] Similar results were obtained in a 1988 statewide survey in Ohio and a 1981 poll in Oklahoma.[8] Even the most powerful state legislators are little known by the public. When New Yorkers were asked in 2009 their opinion of Assembly Speaker Sheldon Silver, more than one-third of them could not offer one, suggesting that they were unfamiliar with Silver's name even though he had been the top leader for 15 years.[9] More directly, a 1998 survey in New Jersey asked if respondents could name the Assembly speaker or the state Senate majority leader. Only 2 percent could name the speaker, which was actually better than the 1 percent who could name the senate majority leader.[10] In 2003, only one in five New Jersey respondents could correctly identify which party controlled either house of their state legislature.[11] Perhaps not surprisingly, a survey conducted just two weeks before the 2007 state legislative elections in New Jersey revealed that three-quarters of the state's registered voters were unaware of the impending contests.[12] Collectively, these data suggest that although many people may express an opinion about their state legislature's job performance, there may not be much substance behind those evaluations.

HOW MUCH INFORMATION ABOUT STATE LEGISLATURES IS AVAILABLE?

Americans appear to know little about their state legislatures. But how much information about the legislatures and their members is available to them? The answer is that there are fewer and fewer stories from the state capitol printed in the newspapers and broadcast on television and radio every year. For some time, observers have lamented decreases in the number of reporters assigned to cover state legislatures.[13] In California, for example, only one full-time and one part-time capitol television bureau now cover the statehouse, with those few reporters and camera operators being shared by a number of stations across the state.[14] In New York, only two television news organizations maintain a presence in the capitol, and consequently, many state legislators hold their news conferences in New York City rather than in Albany so as to increase their chances of getting coverage.[15] The decline in the number of reporters focused on the capitol has consequences. A veteran statehouse reporter in Florida, concerned by the loss of colleagues in Tallahassee, recently observed, "Twenty years of reporting from here have taught me that lawmakers behave differently when they know a hometown reporter is watching."[16]

Events in the Massachusetts House one notable night in 2000 support this assertion. According to one analysis of the incident:

> Massachusetts legislators drank, caroused and slumbered through an all-night session while their leaders added nearly $200 million to the state budget, apparently illegally recording the votes of absent members while the rank and file chanted "Toga! Toga! Toga!" on the House floor. Lawmakers partied in a committee office, purportedly shaved a freshman colleague's leg as a prank while he was sleeping, then fell asleep themselves in a cloakroom, snoring so loudly they could be heard outside in the hall. "Will the House please come to order?" one member implored. "No!" his giddy, giggling colleagues shouted back.
>
> But one thing was left out of the follow-up [news] coverage: There had been no reporters in the chamber that night, out of a Statehouse press corps that numbers in the dozens. It took days before the legislators' most egregious personal conduct was reported.[17]

Reflecting on these events, the house speaker admonished journalists about meeting their professional obligations, placing some of the blame for the ugly episode on them, "You bring in the light, and in the light we have to make these decisions."[18]

But beyond influencing legislative behavior, the lack of media coverage also impacts voters. Without newspapers, television, and radio paying attention to the state legislature, it becomes much more difficult for people to learn about their lawmakers and the decisions they make. One study revealed that people living in and around Richmond, Virginia, where because it is the state capital, the local newspaper gives considerable coverage to state governmental affairs, were much better informed about state politics than were people in the rest of the state who read local papers that focus on other kinds of stories.[19] Thus, it appears that people are not averse to learning about their state legislature, but they have to be immersed in information about it for it to penetrate their consciousness. Unfortunately, a 2008 study revealed that considerably more newspapers were cutting back on coverage of state government and politics than were increasing it.[20] Current media trends indicate that people in the future will be exposed to less information about state government through newspapers, television, and radio.

Potentially filling this information vacuum, at least partially, is an increasing cadre of citizen bloggers who cover their state legislatures on a daily basis.[21] These bloggers are of many different types, from professional journalists to volunteers for some association or another, to political junkies. In many cases, bloggers are providing more detailed information about day-to-day legislative events than newspapers provide. Unlike most mainstream media, however, some of these bloggers have a definite ideological perspective. Although the quality of the blogs varies, there is little doubt that because of them the flow of information about state legislatures and their activities today is more voluminous and represents a broader range of perspectives than what was available through the mainstream media in the past. There is no evidence, however, that many citizens take advantage of these blogs.

Institutionally, state legislatures have responded to the decline in attention from the mainstream media by exploiting new technologies to create alternative avenues to reach citizens. Every state legislature has developed a website to make information available to constituents. The quality of these websites varies; wealthier states with better educated populations have pages that are much more accessible and interactive than those in poorer and less well-educated states.[22] By and large, state legislative websites have tended to foster civic engagement rather than interaction between the representative and the represented. They do, however, appear to be reasonably well used, with reports of 1.5 million visits each week during legislative sessions.[23]

E-mail has also increased the ability of constituents to contact their state legislators. Lawmakers have found it to be useful in interacting with constituents, although this is more the case with members of less-professional legislatures than with their counterparts in more professional bodies. Legislators, however, are less sanguine about their e-mail interactions with interest groups.[24] Indeed, they have reacted negatively to blanket e-mailing efforts intended to influence them. A North Carolina senator, for example, took to the floor to vent about an e-mail he had received opposing proposed cuts in spending on public schools. By mistake, instructions from a school principal to her staff detailing how the message could be sent on to state legislators had been left on the message. The senator complained to his colleagues, "It looks like they're using e-mail not so much to inform and request assistance, but to harass us."[25] For similar reasons, an Idaho senator got his state's technical staff to change the Senate's system so that people could not send e-mails to every lawmaker simultaneously. A member of the Idaho House sympathized with the Senate's decision, noting, "E-mail in the beginning was a personal expression of opinion from somebody in my district. E-mail is starting to become like getting 500 postcards that all say the same thing."[26]

State legislatures have adopted other new technologies to connect with the public. By 2009, 23 state legislative caucuses maintained a blog, 25 had either a Facebook or MySpace page, 20 were on Twitter, and 14 posted on YouTube.[27] Some individual lawmakers have taken to blogging as a way of keeping in touch with their districts, and a few have started to use social networking sites.[28] But given that state legislators are disproportionally drawn from the ranks of older generations, it may take a while for these innovations to catch on. For instance, the first lawmaker in South Carolina to post regular vlogs on YouTube, a middle-aged lawyer, reflected, "Who would've thought it would've been me? I was dragged into the new age by my daughters."[29]

More systematically, by 2009, 47 states provided live video or audio webcasts of legislative floor proceedings; 27 states also had webcasts of committee hearings. Television broadcasts of legislative sessions—essentially state versions of C-SPAN—were available in 28 states.[30] How many people take advantage of these offerings, however, is questionable. For 2007, for example, the Public Information Services for the Minnesota House of Representatives reported that its live and archive webcast streams had 11,652 distinct (meaning unique Internet Protocol address) visitors; an unimpressive number in a state with a population of more than five million. Perhaps even more depressingly, the Virginia Senate estimated that it had only 70 to 100 daily users of its streaming video.[31] Twitter usage data also are disappointing. As of July 2009, very few state legislative caucuses had more than 1,000 followers, and several had far fewer—Delaware House Republicans, for example, had only 168 followers. Clearly, when it comes to covering events at the statehouse, these new media still do not yet enjoy the reach of the mainstream media.

DO STATE LEGISLATORS REPRESENT THEIR CONSTITUENTS?

Given that people know very little about their state legislatures, we might surmise that legislators might not feel constrained by constituent opinion. After all, nobody appears to be watching them. A recent survey of state lawmakers offers some support for this notion. Far more of them leaned toward a "trustee" orientation, meaning that they placed greater weight on pursuing policies that they considered to be right for their state, than toward a "delegate" orientation, one in which they would strive to accurately represent the preferences of their constituents.[32] This finding might indicate that most state legislators feel comfortable substituting their own judgment on issues for those expressed by their voters.

Yet, as discussed in Chapter 6, analyses of roll-call voting in state legislatures suggest otherwise. Lawmakers' votes generally align with the preferences of the voters in their districts.[33] Indeed, legislators work hard to match their representational styles to the characteristics and needs of their constituents.[34] And in a survey of state legislators, 88 percent of them assessed their performance in representing their constituents as either "excellent" or "good."[35] Legislators take to heart what little they hear from their constituents. A Kansas lobbyist observes, "The home constituent who takes the time to contact their legislator can have a tremendous impact on the process. When a constituent wakes up and calls in on a property tax issue or a school finance issue, [legislators] pay attention."[36] Another Kansas lobbyist agrees, saying "Legislators have been known, if they got four letters for it and two against it, to vote for it. They say, 'Well, I've got a mandate from the people.'"[37] Indeed, a Missouri representative recently confessed that he changed his vote on an important bill because "I got more calls telling me to vote for it than I did against it."[38] Ample examples support the assertion that rather than ignoring the folks back home, state legislators are actually obsessed with voter opinion and do a very good job of representing the policy views of their constituents.

More evidence along these lines is presented in Table 7-4, which gives interest group ratings for four lower house members in 2005 and 2006. Although the voting public may not pay close attention to their state legislators, as noted in Chapter 6, interest groups do. Some interest groups publish ratings based on how lawmakers vote on legislation of interest to the organizations. For voters who are sufficiently motivated to find these ratings, they can provide considerable insight into their legislators' policy preferences. Most of these scores are given on a scale of 0 to 100, where a higher score indicates greater support for the rating group's policy positions. Occasionally, a group gives out letter grades.

The first thing to note in Table 7-4 is that the number of interest group ratings varies substantially across the four cases examined here. In California, interest group ratings are numerous (indeed, not all of the available ones are included here). Consequently, a constituent interested in assessing the votes of his or her local lawmaker can wade through a great deal of information. In contrast, comparatively few ratings are available in Tennessee. Voters in Maine and Missouri have a fair number of ratings at their disposal, probably enough for voters to gain a handle on the sorts of decisions their state legislators make.

What do the ratings in Table 7-4 reveal about the legislators they rate? Generally, they show that, as we might expect, Democrats do well with liberal groups and poorly with conservative ones, and the obverse holds for Republicans. But they also suggest that legislators in competitive districts tend to temper their voting behavior while their colleagues who are more electorally secure are free to vote ideologically. Take, for example, the ratings of Loni Hancock, a Democratic member of the California Assembly who represented a district centered on Berkeley, home of the University of California. Hancock's constituents were overwhelmingly liberal, which has two important implications. First, Hancock enjoyed a safe seat; no Republican or minor party candidate had a prayer of defeating her. Indeed, her GOP opponent in 2004 got only 18 percent of the vote. Second, if Hancock accurately reflected the policy preferences of her constituents, she should have a very liberal voting record. The ratings listed in Table 7-4 document that she did just that. Hancock almost always sided with liberal groups on bills involving abortion, animal rights, civil liberties and civil rights, the environment, government reform, labor, and women's issues. On the flip side, more conservative groups, such as the Farm Bureau, the National Rifle Association (NRA), taxpayer organizations, and the California Republican Assembly, gave her voting record very low marks. Of course, although it is clear that Hancock voted the way most of her constituents preferred, it is important to note that her record also reflected her own very liberal proclivities.

TABLE 7-4 INTEREST GROUP RATINGS OF FOUR LOWER HOUSE MEMBERS, 2005–2006

LEGISLATOR	LONI HANCOCK (CALIFORNIA—DIST. 14, DEMOCRAT)	GEORGE FRALEY (TENNESSEE—DIST. 39, DEMOCRAT)	ED ROBB (MISSOURI—DIST. 24, REPUBLICAN)	SUSAN AUSTIN (MAINE—DIST. 109, REPUBLICAN)
2004 vote percentage	78	53	56	61
Issue area for 2005 and 2006: Abortion	Planned Parenthood Affiliates of California (2006)—100 Planned Parenthood Affiliates of California (2005)—100 NARAL Pro-Choice California (2005–06)—100		NARAL Pro-Choice Missouri (2006)—Anti-Choice	Planned Parenthood of Northern New England (2006)—0 Family Planning Association of Maine (2005)—0
Agriculture	California Farm Bureau (2006)—10 California Farm Bureau (2005)—0		Missouri Farm Bureau Federation (2005–2006)—100	
Animal rights	PawPAC (2005)—100			
Budget spending and taxes	California Taxpayers' Association (2006)—24 California Taxpayers' Association (2005)—25 Howard Jarvis Taxpayers Association (2006)—16.7 Howard Jarvis Taxpayers Association (2005)—6			

	California	Tennessee	Missouri	Maine
Business and consumers	California Chamber of Commerce (2006)—18 California Chamber of Commerce (2005)—17 California National Federation of Independent Business (2006)—15 Consumer Federation of California (2006)—100 California Manufacturers and Technology Association (2005–2006)—8	Tennessee National Federation of Independent Business (2005–2006)—67	Missouri National Federation of Independent Business (2005–2006)—100 Missouri Chamber of Commerce (2005)—100	Maine Economic Research Institute (2006)—95 Maine National Federation of Independent Business (2005–2006)—100
Civil liberties and civil rights	Asian Americans for Civil Rights and Equality (2006)—100 Asian Americans for Civil Rights and Equality (2005)—100 Lambda Letters Project-HIVAIDS (2006)—100 Lambda Letters Project-HIVAIDS (2005)—100 Lambda Letters Project-LGBTI (2006)—100 Lambda Letters Project-LGBTI (2005)—100 Equality California (2005–2006)—100			

(Continued)

TABLE 7-4 (CONTINUED)

LEGISLATOR	LONI HANCOCK (CALIFORNIA—DIST. 14, DEMOCRAT)	GEORGE FRALEY (TENNESSEE—DIST. 39, DEMOCRAT)	ED ROBB (MISSOURI—DIST. 24, REPUBLICAN)	SUSAN AUSTIN (MAINE—DIST. 109, REPUBLICAN)
Conservative politics	California Republican Assembly (2006)—0 California Republican Assembly (2005)—0			
Education			Missouri National Education Association (2006)—73 Missouri National Education Association (2005)—20	Maine Education Association (2005–2006)—14
Environment	California League of Conservation Voters (2006)—100 California League of Conservation Voters (2005)—100 Sierra Club California (2006)—100 Sierra Club California (2005)—100	Tennessee Conservation Voters (2006)—8 Tennessee Conservation Voters (2005)—80	Missouri Votes Conservation (2006)—75 Missouri Votes Conservation (2006)—67	Environment Maine (2006)—38 Maine League of Conservation Votes (2005–2006)—33
Family and children	Children's Advocacy Institute (2006)—92 Children's Advocacy Institute (2005)—95			
Government reform	California Public Interest Research Group (2006)—100			

	California		Missouri	Maine
	California Public Interest Research Group (2005)—100			
Guns	Gun Owners of California (2006)—F National Rifle Association Political Victory Fund (2006)—F	National Rifle Association Political Victory Fund (2006)—0	National Rifle Association Political Victory Fund (2006)—A	National Rifle Association Political Victory Fund (2006)—A
Labor	California Labor Federation, AFL-CIO (2006)—96 California Labor Federation, AFL-CIO (2005)—100		Missouri AFL-CIO (2005)—15	Maine AFL-CIO (2006)—0 Maine AFL-CIO (2005)—10
Liberal politics			Missouri Progressive Vote Coalition (2006)—30 Missouri Progressive Vote Coalition (2005)—0	Maine People's Alliance (2006)—13 Maine People's Alliance (2005)—0
Senior citizens	California Alliance for Retired Americans (2006)—100 California Alliance for Retired Americans (2005)—94 Congress of California Seniors (2005)—100			
Women	California National Organization for Women (2006)—100 California National Organization for Women (2005)—100			Maine Women's Lobby (2006)—17 Maine Women's Lobby (2005)—11

Source: Data gathered by the authors from Project Vote Smart.

Republicans holding relatively safe seats were similarly able to take ideo-logically consistent positions on proposed legislation. Susan Austin, who held such a seat in the Maine House, was generally free to vote her constituents' (and her own) conservative convictions. She took consistently pro-life positions on abortion bills and got very high ratings from business organizations and the NRA. Liberal groups assessing her record on education, the environment, labor, and women's issues were much less generous in their evaluations.

More competitive districts were held by Democrat George Fraley in Tennessee and Republican Ed Robb in Missouri. They each had to worry about holding their seats, and each had to appeal to voters beyond their own partisan base. So their voting records reflect their need to moderate their partisan leanings. Fraley, for example, received reasonably good marks from the Tennessee National Federation of Independent Business, an organization that usually backs Republicans. Similarly, Robb, who represented a district focused on the university town of Columbia, voted conservatively on abor-tion and gun issues but took more moderate stances on education and the environment. There is even evidence that Robb's voting record became more liberal as his 2006 reelection campaign approached, while Fraley's became more conservative. Legislators in competitive districts often moderate their voting records to survive electorally.[39]

Overall, these interest group ratings support the notion that state legisla-tors vote the way their constituents prefer. But accurately reflecting the issue preferences of the voters does not necessarily mean that lawmakers are doing a good job of lawmaking. Indeed, in the survey of legislators men-tioned above, they gave themselves considerably lower scores on legislating than on representation.[40] As is shown in Politics Under the Domes 7-1, there are occasions where acting as a faithful representative clashes with acting as a good public policymaker. In the Iowa case study, it is clear that state legis-lators were closely following their constituents' preferences, and in doing so, they were making the correct political calculation. But in deciding to keep a popular yet deeply flawed policy in place, lawmakers were actually making the achievement of the policy goal on which there was unanimous agree-ment much less likely to be achieved.

POLITICS UNDER THE DOMES 7-1

When Politics and Policy Collide in the State Legislature

State legislatures are important institutions because they make public policy. Policy decisions, however, are rarely driven only by sterile analy-ses. Instead, politics typically drives policy. It is not unusual for objective policy analysis to suggest one course for public policy and for politics to follow a different course, as the following case study demonstrates.

In 2002, the Iowa state legislature passed a strict law preventing registered sex offenders whose victims were minors from living with 2,000 feet of a school or child care facility. The legislature held that failure to comply with the residency restrictions would constitute an aggravated misdemeanor, punishable by up to two years in prison and a $5,000 fine. Republican state Senator Jerry Behn introduced the measure after a constituent from his hometown had called him to complain that a sex offender there was living in a home overlooking a school yard. As might be expected, Behn's proposal was politically appealing, and it met with virtually no opposition. Senator Johnie Hammond, a Democrat, was the only legislator in either house to vote against it, later explaining: "It was not that I like sex offenders and it was not that I do not want to protect children. But I do think I have to abide by the constitution and I have concerns about if we are doing that."

Senator's Hammond's legal concerns proved to have some merit. In 2004, a federal district court judge ruled the residency restrictions unconstitutional. A year later, however, the United States Court of Appeals for the Eighth Circuit overturned the lower court's decision. When a few months after that the U.S. Supreme Court declined to take the case, the sex offender law went into effect.

Unfortunately, although wildly popular, politically, the residency restrictions policy proved to have unanticipated negative consequences. In June 2005, before the law went into effect, the Iowa Department of Public Safety did not know the whereabouts of 142 registered sex offenders. Six months later, after the law was implemented, that number had more than doubled to 346. By establishing a 2,000-foot perimeter around schools and day care facilities, Iowa legislators prevented sex offenders from openly living in much of the state's residential areas. This prompted many sex offenders to fail to register their addresses, in essence driving them underground. Trying to find the missing offenders started to consume law enforcement resources. One county sheriff, for example, complained that before the 2,000-foot law went into effect, he knew where almost every registered sex offender in his jurisdiction lived. After it was implemented, he had to devote three of his department's ten members to tracking offenders rather than being able to use them for other law enforcement activities.

Before the start of the 2007 Iowa legislative session, law enforcement groups and victim advocacy organizations joined together to call for repeal of the residency restrictions. Speaking for the coalition, Corwin Ritchie of the Iowa County Attorneys Association observed, "Good public policy needs to protect children. This residency requirement doesn't do that. We find no correlation between where an offender resides, or sleeps, and whether that offender might re-offend." Critics of the residency

(Continued)

POLITICS UNDER THE DOMES 7-1 (CONTINUED)

requirement went on to argue that because the residency requirement made it less likely that sex offenders required to register would actually do so, the law made children less safe, not more safe.

As public policy, the residential restrictions proved to be a failure. But politically, they still had a powerful appeal. Despite the call for repeal from law enforcement officials, the Democratic chair of the Senate Judiciary Committee confessed, "It is very politically risky to even hold hearings" on the topic because doing so might make legislators look "soft on crime." Eventually, hearings were held, taking testimony from "sex offender experts, statewide law enforcement associations, prevention experts and victims—who uniformly criticized the state law banning sex offenders from living within 2,000 feet of schools or child care centers."

Even with clear evidence that the policy was not working as intended, state legislators were extremely cautious about repealing it. The Democratic Senate Majority Leader admitted, "I think people are concerned about political liability." The Republican Minority Leader made such concerns seem valid when she noted that her party would only support additional funds for monitoring sex offenders, not a repeal of the residency law.

The legislature's reticence to change the failed policy exasperated reform advocates. The county attorneys associations' spokesperson complained bitterly that:

> There were about five weeks of testimony presented by knowledgeable Iowa people who work with sex offender issues. There was not one, not one shred of evidence presented that residency law provides safety for children. In fact, there was a significant amount of evidence presented that the law might actually decrease child safety. Even the clear evidence that enforcement of the law is wasting valuable law enforcement resources has had no effect.

One county sheriff offered an even harsher assessment of the lawmakers, saying, "They're just afraid to take action and the people of Iowa should be ashamed. It's absolutely politics at its worst." An offer by law enforcement officials to campaign on behalf of legislators who voted in favor of repeal was not enough to get legislators to make such a potentially risky vote.

In the end, none of the possible reform ideas floated proved politically acceptable, and the legislature opted to leave the law unchanged. In the final days of the legislative session, one Republican state representative involved with the repeal effort urged his colleagues to "Take a deep breath and wait. We don't want to screw it up again this year." In fact, no reform passed until 2009, when the governor and the legislature finally agreed to create new sex offender exclusion zones around schools, child care facilities, and public libraries. But they also decided to allow lower-risk offenders to live anywhere as long as it was outside an exclusion zone. The most serious sex offenders, however, still had to abide by the 2,000-foot rule. Thus, when push came to shove, politics largely triumphed over policy, even in Iowa, a dead-end legislature where taking an unpopular stand risks only a $25,000 a year position.

Sources: Elizabeth Ahlin, "Iowa Sex Offender Residency Under Fire," Omaha *World-Herald*, February 16, 2007; Jason Clayworth, "New Sex Offender Restrictions Signed into Law by Culver," *Des Moines Register*, May 21, 2009; Monica Davey, "Iowa's Residency Rules Drive Sex Offenders Underground," *The New York Times*, March 15, 2006; *Des Moines Register*, "Fix Mistake: Change Sex-offender Law," April 25, 2007; Dan Gearino, "Coalition Wants to Scrap 2,000-foot Law," *Quad-City Times*, December 12, 2006; Kylie Greene, "New Law Limits Sex Offenders' Options; 'Enormous Area': Iowa Legislation Prohibits Those Convicted of Abusing Minors from Living within 2,000 Feet of a Child-care Facility or a School," Dubuque *Telegraph Herald*, June 24, 2002; Wendy Koch, "Sex-offender Residency Laws Get Second Look," *USA Today*, February 26, 2007; *Quad-City Times*, "Protect Children by Repealing Perimeter Law," December 14, 2006; Lee Rood, "Critics Rake Inaction on Offender Law," *Des Moines Register*, April 24, 2007; Lee Rood, "Sex Offender Legislation in Doubt," *Des Moines Register*, April 24, 2007.

THE DYNAMICS OF REPRESENTATION AT THE STATE LEVEL

Earlier, we pointed out that the public seems to hold individual legislators in higher regard than they hold the legislative institution. We are not the first to note this; it is a phenomenon long recognized at the congressional level and more recently at the state level.[41] As others have documented, the public appears to judge the institution and the individual lawmaker on different criteria. More precisely, the judgment is made on different aspects of representation.

THE COMPONENTS OF REPRESENTATION

Representation is a complex concept; political theorists and political scientists recognize that it is a relationship in which designated agents (in this case elected officials) are responsive to the needs of the people they represent.[42] But there are numerous ways to be "responsive." "Policy responsiveness"—voting on legislation in a manner consistent with the district's wishes—is one obvious and important aspect discussed in Chapter 6.

But there are other aspects of responsiveness. One is *service responsiveness*, what we call "casework" or "constituent service," is discussed in several places throughout this text. This entails helping individual constituents with a problem. In its simplest form, it may entail nothing more than providing information, but as one political scientist describes it, it often involves "redressing grievances."[43] In these instances, the representative becomes an "ombudsman," acting as an intermediary and advocate for individual constituents in their dealings with state (or even federal or local) bureaucracies. Many representatives take this part of the job very seriously, as one northeastern state legislator exemplifies:

> I think that one of my personal priorities for any particular day is making sure my constituent stuff is done. I call people back. I let them know that I'm working on their problem immediately. . . . People ought to know that their representatives are responsive, and that they care and that they are going to try to help folks out.[44]

Another component is *allocational responsiveness*, which involves "securing government funds for the constituency."[45] This ranges from construction projects within the district to efforts to redefine funding formulas for state aid to local school districts.[46] A good example of allocational responsiveness is the reaction by Idaho State Senator Shawn Keough when the State Department of Transportation advisory board reordered the priority list of infrastructure projects in early 2009. The Board, arguing that they needed to "spread the wealth" among all parts of the state, moved refurbishing of a much-traveled bridge in the senator's district from the top priority to number seven on the list of projects. "I'm just astounded. . . . I think it's breathtaking that they would take the worst bridge in the state and . . . treat it in the manner they did. It's a pretty important issue for my district."[47]

By raising the issue publicly, Senator Keough put the transportation board on the defensive and forced the governor to take up the issue. As discussed in Chapter 6, budgets in most states must be balanced, and this requirement means that it is more difficult for a state legislator to "deliver the pork" than it is for members of Congress. Nonetheless, there are almost always some building projects to be funded, and legislators seek to exert their discretion over those funds.

Several students of legislatures identify another aspect of representation as *communication between the constituency and the representative*. Earlier we noted that legislators are using newer technologies such as e-mail and blogging to stay in touch with their constituents. But there are more traditional ways that legislators seek to do this as well. During the session, many legislators write and mail newsletters in an attempt to keep their constituents updated on the issues before the legislature. Some write weekly columns for hometown newspapers. And when in the home district, most legislators feel compelled to attend as many local events and meetings as possible. As one Massachusetts legislator put it, "There are always more events, meetings, and conferences to attend than one human can accomplish. . . . Legislators, as representatives, have to be constantly available to one and all."[48] Most legislators recognize the value of the service, allocation, and communication aspects of representation, and they work assiduously at them. It seems it is often on the basis of these activities that state legislators are evaluated by their constituents.

THE CHANGING DYNAMICS OF THE JOB

In Chapter 3, we noted widespread variation among state legislatures on a number of dimensions, including the resources available, the compensation level, and the time in session. But it turns out, the job entails more than just the time in session. For one thing, casework does not end when the session ends. And the obligation to attend meetings in the district does not end. It is almost certainly the case that the general public overestimates the amount legislators are paid and underestimates the amount of work that is involved. The legislators themselves recognize early on that the job is far more than it seems on the surface. Many legislators would agree with this statement by a Connecticut legislator:

> I think in fairness, for somebody to do their job adequately, if you factor out the whole year, the extra hours to count when you're in session, campaigning, responding, you're really getting paid half-time for a full-time job. . . . To do the job adequately takes full time. I just don't think people recognize that.[49]

The job has changed in part because the number of constituents has increased. Since 1970, the population of the United States has grown by about 50 percent; because state legislatures do not add seats to accommodate population growth, the typical state legislator today has 50 percent more constituents than his or her predecessor did a generation ago. A study conducted in the 1990s asked veteran state legislators—those who had been in office for a *minimum* of 15 years—about the changes that had occurred during their time in office. More than 91 percent said the pressures of the legislative job had increased, and more than 87 percent said the demand for constituent service had increased.[50] And in some states, of course, the population growth has been even greater—doubling during this time period in at least seven states and more than *tripling* in Arizona and Nevada.

One recent study found that about three-quarters of state legislators believed that the legislative job was *at least* a half-time position. Another study finds very similar results; a typical state is Maryland, where 83 percent of the legislators claimed to work at least 50 hours per week during session and at least 15 hours per week when not in session.[51] As pointed out in Chapter 1, the number of legislators has declined over the past generation or two. The populations they serve, however, have grown over that same time, as have the demands of the job.

The key thing here is that communication with constituents and case-work are the activities that correlate highest with legislators' assessment of the amount of time they spend on the job.[52] And legislators believe it is an important part of what they do: constituent service was rated as the "most important task" of the legislator in surveys of the Connecticut and New York legislatures.[53]

A FINAL ASSESSMENT

In 2005, a budget battle between the governor and the state legislature forced the Minnesota government to shut down for several days. Legislators feared that constituents would vent their unhappiness over the legislature's role in the political mess when they saw them during public events, such as parades. One state senator reported that the senate majority leader actively avoided any such abuse by marching with several neighborhood kids. "He spent the whole day with them. And he said it was great. Not one person yelled at him. He figured nobody would get mad at him if he had four little children walking around with him."[54]

Fortunately, the vast majority of state legislators do not need a pint-sized posse to protect them from the public. Generally, people like their lawmakers and are accepting of, if somewhat ambivalent about, the institutions in which they serve. Yet except in rare circumstances, people actually know little about the legislature, its members, or the decisions they make. Unfortunately, little is likely to change about this reality. The mainstream media is becoming less and less useful as a source of information about the state legislature, as news-gathering resources are drawn away from the capitol. Legislatures have seized on new technologies to try to reach their constituents, but it does not appear that people are all that interested in taking advantage of these new opportunities. Elections could conceivably help alleviate the lack of informa-tion, but that can only happen when candidates, particularly from the oppo-sition, have sufficient resources to make their case to the voters.[55] Sadly, most state legislative elections are uncompetitive; indeed, in a shocking number of cases, legislative seats go uncontested. That means much of the burden for overseeing the legislature falls onto interest groups. The good news is that the number of such groups is increasing in every capitol, meaning there are more and more eyes trained on the legislature. The bad news is that each interest group tends to see only its own policy trees and not the larger forest.

But people may be comfortable with this situation. Although state legis-latures are flawed in some regards, with occasional scandals, policy mis-takes, and an absence of political courage or policy boldness, voters still return incumbents to office in overwhelming numbers. And perhaps more tellingly, state legislatures do well in comparison with other legislative insti-tutions. When a national sample was asked in 2007 which governmental body it trusted more when it came to matters of government spending and fiscal responsibility, 18 percent said Congress and 60 percent picked their state legislature.[56] Similar results were obtained in a 1988 survey in Ohio.[57] Thus, when asked to evaluate the performance of state legislatures, a reasonable response may be, "Compared with what?" Although state legislatures are far from perfect institutions and citizens may express some discontent with them, they appear to be preferred to many of the alternatives.

ENDNOTES

1. William D. Berry, Michael B. Berkman, and Stuart Schneiderman, "Legislative Professionalism and Incumbent Reelection: The Development of Institutional Boundaries," *American Political Science Review* 94 (2002):859–874; John M. Carey, Richard G. Niemi, and Lynda W. Powell, "Incumbency and the Probability of Reelection in State Legislative Elections," *Journal of Politics* 62 (2000):671–700.
2. Quinnipiac University Poll, "Pennsylvania Voters Have Little Confidence in Tax Fix, Quinnipiac University Poll Finds; Anti-Incumbent Feeling is Strong," December 8, 2005.
3. These data are taken from Rasmussen Reports, *Illinois Toplines*, December 19, 2007.
4. Half of the respondents were asked how much trust they had in each institution, the other half were asked how much confidence they had. The two samples behaved similarly and are combined in the table.
5. Peverill Squire, "Professionalization and Public Opinion of State Legislatures," *Journal of Politics* 55 (1993):479–491. See also Christine A. Kelleher, and Jennifer Wolak, "Explaining Public Confidence in the Branches of State Government," *Political Research Quarterly* 60 (2007):707–721.
6. Squire, "Professionalization and Public Opinion of State Legislatures;" Cherie Maestas, "The Incentive to Listen: Progressive Ambition, Resources, and Opinion Monitoring among State Legislators," *Journal of Politics* 65 (2003):439–456; and Nathan S. Bigelow, Representation in State Legislatures: Searching for Responsiveness in an Age of Polarization," (Ph.D. dissertation, University of Maryland, 2006).
7. Bob Bernick, Jr., "Utahns Fail Quiz on Own Legislators," *Deseret News*, March 20, 2006.
8. The Ohio results are reported in Samuel C. Patterson, Randall B. Ripley, and Stephen V. Quinlan, "Citizens' Orientations toward Legislatures: Congress and the State Legislature," *Western Political Quarterly* 45 (1992):315–338; the Oklahoma results are found in Donald Songer, "Government Closest to the People: Constituent Knowledge in State & National Politics," *Polity* 17 (1984):387–395.
9. Siena Research Institute, "Voters See Senate Fight as a Farce—Bad for NYers," June 22, 2009. For job approval figures revealing the same relationship, see Quinnipiac University Poll, "New Yorkers Back Gov on Gay Marriage, Quinnipiac University Poll Finds; Patterson Approval Up, But Bloomberg Leads Gov Race," June 12, 2008.
10. These data are from questions qkn9a and qkn9b of the Rutgers-Eagleton Poll of February 1998.
11. These data are from questions qin7 and qin8 of the Rutgers-Eagleton Poll of May 2003.
12. Rutgers-Eagleton Poll, "Cranky Electorate Gives Democrats the Edge in Legislative Campaign," October 25, 2007. See question AE1.
13. See, for example, Charles Layton and Mary Walton, "State of the American Newspaper, Missing the Story at the Statehouse," *American Journalism Review*, July/August 1998, and Charles Layton and Jennifer Dorroh, "Sad State," *American Journalism Review*, June 2002.
14. J. Freedom du Lac, "Media Savvy: Out of Focus," *Sacramento Bee*, January 5, 2005.
15. Michael Cooper, "Remember New York's Capital? Forget It," *The New York Times*, August 3, 2005.
16. Steve Bousquet, "We're Losing a Leash on Legislators," *St. Petersburg Times*, February 9, 2008.
17. Jon Marcus, "Animal Statehouse," *American Journalism Review*, June 2000.
18. Marcus, "Animal Statehouse."

19. Michael X. Delli Carpini, Scott Keeter, and J. David Kennamer, "Effects of the News Media on Citizen Knowledge of State Politics and Government," *Journalism Quarterly* 71 (1994):443–456.
20. Project for Excellence in Journalism, "The Changing Newsroom: What is Being Gained and What is Being Lost in America's Daily Newspapers?" July 21, 2008. See the response to survey question 19.
21. A list of blogs on individual state legislatures is kept by the National Conference of State Legislatures (http://www.ncsl.typepad.com/the_thicket/).
22. Paul Ferber, Franz Foltz, and Rudy Pugliese, "Demographics and Political Characteristics Affecting State Legislative Websites: The Quality and Digital Divides," *Journal of Political Marketing* 7 (2008). These relationships are generally true for e-government in general. See Caroline J. Tolbert, Karen Mossberger, and Ramona McNeal, " Institutions, Policy Innovation, and E-Government in the American States," *Public Administration Review* 68 (2008):549–563.
23. See Jodie Condit Fagan and Bryan Fagan, "An Accessibility Study of State Legislative Web Sites," *Government Information Quarterly*, 21 (2004): 61–81; Paul Ferber, Franz Foltz, and Rudy Pugliese, "State Legislature Web Sites and Public Participation: Designing a Civic Resource," *Atlantic Journal of Communication* 14 (2006):229–246; Paul Ferber, Franz Foltz, and Rudy Pugliese, "The Internet and Public Participation: State Legislature Web Sites and the Many Definitions of Interactivity" *Bulletin of Science, Technology & Society* 25 (2005):85–93.
24. Lilliard E. Richardson, Jr. and Christopher A. Cooper, "Email Communication and the Policy Process in the State Legislature," *Policy Studies Journal* 34 (2006):113–129.
25. David Rice and David Ingram, "Smothering Legislators with E-Mail is More Effective When Less Transparent," *Winston-Salem Journal*, June 12, 2005.
26. John Miller, "Idaho Lawmaker Turns Off Mass Committee E-Mails after Deluge," *Idaho Statesman*, March 6, 2007.
27. See National Conference of State Legislatures, "Legislative Caucus Web Sites and Legislative Social Networking Sites," May 22, 2009 (http://www.ncsl.org/?tabid=13409).
28. A list of state legislator blogs is available at http://ncsl.typepad.com/the_thicket/. See also the discussion of Colorado legislators' MySpace pages at http://www.politickerco.com/legislators-starting-log-social-networking-sites-362.
29. Seanna Adcox, "Lawmakers Connect Through Video Logs," *Charleston Post and Courier*, January 14, 2007; Nancy Hicks, "Some Senators Use Blogs to Keep in Touch," *Lincoln Journal Star*, March 29, 2005.
30. These data are from National Conference of State Legislatures, "Broadcasts of Legislative Floor Proceedings and Committee Hearings," March 16, 2009 (http://www.ncsl.org/Default.aspx?TabId=13479).
31. These numbers are reported in Pam Greenberg, "Is Anybody Watching," The Thicket at State Legislatures, January 29, 2008 (http://ncsl.typepad.com/the_thicket/2008/01/is-anybody-watc.html).
32. Christopher A. Cooper and Lilliard E. Richardson, Jr., "Institutions and Representational Roles in American State Legislatures," *State Politics and Policy Quarterly* 6 (2006):174–194.
33. Gerald Wright, "Do Term Limits Affect Legislative Roll Call Voting? Representation, Polarization, and Participation," *State Politics and Policy Quarterly* 7:256–280.
34. Michael A. Smith, *Bringing Representation Home: State Legislators Among their Constituencies* (Columbia, MO: University of Missouri Press, 2003).
35. Alan Rosenthal, *Heavy Lifting: The Job of the American Legislature* (Washington, DC: CQ Press, 2004), 233–237.
36. Paul Eakins, "How Constituents Can Compete with Lobbyists for Legislators' Time," *Topeka Capital-Journal*, January 7, 2001.
37. Eakins, "How Constituents Can Compete with Lobbyists for Legislators' Time."
38. Terry Ganey, "Missouri Plan Bill Spurs 'Robo-Calls'," *Columbia Daily Tribune*, April 9, 2009.
39. Thad Kousser, Jeffrey B. Lewis, and Seth E. Masket, "Ideological Adaptation? The Survival Instinct of Threatened Legislators," *Journal of Politics* 69 (2007):828–843.
40. Rosenthal, *Heavy Lifting*, 233, 237–241.
41. The classic statement is Richard Fenno, "If, As Ralph Nader Says, Congress Is 'the Broken Branch,' How Come We Love Our Congressmen So Much?" in *Congress in Change: Evolution and Reform*, ed. Norman Ornstein (New York: Praeger, 1975).

42. Hanna Pitkin, *The Concept of Representation* (Berkeley:, University of California Press, 1967); Heinz Eulau and Paul Karps, "The Puzzle of Representation: Specifying the Components of Responsiveness," in *The Politics of Representation: Continuities in Theory and Research*, ed. Heinz Eulau and John C. Wahlke (Beverly Hills CA: Sage Publication, 1978); Malcolm Jewell, *Representation in State Legislatures* (Lexington: University Press of Kentucky, 1982).
43. Alan Rosenthal, *The Decline of Representative Government* (Washington, DC: CQ Press, 1998), 15.
44. As quoted in Grant Reeher, *First Person Political: Legislative Life and the Meaning of Public Service* (New York: NYU Press, 2006), 104.
45. Michael Mezey, *Representative Democracy* (Lanham, MD: Rowman & Littlefield, 2008), 87.
46. Rosenthal, *Heavy Lifting*, 30–31.
47. Betsy Z. Russell, "ITD Board Passes Over Dover Bridge Project," Spokane (Washington) *Spokesman-Review*, January 8, 2009.
48. As quoted in Rosenthal, *Heavy Lifting*, 24.
49. As quoted in Reeher, *First Person Political*, 81.
50. Gary F. Moncrief, Joel A. Thompson, and Karl T. Kurtz, "The Old Statehouse, It Ain't What it Used to Be," *Legislative Studies Quarterly* 21 (1996):57–72.
51. Rosenthal, *Heavy Lifting*, 22.
52. Karl T. Kurtz, Gary Moncrief, Richard G. Niemi, and Lynda W. Powell, "Full-Time, Part-Time, and Real Time: Explaining State Legislators' Perceptions of Time on the Job," *State Politics and Policy Quarterly* 6 (2006):322–338.
53. Grant Reeher, *First Person Political*, 75. The study asked "which is the most important thing" legislators should do—pass bills, committee work, constituent service, try to cause the chamber to move in a particular direction, or "other" A plurality (38 percent in Connecticut; 46 percent in New York) chose constituent service. Legislators in the third state surveyed (Vermont) ranked constituent service third.
54. Annie Baxter, "Who to Blame? Parade Provides Few Answers," Minnesota Public Radio, July 5, 2005.
55. Robert E. Hogan, "Policy Responsiveness and Incumbent Reelection in State Legislatures," *American Journal of Political Science* 52 (2008):858–873. An argument that this relationship raises damning doubts about the representativeness of state legislatures is given in Eric Prier, *The Myth of Representation and the Florida Legislature: A House of Competing Loyalties, 1927–2000* (Gainesville, FL: University Press of Florida, 2003).
56. These data are from a Democracy Corp survey conducted from February 14 to February 19, 2007 by Greenberg Quinlan Research.
57. Patterson, Ripley, and Quinlan, "Citizen's Orientations Toward Legislatures," 317.

INDEX

Note: Page numbers followed by t indicate a Table

Additional Titles in REAL POLITICS IN AMERICA Series

Beyond Red State and Blue State: Electoral Gaps in the 21st Century American Electorate
Laura R. Olson and John C. Green
ISBN: 0-13-615557-X

Celebrity Politics
Darrell M. West and John M. Orman
ISBN: 0-13-094325-8

Clicker Politics: Essays on the California Recall
Shaun Bowler and Bruce E. Cain
ISBN: 0-13-193336-1

Congress and the Politics of Foreign Policy
Colton C. Campbell, Nicol C. Rae and John F. Stack
ISBN: 0-13-042154-5

Electing Congress: New Rules for an Old Game
David B. Magleby, J. Quin Monson and Kelly Patterson
ISBN: 0-13-243867-4

From Inspiration to Legislation: How an Idea Becomes a Bill
Amy E. Black
ISBN: 0-13-110754-2

Lobbying Reconsidered: Politics Under the Influence
Gary Andres
ISBN: 0-13-603265-6

Medium and the Message, The: Television Advertising and American Elections
Kenneth M. Goldstein and Patricia Strach
ISBN: 0-13-177774-2

No Holds Barred: Negativity in United States Senate Campaigns
Kim Fridkin Kahn and Patrick J. Kenney
ISBN: 0-13-097760-8

Patrick Kennedy: The Rise to Power
Darrell M. West
ISBN: 0-13-017694-X

Playing Hardball: Campaigning for the U.S. Congress
Paul S. Herrnson
ISBN: 0-13-027133-0

Presidential Campaign Quality: Incentives and Reform
Bruce Buchanan
ISBN: 0-13-184140-8

Reforming the Republic: Democratic Institutions for the New America
Todd Donovan and Shaun Bowler
ISBN: 0-13-099455-3

Smoking and Politics: Bureaucracy Centered Policymaking
A. Lee Fritschler and Catherine E. Rudder
ISBN: 0-13-179104-4

Stealing the Initiative: How State Government Responds to Direct Democracy
Elisabeth R. Gerber, Arthur Lupia, Mathew D. McCubbis and D. Roderick Kiewiet
ISBN: 0-13-028407-6

Transforming the American Polity: The Presidency of George W. Bush and the War on Terrorism
Richard S. Conley
ISBN: 0-13-189342-4

War Stories from Capitol Hill
Colton C. Campbell and Paul S. Herrnson
ISBN: 0-13-028088-7

Women's PAC's: Abortion and Elections
Christine L. Day and Charles D. Hadley
ISBN: 0-13-117448-7